▲▲▲▲▲▲▲▲▲▲▲▲▲▲▲▲

Also by Dee Brown

The American West

▲▲▲▲▲▲▲▲▲▲▲▲▲

DEE BROWN

PHOTOS EDITED
BY MARTIN F. SCHMITT

CHARLES SCRIBNER'S SONS
New York   London   Toronto
Sydney   Tokyo   Singapore

CHARLES SCRIBNER'S SONS
Rockefeller Center
1230 Avenue of the Americas
New York, NY 10020

Designed by Deirdre C. Amthor

Manufactured in the United States of America

1   3   5   7   9   10   8   6   4   2

ISBN 0-02-517421-5

FOR
THOMAS JEFFERSON EASTERWOOD,
BALLOONIST AND TRAILBLAZER

Acknowledgments

▲ ▲ ▲ ▲ ▲ ▲ ▲ ▲ ▲ ▲ ▲ ▲ ▲ ▲ ▲ ▲

WE ESPECIALLY THANK Sally Arteseros for her editorial work in helping to meld the separate parts of this work. Credit is also due many, many librarians and archivists from the Eastcoast to the Westcoast, without whose help in searching out numerous bits and pieces of Western history this book would not exist. Within these pages is much of my late friend and collaborator, Martin Schmitt, who I hope would approve of what we are doing. And had my editor, Carlo de Vito, not been a persistent and amiable gadfly we would never have got it done. Special thanks to copy editor Debra Makay for her keen eye and long labor.

Contents

▲ ▲ ▲ ▲ ▲ ▲ ▲ ▲ ▲ ▲ ▲ ▲ ▲ ▲ ▲

List of Photographs

▲▲▲▲▲▲▲▲▲▲▲▲▲▲▲

List of Maps

▲ ▲ ▲ ▲ ▲ ▲ ▲ ▲ ▲ ▲ ▲ ▲ ▲ ▲ ▲ ▲ ▲

Introduction

▲ ▲ ▲ ▲ ▲ ▲ ▲ ▲ ▲ ▲ ▲ ▲ ▲ ▲ ▲ ▲

THE AMERICAN WEST as a paradigm for the nation as a whole has become, in recent years, almost a cliché. Academics debate its myths and realities. Popular culturists delve into all its aspects. Filmmakers approach and retreat from its myriad of images. Television documentarians display its pictorial records with solemn commentaries. At one time or another almost every American has examined the nation's Western experience, sometimes with curiosity, sometimes with admiration, awe, incredulity, distaste, or a mixture of all of these.

Some years ago Martin Schmitt and I followed the trail of frontier photographers in our first venture into the American West that was. Over a long period we searched for the most telling graphics that we could find, and let the early photographers and artists show us what the West was like. Out of this came three volumes titled *Fighting Indians of the West, Trail Driving Days,* and *The Settlers' West.* Later we considered the possibilities of additional books that would be similar to them, yet more specialized. We finally decided that within our three volumes we already had included the essence of the Old West. Along with the cowboys and Indians and settlers we had introduced gunfighters and lawmen, wagon trains and railroads, soldiers and explorers, gold and silver miners, newspaper editors, gamblers, entertainers, pioneer women, preachers, doctors, and lawyers. The whole of the West was there.

When we first set out to make a book from our findings, we had the naive idea that all we needed to tell our stories were captions beneath the pictures. We soon learned that although a picture may be worth more than ten thousand words, unless one knows the setting of a picture in time and its relation to other pictures, its ten thousand words are gibberish.

And so we had to write narratives to support our pictures. Much of our writing was based upon first-person accounts, diaries and letters, all of which brought our pictures into focus. This book that you are now reading is a welding of the three projects, with some repetitive material eliminated.

The genesis of the original trio of books was a small collection of photographs relating to the Indian Wars in the West. Some personal information is necessary at this point to explain how we got into the Old West through the Indian Wars. Both Schmitt and I were librarians before World War II swept us away from our books and put us into army uniforms. After a series of misadventures while in training camps, reason miraculously prevailed over military bureaucracy and we wound up in Army Ground Forces headquarters at the old Army War College post in Washington. We had never seen or heard of each other before, but we discovered that we were both Western history fanatics and soon formed a lifelong friendship.

Our duties were quite similar to those of reference librarians in civilian life except that during off hours we were required to engage in a considerable amount of military duty so that we would not forget that we were soldiers in uniform. In other words, we had no spare time.

Schmitt and I were sergeants, and we soon discovered that life was simpler for us than it was for the junior officers, especially the lieutenants, when dealing with the colonels and generals for whom we worked.

As soon as the war ended, most of our duties ended, but the point system of demobilization required that we remain in the army for several more months. On days that we were not assigned to telephone answering or some other minor duty, we had no difficulty obtaining half-day leaves. On some of our wartime assignments we had consulted the Signal Corps photograph files in the Pentagon, and being Western history enthusiasts we had discovered there the old Indian Wars collection. From negatives (some were glass plates) we now could obtain prints at reasonable prices. We soon had in our possession splendid portraits of famous American Indian leaders, a few army officers of the period, forts, tepee villages, and various scenes relating to the wars in the Old West.

Being enlisted men, our funds were strictly limited, and we went a bit reckless ordering pictures we craved, virtually emptying our personal coffers. After we had collected the cream of the Signal Corps files, we began visiting the old Bureau of American Ethnology, the Library of

Congress, the National Archives, and other governmental agencies. About this time we were both assigned twelve hours of Sunday duty at the main telephone, which would ring perhaps once an hour, usually an inquiry from a representative of the print media in search of some name or fact about the recently ended World War II. During these long hours of inaction we turned to our Indian Wars pictures, assembling them in various ways, trying to determine the names of the photographers or artists, and identifying places and persons.

As the dates for our discharges from service became more definite, we also began trading prints with each other. Schmitt had edited and annotated the autobiography of General George Crook (which is still in print after half a century) and he wanted everything relating to the general's career in the West. On one particularly dull Sunday morning we hit upon the idea of arranging the pictures into tribal histories. We began scratching out short captions and text to tie them together. It was all very interesting to us, but the idea of creating a book was not seriously considered.

One afternoon Schmitt took a telephone call originating from the entrance gate of the War College post. A civilian was there, asking permission to enter so that he might consult with Sergeants Schmitt and Brown.

The visitor was F. R. Mansbridge, a senior editor from Macmillan publishers in New York. He was an Englishman, a graduate of Cambridge. He told us that he had come down to Washington to see how much art on the Indian Wars might be available in the museums and government agencies. He said that at almost every place he had visited the persons he spoke with told him that Schmitt and Brown from the Army War College were collecting in that field. They advised him to consult with us before continuing his searches.

Apparently Mansbridge had given little thought to photographs. He probably visualized a volume of exciting action paintings like those the British had published about the Empire's wars in India and Africa. When we brought out our 8 × 10 photo prints with our rough text and captions and sat him down at a table, he was soon so totally absorbed that we had to interrupt him at closing time.

He arose with an air of excitement, thanking us for letting him see what we had assembled and insisting that he be permitted to carry our collection off to New York so that his fellow editors might see it. Well, we were having none of that. Too much time and too many pennies were invested in those pictures and the text to allow a stranger to pack them off. We had legitimate excuses. We needed time to develop a better narrative, the captions could be much improved, and we were still trying to find some acceptably authentic Navajo pictures.

How much time would we need, Mansbridge demanded, and then added that Macmillan was eager to get an Indian Wars project moving.

We agreed on ten days, and for the next ten days we worked like the proverbial beavers. We were still not satisfied because we knew we needed a longer text, but on the tenth day we flipped a coin to determine who would go to New York. I won the toss, and with a two-day pass in my pocket went to call upon Mr. Mansbridge at Macmillan. We had titled our manuscript *Fighting Indians of the West,* a salute to the tribes that resisted invasion of their lands.

In those days the Macmillan offices and personnel were very British. The floors were waxed and the walls were paneled in fine wood (even the elevator had mahogany doors). After treating me to an excellent lunch, Mansbridge arranged a staff meeting around a long baronial table. He helped me lay out the pictures and pages in sequence, and soon a half-dozen or so gentlemen speaking mainly in British accents assembled along the sides of the table. They gradually began expressing enthusiasm for Mansbridge's Indian Wars project, but some cautioned that the expense of reproducing so many pictures might bring the price of the book above what the market would bear. (In that era of metal type and engravings the cost of printing illustrations was relatively high.) At four o'clock, tea was brought in and the conversation turned upon a text that must be written. Could Schmitt and I accomplish this? I assured the editors, of course, that we would write a full text.

Back in Washington, we used all our spare time at drafting narratives to tell the varied stories of the Indian Wars. Alas, we had scarcely begun when Macmillan notified us that an analysis of printing costs prohibited them from risking publication of *Fighting Indians of the West.*

After we wasted a few hours in melancholy, Schmitt came up with the next step. The University of Oklahoma Press had published his book on General Crook and he knew an editor there. Consequently the heavy bundle of photographs and manuscripts was soon dispatched to Oklahoma. The press eventually informed us that they were hopeful of obtaining a grant to pay the heavy cost of engraving.

We were several months out of the army and working as civilian librarians again before we heard further from Oklahoma. No grant had been forthcoming. The manuscript and photos were returned to me in Maryland, Schmitt being in the process of changing jobs and addresses.

Several of the 8×10 prints were badly damaged. (We later learned that an Oklahoma professor had used them in a book.)

After communicating back and forth we decided to divide the collection between us and bring the Indian Wars to an end. Schmitt informed me that in a few weeks he would be coming east on vacation to visit friends, including my family and me, and we would divide the collection then.

A few days later when I entered a bookshop, serendipity guided me to a new book that I was not looking for. It was a heavily illustrated volume about the Civil War, only recently published by Charles Scribner's Sons, a book just about the size I had envisioned for the Indian Wars. When the bookseller informed me that the Scribner's book was selling very well, I went straight home and wrote a letter to Mr. Charles Scribner himself. The quick response surprised me. Mr. Charles Scribner would welcome a chance to see *Fighting Indians of the West*.

Not long after that I was summoned to New York and met Mr. Scribner, who had an old-fashioned Dickensian air about him. He introduced me to the editors he had already chosen for the project, R. V. Coleman and Joe Hopkins. This pair wasted no time listing tasks that Schmitt and I must perform before production could begin. For example, we had to replace the damaged prints, expand the text here and there, and add an occasional picture.

When Schmitt arrived from the West with his share of completed tasks, we spent two or three days polishing our material, and then went up to New York. After a day spent with the two editors arguing over various points, Coleman asked whose name should go first on the title page. We flipped a coin and Schmitt won that one. When we boarded a train and started back to Maryland, we rejoiced that we were free forever of the interminable Indian Wars.

But there was one more hurdle. A letter from editor Coleman requested my presence on the earliest day possible. A few minor points that must be cleared up, he said. A day or so later I took an early train and arrived at midmorning. Coleman and Hopkins greeted me apologetically, explaining that they had not expected their editor-in-chief to take more than a cursory interest in *Fighting Indians of the West*.

The editor-in-chief was the famous Maxwell Perkins. He would be waiting for me in his office. He wears a hearing aid, I was warned, and sometimes he turns it off while conversing. If he does not reply to a question, take no offense. But if he asks you a question, make a direct reply. He doesn't like evasions.

Perkins's office was a long room with high windows along three sides. The sills were wide enough to sit or lie upon. He appeared to be in his sixties, an ordinary-looking man, his graying hair brushed straight back from his forehead. Along the wide sills he had placed all our pictures and text in a sort of time line. He greeted me quietly with a look of curiosity, but with no show of approval or disapproval, and suggested that we walk along the rows of pictures and manuscript beginning with the first chapter. Occasionally he would shift the order of arrangement, glancing at me as if to demand my approval and saying something about a slight alteration of accompanying text being necessary with the change of sequence. At the very end he stood erect and looked straight into my eyes. "Where are the Navajos?" he demanded.

I replied that we had been unable to find enough good Navajo photographs to tell the story of their wars. (Several years later, the very photographs we had hoped to find suddenly appeared in Denver from some lost hiding place.)

Perkins looked unhappy over my reply. "The Navajos are my favorite tribe," he said. Then he shrugged, waved me out of his office, and turned back to his desk. "We'll make a fine book," he called after me. "Tell Coleman it's all right."

Fighting Indians of the West was published in 1948, priced at ten dollars. Adjusted to monetary values of the 1990s that amount would equal about seventy-five dollars or more. Some of my friends believed the book would fail at such a high price, that few readers could afford it. The book was by no means a best-seller. But the reviews were excellent, and Scribner's was soon inquiring if we could produce a follow-up.

By this time I was working in Illinois and Schmitt was in Oregon. After a few telephone conversations and exchanges of letters we reached a natural conclusion. We would assemble a picture-and-text history of cowboys, cattle barons, and trail drives. We had chosen a title almost before we began: *Trail Driving Days.*

At the beginning, our arrangement was for Schmitt to collect the illustrations and I would do the text. Each of us dived into the literature of our subject, dividing the West into regions and outlining various segments of nineteenth-century history of the cattle industry. Between us we became familiar with more than four hundred classical works and about fifty sets of periodicals and other serials on the subject. Unfortunately, in the midst of our project Schmitt fell seriously ill and was unable to continue research that involved very much travel. Over the next year I used my vacation time searching through the Midwest and Great Plains, while he collected some great pictures in the Rockies and Far West.

One of the best Civil War photographers, Alexander Gardner, who for a time worked with Mathew Brady, had made a postwar tour of the early cattle trail towns on the Plains, and I found parts of his unique and essential photographic records in the collections of historical societies in Missouri and Kansas. Without Gardner's photos, exposed on glass plates just about the time that the first cattle drives from Texas were moving up the Chisholm Trail, we would know very little today of the look of trail towns in those early months.

Most useful of all the periodicals that I studied was a file of *The Cattleman,* founded by an association of ranchers and published in Fort Worth, Texas. I discovered that its back issues were filled with the lore of the cattle industry, stories by and about cowboys, numerous biographical pieces, personal accounts of ranch life and trail drives, and bits of bunkhouse humor. Much of the material was contributed by men and women who lived in ranching country and wrote in free and easy fashion. All this gave me a feel for the attitude I should take in writing the history.

I soon realized that I must pay a visit to Fort Worth. At that time the editor of *The Cattleman* was Henry Biederman, a cordial and very helpful gentleman who opened his office files and listened patiently to a greenhorn's inquiries about the past. Biederman steered me in the right directions, offering information about several colorful ranchers I might otherwise have overlooked, and he helped me obtain permission to use the remarkable photographs of Erwin E. Smith. Smith photographed cowboys and cattle roundups around the turn of the century but the clothing and gear and backgrounds were virtually the same as those of a generation earlier.

To tell the story of *Trail Driving Days,* we devoted the first pages to the origins of cowboys with emphasis on how ranching developed in Texas. Through the words of participants we followed typical drives over the trails to the early Kansas cowtowns. A section followed on the daily routines of a typical cowboy—roundups, roping, branding, horsebreaking, with accounts of how duties were divided on trail drives. We introduced personal remembrances of activities in trail towns, anecdotes about outlaws, lawmen, dance hall girls, soldiers, bartenders, all of which involved cowboys. Because Dodge City was the "queen of the cowtowns" we gave it full treatment, with stories of how outlaws and lawmen made their reputations there.

The great cattle barons, Billy the Kid, the long trail drives to Wyoming and Montana, the Indians, the wars between settlers and cattlemen all formed large parts of *Trail Driving Days,* published in 1952. Excellent reviews followed. To our surprise, the editor of the renowned *Atlantic Monthly* saluted the book with a review essay.

After publication of this second work, Schmitt and I had separate endeavors to pursue, and we did not return to another joint-effort type of book until three years later. In his duties as archivist at the University of Oregon, Schmitt unearthed several collections of nineteenth-century photographers who had devoted themselves to reporting life in Western towns. One summer he brought his family to visit relatives near Chicago, and he summoned me and my family to a daylong meeting at the Brookfield Zoo. He had brought along some choice photos with which to seduce me (we had both sworn off ever again working on a time-consuming picture history). After about an hour we were into the inception of *The Settlers' West.* We soon discovered that creating a book about the settlers of the Old West was even more challenging than our first two undertakings. Indians, cowboys, cavalry, trail drives, and cowtowns were exciting and romantic subjects, filled with anecdotes and tales of violence, suspense, humor, raw adventure, and many surprises.

To bring the lives of the settlers into focus we first considered the Western land itself—the vastness, the boundless plains and awesome mountain barriers. The Great Plains were a challenge to Eastern Americans and European emigrants. Those who crossed the Plains knew there was a western end to the flatness, but those who chose to settle there either went mad, often from loneliness, or they learned to love the unending sweep of earth and sky, and boasted that from their homes they could "look farther and see less" than anywhere else on earth.

For settlers of the American West, the ways of reaching a destination in the frontier country were either wretched ordeals or wondrous adventures. Fortunately for us, many of these men and women recorded daily events and their thoughts with such picturesque zest that some accounts of westward journeys have elements of great literature within them. At first they traveled in covered wagons, then by steamboats and stagecoaches. The coming of railroads increased the speed of the journeys, but for emigrant travelers there was little in the way of amenities.

And after homes were built, settlers who went west to live from the land soon found themselves engaged in dramatic battles with the natural elements. Droughts, floods, blizzards, prairie fires, insect hordes, tornadic winds, financial panics, and epidemics of disease all became part of the settlers' experience and were colorfully recorded in numerous letters and diaries.

Paul Bunyan and his blue ox "Babe" were giants, to match the giant trees that grew in the virgin forests. These forests were so vast that there seemed no end to them. Consequently they were the first victims of the spoliation of the "garden of the West." The pioneer loggers, miners, farmers—all wasted what they believed to be an inexhaustible paradise.

Life in the early towns was based upon long-established patterns brought from the Eastern states or Europe. Yet there was more informality, an abandonment of puritanical attitudes, forced improvisations in a world of inadequate supplies. In most towns the buildings carried an air of impermanence. Constructed of cheap lumber they had short lifetimes that ended by fire or rot.

Soon after a town was built, with merchants, lawyers, doctors, lawmen, and other professions established in their proper niches, there was leisure for the "finer things of life." Churches and dance halls were the only providers of music until someone organized a brass band and a choral society. Debating clubs supplied an abundance of oratory. And then an "opera house" would be built for entertainers and lecturers from the East. Traveling troupes of actors presented the latest dramas from New York.

The Western settlers created what we think of as the American West. Explorers came and went, soldiers came and went, miners and others came and went. But the settlers came to stay. John Charles Frémont explored and mapped the West, leaving his name on some parts of it, but he returned to the East to live and die. James Bridger epitomized the fur trapper and army scout in the West, but he retired to the comforts of Missouri. George Custer pursued American Indians throughout the Great Plains, but if he had survived he and his wife, Libby, surely would have returned to their beloved Michigan. George Catlin spent years in the West painting Indian tribes, but he lived out his life in Europe, New York, and Washington, D.C. Francis Parkman and Washington Irving explored the West to write great books about it, but both preferred to live in the East. John Butterfield established and operated his Overland Mail across plains and mountains to California, but he kept his headquarters in New York and died there. Teddy Roosevelt made himself into a quintessential cattle rancher in the Dakotas, sometimes contending with his testy neighbor, the Marquis de Mores, who also adopted Western ways and dress. Roosevelt returned to the East to become president; the Marquis returned to France.

No, it was the nameless settlers who stayed where they were, who put down roots, who largely contributed to making the West what it was. Most of them believed in Manifest Destiny. They were confident that Providence had guided them to their frontier homes. They were certain they had been brought there to "civilize the wasteland" of the West.

Their descendants view the Old West in a reverse mirror. They see the exploitation, the depredations, the violence, avarice, and waste— of which there was a plentitude. Yet there was also self-reliance, hospitality, generosity, exuberance, self-confidence, and humor (although sometimes black).

Today it is fashionable to mock the myths and folklore of the American West. Yet if we trace the origin of almost any myth and tale we will usually find an actual event, a real setting, an original conception, a living human being. We must accept the fact that the Old West was simply a place of magic and wonders. Myths and folktales form the basis of almost every enduring saga in the literature of the American West. They are the comfort and joy of screen and television scriptwriters.

But let us be wise enough to learn the true history so that we can recognize a myth when we see one.

CHAPTER 1
Westward March

▲ ▲ ▲ ▲ ▲ ▲ ▲ ▲ ▲ ▲ ▲ ▲ ▲ ▲ ▲ ▲ ▲

"Thare is good land on the Massura for a poar mans home."

THIS THEME, PENNED IN AN 1838 LETTER from Arkansas to Tennessee, appears with its variations as the moving spirit of western migration. The frontiersman who scrawled out the good news from the banks of the White River probably had no conception of the wide reach of land between his few acres and the Pacific shore. He dreamed no dream of empire. His eye was on the good land he had found, where a "poar man" could prosper.

To settlers on the bottom lands of the great midwestern rivers and on the forested fringes of the Great Plains, the West of the 1830s was a rumor of indefinite obstacles. Known in its parts by a few trappers and explorers, it was grasped as a whole by no one. The sources of its great rivers, the extent of its mountain ranges were a matter of vague conjecture by geographers, who often depicted the continental features as they "must be" rather than as they were. These maps of the literate were only a little more useful than the rumors of the semiliterate.

The great desert and the "shining mountains" stood as a barrier to the settlers who had flowed across the Alleghenies. Even the approaches to the mountains were forbidding. Between the western edge of settlement and the Great Divide lay the treeless plains, where wind and alkali dust accompanied fierce storms, and tribes of Indians roamed in search of buffalo.

Beyond the horizon of the settlers were the trappers and traders, less concerned with rumors, correcting the maps while they read them. "The Rocky Mountains," wrote trader Joshua Pilcher in 1830, "are deemed by many to be impassable, and to present the barrier which will arrest

MOUNTAIN BARRIER

To the westward-pushing settlers, the land beyond the Missouri was barricaded by mountains that could not be crossed by wagons. Sometimes referred to as the "shining mountains," they were eternally snow covered. (Photograph courtesy of F. J. Haynes Studios, Inc., Bozeman, Montana.)

the westward march of the American population. The man must know little of the American people who supposes they can be stopped by any thing in the shape of mountains, deserts, seas, or rivers."

That same year the company of Smith, Jackson and Sublette, fur traders, demonstrated that the plains, at least, could be crossed by wagons "in a state of nature." In April 1830, a caravan of ten wagons and two dearborns left St. Louis and crossed to rendezvous in the Rocky Mountains. Twelve cattle and a milk cow were driven along "for support." Grass was abundant, and buffalo beyond requirements, so that the expedition returned, rich in beaver pelts, with four oxen and the milk cow.

"The wagons," wrote the partners, "could easily have crossed the Rocky Mountains over the Southern Pass." Actually, they agreed, the route from the Pass to the great falls of the Columbia River was easier than the eastern slopes, except for a "scarcity of game."

Two years later, the steamboat *Yellowstone* ascended the Missouri to Fort Pierre on behalf of the American Fur Company, and so demonstrated a second practical means of western travel. The desert was vulnerable by land or water. The way was open for the "poar man" with his family and household goods to find good land "on the Massura"—or beyond.

The settlers came. They were not stopped by anything. They came, first, for good land; and when gold was discovered the gold-hunters joined the ranks of the land-hungry. First a trickle, then a torrent, the migration westward became a phenomenon in American history unique in numbers and distances. For fifty years the westward migration continued, until the good land from the Missouri to the Pacific was peopled, and the frontier was declared to be past tense.

Crossing the plains and mountains, easy for the professional fur traders and explorers, offered greater obstacles to the land-seekers, amateurs in the business of travel in a tree-less, water-poor wilderness. The emigrants carried more than "twelve cattle and a milk cow." Hunting buffalo was a new experience. The overlanders had not the contempt for difficulties bred by familiarity into the mountain men. Men and women loaded their children and their goods into wagons, and on horseback. Most found a canvas-covered wagon the best vehicle. Wide tires kept the wheels from sinking into the sand. During the travel season, May to September, lines of these prairie schooners stretched from the Missouri River to the Snake.

For settlers with no baggage or little money, the luxury of a prairie

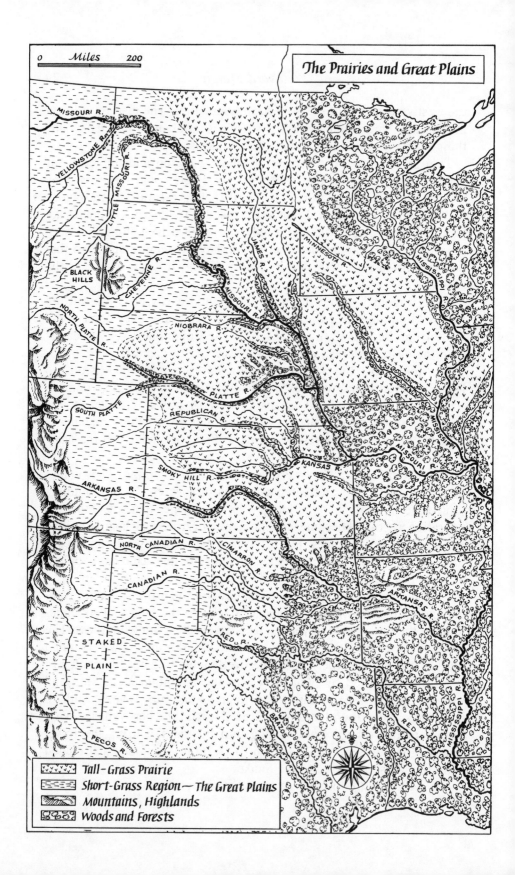

The Prairies and Great Plains

0   Miles   200

MISSOURI R.
YELLOWSTONE R.
LITTLE MISSOURI R.
BLACK HILLS
CHEYENNE R.
NORTH PLATTE R.
NIOBRARA R.
SOUTH PLATTE R.
PLATTE R.
REPUBLICAN R.
ARKANSAS R.
SMOKY HILL R.
KANSAS R.
NORTH CANADIAN R.
CIMARRON R.
CANADIAN R.
ARKANSAS R.
STAKED PLAIN
RED R.
PECOS R.
BRAZOS R.
MISSOURI R.
JAMES R.
MINNESOTA R.
MISSISSIPPI R.
MISSOURI R.
MISSISSIPPI R.
RED R.

Tall-Grass Prairie
Short-Grass Region—The Great Plains
Mountains, Highlands
Woods and Forests

SAN FRANCISCO HARBOR, 1851

For western travelers with money, sailing or steaming around the Horn, or via the Isthmus to the Pacific coast, was a way of escaping alkali dust. During the California gold rush, passengers and crew alike abandoned ship in San Francisco harbor to seek their fortunes. Ships were anchored helplessly until repentant sailors, disappointed in the diggings, came back to work. Passage on 'Frisco-bound vessels was less hazardous than over-land trips, but scurvy, storm, starvation, and lack of water took their toll. (Courtesy of the California State Library.)

schooner was abandoned in favor of carts. Many people simply walked across the plains, pack on back. There were instances of persons starting the journey pushing wheelbarrows. To all of the emigrants the trip was a series of new, strange, and often terrifying incidents.

Trail customs became standardized by experience and force of circumstance. Every well-run wagon train formed a corral of vehicles at the end of the day's journey for protection against Indians, and to provide a fenced enclosure for livestock.

All Western rivers could be forded at some point. At an easy crossing, the stream was shallow, and the ox teams simply pulled the wagons through. At deeper crossings, oxen and cattle had to swim; the wagons were converted into crude boats. Accidents at fords were common, and many an emigrant ended his journey swept down the river.

Mountain trails were also an impediment to travel. Space between the water's edge and canyon walls was sometimes barely enough for wagon wheels. When the cliffs pressed too closely, wagons waded to the other side, or used the streambed as a road. At one point on the Mullan Road (in Montana), regarded as an improved route, the St. Regis River had to be crossed nineteen times in six miles.

The average emigrant was not wealthy. By contemporary account, "His tone was dim, not to say subdued. His clothes butternut. His boots enormous piles of rusty leather, red from long travel, want and woe. From a corner of his mouth trickled 'ambeer.' His old woman, riding in the wagon, smoked a corn-cob pipe, and distributed fragments of conversation all around." (So many of them seemed to come from the Pike country in Missouri that the place achieved lasting fame in an overland ballad.)

Many of the first pathbreakers wrote letters home, and prepared itineraries for neighbors and kin who were to follow. "Guides" were published for the aid and comfort of the emigrant. Advice in such literature was based on tragic experience.

"Build strong wagons, with three-inch tires held on by bolts instead of nails."

"Obtain Illinois or Missouri oxen, as they are more adaptable to trail forage, and less likely to be objects of Indian desire."

"Every male person should have at least one rifle gun."

"Of all places in the world, traviling in the mountains is the most apt to breed contentions and quarrils. The only way to keep out of it is to say but little, and mind your own business exclusively."

Much of the hardship associated with overland travel could be avoided

CROSSING THE KAW

As the Western emigrant trails became established, enterprising persons rigged ferries across the larger streams along the route. Such ferries were usually the cable and scow type, motivated by the river current. Ferry proprietors were necessarily rough characters, as they had to defend their business from competitors and from persons offering shotgun toll. This ferry crossed the Kaw River. (Photograph by Alexander Gardner. Courtesy of the Kansas State Historical Society.)

by taking passage on a Missouri River steamboat to Fort Benton (northwest of Great Falls in Montana), head of navigation. While steamboat travel upstream was slower than a brisk walk, it was also more comfortable, and usually safer. Though most important as carriers of freight, steamboats brought many emigrants on the first leg of their trip to the new land.

Whatever the size of outfit or means of travel, the emigrants shared certain experiences common to all who came to the West. Their experiences have become symbols of the trek: the ferries and fords, Chimney Rock, Devil's Gate, the first buffalo, boiling springs, the Pass, alkali deserts. And Indians, who were also a hazard of the trail. "As long as I live," warned Red Cloud of the Sioux, "I will fight you for the last hunting grounds of my people." The United States Army garrisoned the plains routes, but the few soldiers could not protect every dangerous mile of the road. The sight of death on the trail was a universal experience—death by cholera, death in childbirth, "mountain fever," or a violent death in battle. The graves, quickly dug and marked, were part of the price paid for the free land and the great opportunity at the end of the trail.

To the poor man or woman in search of a better home, the wilderness that was the Oregon Country was very inviting. Traversed by Lewis and Clark, stronghold of the Hudson's Bay Company, and enthusiastically described by missionaries, the Willamette Valley drew settlers two thousand miles over desert, mountain, and plain.

The most well known of these trails was the Oregon Trail. Stretching from Independence, Missouri, to the Dulles, Columbia River, in Oregon, the trail became the main thoroughfare to the Pacific Northwest. After Lewis and Clark, the infamous John C. Frémont, with the help of the colorful guides Kit Carson and Thomas Fitzpatrick, was sent by the War Department in 1842 to do a more extensive survey, ensuring better and somewhat safer passage.

For those emigrants whose destination was the Pacific coast and who had more than average means, the sailing ship and steamboat offered a way of reaching the new land without the hardships of the overland route. Many voyagers found, to their sorrow, that they had exchanged one set of hazards for another.

Gradually the major Western routes became well defined, the worst gullies were smoothed over, the roads kept free from fallen trees, and the steepest grades eased. The Indian threat was subdued. Travel was less hazardous. Toll roads and ferries were established by enterprising persons who tarried on the route, grasping their opportunity on the spot. By the time of the Civil War it was possible to ride an overland stage from Missouri to San Francisco. The stage was comparatively fast, but, as one passenger declared, the ride was "twenty-four days of hell."

Efforts to improve means of overland travel led to some odd innovations. During the 1860s, both Joseph Renshaw Brown of Minnesota and Thomas L. Fortune of Mount Pleasant, Kansas, conceived the idea of a steam-propelled wagon, a prairie motor, designed to haul freight over the plains. But both the Fortune wagon and Brown's device proved impractical for freight work.

Not all western migration was pointed beyond the mountains. The "desert" of the Great Plains lost much of its terror, and attracted the land-hungry. To the settlers who came from timbered country, the plains were a "perfect ocean of glory." Here one could strike a sodbuster and circle a section of land without more obstacles than a few buffalo chips. Water was scarce, but the land was good, and a person could always hope.

As the railroads advanced westward with the aid of the land-grant system, settlement of the plains progressed more rapidly, and with a new pattern. The railroad companies recognized the economic importance of population along the right-of-ways. As they laid track, the lines competed for settlers, and offered attractive inducements to prospective emigrants.

In 1885 the Union Pacific posted special rates of forty-five dollars from the Missouri River to Portland, Oregon, with a free baggage allowance of 150 pounds. Berths in emigrant sleeping cars were free. "The emigrants," said a company leaflet, "are hauled in their own sleeping cars attached to the regular passenger trains."

Agents working for, or in cooperation with, railroad lines sponsored colonies. To settle the vast prairie lands, the railroad immigration agents sought out entire congregations and villages. As Jay Cooke, financier of the Northern Pacific, phrased it, "The neighbors in the Fatherland may be neighbors in the new West." To encourage colonists, the Northern Pacific built reception houses for the trainloads of new settlers, sold "ready-made" homes, offered terms of 10 percent down and the balance in ten annual payments. The company offered to donate a section of land to each colony for religious purposes.

To the railroad colonies came groups of Civil War veterans looking for a new start, entire congregations from England, and shiploads of emigrants from Europe. Max Bass, remarkable promotion agent of the

THE CROOKED STRAIGHT, ROUGH PLACES PLAIN

Mountain travel was made easier when toll roads were established. Road builders constructed easier grades, kept the road free from fallen trees, and filled in the worst holes. Dollarhide's Station *(above)* on the toll road across the Siskyou Mountains from California to Oregon was a major travel point. Through these gates passed stagecoaches, freight wagons, circus trains, pack mules, gold-hunters, itinerant preachers, and travelers whose business was best not asked. It was a lively spot to be. (Photo by Peter Britt, courtesy of the University of Oklahoma.)

Great Northern Railroad, gathered a colony of Dunkers from Indiana and settled them in North Dakota. The special train made up to transport the colony was routed through Indiana, Illinois, and Wisconsin by daylight, so the public could read the banners hung on the cars: "From Indiana to the Rich, Free Lands in North Dakota, the Bread Basket of America!" The train stopped in the Union Station at St. Paul, where Max Bass arranged to have a photograph taken. On March 3, 1894, the Dunkers arrived at Cando, and began a new life as wheat farmers.

Many of the hopeful land-seekers were disappointed in the land, the climate, and in their neighbors, but the stubborn ones endured the first hardships, and stayed.

Whether on a wheat ranch, in the gold fields, or on an Oregon donation land claim, the first consideration of the pioneer was for a house. Shelter for the family, rather than architecture, was the primary concern.

The "axe and augur dwelling" was the most common arrangement in a land where timber was easily available. As the name implies, such a house was built of logs, held together by wooden pins and gravity. The result of a workmanlike job was a "snug home in the wilderness." Inept or careless work produced a house "as tight as the end of a woodpile." A mud, stone, and sod chimney and fireplace heated the cabin, and provided cooking facilities. The primitive bed, referred to as a "prairie rascal," was the only fixed piece of furniture. Tables and chairs, other than those brought from the East, were rough-hewn. Windows were greased paper or parchment. Not everyone could afford such a house; there were settlements where log-house dwellers were considered "tony," while their more democratic neighbors existed in dugouts and tents.

On the treeless plains, the sod house became a common style of building. With a breaking plow, the settler drove a sixteen-inch furrow through heavy sod. The strip was cut into convenient lengths, and the sections laid like brick. Rafters, covered with hay and then with sod, provided a roof. Some of the prairie homes were neat, others simply holes in the ground. Well made, they were comfortable; ill made, they drove the pioneer housewife mad.

The ranch-type home, a one-story, flat-roofed, rambling structure, flourished in country where there was little rain or snow. It was essentially an imitation of the successful adobe of the Southwest.

The Latter-Day Saints, creators of many Western monuments, were especially remarkable from an architectural point of view. Their temple

RUSSIAN EMIGRANTS AT BISMARCK

To the treeless plains came families from Russia. To them, the scenes of North Dakota looked familiarly like the steppes of their native land. (Photograph courtesy of F. J. Haynes Studios, Inc., Bozeman, Montana.)

and tabernacle are noteworthy in the annals of Western building. In his multiple dwelling a Saint could live in peace with his wives and family.

As the settlers prospered, they built homes more closely resembling those they might have left behind. Sawmills were established, and lumber made available. The log house and "soddy" gradually vanished, and the frame house with a shake roof took their place. The wealthy imported ideas and habits from the East, hired labor skilled with a scroll saw, and built stately mansions with crusty decorations, a style known as "steamboat gothic."

The interior of a prosperous frontiersman's home offered opportunity for refinement and display of taste. The G. S. Barnes home at Fargo, North Dakota, was noted in 1883 for its quantity of Victorian decoration, imported artwork, and for its inclusion of every elegant detail. The Barnes family, bankers, had come as far as possible from the "prairie rascal" string bed of the frontier log house, from the one-room, all-purpose soddy that served the emigrant family. Here was splendor on the Western frontier.

Once the West was marked by trail, rail, and road, memories of the early-day adventures, hardships, and privations began to assume the qualities of a romance. The "pioneer" appeared as a special type, imbued with the spirit of Manifest Destiny, the major character of a national saga, rather than a person of average quality in search of more and better land. Pioneer societies were formed among the "first comers."

As the pioneers aged and prospered, they reminisced in a romantic spirit. The story of their adventures became a saga. Some of the longer-lived and more vocal devoted much time and effort to recollecting the picturesque past. Such a one was Ezra Meeker, who crossed the plains in 1852. Meeker, prototype of the Far West's "oldest inhabitant," spent his latter years retracing the Oregon Trail.

Encouraged by a sympathetic public, and assisted by the sale of postcards depicting himself, Ezra set his trail eastward in 1906, with a covered wagon and a team of steers. He called his trip "the Oregon Trail Monument Expedition." The old pioneer finally reached Washington, D.C., where he shook hands with the cowboy in the White House, Teddy Roosevelt. Meeker did much to stimulate popular interest in the history of overland migration, and the "Oregon Trail" cult dates from his efforts.

In contrast to Meeker was Sallie Long, pioneer daughter, who re-

ferred to the societies of emigrants as "pioneer imbeciles," and proph-
esied that "If the public and private words and deeds of most of them
were all published, it would prove a record alike discreditable to them
and their descendants."

Meeker's efforts appealed to the romantic heart of America, and the
story of the winning of the West became a popular theme for poetry,
drama, and fiction. Western ways were adopted by Westerners who
never before realized the obligation. The ideal of the pioneer was attached to commercial ventures, and the covered wagon hid a multitude
of promotional sins. The "Western" movie and the fictional Western
developed a formula of the Great Plains as seen from a car window,
not of the West as it looked from the papered windows of a sod house.

Somewhere between the uncritical enthusiasm of Meeker and the
irritation of Sallie Long stands the veritable Westerner, the pioneer,
the "poar man" who looked for "good land on the Massura." "I have
always lived in the West," said Ed Howe, "and the many pioneers I
have known seemed to feel they were better off than they had been
before."

In the chapters that follow, the faces of the Western pioneer appear—
from the days when the trail over desert and mountain was first cut by
wagon wheels, to the coming of the railroad, and the time when the
frontier became folklore. Here are the Westerners at work, at play,
building a civilization to conform to their environment, practicing their
religion, devising their politics, irrevocably changing the wilderness.
Here, too, are the faces of the Native Americans they encountered.

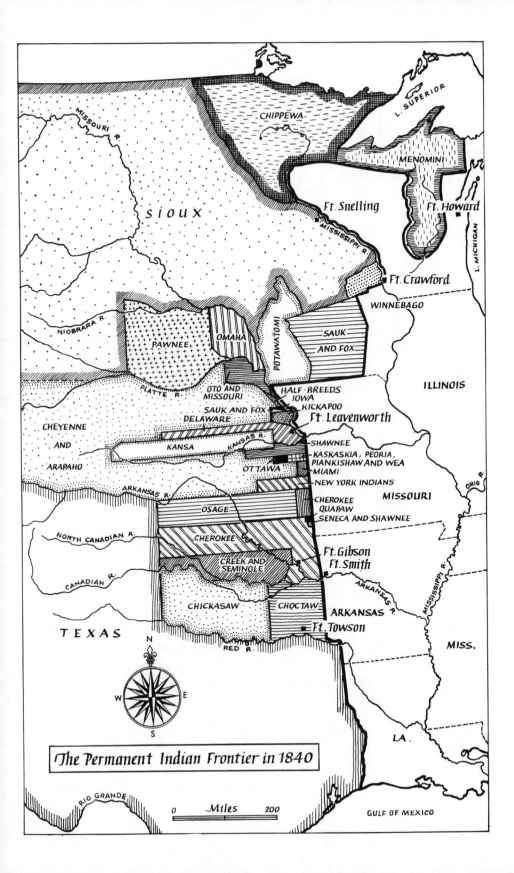

The Permanent Indian Frontier in 1840

CHAPTER 2
Longhorns and Pioneers

▲ ▲ ▲ ▲ ▲ ▲ ▲ ▲ ▲ ▲ ▲ ▲ ▲ ▲ ▲ ▲ ▲ ▲

THE CATTLE CAME OVER with the Spaniards, two years behind the gold-mad adventurers led by Hernando Cortés. They landed at Vera Cruz in 1521, six heifers and a young bull of sturdy Andalusian stock, sharp-horned fighters fast as wild deer.

Gregorio de Villalobos was the first cattleman. He had brought them to Mexico, these offspring of cattle transported first from Spain to Santo Domingo. Accustomed to tropical weather and tropical insects, they grew fat on the steamy coastal grasslands. They increased rapidly in numbers and were joined by other small herds making the sea voyage, and in a decade the tougher ones, the wiry ones with the sharpest-pointed longest horns, were moving north and west.

Twenty years later, Don Francisco Vásques de Coronado was seeing visions of the Golden Cities of Cibola. But as he prepared to march north out of Mexico, he was practical enough to take along some of the progeny of the six heifers and the young bull. Coronado was the first trail driver, with five hundred head of cattle, moving north toward the golden mirage on the high plains. Three centuries later on those same plains where Coronado's visions evaporated, the golden mirage proved true when thousands of cattle herds came driving into the trail towns of Kansas.

During those three centuries, the Longhorns and the cowboys and ranching slowly developed; the Spanish cattle mutating and evolving, the vaquero perfecting his costume and the tools of his trade. The Spanish names still cling, if not in spelling, in pronunciation: chaps, quirt, riata, rancho, sombrero, lasso, corral. And during the three hundred years, the Spaniards became Mexicans, spreading into Texas, seeking more ranching room for their ever-increasing cattle, which served as their main source of food and of leather for boots and saddles. There was always a surplus of livestock, and as the years passed, wild herds of both cattle and horses were roaming over the Southwest—in the grasslands, the sparse brush country, the dry plains, and the rugged mountains.

By the time Texas had won its independence, there was a ratio of six cattle for each Texan. No market existed for beef, but the industrial revolution in the northern United States was creating a demand for hides, tallow, hooves, and horns. The carcasses, considered worthless, were usually left to the vultures and the coyotes.

As early as 1842, however, Texans were driving herds of wiry Longhorns into Shreveport and New Orleans. In 1846, while the Texas-Mexico issue was being settled by a national war, an enterprising young man named Edward Piper drove a herd all the way north to Ohio. And when the California gold rush of 1849 created a small but profitable market on the west coast, some Texans moved cattle overland to San Francisco. W. H. Snyder was one of the pioneers of California driving. His outfit followed the Rio Grande north to the Continental Divide in Colorado, crossed parts of Wyoming, Utah, Nevada, and moved on to San Francisco. It was a two-year operation. Captain Jack Cureton of the Texas Rangers drove 1,100 Longhorns over the dangerous southern route across New Mexico and Arizona, dodging Apaches all the way. But Cureton figured the drive worth the risks. When he sold his steers to the meat-hungry miners, he took a profit of twenty thousand dollars, a goodly fortune in those days.

The great market, however, lay to the north and east, and among the pioneer trail drivers who pointed the way for the development of the Southwest's great cattle empire was Tom Candy Ponting of Illinois. Ponting's first drive set a record for long-distance trail driving that probably was never equaled.

Late in 1852, Tom Ponting and Washington Malone left Christian County, Illinois, for Texas. They were wearing buckskin belts filled with gold to buy steers.

After crossing Missouri and Arkansas, they traveled into the ranching country near Bonham, Texas, and found a place to board with a family named Clutter. "The money we had been carrying around was very heavy," Ponting later recorded, "and it was hard on us, so I took Mrs. Clutter aside and told her our business. This was the first time we had told what our business was. I asked her if she would take the money and put it under her mattress and not mention it to anyone, not even her husband. She promised me she would do so, and we left the money with her, and she kept it safely until we called for it."

When they had gathered about six hundred cattle, Ponting and Malone crossed Red River into Indian Territory and pastured their herd at Boggy Depot. Leaving Malone in charge of the stock, Ponting went to Armstrong's Academy in search of more cattle and chanced to meet there Jesse Chisholm, who a few years later would give his name to the greatest cattle trail of all. Ponting went with Chisholm up the Canadian River to an Indian council. As he found only a few cattle for sale among the Indians, Ponting sought out a rancher named Pussly, who sold him eighty 1200-pound steers for nine dollars a head.

Most of their gold was gone now, and the two cattle-driving pioneers headed their herd of seven hundred bawling Longhorns northeast for the Illinois cornfields. They had their troubles on the way. It was a rainy spring, and near Fort Gibson they had to hire Cherokees to help swim the cattle across the Arkansas River; they built rafts to float the supply wagons over. Unfriendly Indians hovered in the vicinity of their night camping spots, trying to start stampedes.

"I sat on my horse every night while we were crossing through the Indian country," said Ponting. "I was so afraid, I could not sleep in the tent; but we had no stampede."

Near Baxter Springs, Kansas, they crossed into Missouri, following the trail to Springfield, where they had their horses shod. "Sometimes while traveling we would forget what day it was and there would be days when we would see no man except those in our company. We would stop at the farmhouses in Missouri and get butter, eggs and bacon. The people did not want to charge us for them, said there was no market for them, and that we were perfectly welcome to them, but we always gave them something, especially if there were any children around."

At St. Louis, they crossed the Mississippi by ferry. "We had hard work to keep the cattle from plunging in the river." On July 26, 1853, they camped for dinner at the old Colony house in Stonington, Illinois, back in Christian County where they had started their journey.

Here the Longhorns got a winter's rest, but in the early spring of 1854, Ponting and Malone selected the best 150 of the cattle and started them east, pasturing them every night until they reached Muncie, Indiana. "When we got to Muncie, near the Ohio line, we found we could get cars on to New York. We made arrangements and put the cattle on the cars. Up to this time there had been very little of this work done.

We unloaded them at Cleveland, letting them jump out on the sand banks. We unloaded them next at Dunkirk, then at Harnesville, and then at Bergen Hill."

On July 3, 1854, from Bergen Hill in New Jersey, Ponting and Malone ferried their much-traveled Longhorns across the Hudson to New York and took them to the Hundred Street Market, completing a two-year journey of 1,500 miles on foot and 600 miles by rail. They were the first Texas cattle to reach New York.

The *Tribune* reported: "The top of the drove are good quality beef, and all are fair. A lot of twenty-one, short eight cwt., sold to Weeks at $80. These cattle are rather long-legged, though fine-horned, with long taper horns, and something of a wild look." The *Tribune* also pointed out the costs of the drive. "The expense from Texas to Illinois was about $2 a head, the owners camping all the way. From Illinois to New York, the expense was $17 a head."

It would be some time before Longhorn beef was commonplace in New York City. The distance and the risks were too great. But in a few years, Texas cattle became so common on the New York streets they interfered with traffic. "Through the very busiest part of town they go," said a contemporary journalist, "stopping business, frightening horses, filling eyes, mouths and clothes with dust, stopping travel, getting even into Broadway, and at last reaching the pens or the slaughterhouses on the east side of the town."

Meanwhile in Texas, the cattle continued to multiply. And while most Texans seemed to be raising cattle, a few were trying to find ways to preserve the meat for long-distance shipments to the eastern markets. One of the more successful was Gail Borden, who had gained considerable local fame in Galveston by his efforts to invent a land schooner, a covered wagon propelled by a sail. Borden's wind wagon was designed for travelers heading west over the plains. It worked very well, but on a test run dumped its occupants into the Gulf of Mexico. Discouraged, young Borden turned to dried beef biscuits, which he hoped to sell to the army and navy and to Western travelers.

When Borden announced he could use one-third of the cattle produced in Texas every year, the cattlemen became interested, and began avidly reading the young inventor's advertising pamphlets. By 1851, he had a meat biscuit factory in operation at Galveston, and the *Galveston News* reported as follows:

"We stepped into this establishment the other day, for the purpose of noting the *modus operandi* whereby beef cattle are converted into biscuit. The arrangements and the machinery are on a much more extensive scale than we had previously imagined, and the whole establishment exhibited a neatness and a cleanliness which we did not expect to see."

Borden's patented process was to boil about 120 pounds of beef down to a molasses thickness of ten pounds and mix it with flour to form biscuits. He won much publicity, but when he lost the army contracts he had hoped for, his packing plant failed. Borden later went to New York and founded the evaporated milk business which still bears his name.

Another Texan who tried to preserve meat was Captain Richard King, who embalmed his beef by infusing the veins with brine. The experiment failed. Consumers wanted fresh meat, not biscuit or embalmed meat. As did Borden, King took another course, and became the first great rancher in Texas.

The story of the King Ranch begins before the Mexican War, when Richard King came to Texas "possessing only a horse, a saddle, and ten dollars in cash." In 1846 he was operating a steamboat on the Rio Grande, hauling American soldiers and supplies to Mexican invasion points. By 1850, King and his partner, Mifflin Kenedy, owned a score of boats, running a profitable cargo business up the Rio Grande from Brownsville. In 1852, while riding with a young lieutenant named Robert E. Lee across the mesquite flats between the Nueces and the Rio Grande, King remarked on the luxuriant grass along the coastland. He thought it would be fine for cattle raising if there were only a market for beef. Lee replied that possibly a market could be found if a man tried hard enough.

Richard King mulled over the idea for a long time, discussed it with Mifflin Kenedy, and then finally bought the Santa Gertrudis tract of 75,000 acres on the Nueces River. He took his savings and began digging wells, buying Longhorns and horses, and hiring an army of Mexican vaqueros. He was so sure of the future, he went down to Brownsville in 1854 and married Henrietta Chamberlain. Six years later the Santa Gertrudis ranch was the major cattle enterprise on the coastal plain, and in 1860 King took Mifflin Kenedy in as a ranching partner. Combining their resources, the two men increased their land holdings and imported Durhams from Kentucky in order to improve their stock.

For them the coming of the Civil War only brought more prosperity, because their boats were in demand for hauling cotton to Brownsville where it was loaded on British merchantmen. By the close of the Civil

War, the Running W brand of the Santa Gertrudis roamed over 300,000 acres. In 1868, King and Kenedy halved the ranch between them, but when trail driving finally opened a vast new market, King began to expand again. When he died in 1885, the King Ranch enclosed half a million acres.

Without his steamboat business, however, even Richard King might never have survived the Civil War as a cattleman. Few other Texas cattlemen did last out the war in a state of solvency. Some of them had driven their herds across the Mississippi to supply the Southern armies, exchanging their by then worthless cattle for Confederate money that was also worthless long before Appomattox. Most of the younger men went off to Virginia and Tennessee for four years of fighting. When they returned home, they found their stock scattered in the brush and in the arroyos. There were more Longhorns than they knew what to do with. The cattle were grass fat and ready for market. But there was no market.

Several weeks after Lee's surrender, Generals Kirby Smith and Joseph Shelby were still leading small bands of unreconstructed rebels in Texas, and there was strong talk of continuing the war from the Southwest.

The majority, however, were weary of war, and even the few who would not surrender and who rode south across the Rio Grande into Mexico knew in their hearts that the fighting was done.

In a final gesture of defiance, they buried the Confederate flag in the great river. This ceremony marked the end of an era, the beginning of a new and exciting period in Western history. The Civil War was ended, but for many a year Texans would carry on the feud in Kansas cowtowns, baiting the Yankee peace marshals, releasing lusty energies in violent barroom brawls or in sudden explosive gun battles on the streets.

During these same times, the victors to the north were also fitting together the broken pieces of their lives and fortunes. Populations were shifting into cities, but the people wanted meat on their tables—meat formerly obtained in the forests or raised on their farms.

In Chicago a man who had made a fortune selling pork to the Union Army established a packinghouse. His name was Philip Danforth Armour. One of Armour's packers was an Irishman, Michael Cudahy. A few years later, Gustavus Franklin Swift, a New England Yankee, also read the future correctly and selected Chicago as the future meat center. They would all play big roles in the development of the Western cattle trade.

Christmas Day, 1865, on a 345-acre tract where nine railroads converged, the Chicago Union Stock Yards opened for business. And by early spring of 1866, rumors had reached the Texas cattle country that a steer worth five dollars in useless Confederate money would bring forty dollars in good United States currency in northern markets, such as Chicago.

Like a spontaneous seasonal migration, cattle began moving north from the brush country, the coastal regions, the plains, and the mountains. The Longhorns were there for the taking, unfenced and unbranded. All a man needed were horses, saddles, a few supplies, and some good drivers working on shares. The goals were the nearest railheads, and these were in Missouri. Railroad building, halted by the war, was slowly beginning again, and from Chicago the rails were pushing south and west.

Sedalia, Missouri, was the nearest railroad point for Texans, and in the first warm days of early spring, thousands of cattle from south Texas were driven north along the Sedalia trail, passing Forth Worth and heading for the crossing of Red River. After driving past Denton and Sherman to Red River, crossings were usually made at Rocks Bluff Ford or Colbert's Ferry. The herds then rumbled on through Boggy Depot to Fort Gibson, following approximately the trail used by Tom Candy Ponting thirteen years earlier.

Instead of attacking and scalping, the Indians of the territory used modern tactics to harass the drivers. They stood on their legal rights by demanding ten cents toll per head of stock, and usually obtained the assessment. Later it became the custom of cattlemen to pick up strays from other herds and use them for toll payments.

Except for occasional bandits, fierce thunderstorms, unseasonal cold weather, stampedes, and flooded river crossings, the cattlemen had no great difficulty in driving on into Baxter Springs, Kansas. It was here that they encountered real trouble. From Baxter Springs northeastward to the Sedalia railhead, the country was thick with new settlers, Jayhawker farmers, most of them recent battlefield enemies of the Texans. They did not want their fences wrecked and their crops trampled.

Some of the settlers also feared Spanish or Texas fever, a fatal cattle disease transmitted by ticks carried on the Texas cattle. The Kansas and Missouri farmers did not then know how the disease was communicated, but they refused forcefully to permit any Southern herds to cross their properties.

And so, thanks to these vigilant Jayhawkers, Baxter Springs became the main cowtown of 1866, the first in a series of colorful, sinful trail towns of Kansas.

Over 100,000 cattle were dammed up around Baxter Springs through the summer by the blockade, and occasional violent skirmishes flared between the Confederate Texans and the Unionist Jayhawkers. At last the summer waned. The grass died, or was burned off by the defiant farmers. Dishonest cattle buyers bought herds with bad checks. The unsold cattle died. By autumn, the great spontaneous drive of 1866 was ended. For the Texans it had been a financial bust.

A less optimistic folk might have gone home defeated. But not the cowmen of Texas. By the spring of 1867, many were ready to drive their Longhorns north again.

And in 1867, thanks to an enterprising Yankee stockman of Illinois, a convenient railhead and shipping point would be waiting to welcome their coming.

At the end of the Civil War, Joseph McCoy of Springfield, Illinois, had started a business, buying livestock for resale to the new packinghouses in Chicago. McCoy learned of the Baxter Springs debacle from another Illinois stockman, William W. Sugg, who had bought a herd in Texas, driven it north, and had then been caught in the "big bust." It was a doleful tale of lost fortunes.

McCoy realized immediately that good business demanded an open trail from the cattle country to a shipping point on a railroad. His desire to establish a cattle-shipping town soon became an obsession, in his own words, "a waking thought, a sleeping dream."

He studied the maps, and early in 1867 went out to Junction City, Kansas, where he tried to interest the local businessmen in building a stockyard. He received no cooperation, but he made up his mind that somewhere on the Kansas plains was the logical place for a railroad cattle-shipping point.

Returning to St. Louis, he visited the offices of both the Missouri Pacific and Kansas Pacific* railroads. The president of the Missouri Pacific stared at McCoy's rough unblackened boots, his slouch hat, and wrinkled clothes, and then ordered him out of the office. The president of the Kansas Pacific was polite enough to listen to his visitor's plans, but was not interested enough to risk any money on the enterprise.

Doggedly, McCoy went back to Kansas, where he was rebuffed also by the leading citizens of Solomon City and Salina. He later recorded

---

*The Kansas Pacific Railroad later became the southern branch of the Union Pacific.

that he "was apparently regarded as a monster threatening calamity and pestilence."

But at last, near the end of the rail line of the Kansas Pacific, he found the place he had been seeking. "Abilene in 1867," said McCoy, "was a very small, dead place, consisting of about one dozen log huts, low, small, rude affairs, four-fifths of which were covered with dirt for roofing. . . . The business of the burg was conducted in two small rooms, mere log huts, and of course the inevitable saloon also in a log hut, was to be found."

Abilene, however, met all the requirements for a cattle-shipping town. It was west of the settled farming country. It had a railroad, and a river full of water for thirsty cattle. On the prairies for miles around was a sweeping sea of grass that could be used for holding and fattening stock at the end of the drives. And nearby was Fort Riley, offering protection from Indian raids, as well as a potential market for beef.

After McCoy had purchased a tract of land adjoining the town, he settled down to work in earnest. It was already July, and the cattle herds were moving north from Texas. He allowed himself sixty days to construct a shipping yard, a barn, an office, and a hotel.

He arranged for lumber shipments from Hannibal, Missouri, and he wheedled railroad ties from the close-fisted Kansas Pacific in order to build shipping pens sturdy enough to hold wild Longhorns. For the convenience of the drivers and buyers, he built a three-story hotel, naming it the Drover's Cottage.

Meanwhile he had sent his friend, William Sugg, south to meet the cattlemen from Texas and inform them of Abilene, "a good safe place to drive to, where they could sell, or ship cattle unmolested to other markets."

The first herd to arrive was driven from Texas by a man named Thompson who had resold in Indian Territory to a company of cattle buyers, Smith, McCord & Chanler.

The arrival of the second herd was more dramatic. Owned by Colonel O. W. Wheeler of California, it had been assembled in Texas, 2,400 cattle and fifty-four cowboys armed for Indian fighting. Leaving San Antonio in early summer, Wheeler headed north, intending to drive to California over the South Pass route. But when the herd reached Kansas, rumors of cholera epidemics and hostile Indian activities alarmed Wheeler's drivers. Wheeler bedded his stock down thirty miles from Abilene, raging like a sea captain faced with mutiny. When he heard of McCoy's shipping pens, he drove into Abilene and sold out.

Other cattlemen began arriving, but the season was late. Not until September 5 did the first shipment move eastward on the Kansas Pacific, and then on to Chicago over the Hannibal and St. Joe Railroad.

One reason for delay was the reluctance of the Kansas Pacific to build a switchline. The railroad insisted on waiting until several herds arrived, and then announced they would build a twenty-car switchline, using cull ties, adding that they expected they would have to take up the tracks the following year. McCoy was so exasperated he held out for a hundred-car line, and finally got it.

Born showman that he was, McCoy arranged for an excursion of Illinois stockmen to come from Springfield "to celebrate by feast, wine, and song, the auspicious event."

When the visitors arrived at Abilene, they found several large tents prepared for their reception, as the Drover's Cottage was not yet ready to open for business. "A substantial repast was spread before the excursionists, and devoured with a relish peculiar to camp life, after which wine, toasts, and speechifying were the order until a late hour at night."

On the following day, "before the sun had mounted high in the heavens, the iron horse was darting down the Kaw valley with the first trainload of cattle that ever passed over the Kansas Pacific Railroad, the precursor to many thousands destined to follow." Even with the late start, Abilene shipped over 36,000 cattle that first year.

Joseph McCoy wasted no time in preparing for the coming season of 1868. He realized that the most important link to be completed in his plans was a well-advertised route from Texas to Abilene. Upon investigation, he discovered that such a trail was already in existence from Texas across Indian Territory as far north as Wichita.

In 1867 the trail bore no name, but by historic justice it should have been called Black Beaver Trail. Black Beaver, a shrewd old Delaware scout, had used the route in guiding Captain R. B. Marcy's exploring parties and various other expeditions of gold rush days. When the outbreak of the Civil War trapped Colonel William H. Emory's Union forces in Indian Territory, Black Beaver used the same trail as an escape route over which the scout guided the soldiers to safety in Kansas.

As a cattle trail it ran directly south from Kansas for several hundred miles through Indian Territory to Red River and on into Texas.

But the trail was named for a half-breed Cherokee trader, Jesse Chis-

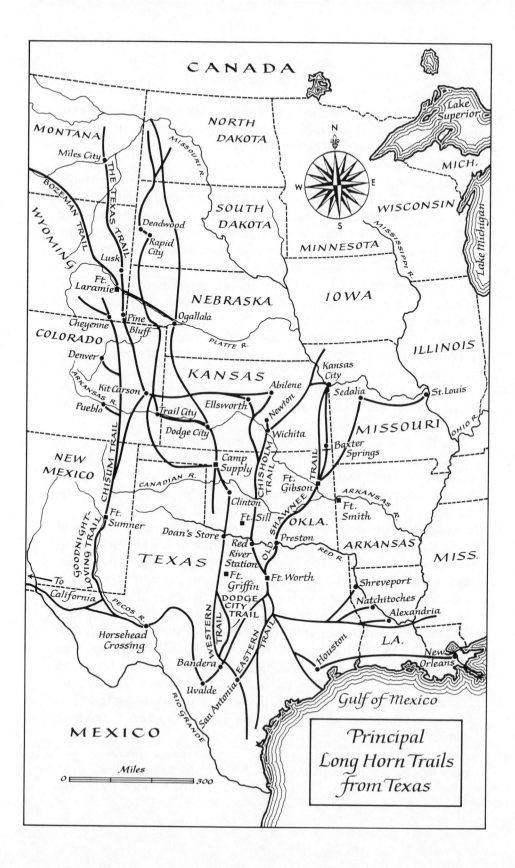

Principal Long Horn Trails from Texas

holm.* In the autumn of 1864, Jesse Chisholm hauled goods over this route south from Wichita and returned in the spring of 1865 with buffalo hides and some cattle. Chisholm retraced his journey in 1865–66, marking the road plainly, and it became known as Chisholm's Trail.

McCoy's contribution to the Chisholm Trail was its extension north from Wichita to Abilene. During the winter of 1867 he sent circulars to every Texas cattleman whose address could be found, extolling the advantages of Abilene as a shipping terminal and inviting the drovers to bring their cattle to his pens. He also sent two agents to Texas to make personal calls on the ranchers, and at the same time he published advertisements in the newspapers of Chicago and other cities, inviting cattle buyers to come to Abilene.

To complete the trail from Wichita to Abilene, McCoy employed a party of engineers to mark the route by throwing up mounds of earth at regular intervals. When this was done he sent his old friend, William Sugg, south to direct herds over the new trail.

As he was completing every detail to ensure a successful cattle-shipping season in 1868, a new obstacle arose which threatened disaster to all of McCoy's plans.

A sudden wave of rumors concerning Spanish fever, and its effects on Longhorns and Texas beef, began spreading across the country. "It was the subject of gossip by everybody," said McCoy, "and formed the topic of innumerable newspaper articles, as well as associated press dispatches. A panic seized upon owners of domestic herds everywhere. . . . The butchers, vendors, and consumers were alike alarmed and afraid to buy, sell, or consume beef of any kind." Several Northern and Eastern states were considering laws prohibiting importation of Texas cattle or beef.

In the spring of 1868, a considerable delegation of buyers arrived at the Drover's Cottage in Abilene. McCoy anxiously awaited the coming of the cattle. In June they came, long winding herds of Texas Longhorns,

---

*Confusion over the origin of the name Chisholm Trail is to be found throughout the history of the cattle trade. In 1866, Thornton Chisholm was trail boss on a drive from Gonzales northwest to Indian Territory and then northeast by way of Topeka into St. Joseph, Missouri. His route was known for a time as Chisholm's Trail. John Chisholm of Paris, Texas, also has been given credit for the origin of the name. And John Chisum of New Mexico gave his name to a "Chisum Trail" in that state. The Chisholm Trail that ended in Abilene, however, was named for Jesse Chisholm. Earliest use of "Chisholm Trail" in print was probably 1870.

JESSE CHISHOLM

Jesse Chisholm, a half-breed Cherokee trader, had already marked a trail suitable for driving cattle north across Indian Territory into central Kansas. Along this route in 1867, Joseph McCoy sent agents to direct the cattlemen into Abilene. From the beginning it was known as Chisholm's Trail. (Photograph courtesy of the Oklahoma Historical Society.)

splashing across the shallow Smoky Hill River into Abilene. Almost 20,000 were sold in that month.

But in a few weeks 50,000 more had arrived, and the Spanish fever excitement had killed the market. The buyers departed for Chicago; the Texas drovers began talking of moving their herds elsewhere. McCoy saw his dream collapsing, but he was not beaten yet.

Always resourceful, he suddenly announced a plan that would have done credit to his contemporary, P. T. Barnum. He hired several expert lassoers, led by a Texan named Mark Withers, to capture a carload of buffalo. Then he reinforced a stock car with stout planking, loaded another car with some smart Texas cow ponies, hitched on to a Kansas Pacific work train, and headed west for the buffalo feeding grounds.

Withers and his cowboys went to work, and in two days they had the full-grown buffalo bulls roped and tied. However, they had to spend several more days completing the job of getting the animals into McCoy's reinforced stock car. The buffalo bulls refused to be pushed, coaxed, or dragged into the car, and McCoy had to bring out a rope and tackle to haul them aboard.

Long canvas streamers were then hung on each side of the car, and "flaming advertisements were painted in striking colors" proclaiming the wonderful cattle bargains at Abilene. As it rolled through St. Louis on its way to Chicago, the newspapers hailed the progress of the "buffalo train," and upon arrival in Chicago, the buffalo were turned into a grass plot in the Union Stock Yard for public display.

McCoy's clever stunt worked like magic. Chicago buyers came back on a special excursion train, the market revived, and the 1868 season closed successfully. "Indeed," said McCoy, "Texas cattle became suddenly very popular and in great demand."

The following year, Joseph McCoy saw 160,000 cattle pass through his Abilene shipping pens. In 1870, the number rose to 300,000. The Kansas Pacific was kept busy moving the cars, and could scarcely find enough equipment to handle the loads. By this time the Chisholm Trail was worn deep like a river, two hundred to four hundred yards wide, with circular bedding grounds at regular intervals trampled by the passing herds.

By 1870, Abilene boasted ten boardinghouses, ten saloons, five general stores, and four hotels. During the summer shipping season, the town was hot, with little swift-turning whirlwinds spinning the powdery dust in the streets. It was noisy with the continual bawling of cattle, the cries of the cowhands, the dust-muffled beat of horses' hooves. And

WHEN ABILENE WAS WILD

By 1870 Abilene boasted ten boardinghouses, ten saloons, five general stores, and four hotels. Texas Street was a double line of false-front buildings, most of them painted and graying in the weather. Here were the saloons, the honky-tonks, and the stores dealing firearms, boots, hats, and horse blankets. Here waited the Calico Queens and the Painted Cats, ready to entertain the gallants from Texas. (Courtesy the Kansas Historical Society.)

over all was the pungent odor of the new pine lumber in the buildings of Texas Street, mingling with the smell of the excited animals crowded in the shipping yards by the town.

Texas Street, a prong-shaped thoroughfare running parallel with the railroad, was a double line of false-front buildings, most of them unpainted and graying in the weather. Here were the saloons, the honkytonks, the stores dealing in firearms, boots, hats, and horse blankets; here waited the Calico Queens and the Painted Cats, ready to entertain the gallants from Texas.

Rowdiness was increasing, and quarrels mixed with whisky and pistols produced several gunfights. According to Stuart Henry, who was a young boy living in Abilene at this time, "when you heard one or two shots, you waited breathlessly for a third. A third shot meant a death on Texas Street."

Abilene had no law. The leading citizens, including Joseph McCoy, hastened to incorporate the town, pass some ordinances, and build a jail. They posted notices along all the roads leading into town, forbidding the carrying of firearms within the city limits. The cowboys read the notices with interest, and jauntily filled them full of bullet holes.

As soon as the jail was built, a party of celebrating cowhands rode into town and tore it down. It was rebuilt under day-and-night guard, but when a camp cook was incarcerated for being drunk, he was freed in a few hours by his boys. They chased the jailer, broke the lock, and rode away with the cook.

To cool down the celebrating Texans, Abilene employed a marshal on July 4, 1870. His name was Thomas J. Smith, and he took the job at 150 dollars a month, with 2 dollars additional for each conviction of persons arrested by him.

Tom Smith was not a talkative man, but he had learned how to handle street gangs while on the New York City police force. Because of his reputation for breaking up a riot in Bear River, Wyoming, he was called Bear River Tom. A broad-shouldered man with gray-blue eyes and a well-kept mustache, he was quite impressive as he patrolled Texas Street on his gray horse.

Bear River Tom's first act was to post broadsides strategically in the saloons of the town: ALL FIREARMS ARE EXPECTED TO BE DEPOSITED WITH THE PROPRIETOR. His first showdown following this was with a rowdy cowboy called "Big Hank," who was wearing his pistol on the street. When Big Hank refused to disarm,

Smith calmly stepped in, struck him a terrific blow on the chin, took his pistol away from him, and ordered him out of town.

News of the bulldozing of Big Hank spread through the cow camps that night, and next morning a man named Wyoming Frank came into town to even the score with Bear River Tom. Wearing two guns, Wyoming Frank sought out the marshal. He received two smashes on his chin. This time, Bear River Tom took one of the challenger's pistols, beat him over the head with it, and told him to leave town and never return.

There were no gun killings during Tom Smith's reign in Abilene, but soon after the cowboys departed in the autumn, a local settler became enraged over a land boundary dispute and ended the marshal's career with a bullet and an ax.

CHAPTER 3
Cattle, Horses, and Cowboys

▲▲▲▲▲▲▲▲▲▲▲▲▲▲▲▲

AS TRAIL DRIVING developed into a major activity in the Southwest, the work of rounding up cattle and getting them to market gradually became routinized. But in the early years, it was more like a hunt than a cattle roundup.

The wild Longhorns hid in the brush and chaparral, and had to be pulled out by force, or lured out with tame cattle decoys. James H. Cook, a trail driver who later became one of the great cattlemen of the West, has described a wild Longhorn roundup.

"We went about five miles from the home ranch and camped near an old corral. The corrals in that country were all made about alike. A trench some three feet deep was dug in the ground. Strong posts about ten feet long were then placed on end, closely together, in these trenches, and the ground tramped firmly about them. They were then lashed together about five feet above the ground with long strips of green cowhide. . . . The following morning about sunrise we left the corral, taking with us the decoy herd."

As soon as wild cattle were observed in a dense clump of chaparral and mesquite, the roundup crew led the decoys into the brush, surrounded the place, and began singing a peculiar melody without words.

"A few minutes later," said Cook, "some of the cattle came toward me, and I recognized a few of them as belonging to the herd which we had brought from our camp. In a few seconds more I saw that we had some wild ones, too. They whirled back when they saw me, only to find a rider wherever they might turn. The decoy cattle were fairly quiet, simply milling around through the thicket, and the wild ones were soon thoroughly mingled with them."

It was an easy matter to drive the mixed herd into the corral, but several days were required to bring the wild Longhorns under control for a trail drive. They were usually left in the corral until they were so hungry that grass appealed to them more than flight.

Other methods were used to capture Longhorns in the open. Moonlit nights were considered favorable times for rope hunting, and when caught the cattle were tied down by all four feet. Next day tame cattle would be driven out and the wild ones released among them. "If they had been left for several hours, their legs would be so benumbed and stiffened that they could not run fast. . . . Sometimes when regaining their feet they would charge at the nearest live object and keep right on through the bunch of cattle and line of riders. It would then be necessary to rope and throw them again."

In a few years, however, range cattle became accustomed to seeing mounted cowboys. An outfit of good riders on fast cow ponies could gather a herd in relatively smooth fashion.

The success of a roundup usually rested largely upon the shoulders of the range boss, who in the early days was the ranch owner. As big ranching developed, the owner would select an experienced and respected cowhand for the job. During a roundup, the authority of the range boss was as ironclad as that of a ship's captain, but to keep his job he had to know how to manage three of the most unpredictable members of the animal kingdom—cattle, horses, and cowboys.

Roundups for assembling a trail herd were begun early in the spring, with every cattleman eager to hit the trail first in order to ensure plenty of grass along the route to Kansas. At the beginning of a "gather," the roundup boss would assemble an outfit of about twenty cowhands, a horse wrangler to look after the mounts, and, most important of all, a camp cook.

On range or drive, the chuckwagon was home, and a good cook was supposed to be proficient at more than the culinary arts. He had to be a combination housekeeper, morale builder, and expert wagon driver or "bull whacker." The cowhands usually referred to the cook as the "Old Lady," but they were careful not to offend him. He had too many subtle ways of evening the score. The cook was the aristocrat of the roundup and trail drive, a man who prized his dignity, was seldom a good rider, and had slight use for the temperamental cattle.

As for the chuckwagon, it was a work of utilitarian art, an invention of a master cattleman, Charles Goodnight. The chuckwagon was a commissary on wheels, a stout wagon covered with canvas and equipped with a box at the rear for storing tin dishes, a Dutch oven, a frying pan, kettle, and coffee pot. The standard staples also had their exact places: green-berry coffee, salt pork, cornmeal, flour, and beans. For fresh meat, of course, there was always plenty of beef handy. A folding leg was usually attached to the chuckbox lid, so that it formed a table when lowered for action. The main body of the wagon was packed with bedrolls, slickers, extra clothing. Fastened securely in the front was a water barrel with a convenient spigot running through the side of the wagon. Beneath the bed was a cowhide sling for transporting dry wood, kindling, or buffalo chips. And in a box below the driver's seat, the cook usually kept necessary tools such as axes, hammers, and spades.

The first day of a roundup, the men would be up before dawn to eat their breakfasts hurriedly at the chuckwagon, and then in the graying light they would mount their best ponies and gather around the range boss for final instructions.

As soon as he had outlined the limits of the day's roundup, the boss would send his cowhands riding out in various directions to sweep the range. When each rider reached a specified point, he turned back and herded all the cattle within his area back into the camp center. All day the men worked the animals back, seeking them out in brush thickets and in arroyos. By evening a restless, noisy herd would be assembled beside the camp. As darkness fell, the cattle usually quieted and gathered close together to rest or sleep on the ground, and the roundup boss assigned night herders to hold the herd in place by patrolling its borders.

After supper in a cow camp, while the cook was washing the pots and pans, the cowboys who were free of duties liked to assemble around the fire for some singing. If they were lucky, a fiddler would be among them. They sang rollicking songs, sad songs, unprintably ribald songs, but usually ended with a sacred hymn. Soon afterward, all except the night herders would be in their bedrolls; the next day's work would begin before the sun was up.

The second operation of a roundup began as soon as a herd had been collected. This next step was to separate from the herd the mature animals which would be driven north to market, and the calves which were to be branded for return to the range.

"Cutting out," it was fittingly called, and this performance was, and still is, the highest art of the cowboy. Cutting out required a specially trained pony, one that could "turn on a dime," and a rider who had a sharp eye, good muscular reflexes, and who was an artist at handling a lariat.

After selecting an animal to be separated from the herd, the rider and his horse would begin an adroit game of twisting and turning, of sudden stops and changes of pace. Range cattle were adept at dodging, and if a cowboy's pony was not a "pegger" the chased animal would soon lose itself in the herd. Some horses never learned the art of cutting out; others seemed to sense instinctively what was demanded of them. For the latter the work was pure sport and show. Working with the best type of cutting pony, a cowboy could drop his reins over the saddle horn and by pressure of a knee indicate the cow he wanted, leaving the rest of the action to his mount.

If calves were being cut out, the objective was usually the mother cow. The calf would follow her out of the herd into the open where it could be roped with ease.

Roping, the final act of the cutting-out process, also required close cooperation between pony and rider. As soon as a steer or calf was clear of the herd, the cowboy lifted his coiled lariat from its place beside the saddle horn, quickly paid out an oval-shaped noose six or seven feet in diameter, and spun it out over his head with tremendous speed. An instant before making the throw, he would draw his arm and shoulder back, then shoot his hand forward, aiming the noose sometimes for the animal's head, sometimes for its feet.

As the lariat jerked tight, the rider instantly snubbed it tight around the saddle horn. At the same moment, the pony stopped short, practically sitting down. The position of a pony at the moment of the throw was important; balance in motion is a delicate thing, and a sudden jerk of a taut lariat could quickly spill horse and rider.

Forefooting was found to be particularly effective with calves, the noose catching the animal by the feet and spilling it in a belly slide, with no damage done. If roped around the neck, a lusty calf would usually have to be forced to the ground, by "bulldogging" it. Bulldogging is a sort of cow jujitsu, and as seen today is a more modern technique than was used in trail driving days. Old-time "doggers" used no ropes, but were clever enough to select fast-moving animals for their victims. By throwing one arm over a calf's head and quickly twisting its neck, an experienced cowhand could unbalance the animal and drop it to the ground like a surprised wrestler—if it was moving swiftly enough.

Tail-twisting was sometimes an effective method of downing calves, and some of the tougher breed of cowboys thought nothing of grabbing a full-grown Longhorn by the tail, twisting the appendage around a saddle horn, and dumping the luckless animal to the ground. But most working cowboys preferred ropes, leaving bulldogging and tail-twisting to rodeo exhibitionists.

As soon as an unbranded animal was roped, it was immediately dragged or herded to the nearest bonfire, where the branding irons were being heated to an orange red. In Texas, all branding was done in a corral, a legal requirement devised to prevent hasty and illegal branding by rustlers on the open range.

Branding, the heraldy of the range, is as old as Spanish-Mexican cattle ranching. When he established a ranch in Mexico, Don Hernando Cortés started the practice by searing three crosses on the flanks of each of his cows. The first brands in Texas were usually the initials of the owner, and if two cattlemen had the same initials, a bar or a circle distinguished one from the other. One of the earliest Texas brands was that of Richard H. Chisholm (*H.C.*) of Gonzales, entered before the Alamo, in 1832.

During the Mexican War, while most of the Texas ranchers were too busy with other matters to attend to their stock, many cattle reached maturity without being branded. Colonel Samuel A. Maverick owned such a herd near San Antonio. Maverick had taken four hundred cattle as payment for a debt in 1847, and had them delivered to his place on Matagorda Peninsula. As his duties kept him in San Antonio, he had no time to look after the cattle, which multiplied rapidly on the tall grass of the Peninsula, and were as wild as antelopes. So many strayed to the mainland unbranded that when ranchers in the coastal areas saw an unmarked Longhorn, they would say: "That's one of Maverick's," or "That's a Maverick."

As no effort was made to retrieve the strays, other cattlemen picked them up and branded them. Finally, Samuel Maverick received an anonymous note from the Matagorda area: "Send someone to look after your stock of cattle immediately or you will not have in 18 months from this time one yearling nor calf to 10 cows."

In 1853, Maverick sent down a party of cowboys and they managed to round up approximately the same number as had been put on the Peninsula six years earlier. They were driven up to a ranch near San Antonio, while Maverick sought out a buyer for them. He had had enough of absentee cattle ranching.

At last he found a buyer, Toutant Beauregard of New Orleans. The cattle were so wild, however, that Monsieur Beauregard never caught all of them. For years, some of the "mavericks of Matagorda" wandered

BRANDING, NINETEETH CENTURY

The operation of getting a branding iron on a stubborn cow or calf, whether in the open or in a corral, was a plain hard-muscle job. A technique was early developed whereby two men known as flankers tackled from opposite sides. One doubled up the animal's front legs and put his knee on its head. The other flanker braced one of his feet against the animal's hind leg, stretching the other to full length. The brander then pressed the hot iron home, and the checker entered another mark in the roundup tally book. (Courtesy of Oklahoma Historical Society.)

about the plains of southern Texas, and so was created a new word in the American language. To this day any unbranded adult range cow is known as a maverick.

In the early years, friction over unbranded cattle caused many a gunfight. Brand artists could alter marks, easily changing a "C" to an "O"; an "F" to an "E"; a "V" to a "W." Or, for example, JY into OX. By ingenious use of triangles, diamonds, and squares, almost any brand could be changed to suit a rustler's convenience.

Brand blotchers frequently used a running iron, shaped like a poker and used like a pencil. When most states made possession of a running iron illegal, they substituted broken horseshoes, riding bits, or bailing wire. The latter was especially favored because it could be easily twisted to effect any sort of brand desired. To make the changed brands look like old markings, the clever rustlers used wet blankets between the hot wire and the stolen animal's hide.

Public registration of legitimate brands was soon established by law, however, so that cattlemen could detect a blotched brand. In Texas, brands were recorded by counties; other states had state brand books.

As additional identification, ranchers also branded their cattle with ear marks. An ear cut squarely off was called a crop. A nick on the upper edge was an over bit. A nick on the lower edge was an under bit. An angling crop on the upper edge was an over slope. An angling crop on the lower edge was an under slope. A triangular piece cut from the tip was a swallow fork, and the ear split deep was the jingle bob.

Ranchers vied with each other in designing unusual brands, preferably brands which would be difficult to change. Some memorable brands were the Hash Knife, the Bible, the Stirrup, the Dinner Bell, the Andiron, the Scissors, the Buzzard on a Rail, the Hog Eye, Turkey Track, Ox Yoke, Frying Pan, and Pancho Villa's remarkable Death's Head. John R. Blocker designed for himself the Block R. John Chisum preferred a straight bar, calling it the Long Rail, and he also used the jingle-bob ear mark. After winning some large stakes in a fast poker game, Burk Burnett designed his famous Four Sixes, incidentally one of the most difficult brands to alter.

Range heraldy might be romantic, but for the cowboy the operation of branding was his toughest and roughest job. Getting a hot iron on a stubborn cow or calf, whether in the open or in a corral, was never easy or pleasant work. When dragged to the branding fire even the mildest-mannered animal would begin bawling and kicking. The con-

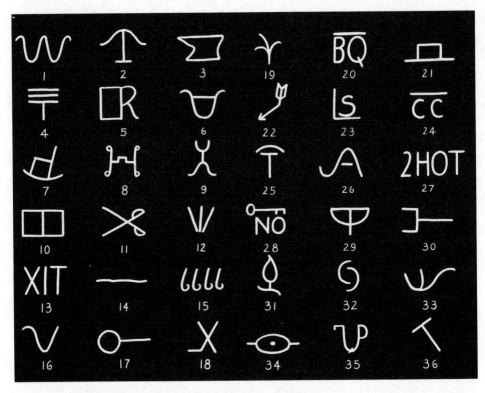

BRANDS OF THE SOUTHWEST

Some of the great brands of the Southwestern cattle ranching are shown above:

1. Richard King's Running W
2. Hash Knife
3. Anvil
4. Curry Comb
5. John Blocker's Block R
6. Stirrup
7. Rocking Chair
8. Spanish Bit
9. Andiron
10. Bible
11. Scissors
12. Hansford's Turkey Track
13. XIT
14. John Chisum's Long Rail
15. Burk Bennett's Four Sixes
16. Matador's Flying V
17. Glidden and Sanborn's Fraying Pan
18. LX
19. Three Feathers
20. Barbeque
21. Hat
22. Broken Arrow
23. LS
24. Henry Creswell's Bar CC
25. Bugbee's Quarter Circle T
26. Goodnight and Adair's JA
27. W. E. Jackson's Too Hot
28. Cabler and Mathis's Keno
29. Captain John Rabb's Bow and Arrow
30. Driscoll's Wrench
31. Mifflin Kenedy's Laurel Leaf
32. Halff's Quien Sabe
33. Pipe
34. Hog Eye
35. Seven Up
36. Tumbling T

(From a drawing by Cody Wade, courtesy of Cody Wade, Jayton, Texas.)

tinual dust almost suffocated the struggling cowboys, and over everything was the acrid smell of burned hair and hide.

As soon as the work of branding was completed, preparations for the trail drive would begin in earnest. One of the first things to be done was to acquire a plenitude of horses. Wild horse herds were the usual source, and they were rounded up much like the wild Longhorns, although mustangs were much more difficult animals to tame.

Each cow waddy going up the trail had to have six to ten mounts, because horses, like people, possess varied qualifications. One might be superior at cutting out, but inferior at night herding; another might be excellent for work around a cow camp, but poor on the range or drive. And on a long drive, with no grain for feed, mounts had to be changed frequently so that they could be kept in good riding condition on their diet of wild prairie grass.

Wild horses not only had to be corralled and branded, they had to be broken to the saddle and bridle. The process was sometimes rough on both horses and men. In the early years of the range, quirts and spurs were freely used.

Even after a good breaking in, some high-spirited horses just naturally were offended by saddles and bridles. A back fall or roll was one method they used to shake off riders. But a good cowman did not object to spirit in his mount. He knew a lively actor made the best cow pony and could be gentled with the right sort of training.

The horse herd accompanying a trail drive was known as the remuda (pronounced *remoother* in Texas). From 100 to 150 horses formed the average drive's remuda, and they were handled by a young waddy known as the horse wrangler. The wrangler was usually a young boy, the job being considered more or less as an apprenticeship for trail driving. He was the butt of many a cowhand's joke, and always had to ride the poorest horse in the remuda. But the wrangler was responsible for every horse in the herd, and was supposed to know their individual traits and habits.

When the riders selected their mounts for the day, a temporary corral was usually made by the wrangler and two or three cowboys who held a long rope a few feet off the ground. This kept the remuda in place until the men could rope and saddle their horses. Trained cow ponies had great respect for ropes, and the best ones would stand in position through a long session at the chuckwagon if their riders merely dropped the bridle reins on the ground in front of the horses' feet.

As the day for the trail drive approached, each cowboy assigned to

REMUDA

The horse herd accompanying a trail drive was known as a remuda (pro-nounced *remoother* in Texas). From 100 to 150 horses formed the average drive's remuda, and they were handled by a young waddy known as the horse wrangler. When the cattle were halted, a single rope was sufficient to hold a herd of trained range horses in place. (From a photo by Erwin E. Smith, courtesy of Mrs. L. M. Pettis and the Library of Congress.)

make the trip would busy himself at gathering his personal gear for the journey. In describing his first trail drive, James H. Cook says: "When Mr. Roberts informed me that I was to be one of his trail waddies, I immediately moved all my personal belongings over to his camp. I was allowed to take five of the best saddle horses which I had been riding, to be used on the trail. Roberts's trail crew consisted of twelve riders and the cook, besides myself. . . .

"On the trail we were each allowed to take a pair of bed blankets and a sack containing a little extra clothing. No more load than was considered actually necessary was to be allowed on the wagon, for there would be no wagon road over most of the country which we were to traverse, and there was plenty of rough country, with creeks and steep-banked rivers to be crossed. We had no tents or shelter of any sort other than our blankets. Our food and cooking utensils were the same as those used in cow camps of the brush country. No provision was made for the care of men in case of accident."

Although Cook does not describe the clothing he wore, it is certain that every item was designed for utility. And because of its basic practicality, the working cowboy's costume has changed very little. He seldom wore a coat because it retarded freedom of movement, and if he wore a vest he rarely buttoned it because he believed that to do so would cause him to catch a cold. He wore chaps, not to be picturesque, but to protect his legs from underbrush and weather.

He wore high heels on his boots to keep his feet from slipping through the stirrups, and gloves, not for vanity, but because the toughest palms could be burned raw by the lariat he used constantly in his work. He paid good money for a good-sized hat because it was his roof against the elements; he wanted it big like an umbrella to keep off the sun, the rain, and the snow.

As for the bandanna, J. Frank Dobie once proposed that it be made the official flag of the range country, and he has cataloged some of its uses: to protect the back of the neck from the sun; for a dust mask; an ear cover in cold weather; a towel; a blindfold for skittery horses; for tying a calf's legs together while branding it; as a strainer when drinking muddy water; a dish dryer; a hat tie in windy weather; a sling for broken arms; a bandage; as an aid in hand signaling; a face covering for dead cowboys; for hanging horse thieves.

Getting the average trail herd of three thousand cattle under way was as complicated an operation as starting an army on a march across country. The personnel consisted of sixteen to eighteen cowboys, a cook and his wagon, and a horse wrangler for the remuda. As a trail herd usually consisted of cattle from several owners or ranchers, a uniform road brand was sometimes applied. This task was much simpler than regular branding, the cattle being driven through a chute. A light application of the hot iron was pressed on each animal as it moved past the branders.

In the early days, the cattle in a trail herd were a mixed lot—varicolored Spanish cattle with small short horns; brown west Texas cattle with slight stripes down their backs and long shiny blue horns; and the Texas Longhorns, ungainly white-patched animals with half-twisted backs, gaunt bodies, and narrow hips. At the start of a drive they were always jumpy.

To keep a herd in order, the wise trail boss searched out a huge dominating animal and made it the lead steer. Charles Goodnight had one called "Old Blue," a veteran of several drives from the Panhandle to Kansas. After a day or so on the trail, barring an early stampede, the cattle would fall into place each morning like infantrymen on the march, each one keeping the same relative position in file as the herd drifted northward.

It was necessary to move slowly at first until the cattle were accustomed to the routine of the drive. When camp was broken in the early morning, the herd was not pushed but was allowed to graze if sufficient grass was on the trail. A herd on the trail moved like a sinuous snake, the lead steer and the best physical specimens "on the point." In the order of movement, the trail boss rode two or three miles in advance, seeking a watering place for the noon camp. Behind him was the chuckwagon driven by the cook, with the horse wrangler and the remuda on the left or right. Then came the point with the lead steers in front and the point riders on the sides, and strung along the widening flow of the herd were the swing and flank riders, to keep the flanks of the herd from spreading too wide.

John Clay, a Scot who became one of the great ranchers of the West, has left a classic description of a trail herd in movement: "You see a steer's head and horns silhouetted against the skyline, and then another and another, till you realize it is a herd. On each flank is a horseman. Along come the leaders with a swinging gait, quickening as they smell the waters of the muddy river."

The tail or drag riders brought up the rear, the least desirable position on a drive. The drag riders had to keep the lame and weak cattle moving, and all day they rode in clouds of dust, assailed by the generated heat

DRAG RIDERS

The tail or drag riders brought up the rear, the least desirable position on a drive. The drag riders had to keep the lame and weak cattle moving, and all day they rode in clouds of dust, assailed by the heat and smells of the herd. Beginning cowboys usually received this assignment, and as they achieved experience and seniority, moved up toward the point. (From a photo by Erwin E. Smith, courtesy of Mrs. L. M. Pettis and the Library of Congress.)

and smells of the herd. Beginning cowboys usually received this assignment, and as they achieved experience and seniority, they moved up toward the point on later drives.

During a day's march, a herd would average about fifteen miles progress. Each evening the herd had to be bedded down, and the night watch assigned, the men usually working in shifts of two to four hours. That most dreaded occurrence of a trail drive, a stampede, usually originated at night. Sometimes a sudden noise, the crackling of a dry twig, the rattle of a cook's skillet, would set the whole herd into mad flight.

To keep the restive cattle quiet, the night watch rode slowly around the herd, crooning to the animals—"Dinah Had a Wooden Leg," "Hell Among the Yearlin's," "Saddle Ole Spike," "Cotton-Eyed Joe," "Sally Gooden," "The Dying Cowboy." When weary of singing the same old songs, the night herders invented new verses, sometimes chanting with deep religious fervor a string of disconnected profanity, or the text from a label of Arbuckle's coffee, or perhaps an unflattering original discourse on the habits of Longhorns.

The cowboys soon learned that cattle liked slow mournful songs, the sadder the better, which may account for the dolorous quality of so many cowboy ballads.

As on the range, the cowboy's life on the trail revolved around the chuckwagon. First man up in the morning was the cook. After shaking the dew from the canvas which covered his kitchen on wheels, and firing up with buffalo chips, his raucous voice would awaken the sleeping cowboys: "Arise and shine! Come and get it!" Shivering in the cold of the prairie dawn, they would rise from their blankets, pull on their boots, and stumble toward the comforting smells of the chuckwagon. Or perhaps the cook had his own variation of a formula used by a certain celebrated trail driving sourdough artist: "Come, boys, get up and hear the little birds sing their sweet praises to God Almighty; damn your souls, get up!"

Chuck times were the best times of the day, even though food on the trail seldom varied. Black coffee, sourdough biscuit, beans, meat, and gravy. A delicacy was fresh onions, which they could find growing wild as they drove across the Indian Territory into Kansas in late spring.

Except for the short periods of delight offered by the cook and chuckwagon, the trail riders had little time for relaxation. At odd moments there might be a game of seven-up or poker, customarily played for matches on the trail, because there would be no money in their pockets until they reached a shipping town.

But to enliven the daily routine, each outfit usually had at least one practical joker, such as Tommie Newton, who rode with the J. W. Simpson herd. On one drive, Tommie Newton was the only cowboy along who had ever crossed Red River, and when the herd neared that stream, he rode ahead to scout a crossing. For once, he found that treacherous river's waters quite low, with white sand bars glittering in the sun. But at a distance, the stream appeared to be on a wild rampage, and Tommie Newton told the boys it was.

"Better shed your clothes and six-shooters right now," said he, "and put 'em in the chuckwagon. I'll go ahead with the cook and wagon and cross on a ferry boat around the bend."

Dutifully, the boys removed everything but their hats and long drawers. Then Tommie Newton and the cook drove off with the wagon and all the outfit's clothing, and crossed Red River with the greatest of ease. After ordering the cook to drive on a couple of miles, Tommie waited on the north bank, listening with keen delight to the profanity of the cowboys in their long underdrawers as they drove that herd across the Red River sand bars.

But for the most part, trail driving was a tough, dangerous business, a time of unending tension for the trail boss, a time of almost continual weariness and danger for every driver. The weather and the Indians were constant threats. A violent thunderstorm or a party of beef-hungry braves waving blankets could start a stampede in a matter of seconds, and to a cowboy on the trail, the cry of stampede connoted more terror than any other sound in the language.

•   •   •

One of the few trail drivers to keep a diary en route was George Duffield, who drove a herd of about a thousand Longhorns from southern Texas to Iowa in 1866. Stampedes and weather made life miserable for Duffield and his outfit all the way up the trail.

On May 1 he recorded: "Big Stampede. Lost 200 head of Cattle." May 2: "Spent the day hunting & found but 25 Head. It has been Raining for three days. These are dark days for me." May 3: "Day spent in hunting Cattle. Found 23. Hard rain and wind. Lots of trouble."

By May 8, they were ready to travel again. "Rain pouring down in torrents," says Duffield. "Ran my horse into a ditch & got my Knee badly sprained—15 miles." May 9: "Still dark and gloomy. River up. Everything looks *Blue* to me."

On May 14, a crossing of the Brazos was attempted. "Swam our cattle & Horses & built Raft & Rafted our provisions & blankets &c over. Swam river with rope & then hauled wagon over. Lost Most of our Kitchen furniture such as camp Kittles Coffee Pots Cups Plates Canteens &c &c."

Next day things went badly again. "It does nothing but rain. Got all our *traps* together that was not lost & thought we were ready for off. Dark rainy night. Cattle all left us & in morning not one Beef to be seen."

May 16: "Hunt Beeves is the word—all Hands discouraged. & are determined to go. 200 Beeves out & nothing to eat." May 17: "No Breakfast. Pack & off is the order. All hands gave the Brazos one good harty damn & started for Buchanan."

Finally they reached Red River, on May 31: "Swimming Cattle is the order. We worked all day in the River & at dusk got the last Beefe over—I am now out of Texas—This day will long be remembered by me—There was one of our party Drowned today."

June 1: "Stampede last night among 6 droves & a general mix up and loss of Beeves. Hunt Cattle again. Men all tired & want to leave."

June 2: "Hard rain & wind Storm. Beeves ran & I had to be on Horse back all Night. Awful night. Men still lost. Quit the Beeves & go to Hunting men is the word—4 P.M. Found our men with Indian guide & 195 Beeves 14 Miles from camp. Allmost starved not having had a bite to eat for 60 hours. Got to camp about 12M. *Tired.*"

All the way to Fort Gibson, the story was one stampede after another. And by this time the Indians were making trouble. On June 18, however, Duffield recorded one pleasant event: "Cook dinner under a tree on the A K [Arkansas] River Bank with two Ladies." He does not say who they were, but they must have been guests from the fort.

Next day: "15 Indians came to Herd & tried to take some Beeves. Would not let them. Had a big Muss. One drew his Knife & I my Revolver. Made them leave but fear they have gone for others."

After crossing the Arkansas on June 27, Duffield wrote: "My Back is Blistered badly from exposure while in the River & I with two others are suffering very much. I was attacked by a Beefe in the River & had a very narrow escape from being hurt by Diving."

A month later the herd was still in Indian Territory, after driving into Baxter Springs and then turning back to cross Kansas farther west. July 26: "The day was warm & the Flies was worse than I ever saw them. Our animals were almost ungovernable."

Duffield's drive ended October 31, when he reached Ottumwa, Iowa, and sold what remained of the herd. He had fewer than five hundred of the original thousand cattle that started from Texas six months earlier.

. . .

As drivers gained experience on the trail, they learned ways to prevent stampedes. Quite often the cause of a series of stampedes was a single jumpy animal, and if such an individual was spotted it was immediately killed and the meat turned over to the cook. Charlie Siringo says that at the beginning of a drive his outfit tied the hind legs of the worst offenders. "Sometimes we had to sew up the eye-lids of these old 'Mossy-horn' steers to prevent them running for the timbers every chance they got. It required about two weeks time to rot the thread, allowing the eyes to open. By this time the animal was 'broke in.' "

Nothing could be done about the weather, however, and cowboys on the open prairie soon learned to respect the power of lightning in particular. George Brock of Lockhart, Texas, said that when he first saw lightning strike the ground and set the grass on fire, he jerked loose his spurs, six-shooter, and pocket knife, laid them down, and ran away. To wear anything metal was considered fatal in a lightning storm.

A sudden clap of thunder at night was almost certain to start the herd moving in a frantic mass. If the drivers lost control of the frightened cattle during a storm, the herd quickly became a monstrous, irresistible force plunging through the darkness. Sometimes the friction of the speeding cattle caused weird blue flashes to quiver at the tips of their long horns.

In a stampede, it was every man for himself. "It is beef against horseflesh," a trail driving veteran once said, "with the odds on beef for the first hundred yards."

The cowboys in their bedrolls, awakened by the cries of the night herders or by the thundering cattle, quickly mounted their horses and rode toward the head of the stampede to help break the flight. Sometimes this could be done by turning the leaders, by firing revolvers and forcing the cattle into a great milling circle.

It was a rare stampede that left no fatalities. A horse's hoof in a prairie dog hole, a slip on muddy earth, a miscalculation of distance in blinding rain or darkness could mean instant death.

Next morning the cook would remove the spade from beneath the chuckwagon and dig a grave; the trail boss would take the Bible from his saddlebag and read services for the dead.

Teddy Blue has told what is probably the best vernacular account of such an event: "And that night it come up an awful storm. It took all four of us to hold the cattle and we didn't hold them, and when morning come there was one man missing. We went back to look for him, and we found him among the prairie dog holes, beside his horse. The horse's ribs was scraped bare of hide, and all the rest of horse and man was mashed into the ground as flat as a pancake. The only thing you could recognize was the handle of his six-shooter. We tried to think the lightning hit him, and that was what we wrote his folks down in Henrietta, Texas. But we couldn't really believe it ourselves. I'm afraid it wasn't the lightning. I'm afraid his horse stepped into one of them holes and they both went down before the stampede.

"We got a shovel—I remember it had a broken handle—and we buried him nearby, on a hillside covered with round, smooth rocks. . . . We dug a little of the ground away underneath him and slipped his saddle blanket under him and piled [stones] on top. That was the best we could do. The ground was hard and we didn't have no proper tools."

Finally, after three months of mud, dust, rain, rivers, Indians, rustlers, short rations, and stampedes, most of the men and cattle and horses still endured. And when the cowboys heard the whistle of a train on the railroad, or saw the first sprawling false fronts of the trail town buildings, they broke into rebel yells, and sometimes song:

I've finished the drive and drawn my money,
Goin' into town to see my honey.

It was the end of the drive, at last.

END OF THE TRAIL DRIVE

Finally after three months of mud, dust, rain, rivers, Indians, rustlers, short rations, and stampedes—most of the men and cattle and horses still endured. When the cowboys heard the first whistle of a train on the railroad, or saw the sprawling false-fronts of the distant trail town buildings, they broke into rebel yells. (From a photo by Erwin E. Smith, courtesy of Mrs. L. M. Pettis and the Library of Congress.)

CHAPTER 4
Red Cloud of the Sioux

▲ ▲ ▲ ▲ ▲ ▲ ▲ ▲ ▲ ▲ ▲ ▲ ▲ ▲ ▲ ▲ ▲

WITH THE ENDING OF the Civil War in 1865, the lusty and rugged years of national expansion—the migration westward—began. In the countless legends of the 1870s and 1880s the gold-seekers, the frontiersmen, and the United States cavalrymen have usually been the heroes.

But the Indians were also heroic, and the story of their long but futile struggle to keep their bison and their elk, their earth and their sky, is an epic that needs no romancer's gloss.

The story of the advancing frontier and the retreating Indian, told in hundreds of personal narratives and official reports, was also recorded by the pioneer photographers, who arrived soon after the dust of the first great emigrant trains settled along the Platte River.

Daguerreotype, succeeded by various wet-plate processes, was the medium of the early artists of the West. The surviving negatives and prints bear testimony to the handicaps imposed by such slow methods. Pioneer photographers carried all their equipment on muleback or in wagons—portable photographic laboratories, including an astonishing variety of materials, from glass plates to iodine. Each view involved unpacking, sensitizing a plate, exposing the plate, developing on the spot, and then repacking. When such labor was accompanied by threats of Indian attacks, sandstorms, and other hazards of frontier travel, it becomes the more surprising that pictorial records were obtained at all.

• • •

Between the gold rush days of 1849 and the beginning of the Civil War in 1861, thousands of emigrants had been crossing the plains each year, seeking gold, opening trading posts, settling new farms. The Indians of the northwest plains had generally accepted the U.S. government's loose policy that all the land west of the "big bend of the Missouri" was theirs, and they expected the settlers to keep out. For centuries the Indians had pitched their tepees along these streams, and had lived as free as people have ever lived, bound only by the earth and sky. Roaming herds of bison and elk were sacred animals, providing food, shelter, and clothing. The hunting grounds were sacred earth. And in the words of an old song:

> *In a sacred manner I live*
> *To the heavens I gazed*
> *In a sacred manner I live*
> *My horses are many.*

The leaders said: "The free open prairies and the sky-high mountains must not be traded for the worthless offerings of the white men. The tribal rites and customs, the sacred dances and the ceremonies must not be swallowed up in the ways of the white men. Let us follow the trail of our fathers. Let us guard the hunting grounds for our people."

For as long as the tribal calendars had recorded the seasons, the hooves of the buffalo had been drumming against the Western earth.

> *The buffaloes I, the buffaloes I,*
> *I make the buffaloes march around;*
> *I am related to the buffaloes, the buffaloes.*

Not only was the buffalo a symbol of food, shelter, and clothing, he was a symbol of life after death. In the body of each buffalo dwelt a manitou.

But the whites were coming to kill them, destroying the sacred buffaloes by the thousands. The medicine men chanted: "The earth is weeping, weeping." The old men of the tribes held councils and made many smokes and talked.

But the young warriors were angry. They smeared their bodies and the skins of their swift ponies with sacred medicine paint. They donned their warbonnets and their gaudy war shirts and all the emblems of battle peculiar to each tribe. They chanted war songs and danced war dances.

INDIAN RUNNER

From runners Native Americans learned that gold-seekers and adventurers were driving new trails across their beloved hunting grounds. (Photograph by Carl Moon, courtesy of Library of Congress.)

In little bands, without organization, they began to attack the invaders of their hunting grounds. But disciplined and well-armed soldiers of the U.S. government brushed them aside, and the pioneers and gold-seekers kept moving westward. Conflicts resulted. There were fights, and many people were killed.

To meet the demands of the western travelers, army posts were set up along the main routes—the Oregon Trail and the Santa Fe Trail. As more settlers crossed the Mississippi River into the rich farming lands west of the Great Lakes, large tracts of territory belonging to the Indians were declared by the U.S. government to be open for homesteading. And although the dispossessed Indians received annuities as "compensation" for their losses, the agreements were not always carried out. Border incidents occurred with increasing frequency.

For two centuries, tribe after tribe had been forced westward, as treaties had been made and broken by the government with complete disregard of the Indians' rights. But the leaders of the Great Plains tribes, the Sioux in particular, were great travelers. They had seen many things and had heard much talk, and they no longer believed in the promises of the white government.

They were brave people, the Sioux. They realized that there must be an end to retreats if their way of life was to survive. They did not like the railroad spurs that were beginning to jut across the Mississippi, pointing significantly westward toward the rolling prairies. They hated the settlements that were rising rapidly along the lengthening trails and stage lines. They knew that in the rich lands of Minnesota, a band of their own tribe had been forced into a narrow, defenseless reserve along the Minnesota River.

When the whites began their Civil War in 1861, the forts and cantonments of the West were drained of experienced soldiers. The untrained volunteers who took their places were not equal to the native warriors of the plains. In August 1862, a small band of Sioux killed five settlers near New Ulm, Minnesota, and loosed a series of bloody encounters between Indians and pioneers that took the lives of over seven hundred settlers in a week. Finally the Minnesotans organized a militia, and after a small battle, four hundred of the captive Indians were brought into St. Paul. They were tried, and most of them were sentenced to death. President Abraham Lincoln pardoned all but thirty-eight of the ringleaders, who were hanged publicly at Mankato on December 26, 1862.

Little Crow, a Sioux chieftain, continued a fighting retreat up the

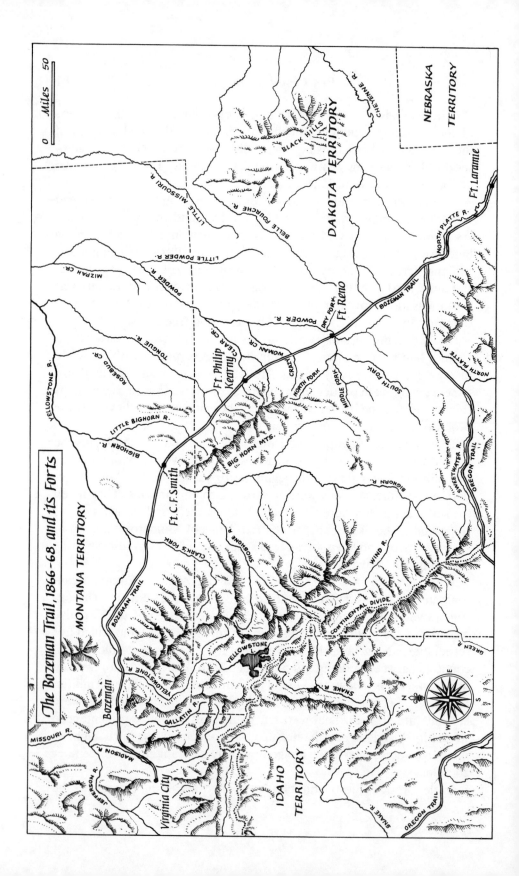

The Bozeman Trail, 1866-68, and its Forts

0 Miles 50

MONTANA TERRITORY

IDAHO TERRITORY

DAKOTA TERRITORY

NEBRASKA TERRITORY

Virginia City

Bozeman

Ft. C.F. Smith

Ft. Philip Kearny

Ft. Reno

Ft. Laramie

Yellowstone L.

BLACK HILLS

BIG HORN MTS.

CONTINENTAL DIVIDE

Bozeman Trail

Oregon Trail

MISSOURI R.
JEFFERSON R.
MADISON R.
GALLATIN R.
YELLOWSTONE R.
CLARK'S FORK
SHOSHONE R.
SNAKE R.
SNAKE R.
GREEN R.
WIND R.
BIGHORN R.
SWEETWATER R.
NORTH PLATTE R.
NORTH PLATTE R.
SOUTH FORK
MIDDLE FORK
NORTH FORK
CRAZY WOMAN CR.
CLEAR CR.
TONGUE R.
ROSEBUD CR.
BIGHORN R.
LITTLE BIGHORN R.
YELLOWSTONE R.
MIZPAH CR.
POWDER R.
LITTLE POWDER R.
DRY FORK
POWDER R.
BELLE FOURCHE R.
LITTLE MISSOURI R.
CHEYENNE R.

N E W S

Minnesota River, but his warriors were routed by General Henry H. Sibley near Wood Lake on September 23, 1862. Little Crow was killed later, and his tanned scalp, skull, and wristbones were put on exhibition.

Now the bars were down.

Twenty-five years of bloody conflict had been started, and the Sioux would be fighting to the end, until that day of final tragedy at Wounded Knee, South Dakota, on December 29, 1890.

During the last months of the Civil War, conditions became so desperate for the settlers that in some sections west of the Mississippi the federal army was forced to use paroled Confederate prisoners to man the forts. By 1864, the Arapahoes and the Cheyennes had joined the Sioux and were raiding the trails along the South Platte River and making forays into Nebraska. In November of that year, nine hundred Colorado militiamen made a surprise raid on the Arapaho and Cheyenne camp at Sand Creek, killing over one hundred men, women, and children. The beaten Indians were presented with a new treaty, and pushed farther back.

The strong Sioux tribes in the Dakotas, Montana, and Wyoming had been left almost unmolested through all these events. But they had watched the encroaching white settlers with wary eyes, and they were determined to resist any invasion of their finest hunting grounds with all the force they could muster. Red Cloud was one of the leaders, and he was a fighting chief.

The time for action came late in 1865, when the government decided to open a road to the Montana goldfields along the Bozeman Trail from Cheyenne northwestward to the headwaters of the Missouri. In the summer of 1865, General P. E. Connor and Jim Bridger with several hundred soldiers were sent on a march, now known as the Powder River Indian expedition, to prepare the way for the new road. The soldiers were continually harassed by superior forces under Red Cloud's leadership, and the expedition finally was abandoned, the army withdrawing when General Connor was suddenly removed from his command.

Early the following year, Colonel Henry B. Carrington of the Eighteenth Infantry was assigned the task of building and organizing a system of forts along the Bozeman Trail in Wyoming. His orders were to open the Bozeman road, either peaceably or forcibly, and he made thorough preparations for his task. Carrington requested a meeting at Fort Laramie with the Sioux leaders, including Red Cloud, the most warlike of the Oglalas. After considerable delay Red Cloud agreed to attend. At

RED CLOUD

Red Cloud began gathering warriors together to defy Carrington's soldiers. He was determined to halt the army's efforts to keep open the trail across Wyoming to the Montana goldfields. "It must be either peace or war," he warned. "If you want peace, return at once to Powder River." The soldiers refused to turn back, and Red Cloud began his fight in guerrilla fashion, biding his time, waiting for the proper moment to let loose all the might of the various Sioux bands and their Cheyenne allies. (Courtesy of the Smithsonian Institution.)

the conference, the proud Sioux chieftain drew his blanket closely around him and disdained an introduction to the military leaders.

In the midst of the negotiations, Red Cloud rose suddenly and faced Colonel Carrington: "You are the White Eagle who has come to steal the road! The Great Father sends us presents and wants us to sell him the road, but the White Chief comes with soldiers to steal it before the Indian says yes or no! I will talk with you no more! I will go now, and I will fight you! As long as I live I will fight you for the last hunting grounds of my people!"

Red Cloud turned and walked out of the council. Not many days would pass before the soldiers would know the meaning of his words.

·   ·   ·

Red Cloud's scouts kept him well informed about the movements of Colonel Carrington and the Eighteenth Infantry, from the day the soldiers marched out of Fort Laramie until they reached the Powder River country.

The Sioux leader knew that Carrington's force consisted of about seven hundred men, a number of civilian woodcutters and choppers, a scanty supply of ammunition, a forty-piece brass band, a dozen rocking chairs, a small beef herd, pigs and chickens, and machinery and tools for building a fort. He knew that wily old Jim Bridger was the guide and trusted adviser of the colonel. Red Cloud also must have guessed that the officers had not been impressed by his threats. Five of them, including Colonel Carrington, brought their wives and children along as confidently as if they were going on a summer outing instead of trespassing into hostile hunting grounds.

But when the expedition arrived at Fort Connor (soon to be renamed Fort Reno) they received a warning of what was in store for them. Raiding Indians captured nearly all the horses and mules assigned to Fort Reno, and an attack was also made on a civilian wagon train farther up the trail.

A few days later, after marching through July heat that caused the spokes of their wagon wheels to break loose, the expedition finally reached Dry Creek. Here they made another contact with the sudden violence that stalked their advance. In the dry basin of the water hole at the campsite they found the scalped and naked body of a dead white man.

Vigilance was redoubled. After they reached Crazy Woman's Fork, some of the men deserted and headed for the Montana goldfields. When a detail of soldiers was sent in pursuit, they were stopped by a band of Red Cloud's scouts and forbidden to proceed farther. In addition, a message from the Indians was sent back to Carrington, ordering him to take his soldiers out of the country. "It must be either peace or war," Red Cloud said. "If you want peace, return at once to Powder River."

But Carrington chose to march on to the Little Piney Fork, where he pitched his tents and started immediately to build Fort Phil Kearny. Although the army officers had brought with them complete plans for a model fort, the site they selected clearly demonstrated their lack of practical knowledge concerning Indian warfare. There was no cover between the fort and its water supply; the nearest fuel and timber supply was five miles distant; and high hills on all sides shut off observation of surrounding terrain. Jim Bridger disapproved of Fort Phil Kearny's location and wanted to march on to the Tongue River, but he was overruled by the military.

Meanwhile, two companies were dispatched northward to construct a smaller fort, C. F. Smith. With Fort Reno behind him as a link to Laramie, Carrington had three forts along the Bozeman Trail. But his men were spread thin. He needed reinforcements, and Red Cloud knew that.

The strategy of the Sioux leader soon became clear. He made no mass attacks. He bided his time, sniping from the brush, picking off a man here, a man there, utilizing the old guerrilla tactics of the Indians. He hoped to cut the ranks of the well-armed invaders to a point where they would be forced either to withdraw from the hunting grounds or to present so weak a front that the Sioux could destroy them in one final smashing attack.

Carrington, however, was a cautious strategist himself, even if he knew nothing about fighting Indians. He forbade his men to venture out in individual or small detachments. Every movement from the fort on the Little Piney was well guarded. Carrington also determined to build an impregnable fort, to perfect a defensive stronghold which no attacking force could storm. From the day the site was selected, the energies of every soldier and civilian were devoted to the construction of the fort. The plans had been drawn up back in Nebraska, and the proper dimensions were staked out on the morning of July 15. Tents were pitched in rows where the buildings were to be constructed; a crude mowing machine which had been hauled all the way from Laramie clipped the grass for the parade ground; woodchoppers and armed soldiers moved out to begin cutting the logs for construction of the thick loopholed walls. By evening of that first day, Red Cloud's scouts on Lodge Trail Ridge, overlooking the fort, must have been amazed at what they saw below them.

The rapidity of the military invasion threatened to break apart Red Cloud's loosely integrated forces. The Blackfeet and the Crows had never accepted him as a leader, and the Cheyennes were vacillating in their allegiance.

Early on the morning of July 16, a few Cheyennes appeared on the hills above the long rectangle of army tents. When they displayed white flags, Colonel Carrington sent out a messenger to welcome them. Meanwhile, he ordered his men to prepare a grand reception in the largest hospital tents so as to dazzle the expected visitors.

As about forty Cheyenne chiefs, warriors, and squaws approached the encampment, the Eighteenth Infantry band marched out to greet them with a rousing military tune. The Cheyennes were impressed.

Black Horse and Dull Knife, wearing elaborate bear-claw necklaces and brilliant beaded moccasins, made long harangues. It was obvious that the Cheyenne chiefs were both fearful and jealous of the influence of the Sioux; they were trying to drive a bargain with the army. Red Cloud's followers, they informed Carrington, were at that moment having a sun dance. And on the previous day the Sioux had made a vain effort to induce the Cheyennes to make common cause with them in driving the whites back to Powder River.

The Cheyennes' inclination to make a strong peace with the whites was probably strengthened by the arrival of four additional companies of infantry late in the afternoon.

But only two days after the powwow with the Cheyennes, the Sioux made a raid on one of the Fort Kearny outposts, seizing several horses. When troops went in pursuit, they were ambushed. Before they could escape, two soldiers were killed, three wounded. About the same time that the casualties were brought in, bad news arrived from farther up the Bozeman Trail. A wagon train had been attacked; six men were dead.

From that time there was no peace. All through the summer and autumn, soldiers and civilians were slain intermittently. Every tactic of guerrilla warfare in the Indians' repertory—from simple ambush to complicated confusion—was used against the invading whites. Red

Cloud even went so far as to teach his braves a few words of English and to dress them in captured blue army uniforms in order to disorganize the soldiers under close attack.

Colonel Carrington obviously did not know what to do. In one communication to headquarters at Omaha he would urgently request reinforcements; in the next he would assure his commander that the situation was under control and that there was nothing further to fear from the Indians. He issued innumerable orders to his men, forbidding them to walk on the grass, cautioning against the use of profanity, restricting them to their barracks after tattoo. With all this, an average of a man a day was being scalped or wounded by Indian attacks in the vicinity of the fort.

When *Frank Leslie's Illustrated Newspaper* sent out one of its artist-correspondents, Ridgeway Glover, he was carelessly permitted to wander two miles from the gates. The soldiers found his body naked and scalped, his back cleft with a tomahawk.

Carrington issued more orders. No soldiers or civilians would thereafter leave the fort without military authority. No large gates would be opened without special permission. All horses of mounted men must be saddled at reveille.

In order that small details of men might be sent to the timber to fell trees and cut logs, a blockhouse was constructed near the pinery, seven miles from the fort. Howitzers were frequently used to shell the woods with case shot before the cutters moved in.

Early in the autumn, Carrington sent Jim Bridger and Bill Williams, a fur trapper and a guide, out on a scouting trip among the Indian tribes. While on their reconnaissance, the two veterans of the Western trails visited a Crow village at Clark's Fork. The Crows, who had originally claimed all these hunting grounds, still hated the Sioux and looked upon them as interlopers. They readily told Bridger and Williams that Red Cloud and Man-Afraid-of-His-Horses had made visits to the village, asking the Crows to join them on the warpath against the whites. Red Cloud had said that he was only waiting for snow weather; then he would surround the fort, cut off its communications, and starve the soldiers out. He planned two big fights, one at the "Pine Woods" (Fort Phil Kearny), the other at "Bighorn" (Fort C. F. Smith).

On their return, Bridger and Williams warned Carrington to expect an attack by winter. They knew that no matter what Red Cloud's exact strategy might be, the real reason the Sioux had not already attacked in force was because of lack of organization among the tribes. But during the late summer and early autumn, the various Sioux bands—the Oglalas, Hunkpapas, Brulés, Miniconjous—had been welded together. And with them were most of the Cheyennes, Gros Ventres, and Arapahoes. As soon as the autumn hunts were over and the tribal stores were filled for the winter, blood would flow on the snow.

Some historians have discounted Red Cloud's importance in the Indians' war along the Bozeman Trail, pointing out that Man-Afraid-of-His-Horses was the head chief of the Oglalas at that time. However, it is evident that Red Cloud, being the younger and more vigorous man, had won over many of the Sioux as a result of his uncompromising stand against the whites at the Fort Laramie peace council. And he had continued to win followers all through the summer of 1866. Man-Afraid-of-His-Horses was old; the pleasures of hunting were no longer so keen, and the evils of the war were many.

After the soldiers moved in and started building the fort on the Little Piney, more and more of the Indians came to believe that Red Cloud was right. The white man must be driven from the sacred hunting grounds.

When the Cheyenne chiefs went down to Carrington's tent camp on July 16, a war party of Sioux angrily watched them from afar, suspecting that the Cheyennes were trying to drive a bargain with Carrington against them. As soon as the Cheyennes departed and made camp, the Sioux warriors dashed among them, demanding to know what they were doing in the soldiers' camp. When the Cheyennes explained that they wanted to make a peace treaty, the Sioux insulted Black Horse and the other chiefs by striking them across their faces with their bows, and then rode off into the night.

"White man lies and steals," Red Cloud told his followers. "My lodges were many, but now they are few. The white man wants all. The white man must fight, and the Indian will die where his fathers died."

In September, he took personal command of war parties raiding the area around Fort Phil Kearny. His braves used white flags and flashing mirrors for signaling, and the frequency of the attacks increased. When they could not get at the soldiers, they raided wagon trains, stampeding or capturing horses and mules. They heaped hay on Carrington's beloved mowing machines and set them afire, stole most of his beef herd, shot up the herders, sent pursuing soldiers limping and crawling back to the fort with arrows driven into their bodies. They even raided the blockhouse near the pinery, fired in through the loopholes, and scalped one luckless private alive.

The soldiers retaliated with their howitzers, which the Indians respected, calling them "the guns which speak twice." But Carrington realized that his infantrymen were no match for the slippery Indians on their swift-running horses. He called for cavalry, and headquarters sent him one company, piecemeal from Fort Laramie.

By October 31, the fort was completed, the stockades, warehouses, and quarters ready for the winter. Colonel Carrington declared a holiday, issued new uniforms to the entire command, and ordered the men out for a band concert and flag raising. "It is the first full garrison flag that has floated between the Platte and Montana," he told the troops. A poem and a prayer were read, the guns were fired in salute, and the band played "Hail Columbia." Meanwhile, up on Lodge Trail Ridge, red-blanketed Indians appeared, riding back and forth on their horses, flashing their mirror signals while they watched the strange celebration below.

A few days later a young infantry captain joined the Fort Phil Kearny staff. His name was William J. Fetterman, and he had served with some distinction through the Civil War. Fetterman sincerely believed that he knew everything there was to know about fighting, and his contempt for the "untrained" Indian was considerable. "Give me a single company of regulars," he boasted, "and I can whip a thousand Indians. With eighty men I could ride through the Sioux nation."

Unfortunately this reckless bravado was shared by two other officers, Captain Frederick H. Brown and Lieutenant George W. Grummond. Brown often had expressed an intense desire to take Red Cloud's scalp personally.

By December, Red Cloud was ready to give them a chance to make good their boasts and threats. He had won the allegiance of several additional bands of the hesitant Cheyennes, and his total warrior force probably numbered more than two thousand.

Early on the morning of December 6, Red Cloud led his camps up along the Tongue and Prairie Dog Creek, spreading the warriors among the foothills near the fort. Then he sent out a small raiding party, following their movements from a high ridge with a pair of captured field glasses. He was trying to set a decoy trap.

When a wood train moved out from the stockade gate into the pine woods, a small force of shouting Indians surrounded the woodcutters and began attacking. The men signaled back to the fort for help. Operating by a prearranged plan, Colonel Carrington sent Captain Fetterman and Lieutenant H. S. Bingham out toward the wagons with forty mounted men, while the commander with Lieutenant Grummond cut across the Big Piney, hoping to intercept the attackers.

The scheme failed. Bingham and fifteen men became separated from Fetterman near Lodge Trail Ridge, and when the junction was made with Carrington the Indians had disappeared. Red Cloud's warriors had turned the tables, killing the officer and two of his men.

For the next two weeks, Red Cloud kept large numbers of his warriors moving about the skylines above the fort, and sometimes at night, parties were sent in near the walls, imitating the cries of wolves. One morning a sentry was found dead inside the fort with an arrow through his chest.

The nerves of the soldiers were on edge. Fetterman went to Carrington and begged for permission to ride out with a company of men and make a bold attack, but the commander refused the request. He chose to watch and wait, hoping for more cavalry reinforcements.

On the twentieth day of December, a large Sioux war party was encamped on Prairie Dog Creek. Here they were joined by their Cheyenne and Arapaho allies, and the ceremonies which always preceded a big battle were begun. A hermaphrodite with a black blanket over his head was sent out to ride a zigzag path over the low hills. The He-e-man-eh, as he was called, made four rides. Each time he came back to chant a report that he had caught soldiers in his hands. On his fourth ride he shouted that he had a hundred soldiers in his hands, and the Sioux warriors cried that this was enough. They beat the ground with their hands, and then the three war parties moved on to Tongue River for a night camp.

The leaders for the coming battle were selected that night, and a young warrior named Crazy Horse was chosen to lead the decoy party. The last time they had failed to trap the soldiers, but this time they would succeed.

At daybreak they followed the Tongue up to the forks, and here Red Cloud asked the Cheyennes and Arapahoes to choose which side of Lodge Trail Ridge they wished to fight on. The plan was to draw the soldiers down the ridge, with the two forces hidden on either side. The Cheyennes and Arapahoes took the upper side, and the Sioux moved over to their position. Then a large party of picked Sioux warriors set out toward the fort.

Meanwhile, inside the fort the bugler had sounded reveille, and the day's routine had begun. It was only four days until Christmas and everyone was looking forward to a holiday celebration. The sun shone brightly, and although snow sparkled in the Big Horns, the air was so warm by midmorning that the men working inside the stockade removed their overcoats for comfort.

A lone wood train moved out of the fort, later than usual that morning, with an extra enforcement of armed guards. About eleven o'clock, the pickets on Pilot Hill began signaling frantically: "Many Indians!" Colonel Carrington was notified, and he stepped outside to join his officers. The women and children also came from their quarters. The next signal informed them that the wood train had gone into corral and that the Indians were attacking. Carrington turned, quietly giving the order to assemble a relief party immediately. Fifty infantrymen and twenty-seven cavalrymen fell into formation, and two civilians who worked at the post, James Wheatley and Isaac Fisher, volunteered their services. Major J. W. Powell was ordered to command.

But Powell had scarcely mounted his horse before Captain Fetterman stepped forward and asked Carrington's permission to command the party. Fetterman, who had been breveted a lieutenant-colonel for his gallantry in the Civil War, claimed seniority. Carrington hesitated momentarily, then gave Fetterman the command. Lieutenant Grummond had already volunteered to lead the cavalry unit, and Captain Brown, unknown to Carrington, joined the group at the exit gate.

Knowing well the impulsiveness of Fetterman, Carrington tersely warned the captain of the cunning of the Indians waiting in the hills. "Ride direct to the wood train, relieve it, and report back to me. Do not engage or pursue the Indians at the expense of the train. Under no circumstances pursue the Indians over Lodge Trail Ridge."

Captain Fetterman saluted, and turned his horse hurriedly toward the open gate. His mounted men galloped after him, the foot soldiers marching on the double behind them. Carrington strode across the parade ground, mounted a sentry platform, and ordered the troops to halt outside. "Under no circumstances," he repeated to Fetterman, "must you cross Lodge Trail Ridge!" Fetterman acknowledged the order, swung about, and led off at a fast pace down the trail toward the embattled woodchoppers. He was commanding eighty men, exactly the number he had declared he would need "to ride through all the Sioux nation."

Watching from high on the ridge, Red Cloud and the other leaders waited until the soldiers were near the corralled wood train. Then they signaled the attacking force to withdraw. While the tricky warriors around the corral were vanishing into the woods, Crazy Horse and his decoy party were dispatched toward the scene of action.

When Fetterman came in view of the woodchoppers, he saw no Indians, and it appeared to him that they had been frightened away at his approach. His desire to slay the "savages" apparently had been frustrated, and he was angry.

But a few moments later, Crazy Horse on his fast white-footed bay dashed out of the brush, leading his warriors in a zigzag trail across a slope in front of Fetterman's men. The soldiers opened fire at once. Fearlessly, the decoy party rode in close, whooping their blood-chilling yells, waving their blankets to frighten the white men's horses. Then they retreated, always moving jerkily back and forth, slowly, slowly up the slope toward Lodge Trail Ridge, the anger of Fetterman growing as he watched them escaping his riflemen.

The sky had become overcast with gray curdled clouds, and the warmth of the morning had disappeared, the cold deepening as if rising perceptibly from the frozen earth. In the forefront were the cavalrymen, eager to spur their horses onward, while the foot soldiers dug their heels in doggedly to climb the slope and keep close. Soon they were past the curving crest of Sullivant Hills, and then they were seen no more by their comrades in the fort.

Ahead of them were the Sioux, the Cheyennes, and the Arapahoes, concealed among the rocks and the brush, waiting silently for the signal to charge. The cavalry moved cautiously now, yards ahead of the panting infantrymen. It was a perfect trap.

Too late Fetterman realized his mistake. As he turned to wave his men back, a hundred "hoka hey's!" shrilled out upon the cold heavy air, the Sioux surging up out of the earth to smother one flank. The Cheyennes and the Arapahoes were up an instant later. The cavalry swung back bravely against a hilltop and stopped, the walking soldiers taking a position behind a pile of large flat stones. But it was all over in a few minutes.

At first the fighting was hand-to-hand, with war clubs and rifle butts; then the arrows began to fly like rain. The foot soldiers were wiped out, and then the Indians pressed the horsemen back against the steep snow-sheeted hill. It was so cold now that blood froze as it spurted from the wounds. In a final charge, the Indians killed the last man of Fetterman's company. When a dog belonging to one of the soldiers came running out barking, a Sioux shot it through with an arrow. Then the warriors picked up their dead and wounded and rode away.

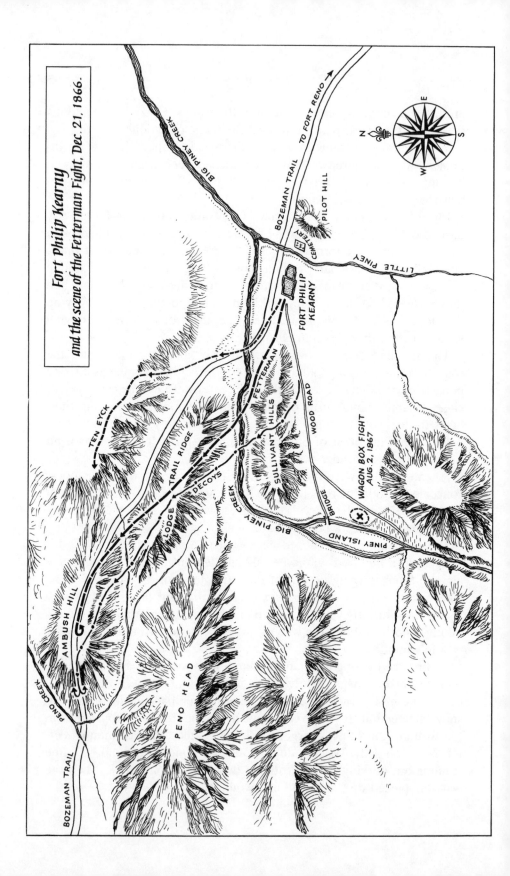

Fort Philip Kearny
and the scene of the Fetterman Fight, Dec. 21. 1866.

. . .

The incidents which followed the so-called Fetterman Massacre were not entirely anticlimactic. As soon as Colonel Carrinton heard the rapid firing from the ambushed soldiers, he sent Captain Tenedore Ten Eyck out with a relief force as large as Fetterman's, but Ten Eyck wisely halted on top of the ridge. He could see literally thousands of Indians moving across the valleys below, and he must have guessed immediately what had happened to Fetterman.

After the Indians had retired from the immediate vicinity of the battle, Ten Eyck's men cautiously retrieved forty-eight of the bodies, returning to the fort with them after dark. By this time the cold had increased in intensity, with the bleakness that usually precedes a snowstorm.

When a volunteer was requested to ride the 235 miles to Fort Laramie to obtain reinforcements, a frontier miner offered his services. His name was John "Portugee" Phillips, and his four-day ride through a blinding blizzard, past Indian encampments, with only a few pieces of hardtack in his pocket, is an epic performance in Western history. When he reached Horse Shoe Station, the news of the battle was flashed over telegraph lines to Fort Laramie.

At dawn on the twenty-second of December, a council was held in the fort, Carrington surprising his officers with a proposal to search for the remaining bodies. Although the number of men at Fort Phil Kearny was not now sufficient for adequate defense, Carrington declared firmly: "I will not let the Indians entertain a conviction that our dead cannot and will not be rescued. We must not give them an idea of weakness here, which would only stimulate them to risk an assault." He proposed to lead the search party himself.

Before departing, he opened the powder magazine and set the fuses so that all the ammunition could be destroyed by a single match. His order was: "If in my absence, Indians in overwhelming numbers attack, put the women and children in the magazine . . . and in the event of a last desperate struggle, destroy all together, rather than have any captured alive."

But the Indians attacked neither the search party nor the fort. It is possible that Red Cloud might have stormed the walls with his enormous forces, but for some reason—probably the weather—he chose not to strike. The blizzard that raged until Christmas piled the snow level with the west stockade, and the soldiers had to shovel continuously to keep a protective trench opened.

When reinforcements finally arrived from Fort Laramie, orders also came recalling Colonel Carrington. Captain H. W. Wessells took over the command. Carrington, his staff, his wife, and his two small sons had to cross Wyoming by wagon train in a blizzard with the temperature as low as 38 degrees below zero.

"There never was a more ill-considered impulse of the American people," he said later, "than that which forced the army into the Powder River and Big Horn countries in 1866, to serve the behests of irresponsible speculative emigration, regardless of the rights of tribes rightfully in possession."

Carrington would spend the remainder of his life trying to justify his actions during his six-month command of the fort on the Little Piney.

•   •   •

After his victory over Fetterman, the fame of Red Cloud spread like magic. All the Indians of the Powder River country heralded him as a leader with "big medicine," and as soon as the long cold winter of 1866–67 came to an end, he began making plans to drive the invaders completely from his country.

Unknown to Red Cloud, however, 700 new breech-loading Springfield rifles with 100,000 rounds of ammunition were brought up to the northern forts during the spring. Previously, the soldiers had used the old muzzle-loaders, weapons which the Indians had found scarcely more effective than their deadly arrows. In battle they merely waited until the soldiers delivered their fire, then when they saw the ramrods in use they would make a wild dash, attacking with arrows and any firearms they might have.

During July 1867, the Fort Phil Kearny woodchoppers opened full operations in the pinery several miles from the fort. A small company of soldiers under major J. W. Powell—whose place Fetterman had taken the day he was slain—was stationed nearby. For defense, Powell had removed the large wooden boxes from the wagon beds and placed them in a rectangular formation.

During the last week of July, Red Cloud gathered his forces together for an attack, but there was considerable disagreement among the chiefs as to the proper place to strike at the whites. Confidence of victory was high among the warriors of all the bands. They had assembled the finest war ponies in the country, and by devious means had obtained many rifles. But the Cheyennes wanted to attack Fort C. F. Smith, while Red Cloud preferred Phil Kearny, where he had already tasted victory. After the smoking of many pipes and the delivery of long harangues, the final decision was made by a simple process. The warriors were divided into two groups. The chieftains and their bands who wanted to attack the upper fort lined up on one side; those who preferred to attack the other fort formed another line. As there were over five thousand warriors present and as the two forces were almost the same in strength, the chiefs decided to attack both forts simultaneously.

The battle at Fort C. F. Smith is now known as the Hayfield Fight, because the soldiers were guarding haycutters outside the fort at the time of the attack. Surrounded inside a barricade of logs and willow boughs, nineteen men successfully fought off hundreds of Indians on August 1, and this assault was a costly failure for the warriors who had not chosen to fight under Red Cloud at Phil Kearny.

Red Cloud, meanwhile, had decided to try his old decoy trick once again, and as before he chose Crazy Horse for the leader. The men stationed outside Fort Phil Kearny under Major Powell offered the easiest target, and Red Cloud decided to slaughter them first, then ambush any relief force that might be sent out from the fort. The night of August 1, wearing their white and green and yellow war paint, their warbonnets, their feathers in scalp-locks, the warriors moved like dark shadows across the rough country north of the Big Piney.

At dawn they prepared to attack, the decoys moving out into the open. But most of the woodcutters fled back toward the fort, while the remainder with the soldiers—thirty-two men altogether—took their sheltered posts behind the wagon boxes. This time the warriors in concealment could not bear to wait for the decoys to lure the men out into the open again. Two hundred sprang out of hiding, stampeding the horses, and then the whole mass of mounted braves began circling the wagon boxes, drawing the noose of the circle tighter and tighter.

But to Red Cloud's consternation the soldiers did not pause between shots to use their ramrods. The screaming bullets spat out continuously and his best warriors went down like grass blades before a blast of wind.

There seemed to be no end to the white men's shooting. Red Cloud signaled the mounted warriors back, and then the Indians tried again, but the same bloody disaster was repeated. For a time there was a pause while the chieftains conferred. In a last charge, almost a thousand warriors who were without horses came swarming up from out of a ravine, while the mounted warriors came in from the other sides. But they could not storm the hail of lead from the new rifles.

When a scout informed Red Cloud that a hundred soldiers were coming from the fort armed with howitzers, he ordered his followers to withdraw. The white man's medicine, this time, had been too strong for him.

For days, Red Cloud thought he had suffered a defeat. In later years he said he had lost the flower of his fighting warriors and had resolved never to fight again. But back east the news of his resistance had at last made a deep impression upon the officials. The Indian Office reported that the government must either make peace with the Indians north of the Powder River or else flood that section of the country with troops and fight a long, costly war.

The government chose to make peace. General William T. Sherman, General William S. Harney, General Alfred H. Terry, General C. C. Augur, J. B. Henderson, Nathaniel G. Taylor, John B. Sanborn, and Samuel F. Tappan were appointed commissioners and were sent to Wyoming to draw up a new peace treaty. The trader friends of the Indians were enlisted by the commissioners in their efforts to persuade the chiefs to sign it. Spotted Tail and Man-Afraid-of-His-Horses were ready to sign, but Red Cloud by this time thought of himself as a conqueror. He was scornful of the commissioners, and he and the young hostiles declared they would remain in the Powder River country until the blue-coated soldiers marched away from the forts.

Finally, in April 1868, in a large tent at Fort Laramie, the terms of the treaty were agreed upon. The U.S. government agreed to withdraw its soldiers from the Bozeman Trail forts. "From this day forward," the treaty began, "all wars between the parties to this agreement shall forever cease." Red Cloud signed on November 6, 1868.

The soldiers were withdrawn from Fort C. F. Smith, Fort Phil Kearny, and Fort Reno. Before the retiring troops were yet out of sight of Fort Phil Kearny, they looked back and watched a band of Indians under Little Wolf setting fire to the hated buildings.

As for Red Cloud, he now believed that at last he had won back forever the sacred hunting grounds of his people. His illusions would vanish all too soon.

STAKING DOWN BUFFALO SKINS, 1870

There was plenty of buffalo meat for pemmican and skins for new lodges in the Powder River country. Here Red Cloud and his people lived after the treaty of 1868. Spotted Tail stayed closer to the Missouri River, near Fort Randall. (Photograph by Alexander Gardner, courtesy of the Smithsonian Institution.)

CHAPTER 5
Black Kettle of the Cheyennes

▲ ▲ ▲ ▲ ▲ ▲ ▲ ▲ ▲ ▲ ▲ ▲ ▲ ▲ ▲ ▲

WHILE RED CLOUD WAS STILL resisting the westward march across Wyoming, another great Indian was striving to settle his differences by diplomatic means. Black Kettle, one of the most famous chiefs of the southern Cheyennes, was the leader of the Colorado tribes whose existence had been menaced by the discovery of gold in that territory.

Black Kettle had tried to keep his people at peace with the invading whites, but in spite of his efforts unavoidable clashes occurred between the Colorado gold miners and the Indians of that region. Upon the advice of Major E. W. Wyncoop, commandant at Fort Lyon, some of the Colorado Cheyennes went to Denver in 1864 to talk with the governor of the territory. As a result of this conference Black Kettle brought his people in to the Big South Bend of Sand Creek, thirty miles northeast of Fort Lyon. To prove his loyalty to the United States, Black Kettle mounted an American flag over his own tepee.

For no apparent reason other than hatred, Colonel J. M. Chivington and his Colorado Volunteers attacked this camp in a surprise dawn raid on November 29, 1864. It has been charged that the goldfield volunteers, fearful of being called east to fight in the Civil War, deliberately attempted to foment an Indian war which would keep them at home. Whatever the reason, the indiscriminate slaughter of the surprised Cheyennes—men, women, and children—was so appalling that some of the most hard-bitten frontiersmen were disgusted. Kit Carson, who could scarcely be called a lover of the Indians, described the Sand Creek affair as a cold-blooded massacre. "No one but a coward or a dog would have had a part in it," he said. In the thick of the battle, Black Kettle had seen his wife shot down as she tried to flee up a streambed.

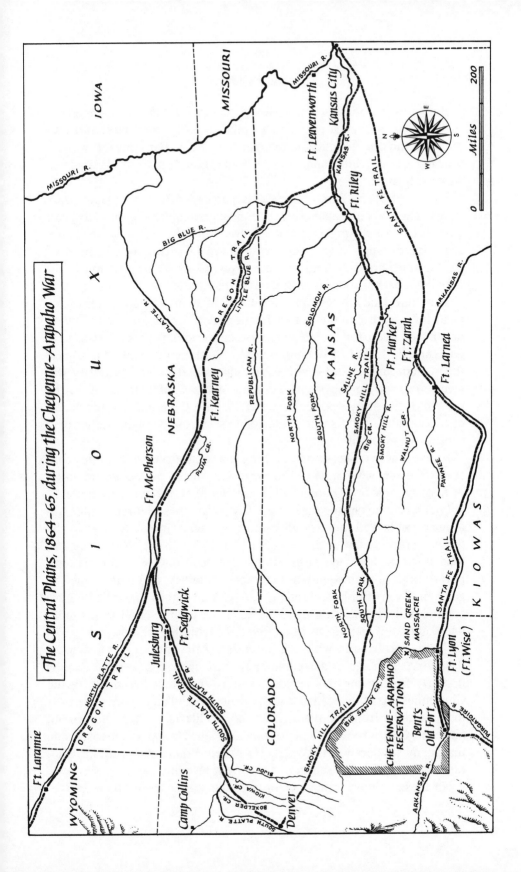

The Central Plains, 1864–65, during the Cheyenne–Arapaho War

But as usual, nothing was done by the officials. The Cheyennes and their Arapaho friends were left to take care of themselves, and they did so in the only practicable manner they knew. For weeks, it was not safe for a lone white man to cross a Cheyenne's path in Colorado or western Kansas.

Finally in 1865, Black Kettle was persuaded to sign a new peace treaty. Then when the government almost immediately ignored its guarantees, he lost his prestige with his followers. In October 1867, after regaining his supremacy over the southern Cheyenne bands, he tried for the third and last time to make a just peace by negotiation in the famed Medicine Lodge Creek Council in Kansas.

This time Black Kettle and the Cheyennes might have retired to a peaceful existence in the Indian Territory reservation assigned to them, had it not been for the rivalry between various factions in the U.S. government. Lack of a definite policy in Washington resulted in a great deal of confusion, and a corresponding ascendancy of authority was given the army in the West. The end of the Civil War added to the growth of the army's power in the West, with the release of thousands of officers and soldiers who preferred to serve on the plains rather than return to civilian life.

Among these officers was a dashing young cavalryman, George Armstrong Custer, who came to the West with the cold-blooded intention of making a glorious career out of the business of slaying Indians.

Ever since the closing days of the Civil War when George Custer was a much-publicized military idol riding up Pennsylvania Avenue in the Grand Army review with his yellow hair flying in the breeze, he had longed for his lost days of glory. He had been reduced from his temporary rank of major-general to a mere captaincy, and that seemed to gall him. Even after he worked himself back up to the rank of lieutenant-colonel with the Seventh Cavalry, he was irascible, cruel to his men, and completely barbarous in his relations with the Indians.

Custer had tried to whip the Seventh Cavalry into shape during the desultory campaign under General W. S. Hancock in western Kansas in 1867. But during this period he more than met his match in the Cheyennes, Arapahoes, and Kiowas, who resisted all the army's efforts to chase them from the plains. The Indians literally ran circles around him, and Custer took his spite out on his men. He was so unreasonable that many soldiers went AWOL. He ordered them shot without trial, then went AWOL himself in order to visit his wife.

For these military crimes, George Custer was court-martialed in November 1867. One year later, however, he was back at the head of the Seventh Cavalry. After reorganizing the outfit, he decided to win back his prestige and even his score with the Indians simultaneously, by some sort of bold stroke. Since he had been unable to best the Indians in open and fair fighting on the plains, he planned to surround the peaceful bands in their winter lodges and wipe them out en masse.

In November 1868, the Seventh Cavalry moved out of Fort Dodge, Kansas, ostensibly "to make the savages live up to their treaty obligations." The "treaty obligations" signed by the Cheyennes, Arapahoes, Kiowas, and Comanches stated that "in case crimes or other violations of law shall be committed by any persons, members of their tribe, such person or persons shall, upon complaint being made, in writing, to their agent, Superintendent of Indian Affairs, or other proper authority, by the party injured, and verified by affidavit, be delivered to the person duly authorized to take such person or persons into custody, to the end that such person or persons may be punished according to the laws of the United States."

The treaty then specifically stated that "such hostile acts or depredations shall not be redressed by force or arms." This provision was meant to protect innocent Indians from being slain for the crimes of the guilty. Yet it was against the villages of peaceful Indians under Black Kettle that Custer was riding in the late autumn of 1868.

General Philip Sheridan agreed with Custer's plans. In fact, he gave the official order: "To proceed south in the direction of the Antelope Hills, thence toward the Washita River, the supposed winter seat of the hostile tribes; to destroy their villages and ponies; to kill or hang all warriors and bring back all women and children."

In fairness to the Washington authorities who backed General Sheridan and Lieutenant-Colonel Custer in their action against the Indians along the Washita, it must be made clear that there had been occasional raids, some cattle had been stolen, and a few farmhouses burned. But these were isolated offenses committed by a few guilty Indians, actions of which most members of the tribes concerned knew nothing. Yet the deeds had been so magnified by distance that in Washington they appeared to be the grossest of crimes.

When Black Kettle and his people went into Fort Larned, Kansas, in July 1868 to obtain the supplies promised them in exchange for moving onto their barren reservation, the authorities refused to give them arms and ammunition necessary for their annual buffalo hunt. This refusal was in direct violation of the Medicine Lodge treaty.

"Our white brothers," said Black Kettle, "are pulling away from us the hand they gave us at Medicine Lodge, but we will try to hold on to it. We hope the Great White Father will take pity on us and let us have the guns and ammunition he promised us so we can go hunt buffalo to keep our families from going hungry."

Finally in August, Black Kettle's old friend of Colorado days, E. W. Wyncoop, now a United States Indian agent at Fort Larned, succeeded in obtaining permission from Washington to give out supplies, including arms and ammunition for the annual buffalo hunt. Soon afterward the Cheyennes departed for the autumn hunt, which was very successful. Black Kettle then led his followers, as directed by the government, to a site on the cottonwood-fringed Washita River. After the strenuous hunts were over, the warriors would return to their lodges to rest, and the women and children would perform many of the tasks necessary for establishing a winter encampment. They would cut the buffalo meat into thin strips, which were hung on pole frames and left to dry in the hot early-autumn sun. Preserved in this manner and then put away into rawhide packs, pemmican was the main winter diet of the plains Indians. The women would also stretch and treat the skins of the buffalo. The texture of the buffalo hide was such that it could not be finely dressed, but it was made into heavy clothing for winter, into moccasins and tent covers. Small hunting parties went out again in the early winter to obtain pelts suitable for bedding and robes.

The Araphoes had followed their Cheyenne friends to Indian Territory and were also busy establishing new winter lodges on the banks of the Washita River. They set up tepees near the villages of the Cheyennes, and awaited the coming of the moons of the short days and deep snows.

For his own lodge, Black Kettle chose a site under a giant cottonwood at the edge of the camp, where he set up his tepee and displayed his brilliantly colored trophies of the chase. He thought that surely now his people had nothing to worry about all winter—nothing except the ugly rumor that the U.S. government was planning to move them into a more restricted reserve and make them live in houses and till the soil like the whites.

Late in November, Black Kettle, Big Man, Little Rock, and some of the other chiefs went to Fort Cobb to talk over this alarming rumor, but they received little consolation. Indeed, they heard further disquieting news. Many soldiers were said to be coming south on a winter campaign. By the time the chiefs returned to the encampment the night

CHEYENNE AND ARAPAHOE CHIEFS

These are the Cheyenne and Arapahoe chiefs who went to Denver, Colorado, in 1864 to make a treaty with the governor. *Left to right, front row:* One-eye, Black Kettle (holding pipe), Bull Bear, White Antelope. *Back row (order uncertain):* Neva, Heap O'Buffaloes, and No-ta-nee (Knock Knee). (Photograph courtesy of the Archives and Manuscript division of the Oklahoma Historical Society.)

of November 26, a blizzard was raging, and if any of the leaders had thought of moving farther south out of range of the approaching army, they would have delayed such action until after the storm had passed.

Custer, however, marched steadily onward until the sky cleared and moonlight shone brightly upon the snow. Meanwhile, his hired Osage scouts brought back the information that Black Kettle's village was directly ahead. There were more women and children than warriors, the scouts said; the Cheyennes' total fighting strength was only about one-fifth that of the soldiers. Custer decided to surround the camp and attack immediately. Certainly now he had a chance to win a "great victory."

At dawn on the morning of November 27, snow blanketed the plains around Black Kettle's village. A film of ice covered the Washita. The old chief must have been filled with foreboding, for he rose earlier than usual that morning and walked out from his lodge to survey the horizon. He was worried about the bad rumor of the soldiers.

If the peaceful winter scene reassured him, his calm was broken a few minutes later by the cries of a squaw running madly down a pony trail just across the narrow river. "Soldiers!" she shouted to her chief.

Undoubtedly the dark memory of Sand Creek must have flashed across Black Kettle's mind, the violent death of his first wife as she ran beside him up the dry streambed. Would this happen all over again? He ran into his lodge, awakened his young squaw, and picked up his rifle. He then stepped quickly outside and fired off the weapon to alarm the village.

From the nearest lodge, his friend Magpie came hurrying to see what was wrong. It was then that the air was split with the blasting of trumpets signaling a cavalry charge, followed by a few shrill bars of "Garryowen." Even when bent on a massacre, Custer was a showman, but the muffled drumming of hooves on the snow soon drowned out the music.

Black Kettle and his wife had no more than mounted their pony when the cavalrymen charged through the village, firing volleys from carbines and pistols, and slashing at fleeing Indians with their sabers.

Magpie ran back a few steps, watching his beloved chief and his chief's wife moving away toward the river on the pony. But Black Kettle had slumped forward, a bullet burning into his stomach, and another must have hit his shoulders for his arms fell limply as the pony splashed into the shallow river crossing. Unable to aid his chief, Magpie watched him slide into the water, dead, and a moment later his wife was dead also, the pony fleeing riderless across the drifted snow.

Although Magpie and some of the others escaped to tell the true story of the massacre, more than a hundred Cheyenne warriors were killed, as well as many more women and children never counted. Their tepees were knocked down and heaped into piles with the winter supply of buffalo hides and pemmican. Then everything was burned. Several hundred ponies were also destroyed. Most of the Indians who were left alive were now captives.

Custer withdrew from the Washita swiftly, fearing retaliation from the Kiowas and other Cheyenne camps nearby. Major Joel Elliott and a detachment of eighteen men, pursuing the fleeing warriors, had all been surrounded and slain by Indians from some of these neighboring villages, but Custer did not know this at the time of his flight.

The army moved hurriedly north to Camp Supply, the troops' winter base, with the prisoners, who were herded on foot through the bitter cold weather. Around the warm campfires at the supply base, the soldiers celebrated their great "victory." One of the features of the evening's revelry was a dance by Custer's hired Osage scouts.

There was one very beautiful captive, Monahseetah, the daughter of one of Black Kettle's subchiefs who had been killed in the battle. Custer took such a liking to Monahseetah that he persuaded General Sheridan to let him keep her with him as an interpreter, though she neither spoke nor understood a word of English. When Custer went back to Fort Hayes four months later to join his wife, he had to leave Monahseetah behind.

As for the remainder of the southern Cheyennes in the Indian Territory, they knew they could never again trust in the word of any white man or in his treaties or scraps of paper. And their friends the Kiowas and Comanches knew also. For a long time the southern Cheyennes would remain scattered and powerless, broken into small bands, wandering over the southwestern plains. Except for some of the unyielding Dog Soldier bands, the Cheyennes were beaten, but the Kiowas and Comanches were still strong with spirit.

During the Battle of the Washita, a visitor called Trailing-the-Enemy from the powerful Kiowa tribe had joined the Cheyennes in the fighting. Now the burden of resisting the invasion of the southwestern hunting grounds would fall upon him and his warrior brothers of the mighty Kiowas—the fighting Kiowas who had lived for generations in the lovely Wichita Mountains and along the waters of the Red, the Washita, and the Canadian rivers.

Outnumbered by vastly more powerful forces and operating in ter-

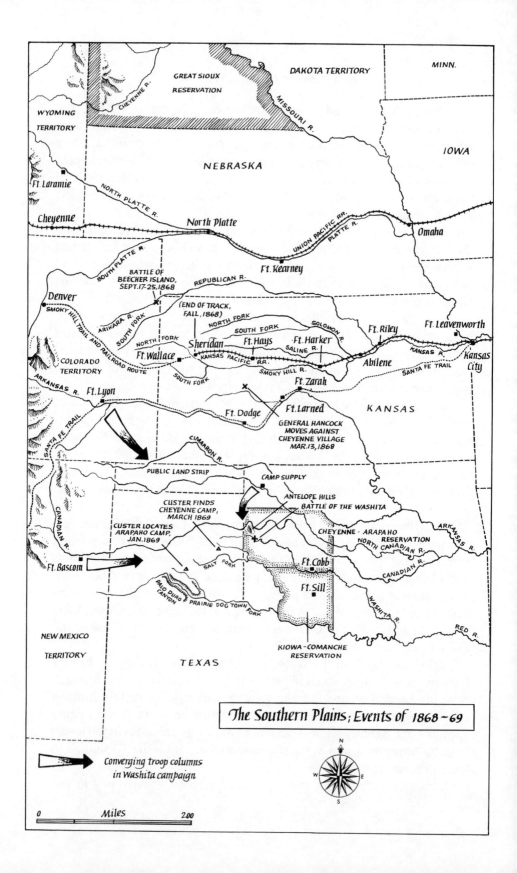

The Southern Plains; Events of 1868~69

Converging troop columns
in Washita campaign

0   Miles   200

ritory filling rapidly with hostile settlers, the Kiowas and the Comanches would wage a continuing guerrilla struggle for almost a decade after Custer's "war to make peace" along the Washita in that winter of 1868–69.

And fittingly enough, it would be the blood brothers of Black Kettle, the Cheyennes in the north, whose might joined with that of the Sioux would finally destroy George Armstrong Custer in the midst of his imagined glory.

CHAPTER 6
Kiowa and Comanche

▲▲▲▲▲▲▲▲▲▲▲▲▲▲▲▲

THE MEDICINE LODGE CREEK COUNCIL which was held in Kansas in October 1867 was a marvelous spectacle in which both the uniformed troops of the army and the bedecked warriors of the southern plains performed splendidly. General W. S. Harney marched his soldiers and wagon trains to the meeting place with considerable pomp and ceremony, but the Indians surpassed him by riding up in a swirling formation of five concentric circles, their horses striped with war paint, the riders wearing warbonnets and carrying gay battle streamers. The great whirling wheel of color and motion stopped suddenly at the edge of the soldiers' positions. Then an opening was formed, and the great chiefs waited dramatically and silently for the outnumbered white men to step inside and prove their bravery and good faith.

As splendid a show as it was, however, the Medicine Lodge treaty accomplished nothing. The government authorities wanted the Indians to retreat to assigned reservations and follow the road of the whites. The Indians wanted to be left free to roam the plains and hunt their buffalo. In spite of Black Kettle's best efforts, and the similar hopes of some of the Kiowa and Comanche leaders, no middle ground was possible.

Attending this council were two Native Americans who would stand out as the great leaders of the southern plains tribes during the turbulent years ahead, chiefs who would carry on a continuous struggle after peace-loving Black Kettle died on the Washita.

These were Satanta, the White Bear, of the Kiowas and Quanah of the Comanches. Both men were merciless killers, but they killed because they knew no other way to keep the lands of their people. They

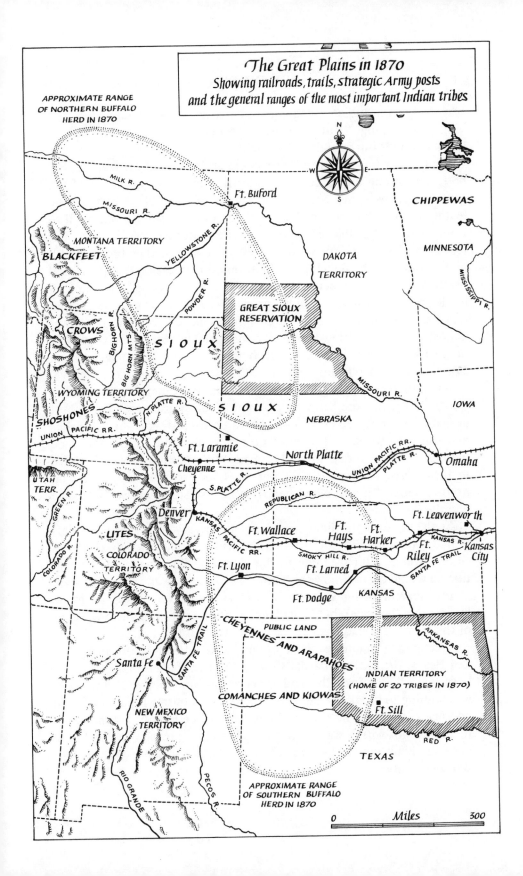

The Great Plains in 1870
Showing railroads, trails, strategic Army posts
and the general ranges of the most important Indian tribes

APPROXIMATE RANGE
OF NORTHERN BUFFALO
HERD IN 1870

MILK R.

MISSOURI R.

Ft. Buford

CHIPPEWAS

MONTANA TERRITORY

MINNESOTA

BLACKFEET

YELLOWSTONE R.

DAKOTA
TERRITORY

MISSISSIPPI R.

BIGHORN R.

POWDER R.

CROWS

BIG HORN MTS.

GREAT SIOUX
RESERVATION

S I O U X

WYOMING TERRITORY

MISSOURI R.

SHOSHONES

S I O U X

IOWA

UNION   PACIFIC   RR.

N. PLATTE R.

NEBRASKA

UTAH
TERR.

GREEN R.

Ft. Laramie

North Platte

UNION PACIFIC RR.

PLATTE R.

Omaha

Cheyenne

S. PLATTE R.

Denver

REPUBLICAN R.

Ft. Leavenworth

COLORADO R.

UTES

KANSAS PACIFIC RR.

Ft. Wallace

Ft.
Hays

Ft.
Harker

KANSAS R.

Kansas
City

COLORADO
TERRITORY

SMOKY HILL R.

Ft.
Riley

SANTA FE TRAIL

Ft. Lyon

Ft. Larned

Ft. Dodge

KANSAS

PUBLIC LAND

CHEYENNES AND ARAPAHOES

ARKANSAS R.

Santa Fe

SANTA FE TRAIL

INDIAN TERRITORY
(HOME OF 20 TRIBES IN 1870)

COMANCHES AND KIOWAS

Ft. Sill

NEW MEXICO
TERRITORY

RED R.

TEXAS

RIO GRANDE

PECOS R.

APPROXIMATE RANGE
OF SOUTHERN BUFFALO
HERD IN 1870

0   Miles   300

admitted to the Indian commissioners that they were raiding and robbing and scalping. "But the white man lies to us and then steals our lands and kills our buffalo," they said.

White Bear was almost sixty years old at the time of the council. His body was strong and lithe, but under the hot winds and suns of the southern plains as his face had become creased and blackened like the leather of an old moccasin. He had come to Kansas in his war paint of brilliant red ocher that covered the entire upper part of his body. His tepee, his shield, and his streamers were red also, and he brought with him an old army bugle which he blew on every occasion that presented itself. At one of the meetings with the commissioners, he rode in blowing his bugle and wearing a blue army coat adorned with epaulets that had been presented to him by General Hancock. But the show was almost stolen by another Kiowa chieftain, Kicking Bird, who wore only his native breech clout and a high black silk hat he had begged from Commissioner Alf Taylor.

When the U.S. representatives told White Bear that the government wanted to provide the Kiowas with comfortable houses upon the richest agricultural lands, the chieftain, who had been resting on his haunches and whittling while he listened to the talk, remained silent for some moments. Then he rose up and replied: "I do not want to settle down in the houses you would build for us. I love to roam over the wild prairie. There I am free and happy. When we sit down, we grow pale and die."

At the time of the final reading of the treaty, many of the chiefs signed, but some did not. Among the Kiowas, only Kicking Bird was sincere when, after listening to the words of the agreement, he said that he would try to follow the whites' road. Lone Wolf refused to sign. White Bear in all his kaleidoscopic glory stepped forward and made his mark on the paper, but he had no intention of obeying the provisions of the treaty. He had already declared otherwise.

Among the Comanches there was much disputation about the treaty. Ten Bears, the old Yamparika Comanche, had spoken plainly. "I was born upon the prairie," he said, "where the wind blew free and there was nothing to break the light of the sun. I was born where there were no enclosures and where everything drew a free breath. I want to die there and not within walls." But he added that he wanted "no blood upon my land to stain the grass," and he urged all the Comanches to sign the treaty.

WHITE BEAR

Finally White Bear was freed from prison, and celebrated his release by going on a buffalo hunt. But at the first report of a raid in Texas, the Kiowa leader was blamed. Even though Indian Agent Thomas Battey testified that White Bear could not have been guilty, he was arrested and put back into a convict's striped uniform. Two years of confinement was all that White Bear could stand. In the autumn of 1876, at the time of the annual buffalo hunt, he slashed the arteries of his neck and legs and leaped from a window to his death. (Courtesy of the Smithsonian Institution.)

Quanah, the leader of the Kwahadi Comanches, however, would listen to none of this talk. Quanah, the half-breed son of a chief and a captured white girl, Cynthia Ann Parker, could see no good in a treaty that would take away from his people their freedom of the range. And so this warlike Kwahadi of the Texas Panhandle left the council before the day of the signing, saying to the other Indians as he departed: "I am not going to a reservation. Tell the white chiefs when they ask, that the Kwahadis are warriors and that we are not afraid."

Black Beaver represented the most peace-loving tribe of all—the Delawares. This veteran scout had been the companion and guide of many great Western explorers. He had led a company of Indians in the U.S. Army during the Mexican War, and had given up his home and farm in Indian Territory to aid the Union forces during the Civil War. Black Beaver believed that his people should follow the whites' road, and live on assigned reservations.

Little more than a year after the much-publicized "peace" council, Sheridan and Custer were destroying the villages of the Kiowas and Cheyennes all along the Washita River. After the slaughter of Black Kettle's Cheyenne band, the Kiowa chiefs decided to move their people to the Fort Cobb agency. As it was midwinter and the soldiers had left them no food, clothing, or shelter, there was no other choice.

To arrange the surrender, White Bear and Lone Wolf approached Sheridan's camp, bearing white flags. Custer went out to meet them, and he was so unfriendly that some of the other Kiowa leaders who were waiting nearby ran away and led their bands into hiding places to the southwest. White Bear and Lone Wolf undoubtedly would have departed also, but Custer put them under armed guard and told them they would be kept as hostages until the Kiowas came in to Fort Cobb. White Bear's son was sent to carry the message back to the other chieftains.

The Kiowas, hiding in the woods, replied that they would come in as soon as their chiefs were released. When he heard this, General Sheridan lost his temper. He informed White Bear that he would hang him and Lone Wolf to the nearest tree at sunrise if their people did not appear in camp by that time. White Bear conferred with his son, who immediately jumped on his horse and rode away. The old chief looked calmly at the general. "When the sun is there," he said, indicating the western horizon, "the tribe will be here."

And so the Kiowas came in to take the white road, all of them except the small bands of Kicking Bird and Woman Heart, who fled to the Staked Plains to join the free Kwahadis.

The whites' road, however, was not easy for these hunters of the plains who heretofore had known no boundaries of time or space. The younger warriors slipped away from the reservation on the slightest pretext, and in the autumn the call of the buffalo hunt was too strong even for the older and wiser ones. Although the government had established Fort Sill in the middle of the Kiowas' reserve in 1869, the soldiers could not keep their charges confined, and as soon as the Indians were outside the limits they inevitably came into violent conflict with the new settlers.

In the spring of 1871, White Bear himself led a raid into Texas. He had heard that the whites were planning to build a railroad across his old hunting grounds, and he could not stand for that. With about a hundred warriors he rode across the familiar prairie, looking for any travelers who might be trespassing there. An unlucky wagon train was surrounded, and seven teamsters were killed before White Bear blew his bugle and called off his braves.

When he returned to the reservation, White Bear was summoned before General William T. Sherman, who had come out from Washington to see the Indian problem firsthand. Sherman was sitting on an open veranda just outside two large windows when White Bear and three other chieftains, Lone Wolf, Sitting Bear, and Big Tree, approached him. Although the sun was intensely hot, the four Indians were wearing heavy blankets.

"Why did you go down into Texas and murder those helpless teamsters who didn't know how to fight?" Sherman asked them directly. "If you want a fight, the soldiers here can always accommodate you."

If White Bear was surprised to learn that Sherman knew all about the raid, he did not betray any evidence on his weather-beaten face. He said that he had heard the Texans were about to build a railroad down there, and he could not permit that. "The road would frighten the buffalo away," he added.

Sherman did not mince words. He told the Kiowas that they were all under arrest and would be sent back to Texas and tried for murder. Upon hearing this remark, Lone Wolf threw off his blanket, cocked his previously concealed carbine, and looked defiantly at Sherman. White Bear and the other two chieftains followed his example, but the window shutters behind the general flew open immediately and the muzzles of two dozen rifles covered the Indians. In the confusion, Lone Wolf managed to escape, but White Bear, Sitting Bear, and Big Tree were caught in Sherman's well-laid trap.

On the way back to Texas for the trial, Sitting Bear was killed while trying to escape. After singing the death song of the soldier society to which he belonged, Sitting Bear had slipped his handcuffs loose and seized a carbine from one of the guards. In the resulting struggle, the old Kiowa's body was riddled with bullets. White Bear and Big Tree were tried and sentenced to death, but on the advice of the Indian agents, who feared a general uprising if the chiefs were hanged, the sentence was commuted to life imprisonment.

But even so, the Kiowas wanted White Bear released. They began a series of retaliatory raids. Kicking Bird, who had returned from the Staked Plains to lead the Kiowas and had set up a village near Fort Sill, had been sincerely working for peace. He told the officials that the trouble would increase if White Bear were not released. Lone Wolf said the same thing. White Horse declared that his band would continue raiding until White Bear was free, and when nothing was done immediately, he and Lone Wolf visited the Cheyennes and tried to persuade them to join in a big war against all the whites.

Finally, in October 1873, the tired old chieftain and his friend, Big Tree, were released from jail and brought back to Fort Sill. Thomas Battey, the new Indian agent, said that the joy of White Bear and his people was "exhibited in a most wild and natural manner."

But the joy was not to endure. At the first report of a raid in Texas, the local authorities and the press blamed White Bear and Big Tree. In November 1874, General Sheridan ordered the two leaders arrested and sent to prison at Huntsville, Texas. Agent Battey declared: "To my certain knowledge Big Tree was at home, sick in his lodge, and White Bear was enjoying, after two years' confinement in prison, the pleasures of the buffalo chase on territory assigned for that purpose." The authorities could not find Big Tree, but White Bear was captured and put back into a convict's striped uniform.

Now the old Kiowa was trapped for good. He lived two years, sprawling morosely on the floor of his cell, or standing for hours gazing out the window. In the autumn of 1876, at the time of the annual buffalo hunt, he cut the arteries of his neck and legs. When the guards tried to save him by taking him to the prison hospital, he grimly outwitted them by leaping out a second-story window. This time he was dead.

. . .

News of the Kiowas and their troubles came occasionally to the camps of the Kwahadi Comanches far to the west. Eagle Heart, White Horse, Woman Heart, and other Kiowa chieftains had taken their bands into the Staked Plains, and they had become strong friends of the Comanches.

When evil days fell upon White Bear and his people, Quanah, the Kwahadi chief, resolved more strongly than ever to stay clear of white people. The Comanches, he said, would never go on a reservation as the Kiowas had done.

Yet the settlers kept coming from the east. The buffalo hunters came by tens and by hundreds, and it seemed that all would be lost. Finally in the spring of 1874, Quanah realized that his people must make a great decision. All the Indians of the southern plains would have to join forces and fight with their concerted might against the buffalo hunters and the settlers, or else all the Indians would have to move on the reservations and live like whites. Quanah called for a great council of the Comanches, and invited their friends who were still free among the Kiowas and Cheyennes.

And so from all over the vast plains the Indians came together for a medicine dance near the mouth of Elk Creek on the North Fork of Red River.

During the dance, the Kwahadis' medicine man, Isatai, convinced Quanah that he had conversed with the Great Spirit. "The Great spirit has at last taken pity on the people," said Isatai. "He will make us strong in war and we shall drive the white men away. The buffalo shall come back everywhere, so that there shall be feasting and plenty in the lodges. The Great Spirit has taught me strong medicine which will turn away the white man's bullets."

Quanah was not certain of Isatai's power, but he permitted him to make a ceremony at the final feast. When Quanah saw that the other chiefs wanted to believe in Isatai, he presented them with a plan of attack. "First we will drive out the buffalo hunters," said Quanah.

Lone Wolf of the Kiowas disagreed. He wanted to raid the reservations and kill the agents and the soldiers. "If Isatai's power is strong," he said, "we shall have nothing to fear from the soldiers." Stone Calf of the Cheyennes, however, was more practical and thought it best to

LONE WOLF

Lone Wolf did not trust Custer, and was preparing to lead the Kiowas west to the Staked Plains to join the Comanches. Learning of this, General Sheridan ordered the arrest of Lone Wolf and White Bear, and threatened to hang them from the nearest tree if they did not order their followers to come into camp and surrender before sundown. Most of the Kiowas came in. Only a small band under Kicking Bird escaped to the Staked Plains. (Photograph courtesy of the Smithsonian Institution.)

attack the small isolated groups of buffalo hunters. The Great Spirit might be displeased if they asked for too much help from him all at once.

At last the decision was made. Quanah would make the plan and lead the Comanches. Isatai would make the strong medicine. Lone Wolf and Stone Calf would lead the Kiowa and Cheyenne warriors.

Quanah's plan was simple. They would attack the southernmost of the buffalo hunters' camps at Adobe Walls in the Panhandle country. After disposing of the hunters there, they would move northward to the next camp, the next, and then the next, always moving more swiftly than the news of the killings, until they had destroyed all the invaders of the buffalo country.

Before dawn on June 27, 1874, seven hundred warriors rode up out of the shadows of the Canadian River valley and spread themselves along the edge of the timber of Adobe Walls Creek. Quanah, in the lead, could see only the smudgy outlines of the buildings of Adobe Walls, picketed and built stockade fashion—two stores, a saloon, and a blacksmith shop. The thirty hunters, who had come to slay the Indians' buffalo and leave the skinned carcasses rotting on the plains, were all asleep.

And so they would have remained asleep had not a drying ridge pole over one of the sheds happened to crack loudly just before daylight. The sharp noise awakened Billy Dixon, the famous Texas scout. Once awakened, Dixon was in no mood to go to bed again. As he walked toward his horse, he saw the animal fling its head back and prick up its ears. Dixon whirled around.

Across the valley, in the graying dawn, hundreds of mounted Indians in their war paint, feathers, and other trappings of battle were sweeping toward the trading post. Dixon had barely enough time to awaken his companions before the first war whoops shrilled out above the drumming hooves. The noise of the breaking ridge pole had probably saved their lives.

The story of the battle of Adobe Walls is only another version of Red Cloud's fight with the Fort Phil Kearny soldiers hidden behind the wagon boxes. This time instead of breech-loading rifles, the buffalo hunters possessed new long-range game weapons. Although Quanah led his warriors in charge after charge, sometimes to the point of beating upon the doors of the stockade with their rifle butts, they could never break into the trading post. The siege continued throughout the day.

KIOWA CALENDAR

The buffalo days of the Kiowas were coming to an end. On this calendar drawn by Anko, a member of the tribe, the outstanding occurrences of the later days are told in pictures. These figures were drawn in brilliant colors, and only the calendars of the Sioux rival this one in beauty and originality of design. (Photograph courtesy of the Smithsonian Institution.)

When the horse of Isatai, the medicine man, was shot from under him, he blamed the failure of his power on a Kiowa brave who had recently killed a rabbit without his permission.

Quanah kept the battle going at intervals for three days, and then he knew he was beaten. He had been wounded in the shoulder, his best warriors were dead or injured, and the news of the attack had already been spread to the north by passing hunters. Worst of all, the power of Isatai had failed.

Even if Adobe Walls had not proved to Quanah that the fate of the southern plains Indians was already sealed, the events of the succeeding weeks certainly must have done so. From Camp Supply, General Nelson Miles was leading an army column toward the Kwahadi country. Colonel Ranald S. Mackenzie was marching from Fort Griffin in Texas. A third column was operating from Fort Sill. And even from the west, a small force was ready to strike eastward out of Fort Union, New Mexico.

The day of the buffalo was over for the Comanches. The wild free days were ended for all of the Indians of Oklahoma and Texas. They could choose either to die or to take the whites' road.

Stone Calf and his band of Cheyennes had been allies of Quanah in the Adobe Walls fight. Remembering the fate of Black Kettle, Stone Calf refused to surrender, and for several months he led his warriors on revenge raids from Texas to Kansas. On one of the raids, the Cheyennes attacked a caravan traveling to the Colorado goldfields. Four girls, the Germain sisters, were taken captive.

In a charge led by Lieutenant Frank Baldwin against the Cheyenne Chief Gray Beard's camp on McClellan's Creek on November 8, 1874, the Cheyennes were routed and driven back to the Staked Plains. Two of the Germain girls were rescued during this engagement. The other two, Katherine and Sophie, were returned unharmed on February 26, 1875, when the Cheyennes surrendered. This incident marked the end of Indian resistance on the southwestern plains.

Quanah chose to take the white man's road. He led his Kwahadis to their reservation and then went to visit the white relatives of his mother, Cynthia Ann Parker. "If she could learn the ways of the Indians," he said, "I can learn the ways of the white man." And the Parkers helped him in his long struggle.

He now called himself Quanah Parker. As the years went by he became a shrewd businessman, built a large house, and successfully

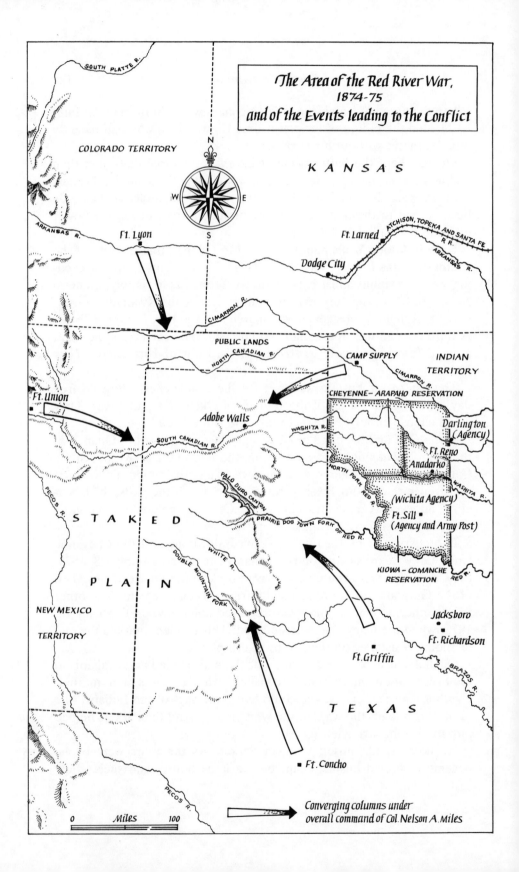

The Area of the Red River War,
1874-75
and of the Events leading to the Conflict

SOUTH PLATTE R.

COLORADO TERRITORY

KANSAS

ARKANSAS R.

Ft. Lyon

Ft. Larned

ATCHISON, TOPEKA AND SANTA FE R.R.

Dodge City

ARKANSAS R.

CIMARRON R.

PUBLIC LANDS

NORTH CANADIAN R.

CAMP SUPPLY

INDIAN TERRITORY

CIMARRON R.

CHEYENNE – ARAPAHO RESERVATION

Ft. Union

SOUTH CANADIAN R.

Adobe Walls

WASHITA R.

Darlington (Agency)

Ft. Reno

Anadarko

PALO DURO CANYON

NORTH FORK RED R.

WASHITA R.

PECOS R.

S T A K E D

PRAIRIE DOG TOWN FORK OF RED R.

(Wichita Agency)

Ft. Sill
(Agency and Army Post)

WHITE R.

DOUBLE MOUNTAIN FORK

P L A I N

KIOWA – COMANCHE RESERVATION

RED R.

NEW MEXICO

TERRITORY

Jacksboro

Ft. Richardson

Ft. Griffin

T E X A S

BRAZOS R.

Ft. Concho

PECOS R.

0   Miles   100

Converging columns under
overall command of Col. Nelson A. Miles

managed his farm and ranch. He traveled all over the country, and went to Washington to ride in President Theodore Roosevelt's inaugural parade. After long years of effort he finally achieved full American citizenship for all the members of his tribe. The old fighting Kwahadi had come a long way down the white man's road.

CHAPTER 7
The Conquest of Cochise

▲ ▲ ▲ ▲ ▲ ▲ ▲ ▲ ▲ ▲ ▲ ▲ ▲ ▲ ▲ ▲

SOUTH AND WEST OF KIOWA-COMANCHE
country the land wore a different face. Here in the "land of little rain"
the sun rose and set on rocky peaks, separated by steep gorges. There
were ashes from a thousand sleeping volcanoes. Water was hidden,
springs and rivers few. Trails were dim, and led through country that
even a mule found difficult.

Wood, water, and grass, necessary trinity of the westward-pushing
settler, were scarce. The few fertile valleys were oases, yielding deer,
bear, and wild fowl in abundance.

This land had been acquired by the United States from the Mexicans,
but there were many who believed it useless. The reward of exploration
and discovery was often death. Nevertheless, the people pushed in, first
from the south into Chihuahua and Sonora, and later from the east and
west alike. The few green valleys of this desert became the goal of
fortune seekers, and life-giving springs became way stations on trails,
or sites for military posts. The lure of gold and silver was greater than
the hardships of the trail, and the barren hills were ransacked for gold;
the valleys became cattle ranges.

Resisting the intrusion of the whites was the Apache, native of Arizona and New Mexico. A mountain people, the Apaches had developed
large chests and great lungs, giving them staying power beyond that of
their enemies. They were true children of their pitiless environment:
cruel, cautious, crafty, cunning. Thievery was their trade, and death
their trademark. The black-robed Christian fathers who had peacefully
conquered other Southwestern tribes found the Apaches unrepentant
and exceedingly skillful sinners.

In the early days, before gold fever drew emigrants a thousand miles in madness, the Apaches, armed with bows and arrows, were not a factor to draw attention in the annual reports of the War Department in Washington. Captain John Pope derided them as sneak thieves who were never known to attack more than ten men at a time. Fighting and running was their way of making war.

But as the settlers trespassed more deeply and permanently into the homeland of this desert people, and when muskets or breech-loading rifles were placed into hands eager and able to use them, the Apaches ranked with the Comanches as the scourge of the Southwest. Guns replaced bows and arrows, and then the Apache became the equal, in fact the superior, of his white foe. For the ways of the Indian were the ways of the land; each rock was a fortress, and every canyon an ambush place.

Intermittent wars flared for half a century. The names of warriors and soldiers—Cochise, Mangas Coloradas, Geronimo, Nachez, Victorio, Crook, Carleton, Gatewood, Miles—are still written in the land of Arizona and New Mexico.

During the Civil War, when the whites were shooting each other, it was a very good time for the Apaches to reestablish their right to the land. White interlopers were robbed and killed. Both Union and Confederate forces were attacked. The helpless citizens abandoned their claims and crowded together in Tucson, Tubac, and various ranches.

Chief enemy of the Apache during this period was Colonel James Carleton, who organized the California Column and fought the Apaches for four years. At the end of that time the great chief Mangas Coloradas was dead, treacherously shot "while escaping arrest." But Cochise, strong, six-foot-tall chief of the Chiricahua Apaches, greatest of the warriors and yet greater as a diplomat, was left to defend his land.

Cochise had a special hatred for the whites. In 1861 he had been accused of stealing a small boy from a ranch near Fort Buchanan. The boy had actually been kidnapped by Pinal Apaches. (Later known as Mickey Free, he became a government scout and interpreter.) Lieutenant George Bascom, Seventh Cavalry, camped near Apache Pass, was determined to make Cochise return the boy. When Cochise came to Bascom's tent for a talk, the soldiers tried to capture him. The fighting chief drew a knife and ripped his way to freedom through the rear of the tent. His companions were seized as hostages.

Cochise gathered his followers and proceeded to capture several white men to assure the safe return of Bascom's prisoners. The exchange was never made, and Cochise rode away to kill the whites he had taken. In retaliation, three Indian hostages were hanged.

Cochise became implacable. "I was at peace with the whites," he said, "until they tried to kill me for what other Indians did; now I live and die at war with them." In his war he is known to have burned thirteen white men alive, tortured five to death by cutting small pieces from their feet, and dragged fifteen to death at the end of a lariat.

The chief made war with all the energy of his nature, but he made peace, too, when it suited his purpose. In September 1871, he consented to meet General Gordon Granger at the Indian agency at Canada Alamosa. He would hear what the whites had to offer, but he would not forget the dismal end of Mangas Coloradas.

General Granger nervously smoked a pipe of peace with the chief, and then quickly spoke. The white government, he said, wanted to live in peace with the Apaches. He would give Cochise mountains and valleys in Tularosa as a reservation, a home for him and his people forever. In return, the Apaches must remain at peace, steal no stock, raid no settlements, and permit the settlers to take over the rest of the country unopposed.

Cochise and his followers retired to consider the general's words. The chief returned to reply with fierce dignity. "When I was young I wandered all over this country, east and west, and saw no other people than the Apaches. After many summers I walked again, and found another race of people had come to take it. How is it? I will not lie to you; do not lie to me. I want to live in these mountains. I do not want to go to Tularosa. That is a long way off. The flies on those mountains eat out the eyes of the horses. The bad spirits live there. I have drunk of these waters and they have cooled me; I do not want to leave here."

A few months later the Apaches at Canada Alamosa were removed to Tularosa valley in the Mogollon Mountains; Conchise and his warriors went back to their home in southern Arizona.

Other Apaches who sought peace left their *rancherias* in the wilds and came in to the army camps for protection. In February 1871, Eskiminzin, chief of the Arivaipa Apaches, came to Camp Grant with 150 followers. They were poor, they said, and hungry, tired of being hunted and killed. They wanted a place to live in peace. Lieutenant Royal E. Whitman, commander at Camp Grant, believed them, and gave them a place near the post on land which had once belonged to the Apaches.

The settlers in nearby Tucson were alarmed. Almost daily they spoke of Indian raids in the vicinity. Eskiminzin and his warriors were blamed. The citizens, when the army did not take their point of view, decided to act themselves. On April 28, 1871, a party of six Americans, forty-eight Mexicans, and ninety-two Papago Indians gathered in Pantano Wash, east of Tucson.

Early on the morning of April 30, the mob, armed by the adjutant-general of Arizona Territory, attacked the unsuspecting camp of Arivaipas. Most of the warriors, including Eskiminzin, were off in the mountains, hunting. Squaws, old men, and children were left to be massacred. In a few minutes 108 of these helpless ones were killed. Twenty-nine children were taken captive and sold as slaves, or kept as servants by residents of Tucson.

Participants in the massacre were later tried in Tucson and acquitted. To murder an Indian was considered no crime.

The other Apache tribes, hearing of the Camp Grant Massacre, commenced making war with new vigor. To combat the new outbreak, the army divided its forces into small commands supplied by mule train. They were to hunt down the Indians in their home *rancherias*. Warriors from among the reservation Apaches were enlisted as scouts to track down their people in their hiding places. The Americans found the scouts wild and unmilitary, but also highly efficient and trustworthy. Through canyons and over mountains these little commands sought out and destroyed the Apache *rancherias* off the reservations.

Rewards were offered for the heads of important hostile chiefs. Delche, a great fighter, had an especially high price on his head. It was brought in several times—a different head each time—and the reward was always paid.

·   ·   ·

On Christmas Day, 1872, Companies L and M, Fifth Cavalry, commanded by Major William H. Brown, accompanied by a detachment of thirty Apache scouts, plodded through the Superstition Mountains of central Arizona. It was a poor holiday. The mountain heights were covered with snow, and cold wet winds chilled the slopes. What fires were permitted were small, hardly enough to warm the hands or dry a pair of moccasins.

During the day Company G of the same regiment, out from Fort McDowell with a party of one hundred Pima Indians, joined Major

APACHE SCOUTS

Warriors from among the reservation Apaches were enlisted as scouts to track down their people in their hiding places. The scouts were wild and unmilitary, but highly efficient and trustworthy. (Photograph by C. S. Fly, courtesy of the Smithsonian Institution.)

Brown's command. The combined parties were in the heart of hostile Apache country, and looking for a fight. The native scouts, under half-breed Archie MacIntosh, worked far ahead of the command looking for the Apache *rancheria* supposed to be hidden in the mountain range known as Matitzal, or Four Peaks.

Only two men of the combined party knew where they were going, Major Brown and an Apache scout, Nantaje, known to the soldiers as Joe. Nantaje had been raised in the Matitzal, and knew the hiding places of his people. He would lead the white men there.

On the evening of December 27, camped in the canyon of Cotton-wood Creek, just at the eastern foot of Four Peaks, Major Brown told his officers of his plan. There was a cave, he explained, in the canyon of the Salado or Salt River. Here the Apaches were supposed to be hidden. The command was going to surround and surprise the place, and deal a crippling blow to Indian power.

All precautions for surprise were taken. The soldiers, learning from the Indian scouts, wore moccasins, and stuffed them with dry grass. With such footwear they could walk softly; the rocks would not betray them. Pack mules and surplus equipment were left behind, under guard. Guns and ammunition were all that was necessary for the business at hand. Bacon, bread, and a little coffee were taken by each man, and a canteen of water hung on each belt. The Apache scouts skinned a mule and feasted in anticipation of the fight.

The approach to the cave began when darkness hid the movements of the men. Silently the fighters followed the lead of Nantaje, who assured them they were close to the cave and would soon find plenty of Indians. The route took them up the steeps of the Matitzal to the canyon of the Salado, and onto the high mesa which bordered it. Fresh Indian tracks were found, and Company G under Lieutenant James Burns was dispatched to follow.

Just before dawn Nantaje and MacIntosh led Lieutenant William J. Ross with half a dozen of the best shots along a rough trail down the canyon of the Salado. It was dangerous work. A slip meant death on the rocks hundreds of feet below. A sudden turn in the angle of the wall revealed the promised cave, in reality a shelf of the great canyon wall, protected on all sides by great, smooth boulders, splintered off the cliff.

A party of Apaches, just back from a raid, were hunched about a small fire. The attackers took aim; each man chose his target silhouetted against the dancing flames. The roar of rifles echoed from canyon walls, and was answered by yells of surprise and hatred within the cave. A few scattered arrows were sent in the general direction of the attack, but Ross and his men were safe, each behind a rock. A quick rush past the cave lodged men on the other side, and the Indians were trapped.

Major Brown called on the Apaches to surrender. The answer was a volley of bullets and arrows, sped with screams of defiance. The Apaches were ready to die. The soldiers directed their shots against the roof of the cave, and the ricochet caught the huddled inmates. Cries of the wounded and wails of frightened children indicated that the indirect fire was effective.

Suddenly a death chant began. It spoke of revenge and despair. A charge followed, driven back with bloody losses, but the death chant continued, punctuated by constant fire against the roof of the cave.

On the rim of the canyon, above the cave, death loomed in a new form. Lieutenant Burns and G Company heard the roar of the fight, and watched the proceedings from above. They decided to roll rocks over the cliff onto the shelf. Destruction fell on the Apaches with a crash. Screams of the dying rose high in the air. Only echoes responded. The death chant was quiet. No rifle spoke. The cave was the house of the dead.

Sixty-six Apaches died in the Battle of Salt Canyon, and the one warrior who escaped alive was killed soon after at Turret Butte, another supposedly impregnable Indian refuge.

The fight in the canyon of the Salado was but one of many which were being forced on the Apaches by a new enemy, General George Crook, who was fresh from victories against the Paiutes in Oregon and Idaho. The "Gray Wolf," as the Apaches learned to call Crook, had sent soldiers from every camp in Arizona with instructions to stay in the field until they had located and subdued the last Apache. Pack mules were equipped and trained as support to these columns, and friendly Indians led the soldiers to the hiding places of their people.

Warfare such as this was too much, even for the Apaches. Peace on the reservations was better. When Crook sent captives out with the news that surrender would be accepted, all the Indians within reach came in. On April 27, 1873, the last of the Apaches surrendered at Camp Verde. Chalipun, Apache-Mojave chief, approached the general and explained his surrender. "You see, we are nearly dead from exposure and want of food—the copper cartridge has done the business for us. I am glad of the opportunity to surrender, but I do it not because I love you, but because I am afraid of the General."

Old Delche came in, too. He had boasted 125 warriors six months before; twenty were left. "There was a time," he complained, "when we could escape the white soldiers. But now the very rocks have become soft. We cannot put our feet anywhere. We cannot sleep, for if a coyote or fox barks, or a stone moves, we are up—the soldiers have come."

General Crook was not only a fighter, but a human being as well. He became a good friend of the Apaches. Under his stern but understanding rule the Apaches settled on reservations and tried to walk the whites' road. They no longer roamed freely over the mountains, but they could rest at night, and live in peace. They tried to forget the old ways.

As quickly as the Apaches came in to the reservation they were put to work—some digging irrigation ditches and raising corn, others cutting hay and bringing it to the agency quartermaster, who bought all of it. Rations were issued to the Indians at the agencies to make up for food that could not be raised or hunted. Apache wars stopped, for a while.

CHAPTER 8
Treaties and the Thieves' Road

▲ ▲ ▲ ▲ ▲ ▲ ▲ ▲ ▲ ▲ ▲ ▲ ▲ ▲ ▲ ▲

AFTER RED CLOUD, the Sioux leader, signed the treaty of 1868, he and his band went up to the Powder River country. Here they found life as it had been. There was plenty of buffalo meat for pemmican, and skins for new lodges. The squaws were busy drying meat and making robes. The horses grew fat on the good grass, undisturbed by the new settlers. The soldiers had gone away, and the forts were burned.

Spotted Tail stayed near the Missouri River, closer to the agency, above Fort Randall. But he, too, had seen enough of the whites. Their whisky and diseases seemed to come up the river on every steamboat. Spotted Tail kept his people far enough away from the agency to dilute the traders' poison. He was content to draw rations and live in peace according to the terms of the treaty.

In the summer of 1870, Red Cloud with seventeen head men and three squaws and Spotted Tail with four Brulé chiefs were taken to Washington for a talk. On their way east they would see how many white people there were, the Americans reasoned, and realize that it was useless to object to whatever might be proposed.

The opportunity to impress the chiefs was not wasted. Red Cloud was told that he must move onto a reservation, near an agency, like Spotted Tail, preferably on the Missouri. The chief was obstinate. "The white children have surrounded me, and left me nothing but an island. When we first had this land we were strong, but now we are melting like snow on a hillside, while you are grown like spring grass. I have two mountains in that country, the Black Hills and the Big Horn Mountains. I want the father to make no roads through them. I have told

RED CLOUD'S HEAD MEN

In the summer of 1870, Red Cloud and seventeen head men were invited to Washington. He stopped at Omaha, en route, where photographs were taken of the visiting chiefs. (*Left to right, seated:* Sitting Bull, Swift Bear, Spotted Tail. *Standing:* Julius Meyer [interpreter], Red Cloud.) (Photograph courtesy of the Smithsonian Institution.)

these things three times, and now have come here to tell them the fourth time. I do not want my reservation on the Missouri."

The treaty of 1868 was then explained to Red Cloud. For the first time he knew the truth of what had been done. It was as the white man had boasted, "The chiefs have sold themselves for another feast of crackers and molasses."

Red Cloud spoke in anger now. "You whites have a chief to go by, but the only chief I go by is God Almighty. The whites think the Great Spirit has nothing to do with us, but he has. After fooling with us and taking away our property they will have to suffer for it hereafter."

When Red Cloud returned to his people, they knew his spirit had been bowed. It was whispered in the lodges that he had allowed the whites to capture his spirit in the black image box, the camera. The chief left the Powder River country in July 1871 and settled near the new agency by Fort Laramie. Spotted Tail also went to a new place on upper White River.

But there were still many Sioux who scorned the example of Red Cloud and Spotted Tail. They refused to move onto the white man's island, believing it was better to hunt buffalo on the Powder than eat wormy pork from the agency. Some of the people who went to the agency in winter always came away again at the time of the new grass. Crazy Horse, Black Moon, Old Bull, and Sitting Bull defied the treaties. Was not this land theirs? Had they not wrested it from the Crows fifty years before, and lived on it and defended it ever since? They had even driven the whites from it a short while ago.

The government let these wild ones alone until 1871, when surveyors for the railroad began measuring the hills. This was bad medicine. Where these strange whites came, others always followed. The surveyors pushed through the heart of the good buffalo land, through the hunting grounds of the Sioux, the Cheyennes, and the northern Arapahoes. The Indians struck back.

Surveyors were attacked. Black Moon with several hundred Sioux and Cheyennes attacked eight troops of cavalry under Major E. M. Baker near Pryor's Fork, Montana, on August 14, 1872. Before the year ended there were five more big fights against trespassers in that country. The Sioux and Cheyennes found that the words of the peace commissioners were hollow.

There was little the warriors could do. They could swoop down, now and then, on the men who were building the iron road, but the soldiers were always on guard. Five times the warriors gathered and attacked

CRAZY-IN-THE-LODGE

Crazy-in-the-Lodge was head warrior under Spotted Tail. (Photograph courtesy of J. Morrow Collection, W. H. Overstate Museum.)

Fort Abraham Lincoln in the Dakota Territory, near Bismarck, for here was the gathering place of the whites who would invade the land of the Sioux. But the old days of victory were gone. The soldiers had too many guns, and even artillery.

Some of the Black Kettle Cheyennes were with Crazy Horse, and from them he learned that among the soldiers in Dakota was the one called Custer, the squaw-killer. He had been sent from the south to do his work among the Sioux. Crazy Horse attacked Custer on the Yellowstone on August 11, 1873. But it was as a flea bite to a charging white bear.

General Sheridan, in command of the Division of the Missouri, believed that a fort in the Black Hills would make it easier to protect the advance of the railroad. In July 1874 he sent a reconnaissance expedition to the Hills under Colonel Custer. The report of this scout, published August 12, 1874, meant the death of the treaty of 1868 and spelled the end of Sioux possession of the Black Hills. Gold—"from the grassroots down"—was what Custer found. News of the discovery spread throughout the depression-ridden East, where it was eagerly received and greatly exaggerated.

The expedition had broken the very words of the treaty; the law books said that Indian lands would never be violated. But gold was reported, and the magic sound brought the whites on a run. The "Thieves' Road," as Fast Bear called Custer's trail, was soon worn deep by fortune hunters.

Now that the Black Hills looked good to the whites, it was time for another treaty. A seven-man commission headed by Senator William B. Allison and General Alfred H. Terry was sent to the Sioux to negotiate for the sale of Pa Sapa, the sacred Black Hills. Spotted Tail went to the Hills to see for himself just what it was the white men wanted. He found another expedition there, escorted by soldiers under Colonel Richard I. Dodge and guided by California Joe, famous Western scout. The government was making sure about the reported gold, and had sent a professor, Walter P. Jenney, to see for them.

The commission met on September 17, 1875. The Indians were in no mood to sell Pa Sapa. That was sacred medicine ground. If it went to the whites, that was just another feast of crackers and molasses for the chiefs.

Over seven thousand Indians gathered at the council. Most of them were hostile, and constant threats were made toward the commissioners by Little Big Man and others. Only a firm stand by the friendly Indians under Young-Man-Afraid-of-His-Horses averted a massacre.

There was much talk. Spotted Tail knew that his people had a hill of gold; he wanted full value for it. Spotted Bear said, "Our Great Father has a big safe, and so have we. This hill is our safe. We want seventy million dollars for the Black Hills." Red Cloud demanded Texas steers for meat for seven generations to come, and much money besides. Little Big Man screamed for war. Crazy Horse, who did not attend the council, observed, "One does not sell the earth upon which the people walk."

The council broke up without any agreement, and the commissioners went home with their bellies full of threats. They did not feel safe until they had crossed the Missouri. But white fortune hunters moved into the Black Hills in increasing numbers. When the Indians found them they killed them. Yet within six months there were 11,000 whites in Custer City alone.

In December 1875, the Interior Department sent word to all the Indians in unceded territory, mostly on the Powder River, to come in to the reservation by January 31, 1876, or be considered "hostile." This was one way of clearing the Thieves' Road since the commission had failed. But it was the middle of a severe winter. Even the soldiers had stopped campaigning in November because of the cold. The Indians could have left their camps and come down to the agency, but they could see no reason for hurry. It was foolish to leave buffalo country for the agency, where everyone knew food was scarce. "We will come when the snow melts," they said.

February 1, 1876, arrived, and the Interior Department notified the War Department that the Indians who had not come in were to be forced. That was the job of the army, and the army had its soldiers waiting. In March 1875, General Crook, who had brought the Apaches onto reservations, had been transferred to the Department of the Platte. He was going to teach these northern Indians to walk the whites' road. He was going to "use a little force." But a little was not going to be enough.

· · ·

It was March, the Moon of Snowblindness, 1876. After a short February thaw the snow was again deep on the ground, and ice was frozen thick on the rivers. Sheltered in a canyon near the mouth of the Little Powder were the lodges of He Dog, of the Oglala Sioux, and Two Moons, of the northern Cheyenne—105 lodges altogether.

He Dog was waiting for the snow to melt before he came in to the agency. Only the month before he had parted with Crazy Horse, who would not come in. There were stories of many white soldiers coming north, but the camp felt safe in the protecting canyon.

At dawn on March 17 a young Sioux left his tent to drive the horse herd to water. He went down a small ravine outside the camp, and was suddenly confronted by a line of cavalry trotting toward the village. With a yell he warned the sleeping lodges. A squaw lifted the flap of her tepee and saw the charge rising from the ravine. "The soldiers are here!"

He Dog, Two Moons, and the other warriors roused themselves quickly, and cut their way out of their lodges, bows, arrows, and guns in hand. The pony soldiers galloped into the village, shooting their revolvers. The warriors shot back, aiming at the horses, for a cavalryman on foot was but half a man.

The squaws and children, half clad, fled into the plum thicket around the camp and clambered up the icy bluffs behind the village. More soldiers followed the first, and drove the horse herd away from camp, almost seven hundred ponies in all.

The soldiers had taken the camp, but Indian warriors were on three sides, shooting, and keeping them from moving on. Suddenly smoke billowed from the lodges. Everything was being piled together and burned, all the buffalo meat and robes, the weapons and sacred medicine things. Nothing was to be left.

But the soldiers behaved strangely under fire. They turned around and left the camp as quickly as they had come. The fight was not going the way they had planned. One of the soldier detachments never reached the village, and those who had could not face the shooting of the warriors. In their hurry they even left their dead behind.

When the soldiers were gone, the Indians came back to their village. A few poor horses which had not been shot by the whites were gathered. Two Moons and He Dog went back to the village of Crazy Horse. Some of the warriors stayed behind to recapture a few ponies. They succeeded in getting back over half the herd, but while driving them along, they ran into another detachment of soldiers, who took the horses away again.

The cavalry attack on the Sioux-Cheyenne village was the only major fight of General Crook's campaign in the winter of 1875–76. The campaign had started from Fort Fetterman on March 1 with ten cavalry and two infantry companies, with pack train and wagons. The detachment in the attack was led by Colonel J. J. Reynolds, Third Cavalry, guided by Sioux scouts.

Reynolds's fight on the Powder made it plain to the Indians that they would again have to unite to make a determined stand against the whites. It would be harder this time, because the soldiers were being helped by agency Indians and traders' sons. Even those who had once shared the lodges of the Sioux were now leading the soldiers against them. Frank Grouard, who had once been welcome in the lodge of Crazy Horse, led Reynolds to the camp on the Powder. The warriors saw him there.

CHAPTER 9
The Big Rolling Land

▲ ▲ ▲ ▲ ▲ ▲ ▲ ▲ ▲ ▲ ▲ ▲ ▲ ▲ ▲ ▲ ▲

Come to the Garden of the West! Come to Kansas! Come to Minnesota! Come to Nebraska, the Great Platte Valley. Soldiers Entitled to a Homestead of 160 Acres. Purchasers, their wives and children carried free in our elegant day coaches. Red River Valley Lands. Homeseekers! A Farm for $3 per Acre! Every Farmer, Every Farmer's Son, Every Clerk, Every Mechanic, Every Laboring Man Can Secure a Home.

THE RICH ROMANTIC PLACE NAMES of the big rolling land beyond the Mississippi echoed across the eastern United States. Broadsides in all the languages of Europe made the strange Indian names of the faraway country familiar to emigrants long before they reached New York en route to the free lands extending to the "shining mountains" and the Pacific. The slow march of settlement which had followed the Homestead Act of 1862 turned into a stampede during the 1870s and 1880s.

Thousands of human beings moved out upon the great plains into an awesome surreal world of limitless earth and sky. For some it was a world of beauty and freedom, but for others it was frightening and sometimes maddening in its loneliness.

The young farming men, women, and children came from everywhere, bringing everything they owned—a few horses or oxen, a coop of poultry, seeds for planting, a plow. Their first days were hard, but a few people like John Ruede from Pennsylvania found time to scrawl letters to the folks back home: "Staked two corners of my claim this morning. . . . Looking for a place to make our dugout." Two days later Ruede recorded: "We got through digging the hole by the time it was dark. The hole is 10 × 14 feet, and in front 4 ft. deep, 4½ behind. On Monday we must look for a ridge pole and dig steps so we can get into the place."

Within the week, sod walls twenty inches thick were up above the ground, and Ruede wrote on Saturday, just nine days after staking his claim: "Used part of the straw on the roof, and covered the whole roof with a layer of sod, and then threw dirt on it, and the 'House' was finished."

Next day, Ruede was planting gooseberry bushes along the west side of his sod house and making arrangements for help with well-digging and sod-breaking.

The new settlers used different words to explain why they moved west, but beyond all their words was the old American vision of a better life beyond the far horizon. "We wanted to come to a new country," said Susan Frances Lomax, "so our children could grow up with the country. We were living on a good farm [in Mississippi]. My husband said he would live ten years longer by coming to a new country. You hardly ever saw a gray headed man. I did not want to come to Texas at all; I dreaded the Indians in those days. . . . It was a hard time on weman; they staid at home and did the work while the men were on their ponies hunting or looking after stock."

Without their yoked oxen, thousands of homesteading families could never have plowed their first fields or hauled wood and water. And in the dark days of the settlers' first blizzardy winters, more often than not it was the dependable ox that was sacrificed for food to keep them alive until spring.

Patient, plodding, stolid—never romantic. That was the ox, a cud-chewing animal now virtually extinct, neglected by both poets and historians. Rarely does this beast of burden appear in Western fiction or motion pictures. Alongside the graceful galloping horse, the colorless castrated ox does not shine in the saga of the West. Oxen, however, were usually considered as members of the family, endowed by their owners with affectionate or dignified names. A Texan called his pair Pollux and Castor.

Everything but land and sky was scarce on the early Western homesteads. Water was usually the scarcest necessity of all. As soon as a settler marked his claim and set up a wagon-cover tent, he started searching for water. The nearest stream might be ten miles away, and water had to be hauled in barrels until a well could be dug. One Ne-

SOD SHANTY ON THE PLAINS

Beyond the tree belt, sod formed the basic ingredient of building. Eighteen-inch strips were cut into suitable lengths and laid like bricks. The floors were pounded earth, the windows oiled paper or glass, depending on finances and personal preferences. To the sod house of western Nebraska with its dirt roof and shored-up walls the rancher brought his bride; here he raised his family. (Photograph by S. D. Butcher, courtesy of the Nebraska State Historical Society.)

FIRST ARRIVALS

The young farming men, women, and children came from everywhere, bringing everything they owned—a few horses or oxen, a coop of poultry, seeds for planting, a plow. "We wanted to come to a new country," said Susan Frances Lomax, "so our children could grow up with the country. . . . It was a hard time on weman; they staid at home and did the work while the men were on their ponies hunting or looking after stock." (Photograph by S. D. Butcher, courtesy of the Nebraska State Historical Society.)

braska farmer hauled water for two years before he could complete digging his well by hand. He dug three hundred feet straight down through hard clay and rock with a pick and shovel.

Edward E. Dale, reminiscing about early days in Oklahoma, recalled asking a farmer why he persisted in hauling water nine miles for his horse and livestock, instead of digging a well. Replied the farmer: "It's just as near to water one way or the other, and I prefer to get mine along horizontal rather than perpendicular lines."

Itinerant well-drillers finally solved the water problem for most Western settlers. The usual charge was twenty cents per foot for a hole six inches in diameter, the owner to furnish the necessary iron casing.

Water was pulled out of the deep wells with windmills, and the first homesteaders built huge ones, assuming that the bigger the wheels the more water would flow. In some areas, Dutch-type windmills were built and used for milling grain as well as for pumping water. "Jumbo" windmills were popular, requiring no tower, being merely a large fan-wheel in a crude box. Travelers were impressed by one early ranch on the plains which had a "double-header windmill with two power wheels twenty-two feet in diameter seventy-two feet from the ground."

Finding fuel for cooking and heating was often another major problem for the plains settlers. In the Southwest, the pioneers dug mesquite sprouts from the dry earth; in other parts of the country the best woodlands were often on Indian reservations, and the Indians collected a fee—about fifty cents a load—for firewood cut by the homesteaders.

During the first decade of settlement following the Civil War, buffalo chips were the surest and most common source of fuel. Gathered into wagons, carts, or wheelbarrows, the chips were stacked in ricks or piled under a shed to ensure dryness; they would not burn when wet.

Later, along the great cattle trails, cow chips replaced the vanishing buffalo dung. But as late as 1880, buffalo chips were still in good supply in some parts of Kansas. The Kinsley *Graphic* carried the following notice on January 17 of that year: "The County Commissioners at their last meeting issued an order to the township trustees that they would allow no bills for coal for the poor, in cases where the poor have teams to gather buffalo chips."

When the buffalo and cow chips, the mesquite roots, and the few trees along the streams were all gone, the plains settlers learned how to burn sunflowers and hay—both in plentiful supply. The sunflower advocates claimed one acre would produce twelve cords of fuel, but unfortunately the twelve cords burned faster than one cord of wood.

WELL-DIGGERS AND WINDMILLS

Everything but land and sky were scarce on the early Western home-steads. Water was usually the scarcest necessity of all. As soon as the settler marked his claim, he started searching for water. The nearest stream might be ten miles away, and water had to be hauled in barrels until a well could be dug. When asked why he persisted in hauling water nine miles instead of digging a well, one farmer replied, "It's just as near to water one way or the other, and I prefer to get mine along horizontal rather than perpendicular lines." Itinerant well-drillers finally solved the water problem for most western settlers. Windmills were also used to pump water up, once the deep wells were dug. (Photograph courtesy of Kansas State Historical Society.)

Hay burned even faster, and in spite of several ingenious hay-burner stoves developed during the 1880s, a common saying of the times was that it required "two men and a boy to keep a hay fire going."

The size of Western farms encouraged mechanization. But few of the early homesteaders could afford even the crude farm machinery of that time. Many a first crop was put in with hoes, spades, and mattocks. Because corn was grown on almost every farm, one of the first "machines" acquired was either a foot or hand corn planter. "This labor saving device," read one advertisement for the hand planter, "is important to the farmers of the West. It is carried or used like a walking stick or cane. It is simple, cheap, accurate, and dependable."

As the settlers prospered, they began buying newly invented machines. Across the expanding wheat country during the 1870s, reapers and binders and harvesters appeared in a variety of types and models. Unaccustomed to anything more complicated than a plow, the horses did not always cooperate. In his diary, a Western farmer proudly noted the acquisition of a stalk-cutting machine, then a few days later laconically recorded: "Finished cutting stalks. The horses ran away and broke stalk-cutter all to hell."

But as early as 1878, the Dickinson County (Kansas) *Chronicle* reported that a young lady of the community was successfully operating a farm with machines: "She does her own plowing—using a sulky plow. This year she has one hundred acres of fine wheat and will cut and bind it herself—using a self-binder."

Newcomers to the West soon discovered that they had less to fear from the highly publicized "savage Indians" than from the violence of nature—especially the capricious weather, which could be more deadly destructive than a war party of savage braves.

The most common enemy was the prairie fire, a particularly awesome spectacle after nightfall. Prairie grass grew as high as a man's head, and during rainless autumns it dried and browned under the sun until it was more inflammable than pitchpine.

"A ribbon of smoke in the distance," wrote Wiley Britton, "it rapidly increased in size, and in a very short time became a great volume of dense black smoke, with tongues of flame shooting high into the air, and a few minutes later we saw hawks and birds of the prairies flying wildly before the sea of surging, writhing and leaping flames. In an incredibly short time the whole visible horizon to the southwest was darkened by the thick black smoke, ashes and flames, and then came

WHEAT-BUYING CENTER, FARGO, DAKOTA TERRITORY

To work the fields from Texas to the Canadian border, machines as well as men were needed to plant and harvest endless acres of wheat. Records of one farm of 60,000 acres show that 150 men were hired for April plowing and 400 during August and September for harvesting. Typical of wheat-buying centers was Fargo, Dakota Territory, as shown in this 1879 photograph. (Photograph by F. J. Haynes, courtesy of F. J. Haynes Studios, Bozeman, Montana.)

PUFFING MONSTERS OF THE PRAIRIES

Before the end of the nineteenth century, steam-powered machines were a common sight on prosperous prairie and mountain valley farms. Each year they seemed to grow more and more gigantic, moving like clanking prehistoric monsters across the big rolling land. (Photograph by Lee Moorehouse, courtesy of the University of Oregon Library.)

antelope, deer, jack rabbits and wolves, racing with the roaring, billowy, writhing flames, in mad flight for safety."

Until settlers learned to plow fire breaks around their fields and cabins, the only methods of defense were to set backfires, beat out the flames with brush, or run a drag over the line of fire. Drags were often hastily improvised, as was Teddy Roosevelt's when he stopped a fire threatening his Dakota ranch by splitting a steer in half and dragging it across the flames.

Contemporary Westerners may believe they have bigger wind and dust storms than the pioneer settlers, but early accounts of the plains country belie these modern claims. Newspapers were reporting dust storms as early as 1860: "The air was filled with bricks, barrels, boxes, tubs, signs, and boards which were blown about like chaff, and the dust so beclouded the air as to shut out the light of day." One old story of a Kansas cowtown tells of a barber who while shaving a customer chanced to glance out the window and see his first dust storm, a solid wall of blackness descending upon the town. "God almighty!" cried the barber, "the end of the world has come. I'm headin' for home to be with my family." He ran out into the street, leaving his customer to meet doom with a lathered face.

The winds were as awesome as the dust they carried before them. The Wichita *Eagle* in 1872 reported winds lifting "ten-pound boulders and two-year-old mule colts off the ground—the squawking flock overhead may be geese, may be jackasses. Those of us who have lost their domestic animals and fowls need not be alarmed, as the chances are that such stock will be blown back by the next wind."

With its fearful roar and death-dealing funnel, the tornado was a terror to lonely plains dwellers. As a defense against this monster, the settlers built storm cellars. They soon learned to make jokes and tell tall tales about twisters and the huge hailstones which usually accompanied them. "The twisting motion of the wind," a newspaper reported, "drew all the milk from one farmer's herd of cows and sprayed it into the air where it became mixed with small pellets of hail and made a veritable downfall of ice cream. Some pretty big hail fell. One chunk will furnish ice to the meat shops for the next 90 days. Another imbedded itself in the ground and is slowly melting, will afford water to stock all summer and also make a fine boating pond."

Blizzard and flood tales of the West are legion, and many are tragic. Both these weather phenomena often came suddenly, the blizzards blowing up late on a hazy warm day, and the floods rushing down dry runs where water was seldom seen. Inexperienced homesteaders were sometimes caught away from home by blizzards, unaware until too late of how rapidly the temperature could drop and of how low was the visibility in a howling snowstorm on the plains.

Not all were so lucky as the Colorado rancher lost in a driving blizzard. Encountering a buffalo floundering around in a deep drift, the rancher quickly slew and disemboweled the animal, then crawled inside, drawing the opening tight to keep out the cold. Next morning when he awoke the rancher found his exit hole frozen shut. He solved his double problem of imprisonment and hunger by eating his way out.

Stories of nature's violence in the West gradually drifted back to the East, reviving old tales of the Great American Desert. To counteract these stories, Henry Worrall of Topkea drew a charcoal sketch, "Drouthy Kansas," depicting huge cornstalks, grapes, watermelons, and potatoes. Worrall's caricature was reprinted all over the country, and tall tales about Kansas soon became the fashion.

In 1884 some Eastern newspapers carried a story of a Kansas farmer who climbed to the top of a cornstalk one evening to inspect the state of the weather. His foot slipped and he fell into a nearby treetop where he dangled precariously by his suspenders all night. When he was rescued the next morning he swore he would buy an almanac and keep himself posted on the weather without resorting to such dangerous methods as climbing tall cornstalks. The Kiowa *Herald* of July 8, 1885, commented on this story: "Coming from an eastern paper, we don't believe it. If he had fallen out of the top of a cornstalk in a field of Barber County corn the blades would have been so thick and strong that they would have sustained his weight and he could reach the ground as easily as walking down a step ladder, and not been put to the painful necessity of hanging all night in a tree top with only his suspenders between him and eternity."

In the summer of 1874, farmers all over the West began seeing strange silvery spots circling in the sunny skies. The puzzled plainsmen soon discovered what the silvery circles were—millions of grasshoppers in flight. Before that summer ended, 1874 was known as the Great Grasshopper Year.

From Oregon to the Dakotas, south to Texas and east into Missouri, the insects descended upon the land in columns 150 miles wide and 100 miles long, beating like hail against the roofs and sides of farmhouses. Tormented homesteaders tied strings around their trouser bottoms to keep the pests from crawling up and biting their legs. At Fort Scott,

YEAR OF THE GRASSHOPPER

In the summer of 1874, farmers all over the West began seeing strange silvery spots circling the sunny skies. The silvery circles were millions of grasshoppers in flight, and before that summer ended, 1874 was known as the Great Grasshopper Year. The insects descended upon the land in columns 150 miles wide and 100 miles long. Efforts to save crops were futile. Hundred-acre cornfields vanished in a few hours. Farmer Swain Finch of Nebraska *(above)* doing battle with the invaders of that year. (Photograph by S. D. Butcher, courtesy of the S. D. Butcher Collection, Nebraska State Historical Society.)

Kansas, a descending grasshopper cloud stopped a horse race, covering the tracks three inches deep. Lighting upon trees, the grasshoppers broke limbs under their weight.

Efforts to save crops were futile. Hundred-acre cornfields vanished in a few hours, the plants denuded to the stalks. When blankets and sheets were spread over precious vegetable patches, the grasshoppers ate the bed clothing. One account tells of a man who lay down to rest beside a road; when he awoke his throat and wrists were bleeding from the bites of starving grasshoppers. They ate harnesses, window curtains, hoe handles, and even each other.

When a dark cloud of grasshoppers landed upon the Union Pacific tracks near Kearney, Nebraska, they stopped all trains, grease from the crushed insects setting locomotive wheels to spinning.

News of this major victory for the grasshoppers came as an anticlimax. Many Great Plains farmers had already given up, and wagon after wagon filled with household goods moved eastward with "Grasshopper" signs on their sides, like the Pike's Peak "Busters" of an earlier decade.

One group of disillusioned settlers, returning through Topeka, stopped there long enough to speak their minds to Henry Worrall of "Drouthy Kansas" fame. "Had it not been for the diabolical seductiveness of that picture," reported the Topeka *Commonwealth,* "they said they would never have come to Kansas to be ruinated and undone by grasshoppers."

Homesteaders who refused to quit—and they were in the majority— were faced with a hard winter. Many had no money, no credit, no food; some had no fuel or clothing. Some settlers earned enough money to live through the winter by gathering the bones of buffaloes and other animals from the stripped land. The bones were symbolic but were not a direct result of the grasshoppers' ravages; they were converted into cash and shipped east to fertilize plants. For the first time in the nation's history, the federal government offered relief to farmers, the Secretary of War issuing a "grasshopper appropriation" for the purchase of food and clothing to be "divided among the naked."

Funds were quickly exhausted, and appeals were made to more fortunate citizens in other states to help with offers of food and clothing. Several Western states issued Grasshopper Bonds to relieve their desperate people. Nebraska passed a Grasshopper Act naming the insect as Public Enemy Number One, requiring every able-bodied male between the ages of sixteen and twenty to serve as legalized vigilantes in a continuous war against the foe.

Western settlers fought the grasshopper hard in 1875. Minnesota established a bounty of fifty cents a bushel on the insects. Happy farmers fastened boxes on their reaper platforms and drove around their fields until the boxes were full. One farmer who had an abundance of the insects chased his neighbors with a pitchfork when he discovered them "poaching grasshoppers" on his land. It was fun while it lasted. But the bounty was in the form of state scrip, and so many grasshoppers were turned in for collection that Minnesota went bankrupt.

In spite of grasshoppers and the violence of nature, Western homesteaders endured and eventually came to prosperity. They experimented with new crops, eagerly sought improved varieties of wheat and corn, and replaced their long-legged sway-backed scrub cattle with blockier, meatier animals. As a means of spreading information among themselves, they organized annual state fairs. Because Western states were large and transportation was poor, the early fairs were held in different towns in succeeding years.

At a Colorado fair held in Denver in 1876, farmers exhibited "all varieties of produce among which are mammoth squashes, beets, potatoes, and melons, besides some freshly cut grass measuring over six feet in height." Premiums included ten dollars for the "best-dressed buffalo robe dressed in Colorado by a white man."

Fair managers favored horse racing but frowned on such things as balloon ascensions and trapeze performers. "They should be left to the domain of the circus," said John Shaffer of Iowa in 1880. "They are no part and parcel of the purpose for which State Fairs were organized. People will come to a fair without them." But Mr. Shaffer admitted that farm families needed some amusement and recommended that side shows be permitted. "They will follow after a fair, anyhow, as persistent eagles will gather together about a carcass. If admitted inside the grounds, any indecent or unmoral exhibition can at once be driven away, or any vices practiced under the canvass can be apprehended and abolished."

As settlement continued, the more populous counties began holding county fairs, offering long and varied lists of awards. In addition to the usual livestock and crop prizes, awards were made for such entries as best lady driver of single horse and double team, best display of evergreens, best ten pounds of Indian corn starch, best fancy painting in oil, best agricultural wreath, best map of the solar system.

Manufacturers of farm machinery and household goods were encouraged to display their wares, and were given medals for the best revolving horse hay rakes, corn shellers, horse collars and shoes, kerosene lamps, washboards, bar soaps, and artificial teeth—all of which reflected the deep-felt needs of hard-working farm families in the West.

By 1884, just ten years after the disastrous grasshopper year, the settlers of the Western plains had proved the Great American Desert to be a myth. In that year they prospered while Eastern farmers suffered alternate droughts and floods. In April, Henry Worrall, the Kansas caricaturist, had the pleasure of drawing a sketch of a gaily draped train loaded with grain—the gift of Western farmers to flood sufferers back East. "The cars were rudely but effectively decorated with designs in color," reported *Harper's Weekly,* which published Worrall's drawing with an account of the event. The grasshopper—rampant and couchant—was much in evidence among the blazing banners.

Transportation, however, remained as a formidable obstacle to farm prosperity in the West. The Missouri was the only navigable river which flowed to markets in the East. And although five great railroads were spanning the continent, there were few branch or intersecting lines to serve thousands of square miles of farmland long distances from the rails. Thirty miles was a long day's journey. One hundred miles required at least a week to come and go by horse team—even longer by ox team.

A Southwestern cattleman could drive his stock overland to trail town railheads, but a wheat farmer had to load his crop in wagons, and then after consulting his almanac, drive off across the prairie behind a twenty-mule team headed for the nearest railroad stop or steamboat landing. If the almanac was in error and heavy rains caught his tandem wagons en route, the wheels soon bogged to the axles. And even if the weather held good, very likely there was no shelter or grain elevator at the railroad loading point.

Typical of wheat-buying centers was Fargo, Dakota Territory. In the larger towns like Fargo, dealers such as J. R. McLaughlin built Farm Machinery Halls, where the latest in plows, wagons, and power machines could be inspected by interested settlers. The center of attraction during Fargo's Fourth of July celebration in 1881 was a fancy chariot advertising Cyrus McCormick's new twine binder.

Some Western homesteaders acquired steam-powered farm machines before they were able to enjoy the benefits of steam-powered rail transportation. In December 1870 a settler near Hell Gate, Montana, wrote to the Wood, Taber & Morse Company, explaining that since railroads had not yet reached his region, "your engine is a rare sight in these mountains. Some of the old mountaineers have come down the valley and camped for two or three days to see the machine and listen to the whistle of my agricultural steam engine."

Before the end of the nineteenth century, steam-powered machines were a common sight on prosperous prairie and mountain valley farms. Each year they seemed to grow more gigantic, moving like clanking prehistoric monsters across the big rolling land.

Successful wheat farming with the new and expensive machines required extensive acreage, and upon the vast land grants paralleling the railroads, bonanza farms began developing in the late 1870s. The Northern Pacific Railroad, which crossed the Dakotas, took the lead in this type of farming, operating farms as large as 100,000 acres in the valleys of the James and Red rivers.

"You are in a sea of wheat," one visitor wrote, "the railroad train rolls through an ocean of grain." Hundreds of horses, dozens of mammoth steam-powered machines, seeders, harvesters, and threshers were required to operate these bonanza farms. "Even the telephone is brought into requisition for the management of such an estate."

Workers as well as machines were needed to plant and harvest these endless acres of wheat. Records of one farm of 60,000 acres show that 150 men were hired for April plowing and 400 during August and September for harvesting. But only a few hands were necessary during the other nine months.

To meet this demand for seasonal labor, migratory harvesting crews moved north across the plains each summer—working the wheatfields from Texas to the Canadian border. Ironically, quite a few of these workers were unemployed cowboys, refugees from bonanza cattle ranches which collapsed after the blizzard of 1886.

"They reached our neighborhood in July," wrote Hamlin Garland, who lived as a youth in the wheat country, "arriving like a flight of alien unclean birds, and vanished into the north as mysteriously as they had appeared. Some carried valises, others had nothing but small bundles containing a clean shirt and a few socks."

Flying dust, cracking whips, glistening straw, a ceaseless ringing humming—that was horse-power threshing as described by Garland. "The wheat came pulsing out the spout in such a stream that the carriers were forced to trot on their path to and from the granary in order to keep the grain from piling up around the measurer. There was a kind of splendid rivalry in this backbreaking toil—for each sack weighed ninety pounds."

Along with bonanza wheat farming, sheep ranching also prospered

THE PRESIDENT VISITS A BONANZA FARM, 1878

When President Rutherford B. Hayes toured the West in 1878, he stopped his special train to have a look at the famed Dalrymple Farm. "It was a sea of wheat, the railroad rolling through an ocean of grain." (Photograph by F. J. Haynes, courtesy of F. J. Haynes Studios, Bozeman, Montana.)

in the late nineteenth century. "The expenses are not heavy," said Major William Shepherd, who made a study of the industry in 1885. "Two men can through the year easily drive two or three thousand sheep. The returns from wool and increase are not exaggerated at twenty-five per cent."

Many additional men were needed at shearing time, however, and sheep shearers, like harvest hands, followed the season north, shearing wool with hand clippers. Beginning in March they moved up from the Southwest into the Rocky Mountain ranges, reaching the Canadian border by July. A good shearer could clip a hundred sheep a day, and might earn ten dollars—very good pay in those days.

Sheepman trailed their stock to grazing lands and to markets, but unlike cattlemen they did not swim the animals across rivers. A sheep bridge was necessary for a river crossing. "It often consists of a single large pine tree, which has been felled, and directed in its fall across the stream. A rough balustrade is added, and a few stones are piled to make a ramp by which the sheep can mount readily on to the log. The banks of the river on either side, above and below the bridge, may be fenced, to prevent the sheep from pushing each other into the water when crowding to cross." Wethers or goats were trained to lead the crossings.

Not all the Western cowboys had turned to harvesting, and certainly very few would drive or shear sheep. The cattle trade still flourished after a fashion, but the range was closed, and no more trail drives could be made across the fenced and furrowed land. Said old-time cowboy Teddy Blue: "Fences and sheep and settlers were coming in, and the old-time big cow outfits was going out, and nothing was like it used to be in anymore." The cowboys spent their time riding within fenced ranges, searching for stray calves to brand, or routing outlaw steers out of hiding places in brakes and arroyos.

Western stockmen also liked to experiment with new breeds of animals. Along the grassy coastlands of Texas, A. P. Borden imported the first Brahmins from India; out in the Panhandle and on the plains of Kansas others crossbred cattle and buffalo. In Bastrop County, Texas, Bethel Coopwood and John Wesley Lanfeer started a camel-breeding experiment, hoping to market their product to the army for transport use across the high dry trails of the Southwest.

By the turn of the century, the trusty ox had practically disappeared. But the horse was in his glory. As the West filled with new settlers, demand for horses reached a peak. The natural supply of wild mustangs was soon exhausted, and horse ranches developed into profitable enterprises.

But the big money crop from Southwestern land during the last years of the frontier was cotton. Texas and Oklahoma took over cotton raising from the Old South, fields of green and white covering the former grazing lands of the Longhorns.

"Cotton is the surees crop to rais in Texas," a shrewd settler wrote to a friend back in Ohio as early as 1833. By the end of the century, the railroad yards at Houston each ginning season were clogged with long lines of boxcars and flatcars stacked high with bales of cotton.

Underneath the rich cotton lands of the Southwest were even greater treasures. The Indians had known of places where brown fluids seeped from the earth, oils which healed battle wounds and skin diseases. Around such seeps were invisible substances in the air that would burn forever—better than pine torches to light the night during times of tribal ceremonies. The first pioneers learned to use the brown fluids for softening leather, lubricating wagon axles, and making ointments. Most Texans despised the stuff; it ruined their water for drinking. In 1886, a rancher near San Antonio drilled 235 feet for water, but hit oil instead. He was disgusted until he discovered he could use it for fuel around the ranch.

Then in 1894, a well being bored for water at Corsicana, Texas, suddenly began spouting oil in a steady stream. It caught fire and started the first oil boom in the West. Corsicana was soon producing petroleum commercially—1,450 barrels the first year. Four years later production rose to more than half a million barrels.

The Corsicana boom encouraged other petroleum drilling in Texas, and on January 10, 1901, an oil gusher big enough to surprise even a Texan blew in just outside Beaumont. Spindletop, the gusher was called—the most famed well in the history of Western petroleum.

The first showing of oil came at around the 800-foot mark, and Al Hamill, the driller, figured he might bring in a fifty-barrel well. With his old-fashioned rig, he drove down another 200 feet. Suddenly the drill pipe shot up out of the casing and knocked off the crown block. "In a very short time," Hamill said afterward, "oil was going up through the top of the derrick and rocks were shot hundreds of feet into the air. Within a very few minutes, the oil was holding a steady flow at more than twice the height of the derrick." Spindletop spilled oil all over the Texas landscape, 100,000 barrels a day.

In a few weeks Beaumont was running a high fever. Wooden oil derricks shot up like weeds. The population jumped from 10,000 to 30,000. Tents, shacks, saloons, and gambling houses sprang up as they had in the old cattle trail towns of an earlier generation. Land values soared from $40 to $1,000,000 an acre.

The railroads ran special weekend trains for tourists, and the obliging oil drillers arranged for new wells to be spouting over the derrick tops every Sunday to entertain the visitors.

But before long another field, Sour Lake, had surpassed Beaumont as a rough, tough boomtown in the true Western Tradition. This pool was so rich that derricks were built with their supports adjoining. "For surging energy," recalls Charlie Jeffries, who worked there as a roustabout, "for unrestrained openness and diabolical conditions otherwise, Sour Lake was head and shoulders above anything Texas had seen up until that time or perhaps has seen since. A short while after operations began, a large part of the field was worked up into such a mess of mud as can hardly be imagined. In saloons, Sour Lake ranked high. These were of all sizes and quality. . . . After payday, when a gang of pipeliners came to town, especially if it happened to be a chilly, drizzly evening, the sidewalk for a block or more would be filled with jabbering, reeling men."

The West's oil fever soon moved into Oklahoma, where homesteaders of recent land rushes were having no easy time of it on 160-acre claims unsuited for plow farming and too small to support range livestock. Many were selling the land off for a few dollars an acre.

Then in 1905 near a sleepy village which the natives called Tulsey Town, wildcatters made a big strike in the Glenn Pool. Gamblers and speculators and the new fraternity of oil men in their big hats and laced boots swarmed into the little town on the Arkansas River. Millions of barrels of oil poured out, breaking prices on the market for a time. The Glenn Pool changed Tulsey Town into Tulsa, Oil Capital of the World.

A mad search for oil spread north and west across the Great Plains, new strike following new strike. Any shift upward in oil prices set off new drillings, sometimes so frenzied that thousands of barrels flowed back into the earth for lack of storage tanks. Often the spouting wells caught fire and burned for days in ominous clouds of greasy boiling smoke.

California had small petroleum fields long before Corsicana and Spindletop were discovered in Texas. But boomtowns and oil fever were lacking; perhaps California was immune to oil fever after its wild gold rush days. Not until the Lake View gusher blew in and poured out 90,000 barrels a day did Californians go a little mad over oil. For months Lake View spouted completely out of control, the richest oil well of all time, the spray covering an area fifteen miles around. "We cut an artery down there," said the driller, "Dry Hole Charlie" Wood. "What we feared most was an early rain. A flash flood could have spread our ocean of oil down over the valley below. So we went up into the hills with an army of 600 men and damned up the mouths of canyons with earth walls twenty feet high and fifty feet thick. Down below we built storage for ten million barrels of oil." Nine million barrels ran into the Lake View reservoir before it could be controlled, a flood of oil that dropped the market price from fifty to thirty cents per barrel.

Half a century before the contagious oil fever struck in the West, pioneers had been searching for riches under the big rolling land. The original wildcatters were gold prospectors, miners with pans and cradles. Men without women, they traveled on foot alongside their trusty burros instead of behind yoked oxen in covered wagons. They traveled light with only a pick and shovel, and needed no rotary rig to wheedle fortunes from the tantalizing earth.

"Stalwart, muscular, dauntless young braves," Mark Twain described them. "Brimful of push and energy. But they were rough in those times! They fairly reveled in gold, whisky, fights and fandangoes."

They panned and cradled for gold; they built crude but ingenious machines to crush hard quartz. One was built in the Black Hills shortly after Colonel George Custer's expedition found gold there in 1875. As the quartz was crushed, water was introduced; the resulting milky mixture flowed out over a framework where quicksilver riffles picked up the precious particles of gold.

Like the homesteaders, miners were often hampered by lack of water and transportation. Gold could not be mined without water, and silver ore had to be transported to stamping mills, sometimes with a train of twenty-mule teams hauling silver ore. Each wagon would be manned by a driver and a swamper, the driver wielding a whip, the swamper hurling stones at the mules to keep them moving.

While homesteaders were plowing the land and prospectors were digging beneath its surface, others were at work in the forests. Demand for lumber was rising rapidly as new towns and cities began to grow. During the era of settlement following the Civil War, the logging industry was first centered in the Lake States of Michigan, Wisconsin, and Minnesota. Here in the vast white-pine forests was born Paul Bun-yan, legendary hero of Western loggers. Here again, the ox is the forgotten pioneer, as in the case of the first homesteaders. Ox wagons brought in veteran loggers from the East, ox teams hauled food and supplies to set up the first lumber camps, and then they went to work skidding logs on go-devils over ice and snow to river landings. Paul Bunyan's best friend was Babe, the Blue Ox.

Like an outdoorsmen, loggers enjoyed eating, but one of their pe-culiar traditions was silence at mealtimes. Stewart Holbrook, historian of the lumber industry, says the origin of this custom of no talking at mealtimes is lost in history: "Some lay it to the cook's desire to have the men fill their gut and get out as quickly as possible." Any violation of the rule was quickly quelled by the cook, who tolerated no sound except the "champing of jaws."

"We seldom ever worked on Christmast," wrote Otis Terpenning, a Minnesota lumberjack. "Some spent their time in playing cards, And listing for the cheerie sound of the dinner horn, Saying come and eat, eat. The cook would always have something extry, and plenty of it. Their was roast beef brown gravy, Good home made bread, Potatoes, Shiny tins heaped with golden rings called fried cakes And close to them a punkin pie baked in a ten-inch tin about one and a half inch deep."

While their contemporaries, the cowboys of the Southwest, were putting brands on cattle, Western loggers were similarly designating ownership with log marks. Both bark-marks and end-marks were used, applied with branding axes. When logs came down tributary streams to the big river booms, sorters worked over the jamming mass of timber, sorting the various brands, which were then joined into rafts for further movement down to the lumber mills. A log in a boom without a brand was like a maverick cow in a roundup; it was anybody's log. And lumber "rustlers" tempted by thousands of unguarded logs sometimes stole choice specimens, obliterating or changing the original brands, and then selling them to the highest bidders.

By the end of the nineteenth century—the end of Western settle-ment—the logging industry had leaped from the Lake States to the Pacific slopes, from white pines to Douglas fir and Ponderosa pine and redwood. As the loggers moved westward with settlement, they took their oxen with them to bring giant pines out of the mountain forests. But in a few years, funnel-stacked engines were puffing into formerly inaccessible areas on narrow-gauge rails. The logging locomotives were equipped with fireproofers to control sparks.

Through all these swiftly changing years, the lumberjacks kept the big rivers of the Western land filled with the felled giants of its virgin forests—logs from which came the millions of feet of lumber that built the towns and cities beyond the Mississippi.

CHAPTER 10
The Story of a Western Town

▲ ▲ ▲ ▲ ▲ ▲ ▲ ▲ ▲ ▲ ▲ ▲ ▲ ▲ ▲ ▲

UNDER THE CANVASES OF THEIR covered wagons, the Western overlanders stowed a little of everything they required to start life in a new, raw land. Clothing, furniture, household equipment, weapons, seeds, medicine, schoolbooks, and a reserve of food were all intended to make the people of the frontier independent. Such independence was short-lived. Powder and lead, if nothing else, tied the settler to the East. Conversely, the income from ranch or mine was worth little except as traded for products and manufactured articles necessary for life or desirable for comfort.

The link between the consumer of the West and the supplier in the East was the town. Often little more than a trading post, the Western town supplied the needs of the settler, and took in return the raw material of the new land. To the trader came fur trappers with their pelts, buffalo hunters with hides and tallow, farmers with grain, miners with dust. To all these the trading post was a place to get powder and shot, tobacco, coffee, clothing, beans, liquor, and news. The firm of Ridenour and Baker, frontier Kansas traders, reported, "Farmers came in from fifty to one hundred miles to trade. Several farmers would get together and send one team, and purchase a wagon load amounting to several hundred dollars. . . . We bought hides, fur, grains, and all the farmer's produce."

Around such primitive enterprises grew the settlements, the centers of population which, in time, became chartered towns with names, and all the accoutrements associated with town life. Here were the centers of trade, communication, transportation, banking, and native industries.

The location of a Western town was usually determined by some natural advantage. Traders did not just pick a good view and settle on it. As overland trails were established, towns developed along the routes at fords, springs, junctions, and other natural stopping points. Waterfalls, heads of navigation, and approaches to mountain passes were geographical advantages favorable to the establishment of centers of population. Oregon City in 1858, at the end of the Oregon Trail and at the falls of the Willamette River, seemed destined to be the major city of the region. No one could have predicted that Portland, a few miles downstream, would outgrow the city by the falls. Some towns developed by a process of gravitation toward the old fur trade establishments and army posts founded by an earlier generation.

Terrain meant nothing when a gold town was on the make. Houses, stores, and streets were crowded into canyons and gulches, or suspended on steep hills. Burke, Idaho, had a main street so narrow the awnings had to be raised to let the train go by.

Mining towns were assembled as rapidly as new strikes were made, and as quickly abandoned. Western geography is punctuated with their names once known to thousands, and now forgotten. Described as "Ophir holes, gopher holes and loafer holes," mining communities were a mixture of success, frustration, and despair. Pioneer City, first gold camp in Montana, lived longer than most, but its glory faded when the nuggets were gone.

Some mining camps outlived their growing pains and developed into commercial and political centers. Helena, Montana, was on July 9, 1865, "a lively camp. Three thousand people were there. The saw and hammer were busy in putting up cabins and storehouses, and in constructing sluice boxes for the washing out of gold. Trade was lively, saloons crowded, hurdy gurdy dance houses in full blast. There was suspended on the limb of a tree a man hung by the Vigilante committee the night before, the eighth specimen of similar fruit encased in leather boots that tree had borne in so many months."

In October 1861 the junction of Blue Canyon and Freezeout Gulch in eastern Oregon was a shelf of barren land like many others in the Powder River country. By the fall of 1862 the shelf supported a tent and cabin town of two thousand miners, traders, saloonkeepers, and floaters. Auburn was a bustling place which had already hanged two men, one legally. A year later, half the population had rushed to the Boise Basin mines of Idaho, and Auburn was on the decline. In a decade the town was a "ghost," and today only the shelf of land remains.

Seaport towns with natural harbors were more permanent. San Francisco, the most striking example of a city which survived the vagaries of a gold rush and desolation by disasters, was recognized as a town site in 1770. It became notorious when gold was discovered, but the harbor was worth more than the mines of the interior.

Bushrod Wilson, sailor and adventurer, described the town of San Francisco on July 3, 1850. "This place is a hard hole. Gambling, drunkenness, and immorality to excess, and a person that has just broke out in life is in great danger of being ruined here. Everything that will effect the senses is resorted to for base ends. The most enchanting music, the various forms of gambling, and obscene pictures, the allurements of women of the town, and drinking."

Wilson had his fling at the mines, and then left the scenes of iniquity to better his fortunes at what he believed would be the greatest city in the Oregon Territory. "Marysville," he wrote in 1851, "is at the head of steamboat navigation. We expect a steamer up here every day. We have a saw and grist mill here, fourteen houses, five stores, one tavern, two blacksmith shops, one cooper, one carpenter, one planing mill factory, and twenty buildings going up, where last year there was only two houses, one old log, and one split board house."

Bushrod Wilson's expectations were not fulfilled. His chosen site was not the head of navigation, and what navigation there was soon declined before a greater force, the railroad. The town of Marysville was just another country settlement kept alive by rural trade.

Geographical probabilities were sometimes ignored in the founding of Western towns. In May 1854, a sheriff, two doctors, a merchant, Indian agent, speculator, and two land agents crossed the Missouri River to the Nebraska side. Here they erected a claim house of logs, and divided the land into town lots. By agreement, donations of property were assigned to the Methodist church, Masonic Lodge, and Odd Fellows. These founding fathers, members of the Council Bluffs and Nebraska Ferry Company, were engaged in the Western frontier specialty of creating a town for speculative purposes.

Two years later, a steamboat crowded with emigrants stopped at the "Omaha City" (named after the nearest tribe of Indians) landing. The town's entire population welcomed the vessel: "Were immigrants coming into the Territory? If so, how many and of what character and condition. Are there probably lot buyers? Do they come with cash, or with hoes and plows, or cards?"

Clark Irwin, one of the steamboat passengers, strolled to the Apex Saloon for a glass of beer. He paid for his drink with an imitation bill of the kind wrapped around a patent medicine bottle. The bill was accepted. "Money and town stock," concluded Irwin, "or any other nicely printed and ornamented paper, were superabundant and equally current."

The founders of Omaha were fortunate in their selection of a town site, though only two of them ever enjoyed residence there. Other town speculations were less rewarding. According to one account, "Intense fever was stirred in the blood of men by the hope and belief that a company of them, or possibly only one or two could get together, take a tract of government land worth $1.25 an acre, and simply by platting it into lots and calling it a town make it worth at once from $1000 to $3000 per acre." John J. Ingalls, Massachusetts lawyer, was attracted in 1856 by a colorful lithograph of Sumner, Kansas Territory. When Ingalls arrived, he found little but platted Kansas prairie. In later years as senator from Kansas he recalled the attractive advertisement as a "chromatic triumph of lithographed mendacity."

All Western towns, regardless of origin, depended on transportation for their existence. Trading posts and their successors, general stores, had to renew supplies and export the raw materials of trade. Before the day of the railroad, transportation services were handled by steamboat and ox-freight lines. Steamboats operated on every navigable river in the West. The Missouri River was the great western supply route. Fort Benton, dominated by the firm of Pierre Chouteau and Company of fur trade glory, was at the head of Missouri River navigation. It had been established in 1846 as a supply post for the American Fur Company. During the Montana gold rush of the 1860s the site boomed, and a town grew up around the post. Steamboats loaded with freight and anxious miners disembarked here. Below this point the waterway was dotted with port towns whose main business was transshipment of steamboat freight via ox team.

From Bismarck and other Missouri River points, freight was hauled overland by ox team to the interior settlements. Pierre, Dakota Territory, was the port of entry for the Black Hills mining region. Overland freighting meant Russell, Majors and Waddell, greatest of all the freight companies, operating out of Nebraska City. Twenty-six wagons and 312 oxen made up one of their supply trains. Thirty bullwhackers kept the train moving, and the company furnished each man with a "pocket Bible as protection against moral contamination, two Colt revolvers and a large hunting knife as protection against Indians."

Towns too remote for wagon trains were supplied via muleback. Min-

SUPPLY DEPOT

Below Fort Benton, the waterway was dotted with port towns whose main business was to maintain the flow of supplies from the East. Steamboats were the lifeline of the frontier. *The Eclipse* is docked at the Third Street landing, Bismarck, Dakota, 1876. (Photograph by F. J. Haynes, courtesy of F. J. Haynes Studios, Bozeman, Montana.)

ing towns in the mountains were likely to have to depend on the mule. Everything from bacon to billiard tables was packed across the narrow trails that connected remote settlements with the outside world. The art of packing, a special skill developed largely by the Mexicans, was euphonious with Spanish terms like *cargadore, aparejo, suadera,* and *cincha.* Some of these terms were mangled into English.

Along the routes of the ox-team freighters, small settlements were established at natural stopping places—water supply and pasturage. The names and locations of many such temporary halts have long disappeared into history. Bakeoven, in eastern Oregon, was named after the enterprising activities of a freighter who was stranded with a load of flour, his team driven off by Indians. He built an oven, baked bread with his flour, and sold the product to miners traveling along the road. The ox freight gradually gave way to the westward-pushing railroad as the major link between Western towns and Eastern markets.

The communication center of a Western town was the express office. The government postal service was unable to cope with the rapid expansion and settlement of the Western territories, and private initiative took over the job. Dominated by Wells, Fargo, the express companies delivered parcels, packages, and mail to the remote towns and mining camps scattered over plains and mountains. A few large companies operated overland, but most of them were local lines whose service depended on connections with the major organizations.

Both Wells, Fargo and the local express companies were represented in the major Western towns by agents who maintained offices in general stores, banks, or other establishments. The Beekman Express of Jacksonville, Oregon, operated in the 1850s from the Beekman bank. To this office came miners with gold dust to be weighed and shipped; into this office came letters and packages addressed to the miners and settlers of southern Oregon and northern California.

Serving the Black Hills population was the Northwestern Express, Stage and Transportation Company of Deadwood. Via the "Custer Route" to Bismarck, a miner could transport mail, packages, freight, or himself anywhere in the world.

Alonzo Delano described the welcome arrival of an express in a California mining camp. "Every pick and shovel is dropped, every pan is laid aside, every rocker is stopped with its half-washed dirt, every claim is deserted, and they crowd around the store with eager inquiries, 'Have you got a letter for me?' "

For the accommodation of human traffic, most Western towns boasted a hotel, or stage stop. Overcrowding was no problem; wayfarers usually carried a blanket or two and floor space was available for fifty cents. One such hostelry was known as the "Six Bit House," the charge being two bits (twenty-five cents) each for supper, bed, and breakfast. The Belle Fourche stage station, stockaded against Indian attack, offered shelter to stage passengers from the Black Hills.

Where transient traffic was heavy, more pretentious hotels flourished. The Capitol Hotel at Bismarck, Dakota, in 1876, was well located. The town enjoyed considerable steamboat and stage business and was close by Fort Abraham Lincoln, outfitting point for many army expeditions. Well kept, such hotels were comfortable, but usually they suffered from invasions of "bed bugs and broad gauge rats."

As Western towns grew, and population increased in density and variety, the institution of the trading post and general store was displaced by specialized enterprises. Butcher shops, drug and cigar stores, stores for hay, grain, and feed, real estate offices, banks, and saloons filled the needs of the community and surrounding country.

Tinned and sacked foods were the major stock in trade of the early groceries. Fresh vegetables were sold in a limited season, if at all. In the tinned line, a patron could get beans packed in Chicago, or oysters from Baltimore.

The Western appetite for the comforts of life was satisfied by a shopping tour in town. E. A. Grant's store in Fargo, Dakota, provided the pioneer of 1876 with wallpaper, stationery, crayons, stereoscopic views for stereoscopes, beauty cream, and other refinements not usually associated with life on the plains.

Combinations of enterprises were common. Usually the furniture dealer doubled as an undertaker, the local carpenter built coffins, the newspaper editor often read law or sold real estate. The hay and grain business was part of a livery stable, and the hotel operated a restaurant on the premises. As one groceryman put it, "You can't make a living selling groceries alone. We sell that line at cost to bring in trade for our other goods."

An institution peculiar to Western towns was the Chinese store. Tea, canned fish, firecrackers, opium, and other esoteric specialties were offered for sale. Excluded from Occidental society, the Chinese maintained much of their native culture in the foreign land.

Even remote settlements were invaded by merchants looking for profitable business. J. L. Niebergall set up a men's clothing shop in Cripple Creek, Colorado. The mining population was in no position to practice the art of making or remaking clothes. For their boots, shirts, coats, and hats they went to Niebergall.

Drug and cigar stores were, in frontier days, just that. They did not sell kitchen equipment, wagons, or sporting goods. They were notable for the modest size of their soda fountains and variety of patent medicines. Their drugs and nickel cigars combined to give the stores an indefinable smell.

Butcher shops in Western towns offered patrons a choice of tame and wild meat. John Audubon visited Western butcher shops to find specimens for his drawings. Customers looking for meat could choose between the usual beef or pork, or buy a bear steak, buffalo hump, antelope, venison, prairie chicken, or whatever the professional hunters had brought in.

Frontier bakers found business especially good among bachelors. The miners of the Coeur d'Alene region were too busy to leave their diggings, and were well served by the muleback bakery. Fresh bread was a treat no miner could resist, even at a dollar a loaf.

Manufacturers flourished in Western towns, and faded with the coming of cheap railroad transportation. Many communities had their own flour mills. Furniture manufacturing and the allied skill of carriage and wagon building were profitable frontier enterprises. Some Westerners manufactured farm equipment, others found breweries more economic. Boots and shoes were made in the West before it became cheaper to import them. Woolen mills were founded in favorable areas, and flourished on government contracts for blankets delivered to the reservation Indians. Ironworks were incorporated, and abandoned. Meat-packing plants, notably that of the Marquis de Mores of Medora, Dakota, were built in defiance of the great slaughtering centers of Kansas City and Chicago.

Bar iron, strap iron, nails, and wire were much in demand on the frontier. The demand could be filled either by shipment from the East or by utilization of iron deposits in the West. The Oregon Iron Works tried to capture the Pacific coast market. Neither the iron nor the available coal was of high enough quality to assure profitable operation.

Few Western industrial efforts survived Eastern competition. Processing of fish, lumber, fruits, and vegetables, or the building of wooden ships, was always economic near the source of raw material, but in general the Western settlers delivered the products of their land to the Midwest and East. The Western towns learned not to depend on manufacturing as a way of life.

THE BAKER

Frontier bakers found business especially good among bachelors. The miners of the Coeur d'Alene region were too busy to leave their diggings, and were well served by the muleback bakery. Fresh bread was a treat no miner could resist, even at a dollar a loaf. (Photograph by F. J. Haynes, courtesy of F. J. Haynes Studios, Bozeman, Montana.)

Western banks, too, reflected the dependence of the frontier on Eastern institutions. Banks rose in confidence, and fell whenever the winds of financial panic blew from the East. Prairie banks issued their own currency, described by one printer as "the substance of things hoped for, the evidence of things not seen." Gold dust was more dependable as currency. Western banks were closely tied to land and cattle prices, unstable at best, and financial indigestion was a chronic condition among pioneer establishments. When a Missouri River steamboat captain tried to bargain for a few cords at a woodyard, the proprietor asked, "What kind of money do ye tote?"

"The best on earth—the new Platte Valley Bank."

"If that be so, I'll trade cord for cord."

Unwitting chronicler of the West was the town photographer. In his home studio, or as a summer itinerant, the photographic artist was early on the Western scene: The urge to send a likeness to the folks back in the "states" was strong among the pioneers, especially the bearded miners. The reaction of one fond father, Samuel G. Crawford of Havana, New York, was forthright. "We received Ronald's ambrotype, and had his name not been inside, we would not have known it. When he left home he was a smooth-faced, good-looking boy, and he sends home the likeness of an ourangoutang with the upper part of his face shaved!"

The variety that characterized Western town life favored pioneers who were adept at a number of skills or trades. Oregonian John Bentley was a carpenter, undertaker, sawmill owner, sheriff, and United States marshal. "One time during a diphtheria epidemic," wrote Bentley, "I worked all night making five caskets for the children of Mr. and Mrs. Ben Ogle. The five of them died of this disease and were buried the same day. My wife held the light for me that night as I made those coffins, and it was morning before I finally completed them." John was familiarly known as "Two-toot Bentley," after the signal for his being wanted at the lumber mill.

The one town institution which most nearly reflected the temper of the West was the newspaper. On the pages of the weeklies is preserved the history of the land and the people who settled it. "A press, ink, paper, type, pistols and coffee" represented the investment necessary for a paper in frontier days. The ability to write well or previous experience was secondary. Under such favorable circumstances the editor and his press followed the covered wagon before the dust of the emigrants had settled.

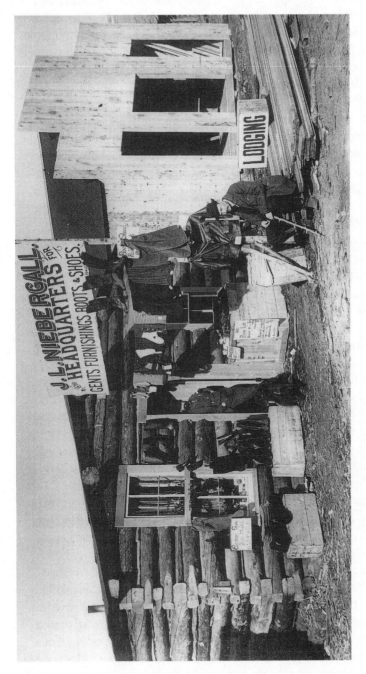

GENT'S FURNISHINGS

Even the most remote settlements were invaded by merchants looking for profitable business. J. L. Niebergall set up a men's clothing shop in Cripple Creek, Colorado. The mining population was in no position to practice the fine art of tailored clothing. For their off-the-rack boots, shirts, coats, and hats, they went to Niebergall. (Photograph courtesy of the Denver Public Library.)

Establishment of a newspaper was a landmark in the progress of a town. Little capital, a minimum of equipment, and a strong personality were the requirements for a country weekly. Even so, newspapers changed hands frequently for personal or political reasons. The first editor of the Prescott, Arizona, *Miner* was killed by Apache Indians. His successor, John Marion, was more careful and produced a lively paper frequently quoted in California dailies.

Independent newspapers did not exist. It did not pay to be independent; an editor's income came from legal notices and job printing rather than from commercial advertising, and political backing assured prosperity. Personal journalism was the frontier style, and involved publication of scurrilous remarks about rival editors. "There is not a brothel in the land that would not have felt itself outraged by the presence of the *Oregonian* of the week before last," wrote Asahel Bush, editor of the *Statesman* from Salem, Oregon. "It was a complete tissue of gross profanity, falsehood, and meanness." One pioneer journalist was described as "formerly editor, proprietor, printer, compositor, roller boy, extra seller, libeller, item gatherer, affidavit maker, slanderer general, and pimp generalissimo."

Now and then editorial remarks concluded with personal violence. George W. Clark of the Van Buren, Arkansas, *Intelligencer* referred to his colleague John S. Logan of the *Frontier Whig* as "Big Mush." Logan responded with "Toady Clark." The two inventive editors fought a duel with rifles at sixty paces. Two shots were fired by each, but no one was hurt. "The smell of powder and bad marksmanship are said to have led to a reconciliation."

The precarious yet congenial atmosphere of frontier journalism was recalled by an 1857 Kansan. "A visit to the printing office afforded a rich treat. On entering the first room on the right hand, three law shingles were on the door; on the one side was a rich bed—French blankets, sheet, table cloths, shirts, cloaks and rugs, all together; on the wall hung hams, maps, venison and rich engravings, onions, portraits and boots; on the floor were a side of bacon carved to the bone, corn and potatoes, stationery and books; on a nice dresser case stood a wooden tray half full of dough, while crockery occupied the professional desk. In the room on the left—the sanctum—the housewife, cook, and editor lived in glorious unity—one person. He was seated on a stool, with a paper before him on a plank, writing a vigorous knockdown to an article in the Kickapoo *Pioneer,* a paper of a rival city. The cooking stove was at his left, and tin kettles all around; the corn cake was adoin', and instead of scratching his head for an idea, as editors often do, he turned the cake and went ahead."

Such were the towns and town institutions of the early West. Many flourishing centers vanished with a sudden exodus of population; others died slowly of economic attrition. Some tasted momentary glory only to subside into semi-oblivion. Those which survived outgrew the pioneer phase, battled flood and fire, and assumed their place in the Western scheme of civilization.

CHAPTER 11
The Finer Things in Life
▲▲▲▲▲▲▲▲▲▲▲▲▲▲▲▲

ALVIRA RAYMOND, wife of an Indian mission employee in the Oregon country, wrote her sister in 1842, "One thing that is discouraging is that the natives of this land are dying off very fast, and all we do for them must be done shortly. A thing that encourages us is that this country is filling up with those who need the gospel more, if possible, than the heathen."

Few Western emigrants were so fortunate as to have an organized mission waiting for them when they arrived at their new home. Overland wagon trains often included "preachers" as members of the company, and when the Sunday "lay bye" was observed, a service might be held. One such occasion, along the Snake River in 1862, was described by Evans S. McComas of Iowa: "Had preaching in our correl by Capt. Bristle, the fighting Capt. of the Iowa City train. Had a sermon from the 8 chapt. and 28 verse of Romans. It was a curious group for to be at church, the men with Bowie knives and revolvers to their belts, in their shirtsleeves and buckskin pants—with one exception. One old fellow sit up, stiff as a churn dash, with a starched shirt and linen coat on. It did not look much like a basket meeting in the States."

The frontier preachers were a miscellaneous lot, and their reasons for migrating westward were not always spiritual. The Reverend James Croke, S. J., noted in 1854 that many of the settlers *"Are* or *have been* preachers. These gentry, finding that farming *pays better* than preaching, have renounced the pulpit for the plough." Father Croke overlooked the circumstance that many of these "renegades" were self-ordained, and that certain Protestant denominations regarded missionary work as impertinent interference with the predestined will of God.

The major church bodies sent representatives to the frontier to preach, marry, baptize, bury, and comfort. The successful missionaries forgot their ecclesiastical feuds in a common effort to ameliorate the spiritual and social condition of the settlers. The first Episcopal communion service in Virginia City, Montana, welcomed Baptists, Methodists, and Lutherans to the Lord's Table.

Churches in the new West had to wait their turn; houses and stores were built first as a matter of practical survival. Few communities had enough members of one denomination to support a building. There were never enough ministers to reach all the disconnected mining camps and settlements on the frontier, and the coming of an itinerant man of God was an event as important as the arrival of a supply train or variety troupe.

In larger Western communities, individual denominations felt strong enough to build their own churches. Subscriptions were solicited from everyone, regardless of creed, for a church was a "good thing" to have in town. The Presbyterians of Moorhead, Minnesota, built a church in the early 1870s which was used by various denominations until destroyed by fire in 1877.

When no church building was available, services were held in private homes, stores, saloons, and billiard parlors. The literal hat was passed by zealous deacons who sometimes obtained contributions at gun point. Settlements cooperated in the erection of religious "Pantheons" for the use of all denominations—"Mormons excepted." Divine worship was attended by emigrants of all and no creeds. "I enjoyed your preaching," said one honest lady, "but I do not believe a word you said about Christ being God; however, if you will come with me and my boys, we will give you a dinner, the best we have."

The itinerant preacher, or circuit rider, was a frontier institution carried west in the same pattern that had developed east of the Missouri. The camp meeting, revival, "protracted meeting," and related devices associated with certain denominations were Westernized. According to Ed Howe, "The first wickedness I ever heard of came with attendance on these camp meetings, for on their edge collected strange men who sold keg beer, and whisky in bottles, and their patrons engaged in rough language and fighting."

Among Western-born revivalists, best known was William Ashley Sunday, orphaned by the Civil War. Billy had worldly talents. As a boy he won three dollars at a Fourth of July footrace in Ames, Iowa. He played professional baseball for the Chicago White Stockings. But he hit the sawdust trail in 1887 after listening to a group of singers from

FIRST CHURCH

In larger Western communities, individual denominations felt strong enough to build their own churches. Subscriptions were solicited from everyone, regardless of creed, for a church was "a good thing" to have in a town. The Presbyterians of Moorehead, Minnesota, built this church in the early 1870s. It was used by various denominations until destroyed by fire in 1877. (Photograph by F. J. Haynes, courtesy of F. J. Haynes Studios, Bozeman, Montana.)

the Pacific Garden Rescue Mission. "I was born and bred in old Iowa," said Billy later. "I am a Rube of the Rubes, a hayseed of the hayseeds . . . and I expect to go to heaven just the same."

The camp meeting, or revival, required no building, and had an emotional and dramatic appeal calculated to stir the hearts of men and women whose relationships with God were casual. At one revival service "was unfurled the bloodstained banner of the Red-Shield Cross, bearing for its inscription, 'Holiness to the Lord.' " Converts came to the altar under emotional stress, and, as Father James Rector said to one of them, "It's good for you, you need a good whoopin'."

Western preachers sometimes sacrificed their lives in the cause of Christ. Valentine Rightmyer, Methodist minister of Gold Hill, Nevada, died on April 11, 1863, of starvation, "having a small salary, a large family, and too much pride." Preacher Henry Weston Smith, first to carry the Gospel to Deadwood, posted a notice on his cabin door on August 20, 1876: "Gone to Crook City to preach, and God willing will be back at three o'clock." God was in this instance not willing. Preacher Smith was killed by Indians a few miles out of town.

The natives of the West were not neglected by those who spread white culture. Religious and educational work among the Indians was simplified by the reservation system. Certain reserves were allotted to one or two denominations by government fiat.

The West offered refuge to the most remarkable religious group ever to form in the United States. To the valley of Salt Lake came the disciples of Joseph Smith, fleeing Gentile persecution. In the desert they built a civilization devoted to cooperative, peaceful enterprise, and a tabernacle for the worship of God as interpreted by their prophets.

Religious specialists, seers, spirit-talkers, and deviates found the West a fair field. They were usually regarded with curiosity or cautious amusement. The "Bulgarian Monk" of Bay Horse, Idaho, dressed in his version of apostolic garb, pronounced jeremiads over the sinful miners and returned to the mountains to gather fresh information for his next visit.

More widely accepted than stray prophets were the phrenologists who traveled through Western settlements reading heads and teaching their art to local enthusiasts.

The churches contributed much to the social life of the settlers. Congregations supported and encouraged temperance organizations and mission societies. Such groups met to transact necessary business, and then bound the ties of Christian love more firmly. The Christian Endeavor Society was a popular center of social and cultural activity. Outings of this society included not only food and fun, but psalms, hymns, and spiritual songs.

Education as well as salvation was important to the pioneer cultural effort. Schoolbooks, advised an overland guide, were important to an emigrant family with children. The problem of educating the young in the new country was more complicated than a matter of book shortages. There was also a lack of teachers. In homes with educated parents, the children learned to read and write by the hearthside. In settled communities families cooperated to build a schoolhouse, hired a teacher, and hoped for the best. The best was usually not much.

Early schools were often one-room shacks attended spasmodically, and supported grudgingly. School architecture was a practical affair. On the plains many settlers lived in sod houses, and their schools were of the same material. In spring, sod schools sprouted greenery. Teachers were itinerant, poorly paid, and often little better educated than their pupils. Well-educated persons on the frontier could find more profitable employment clerking in a store. Thomas J. Dimsdale of Rugby and Oxford was paid two dollars a week per child for teaching school in Virginia City, Montana, during the winter of 1863–64. Dimsdale found better employment as editor of the Montana *Post*.

The problem of keeping frontier schoolchildren under control was much the same as elsewhere. Use of the rod was considered natural and necessary. However, outraged parents could react to real or fancied mistreatment of their offspring.

Early settlers were by no means united in the notion that universal education was a good thing. "Our teacher," wrote an observing pupil in 1863, "has just about taught as long as any man can in this town, and consequently is just about played out. The directors hired him at $40 per month. The people got into one of their contrary ways, and kept their children from school."

Writing schools, spelling schools, singing schools, and painting schools were available on occasion when an itinerant teacher offered short-course specialties. Facility in the Spencerian hand, "training in the vocal voice," and quantities of rose-ornamented chinaware were the tangible results of such educational diversions.

Public-supported schooling of every child gradually gained favor, and territories set up systems of education. Creditable school buildings were erected. The school at Fargo, Dakota, was the pride of the town in 1878.

LITTLE GREEN SCHOOLHOUSE

On the plains, school architecture was a practical affair. The settlers lived
in sod houses, and their schools were of the same material. In spring,
sod schools sprouted greenery. The children who attended this Nebraska
school were likely to amount to something in life. They attended out of
choice, not necessity. Public education depended on community cooperation and enterprise; public schools were attended sporadically and
supported grudgingly. Teachers were itinerant, poorly paid, and usually
ill trained. (Photograph by S. D. Butcher, courtesy of the S. D. Butcher
Collection, Nebraska State Historical Society.)

School interiors also improved. The whipsawed plank benches of pioneer days gave way to standard seats, approved by Eastern educational theory. The curriculum was enlarged and standardized. Teachers were certified. Mass education had begun.

New educational theories and methods were introduced to the West. Children were subjected to physical training by means of organized play, "wand exercises," and similar devices. Such "frills" were especially dear to teachers in city school systems, where drills with wands and dumbbells were expected to "dispense with pale faces and contracted chests so common in schools."

"Higher" education on the frontier was dominated by the "academies," which were little more than grade schools, often established by religious groups. Umpqua Academy, a Methodist institution established in 1855, began with a building 30 by 40 feet, one story, with a second projected. It was, said its founder, "emphatically in a new place— midway between Portland and Yreka."

Female academies, devoted to teaching the arts of hemstitching, needlework, and refined manners, were also founded by religious bodies, though attended by all who could find time and tuition.

Some of these establishments never got beyond the realm of hope; others withered after the publication of a few catalogs and appeals for financial aid. Not until late in the nineteenth century were the frontier states able to support worthwhile colleges, and a few universities. Even then, as one professor testified, "The raw material is very raw."

The informal lyceum, debating society, and later the Chautauqua provided cultural opportunities at varying levels. The Chautauqua was begun in 1874 as a "Sunday School Teachers' Assembly," and towns prided themselves on Chautauqua hills. The circuit or tent Chautauqua, which brought culture into every Western community, was devised by J. Roy Ellison, born in a Nebraska sod house. The Cautauqua specialized in lectures on temperance, literature, "the battle of life," and similar elevating subjects.

According to one Kansas emigrant, "I have listened to most animated and profound discussions of the immortality of the soul, whether the Bible was inspired, foreordination, transsubstantiation . . . the doctrines of John Calvin, and the infallibility of the pope." Hours of serious debate were held about whether true beauty was to be found in nature or in art, whether fire was more destructive than water, and whether the fear of punishment was a greater incentive than the hope of reward. Fundamentally, the "cultural" society served a social purpose, well expressed in a note received by a young Iowa woman: "Will you go to Literary with me a-Friday night? If so, please let me know by a-Tuesday night."

The lack of general education in the West was reflected in the condition of the arts generally. What literature, music, and drama existed were largely imported. There was almost no sustained creative activity. The overland diarist, quite unconsciously, was the first frontier literary figure. A few of the early travel journals were deliberately assembled for publication as guidebooks. Most of them were written for their keepsake value; their literary or historical merit was discovered by a later generation.

The frontier poet was a special case. The literary urge quiescent in the breast of the emigrant erupted early in poetry production. When newspapers were established, the settler-poets showered local editors with political, social, and religious opinions in verse. A few of the grassroots poets attempted flights of fancy; others felt that humor was their forte. All of them imitated popular Eastern poets. The earliest literary publication of the Dakota Territory is the "Ballad of Love's Independence," published in broadside at Fort Rice, and written by Sergeant P. A. Morgan.

Now and then territorial verse writers defied literary probabilities and produced either quantity or quality enough to deserve recognition. Of the quantity school was Captain Jack Crawford, dubbed the "Poet Scout." The captain dashed off reams of verse on frontier themes, and made his living as a free-lance army scout. Crawford published his work, and tried in vain to sell it. There were no remainder houses to resolve Crawford's predicament, so he resorted to the inducement of "autograph, presentation" copies, with additional holograph poems on the flyleaf.

Captain George Waynefleet Patten, Western Indian fighter, known to his fellow soldiers as "He-he-be-God Patten," was unofficially considered "poet-laureate of the United States Army," in recognition of his Western "poetical effusions." Patten was fond of "The Emigrant's Dying Child" and similar lugubrious themes. Sitting Bull, the great Sioux medicine man, was a poet, at least by repute. *The Works of Sitting Bull,* published in Omaha and Chicago under the able editorship of Lieutenant Robert D. Clarke, a military friend, went through two editions in their original French, German, and Latin. According to the introduction, S. Bull had early in life been a classical scholar at the Sorbonne.

Joaquin Miller and Eugene Field were poets of the frontier environment, respected for their quality. Miller was not popular in his home territory of California and Oregon, but was feted as a literary prodigy in the East and abroad. He doubled as his own press agent, and his success in that line outran his literary talent. Field was a Denver newspaperman who published verse in Western dialect, then turned to poems for children.

Native frontier fiction writers left almost no impression on early Western literary history. Most states and territories saw one or two outbursts of fiction, like that of Margaret Jewett Bailey's *Grains, or, Passages in the Life of Ruth Rover*. This true-confession novel, published in Oregon in 1854, caused a temporary sensation, but did not found a literary movement.

Edgar Wilson "Bill" Nye, hailed as a humorist, practiced his style in the young city of Laramie, Wyoming. Arriving in Wyoming in 1876 with thirty-five cents in his pocket, he undertook several offices and jobs, including justice of the peace, United States commissioner, postmaster, editor, and staff correspondent for regional newspapers. When Oscar Wilde, en route to San Francisco, stepped off the train at Laramie for a breath of air and an interview, the editor met him at the station. "We told him our name was Nye, the great Wyoming aesthete." Nye combined his breezy talents with the reputation of James Whitcomb Riley. Between them they published a railway guide. "What this country needs," said Nye, "is a railway guide which shall not be cursed with a plethora of facts or poisoned with information."

Though the pioneers wrote little, they read much. "My literature is a volume of Shakespear, Dr. Gunn's Family Physician, and an agricultural report," wrote a young lady in 1870. "I have read the Shakespear till I feel my morals are damaged, Dr. Gunn till I am a first-class family physician myself, and the agricultural report till I can discuss stock and soil with anyone."

Literary traffic in books and periodicals from the East was surprisingly heavy on the frontier. "Horace Greeley's Weekly Tribune furnished our political economy, and Harper's Weekly was a regular visitor," recalled one Kansan, "while Petroleum V. Nasby furnished the humor of the day." Booksellers' records and newspaper advertisements indicate that the settlers pined for and bought the same mixture of classic and yellow-back literature popular in the "states."

The Westerner who wanted more than the good cheer of a book could attach himself to the Freemasons, Odd Fellows, Red Men, or

U. S. MAIL BY PROXY

In a Western town the communication center was the express agent. The government post office was unequal to the task of providing mail and parcel service to the scattered settlements of the vast area beyond the Missouri. Express companies, founded by private enterprise, took over the work. Best-known of the companies was Wells Fargo, which operated overland, and by connections with local concerns, penetrated wherever express service was established. (Courtesy of the Railway Express Company.)

Good Templars, social importations from the East. The frontier produced some home-grown organizations, notably the E Clampus Vitas of the California miners, and the P.E.O., devised by two young ladies of Iowa Wesleyan College in 1869. Few pioneer biographies could be written without mention of membership in one or more fraternal associations.

So far as painters and sculptors were concerned, the Western Indians exhibited more talent than the emigrants. Eastern artists were early attracted by the scenic and human values of mountains and plains. The names and reputations of John Mix Stanley and George Catlin are permanently associated with the West.

Greater than the impact of prose, poetry, or social assembly was the cultural effect of frontier drama. Traveling players penetrated the mining towns, villages, and crossroads settlements. Towns with no church or school boasted an "Opera House."

"An enormous nose and a powerful voice" was enough to please some Western audiences. Others were more critical. In 1881 the divine Bernhardt played *Camille* in Tootle's Opera House, St. Joseph, Missouri. As Ed Howe of the Atchison *Globe* saw the performance, "At exactly 8:31 last night Sarah Bernhardt made her appearance on the stage of Tootle's Opera House, walking down the centre as though she had but one joint in her body, and no knees. . . . Her dress was of white and costly stuff, and cut so low in front that we expected every minute that she would step one of her legs through it. . . . With reference to *Camille* in French, it is about as interesting to an American as five acts of a Chinese drama running three months."

Much frontier theater was crude, "thirty lightning acts in succession, no long waits." But the audiences were not especially critical. Variety was to pioneer audiences the spice of theatrical life. McDaniel's New Theatre of Cheyenne offered the miner, Indian fighter, cowhand, or floater something to suit every taste. The traveling companies starved from one engagement to the next, though as Chris Fletcher, theater manager of Hartville, Wyoming, complained, "As soon as they get the wrinkles out of their bellies they go temperamental."

Theaters doubled as gambling houses and dance halls. The Bella Union, first theater in Deadwood, specialized in variety acts. When the show was over, the house was cleared for action of various kinds. The seventeen curtained boxes of the Bella Union were then used by the female players, as one chronicler phrased it, "to sell themselves."

Except for the fiddle at a dance or a melodeon at home, frontier music, in its cultural aspects, was largely confined to amateur bands with plenty of oompah. Carl Klaermer's band of Fredericksburg, Texas, was German in both style and composition, the town having been settled by German colonists. The musicians were well trained, some of them, no doubt, by Jacob Brodbeck, local music teacher. Brodbeck was a man of parts. He invented an airplane twenty-eight years before the Wright brothers. It was powered by coil spring, and flew to treetop level. (The inventor could never figure a way of rewinding the spring in flight.)

Musical organizations of varying quality traveled through the West from one "booking" to another. The DeMoss Concert Entertainers, a musical family known as the "Lyric Bards," was formed in 1872 by the father, James M., the mother, two sons, and three daughters. The DeMoss quartet, brothers and sisters, traveled throughout the United States, Canada, and Europe, and were Washington D.C. guests of Vice-President Adlai E. Stevenson.

Among the greatest of the stage figures produced in the West was Lotta Crabtree, born in California and trained by Lola Montez at Grass Valley. Crabtree was raised in the tradition of troupers like the George Chapman family, who invented the showboat business on the Mississippi River, and put it on muleback for California miners. Crabtree first hit the California stage as a child actress. Under the clever management of her mother, she became the Queen of Variety. Lotta could perform anywhere, from the Bella Union of San Francisco to a redwood stump in the wilds.

The larger Western cities prided themselves on fancy theater accommodations. Top-rank performers attracted full houses. Denver's Broadway Theater opened on August 18, 1890, with the Emma Juch Grand Opera Company playing *Carmen*. The Broadway was said to be the first theater to provide a bathtub in the star's dressing room.

Variety and vaudeville gradually centered in the larger Western towns and cities. One-night stands by second-rate companies kept the hopes of many small-town opera houses flickering, but around the turn of the century the Keystone Kops on the screen pushed *Uncle Tom's Cabin* from the stage.

BERNHARDT VS. HOWE

Established stars took some risks when playing before Western audiences. When Sarah Bernhardt played *Camille* in Tootle's Opera House, St. Joseph, Missouri, in 1881, the young editor of the Atchison *Globe* was on hand. As Ed Howe saw it, "At exactly 8:31 last night Sarah Bernhardt made her appearance, walking down the centre as though she had but one joint in her body, and no knees. Her dress was of white and costly stuff, and cut so low in front that we expected every moment that she would step her legs through it." (Photograph by Melandri, courtesy of the Harvard Theater Collection.)

CHAPTER 12
The Myth and Its Makers

▲ ▲ ▲ ▲ ▲ ▲ ▲ ▲ ▲ ▲ ▲ ▲ ▲ ▲ ▲ ▲

BUSY WITH AX AND PLOW, with the essentials of ex-
istence, the Western settlers were too preoccupied to produce a written
chronicle. Private diaries or letters published in Eastern hometown
newspapers reflected the genuine pioneer, but popular delineation of
the West as a cultural entity was in general left to Easterners, to "for-
eigners" whose approach to the region was in the tradition of American
mythology. What had been the Great American Desert became the
habitat of Western gods and demigods—Jim Bridger for the mountain
men, Pecos Bill for the cowboys, Wild Bill Hickok for the gunmen,
Buffalo Bill for the nation.

Prototype of the Western legend, of the tall tales, the Texas brags,
was Colonel Davy Crockett. Like most folk heroes of the West, Crockett
was flesh-and-blood transformed. He was a myth even before he died
bravely at the Alamo. "I can walk like an ox, run like a fox, swim like
an eel, yell like an Indian, fight like a devil, spout like an earthquake,
make love like a mad bull, and swallow an Injun whole without choking
if you butter his head and pin his ears back."

He was the indestructible Westerner, the superman, bragging, brawl-
ing, outlandish, the good hero who invariably subdued single-handedly
the vast powers of evil.

For a generation after the Alamo, the mythical Davy Crockett flourished as a folk hero in oral tradition, in newspapers, and in a series of
almanacs whose authors were mostly anonymous. The Crockett Almanacs set a pattern for the Western myth which was to unfold as a
literary form in a flood of dime novels following the Civil War.

While the Westerners were pushing toward the beaver country, the
mines, and the good land, a young Irishman named Mayne Reid was

traveling in Western America, living with trappers, hunting buffalo, trading with Indians. After some years of adventure, he visited Philadelphia, became a close friend of Edgar Allan Poe, and decided to try his hand at writing for magazines. Reid was working for Wilkes's *Spirit of the Times* when the Mexican War began. He joined up in 1846, and spent the next three years soldiering the traveling in Mexico and the Southwest.

After the war, Mayne Reid settled down in London to begin a thirty-year career of writing adventure novels, most of them based on his exciting decade spent in North America. Reid's plots were rambling and picaresque, but his details of landscape, vegetation, accoutrements, and customs were usually exact. He sometimes appended glossaries of Western words to his novels. He introduced the treacherous Apache and the mounted horseman with jingling rowels. The speech and dress of his non-Indian characters are still used by writers of Western fiction, but his Indians all spoke pure Oxford English, and the tribes were often mixed geographically.

In contrast to the Crockett Almanacs' bragging superman, Reid favored an indomitable hero who was usually taciturn, possessed of a mysterious romantic past, and who occasionally bore traces of the medieval knight. During the 1850s and 1860s, Mayne Reid produced a sizable shelf of Western American fiction. His works were later reprinted as dime novels and with the tales of James Fenimore Cooper served as prime sourcebooks for thousands of paperback Westerns. By the mid-nineteenth century, the Eastern public had come to expect certain things from the Western scene, and the Western myth was rapidly being established.

In 1859, Horace Geeley, editor of the New York *Tribune,* made an overland journey to California, enthusiastically reporting everything he saw in the form of letters to his newspaper. At that time Greeley was the most widely read writer in the nation; the weekly edition of his "Try-bune" was a national newspaper, circulating to every village and crossroads. His vivid accounts of the wild West, read eagerly by thousands of subscribers, fixed in the American mind romantic impressions of that far-off land that have not entirely disappeared to this day.

Greeley was too good a newspaperman to disappoint his readers. The Western myth, the Crockett flair for exaggeration, struck him as he crossed the Mississippi. "I know that a million buffalo is a great many, but I am certain that I saw that many yesterday." He revived the latent myth of the Great American Desert, placing it between Leavenworth, Kansas, and Denver. (The summer of 1859 *was* hot and dry, and he traveled that section in a slow-moving stagecoach.) And he could not resist adding his bit to the legend of continuous gunfire in Western saloons. The gamblers, he said, "had a careless way, when drunk, of firing revolvers, sometimes at each other, and other times quite miscellaneously." He also discovered the perfection of California's climate.

Perhaps the most permanent contribution made by Horace Greeley to the Western legend is the story of his ride with Hank Monk, who has become the symbol of the speedy stagecoach driver who always brought his passengers through on time. Mark Twain recorded the incident in *Roughing It:* "Drivers always told it, conductors told it, chance passengers told it . . . I never smelt any anecdote so often as I smelt that. . . . When Greeley was leaving Carson City he told Hank that he had an engagement that afternoon at Placerville and was anxious to go through quick. Hank cracked his whip and started off at an awful pace. The coach bounced up and down in such a terrific way that it jolted the buttons all off Greeley's coat, and finally shot his head clear through the roof of the stage. He yelled at Hank to go easier—said he wasn't in as much of a hurry as he had thought. But Hank stuck to his first orders. 'Keep your seat, Horace,' he said reassuringly, 'keep your seat and I'll get you there on time!'—and you bet he did, too—what was left of him."

In the autumn of 1860, Americans in some Eastern areas were puzzled to find a mysterious advertisement in their newspapers, on signboards, on barn walls, and on sidewalks: "Who is Seth Jones?" A few days later the question was answered with the publication of a dime novel, *Seth Jones; or, The Captives of the Frontier.* Thus appeared the first successful dime novel depicting the frontiersman as hero. *Seth Jones* sold half a million copies, and for a generation various reprints were made. It convinced Beadle & Company, the publishers, that "a new mine had been opened."

Edward Sylvester Ellis, author of *Seth Jones,* was a twenty-year-old schoolteacher who had lived most of his life in New Jersey. Offered a contract to write four similar dime novels a year, Ellis fulfilled it in a few days, and began writing other stories under fifteen different pseudonyms. For thirty years he spun out millions of words of Western mythology for millions of entranced and credulous readers.

The West's paramount flesh-and-blood folk hero began his astounding literary career without fanfare on December 23, 1869, in Street and Smith's *New York Weekly.* The creator of Buffalo Bill was Edward Z.

C. Judson, a veteran author of yellow-backed novels who wrote under the pen name of Ned Buntline. Unlike most dime novel writers, Judson traveled widely, basing his tales upon actual events and persons. He met William Frederick Cody by chance while touring the West in search of story material. Three years after the appearance of *Buffalo Bill, the King of the Border Men,* Judson persuaded Cody to visit New York and act in a stage play. Within a short time Buffalo Bill was permanently established as king of the gods in the mythology of the West.

The legend of Buffalo Bill, though aided by his Wild West Show, was best sustained by Colonel Prentiss Ingraham, who took over where Judson left off. Ingraham invented legends about Cody while traveling with him in the West and sometimes acting as advance agent for the show. Between 1870 and 1900 he published at least eighty different Buffalo Bill dime novels, most of which were reprinted year after year. Few Americans of that era escaped reading at least one of them, and many undoubtedly accepted the West as a place of pure melodrama with Buffalo Bill the imperishable hero.

It was not only Easterners who read and believed. San Francisco's flourishing bookstores of that period kept large stocks of Western yellow-backs, and the pioneers who crossed the plains read them as they rode. "This wagon," recorded Thomas Creigh, overlander of 1866, "is termed the 'Reading Room,' having no small number of 'Beadles' and other interesting reading matter."

While dime novel authors were writing endless pages of manufactured romance, a modest Texan, John C. Duval, proved with one little book that a straightforward account of a real Western hero could be as exciting as a synthetic one. In 1870 Duval published his *Adventures of Big-Foot Wallace, the Texas Ranger and Hunter.* Big-Foot (William A. Wallace) and the Rangers were so popular that a publisher in the East reprinted the book a few months later; it went through more than six editions and remained in print for decades.

Although John Duval peopled his story with stock characters—virtuous maidens, indefatigable heroes—he knew his country and depicted it faithfully. His Indians, along with his mustangs, buffalo, and rattlesnakes, were more real than anything readers could find in their dime novels. "I did not think I was capable of writing a book like those of Mayne Reid," said Duval afterward. "But my young friends said that boys didn't care much for style or literary merit, that all they wanted was a truthful account of scenes and incidents that had actually oc-

MEXICAN JOHN

The trail cook usually traveled with the chuckwagon, or chuckbox, based on Charles Goodnight's design; was always valuable on drives; and became an integral cast member of Western lore. Mexican John was a well-known trail cook, and was famous for his baked pies. (Photograph by L. A. Huffman, courtesy of the University of Wyoming Library.)

curred, not fictitious ones that never had an existence except in the imagination of the author."

After the fashion of Duval, Western writers began to base their characters on living persons, some of whose real exploits were being recorded contemporaneously in the press. Actual events in the lives of Kit Carson, Wild Bill Hickok, California Joe, Joaquin Murietta, Billy the Kid, and many other Western gods and demigods furnished departure points for wild plotting and violent action. A friend once showed Kit Carson the cover of a dime novel which pictured the plainsman slaying seven Indians with one hand while he clasped a fainting maiden with the other. The old scout studied the lurid cover through his spectacles for a long time, finally drawling, "That there may have happened, but I ain't got no recollection of it."

Readers of popular Western literature could never be sure which of their heroes were real and which invented. Deadwood Dick became an object of serious tourist search in Deadwood, South Dakota, and the chamber of commerce decided to resurrect the popular myth. They selected a long-haired, loquacious old rascal named Dick Clarke to play the role. He proved to be as good a storyteller as Edward L. Wheeler, creater of the Deadwood Dick novels. Clarke improved on the history of Custer's Last Stand. He also sold locks of his hair to women tourists, rusty rifles and pistols to the men, and photographs of himself to everybody.

The self-reliant, free-swinging, sassy Western women also found their chroniclers among the myth makers. There were numerous "queens" of the West, girl dead-shots, Denver Dolls, Wild Ednas, Arkansas Sal, and of course, Jane Canary, better known as Calamity Jane.

On higher levels of literature the Western myth was also in creation. Like a strong breeze out of the West came Mark Twain with his *Celebrated Jumping Frog of Calaveras County* and *Roughing It.* Americans who had laughed over the Crockett Almanacs could laugh again, for here in a wild Western setting was Crockett reborn, the genuine native humor of exaggeration, the tall tales of the frontier. Mark Twain rode his frog around the world, and to millions of his listeners and readers, the American West and those who people it became a boisterous extravaganza, fantastic and superhuman.

Contemporaneous with Mark Twain was another Westerner, Bret Harte, whose sentimental harlots and noble gamblers have persisted as lively actors in the continuing legends of the Old West.

By 1876 every American east of the Mississippi surely must have felt in some degree the presence of that fanciful land of buck-skinned giants somewhere beyond the river's western shore. If there were a few who had somehow escaped the legend, they discovered it dramatically early in the summer of that eventful centennial year. For it was in June of 1876 that George Armstrong Custer led his Seventh Cavalry to doom along the Little Big Horn, focusing the attention of the world on the American West.

Before the Last Stand, Western cavlarymen had played minor roles in the popular literature of the West. But by the time the newspapers and magazines had told and retold the story of the valiant Seventh Regiment, there was a vast demand for tales in which the cavalryman was hero. None was better suited to fulfill this demand than Captain Charles King, a cavalryman himself, who had participated in that Sioux campaign of 1876. King was exact in his details of action, equipment, terrain, and weather, but he loved to spin out tales of young lieutenants fresh from West Point, suffering from mysterious pasts, who blundered and then redeemed themselves by gallant fighting. He included heroines who appeared to be Indians but were not, Irish sergeants who swore and drank heavily but always died bravely on the battlefield. For thirty years Charles King wrote of cavalrymen; his plots and characters are still in use today.

Mythology must have its singers, and as has been noted, the West was no exception. John Wallace Crawford, or Captain Jack the Poet Scout, preempted the field while Joaquin Miller was sulking on mountaintops or preening himself in Europe. "Often without the least provocation," Jack once said modestly, "I have been in the habit of reciting my poems and singing my songs whenever I could corral a squad of friends and old comrades possessing vitality enough to survive the affliction."

The cowboy came late into Western mythology. As there was no cattle industry until after the Civil War, mid-nineteenth-century writers had no sources on which to draw. Thomas Pilgrim, using the pseudonym Arthur Morecamp, published *Live Boys,* an authentic fictionized account of cattle trailing in 1878, but not until 1885 did a real cowboy write a book about his experiences. The author was Charlie Siringo; the book was *A Texas Cow Boy; or, Fifteen Years on the Hurricane Deck of a Spanish Pony.*

Charlie Siringo, born in Texas, was a cowboy by nature, but a writer by chance. "I happened to pick up a small scrap of paper and read: 'To the young man of high aim literature offers big inducements, providing he gets into an untrodden field.' " Siringo decided rightly that cowpunching, the only field he knew, was untrodden. "My excuse for writing this book is money—and lots of it," was his opening sentence. The excuse was valid, for *A Texas Cow Boy* sold close to a million copies. It must have been a rich sourcebook for the dime novel factories, though there was little romance in Siringo's simple telling of his boyhood, of how he went "on a tare" in Wichita, of the Chisholm Trail. He wrote like a cowboy talking. Charlie Siringo proved that folklore is not invented, and that perhaps the Western myth was true after all.

The reality of *A Texas Cow Boy* was not to endure. In 1902 *The Virginian* appeared. He and the long line of soft-voiced knights on horseback who succeeded him have since dominated the legend.

> The Virginian's pistol came out, and his hand lay on the table, holding it unaimed. And with a voice as gentle as ever, the voice that sounded almost like a caress, but drawling a very little more than usual, so that there was almost a space between each word, he issued his order to the man Trampas:—"When you call me that, *smile.*"

That is the most famous scene in Western fiction, from the book that J. Frank Dobie has called the "classic cowboy novel without cows." The author was Owen Wister, Harvard graduate and Philadelphia lawyer, who went west on a visit for the first time in 1885, the year Charlie Siringo's *A Texas Cow Boy* made its appearance.

The image of the horseman as cavalier had moved across the Old South into Texas, and then as the Texas cattlemen went north into Wyoming and Montana to claim the open ranges as feudal barons, they carried with them this vision of knighthood. The ranchers were the last cavaliers, the knights of the range, in strong contrast to the Crockett Almanacs' bumptious vulgarians. Owen Wister no doubt met a few real cowboys, but his associates were in the main wealthy ranch owners, feudal barons derived from Texas or directly from Britain. All around him were cavaliers on horseback wearing chaps instead of armor.

The Virginian became a best-seller immediately, and for the first time a Western story achieved respectability. It was bound in cloth, stocked in public libraries, and could be read by Americans openly in family living rooms. Made respectable by *The Virginian,* the Western story began to flourish in cloth covers. Emerson Hough compromised with historical truth for the sake of the myth; Zane Grey averaged almost two titles a year for a generation as a prolific make-believer. Bertha Muzzy Sinclair, one of the few women writing Westerns, created *Chip of the Flying U* in 1906. Chip and his punchers rode the Montana ranges in book after book, cavorting and conversing with all the good clean fun of the Rover Boys.

Probably the most enduring of all make-believe cowboy folk heroes, Hopalong Cassidy was born in 1910, the creation of Clarence E. Mulford. Hopalong was Don Quixote played straight, and like some other synthetic Western heroes owes his fame more to the moving pictures than to the printed word. For in those innocent buoyant years of the new century, when Americans were reading *The Virginian* and its many imitations, a new invention brought nickelodeons into downtown streets. The makers of these moving pictures quickly discovered that the Western scenarios were among the most popular, and during their heyday one of the anxioms of that industry was that a "horse opera" rarely lost money.

Like all early moving pictures, the first Westerns were simple in plot and characterization, with good and evil in sharp, unreal contrast. In one of these first ventures, *The Life of a Cowboy* (1906), there are four standard scenes—a bar, a stagecoach, a holdup, and a chase. For many decades the pattern remained the same.

Real cowboys, of course, rarely ever saw a stagecoach, and when they did the chances of its being held up were remote. They visited saloons much less frequently than New Yorkers, and seldom chased anything more villainous than a bad-tempered steer. But from that day to this the myth has thrived, with shadow heroes subduing evil in a shadowland of gods and demigods, a West the pioneers never knew and probably never imagined in their wildest dreams.

CHAPTER 13
Rip-Roaring Trail Towns

▲ ▲ ▲ ▲ ▲ ▲ ▲ ▲ ▲ ▲ ▲ ▲ ▲ ▲ ▲

WHEN THEY REACHED A TRAIL town at the end
of a drive, the cowboys sometimes drove the herd right through the
streets. As soon as the cattle were bedded down, all except a few herd
riders were free to go into town. (Some unlucky cowboys had to stay
with the herd while the lucky ones made merry in town. But no matter
what hour the noisy celebrators returned to camp, the relieved first-
shift guards would gallop off to town to salvage what joys they could
from the waning night.) It was customary to pay off the men as soon
as the drive ended, and with money jingling in their pockets, the cowboys were ripping and raring and ready to go. After three hard months
on the trail, no one could blame them for cutting loose and raising hell.

No cowboy entering a trail town ever permitted his horse to walk or
trot; all horses went in at a lope or a gallop. Pistols were fired off, but
they were usually pointed skyward. With their horses' hooves pounding
the streets, their bridle chains rattling, and their voices whooping out
rebel yells, they made plenty of noise. But unless they were frustrated
by some undiplomatic town marshal, their spontaneous hurrahing did
not last long or create much havoc.

The usual first action of a trail's end cowboy was to get a haircut and
have his mustache or beard properly shaped and blacked. Then he
visited a clothing store for a new outfit. Emerging with new clothes,
the hat and boots embellished with Texas stars, he was ready for fun
and frolic.

"I remember it like it was yesterday," said Teddy Blue. "I had a new
white Stetson hat that I paid ten dollars for and new pants that cost
twelve dollars, and a good shirt and fancy boots. They had colored
tops, red and blue, with a half-moon and star on them. Lord, I was

proud of those clothes! They were the kind of clothes top hands wore, and I thought I was dressed right for the first time in my life."

After drinking some of the strong whisky which was brought into the town in carloads, and bucking the tiger with the faro dealers, the men were ready for a hoe-dig with the Calico Queens of the honky-tonks.

"The cowboy," said Joseph McCoy, "enters the dance with a peculiar zest, not stopping to divest himself of his sombrero, spurs, or pistols. . . . A more odd, not to say comical, sight is not often seen than the dancing cowboy. With the front of his sombrero lifted at an angle of fully forty-five degrees, his huge spurs jingling at every step or motion, his revolvers flapping up and down like a retreating sheep's tail, his eyes lit up with excitement, liquor, and lust, he plunges in and 'hoes it down' at a terrible rate in the most approved yet awkward country style, often swinging his partner clear off of the floor for an entire circle, then 'balance all,' with an occasional demoniacal yell. . . . All this he does, entirely oblivious to the whole world and to the balance of mankind. After dancing furiously, the entire 'set' is called to 'waltz to the bar,' where the boy is required to treat his partner and, of course, himself also; which he does not hesitate to do time and again, although it costs him fifty cents each time."

Most cowboys trailing to Kansas cowtowns were from Texas, but even those from other sections were called "Texans." A Kansas traveler of the day described them: "In appearance a species of centaur, half horse, half man, with immense rattling spurs, tanned skin, and dare-devil, almost ferocious faces."

A New York *Tribune* correspondent observed: "And here are . . . the identical chaps I first saw at Fair Oaks and last saw at Gettysburg. Every man of them unquestionably was in the Rebel army. Some of them have not yet worn out all of their distinctive gray clothing—keen-looking men, full of reserved force, shaggy with hair, undoubtedly terrible in a fight, yet peaceably great at cattle-driving and not demonstrative in their style of wearing six-shooters."

James Butler (Wild Bill) Hickok, who had fought against these men as a scout and spy in Missouri and Arkansas, understood them well, and shortly after he became Abilene's marshal in 1871, Hickok announced that the cowboys could wear their revolvers wherever and whenever they pleased. This was a welcome change from the rules established by the late Bear River Tom Smith.

A tall, graceful man and a spectacular gunfighter, Wild Bill patrolled Texas Street by walking in the center. His long auburn hair hanging in

WILD BILL HICKOK

James Butler (Wild Bill) Hickok, who had fought against these men as a scout and spy in Missouri and Arkansas, understood them well, and shortly after he became Abilene's marshal in 1871, Hickok announced that the cowboys could wear their revolvers wherever and whenever they pleased. A tall, graceful man and a spectacular gunfighter, Wild Bill was popular with most of the cowboys. (Courtesy of the Kansas Historical Society.)

ringlets over his shoulders and his small, finely formed hands and feet gave him a feminine appearance. But everyone respected Wild Bill as a quick-draw artist. He usually wore a pair of ivory-hilted and silver-mounted pistols thrust into a richly embroidered sash. His shirts were of the finest linen and his boots of the thinnest kid leather.

As Wild Bill's salary was rather small, he augmented his earnings by frequent gambling. He was popular with most of the cowboys.

Some other Abilene citizens were as colorful as Wild Bill. Josiah Jones was a fat and jolly saloonkeeper who kept a colony of prairie dogs for fun. When Eastern visitors began offering him five dollars per pair for the prairie dogs, Jones's hobby became such a business that he complained he had no time for running his saloon. He engaged small boys to sell the animals to travelers on the Kansas Pacific.

Lou Gore and her husband, J. W. Gore, operated McCoy's Drover's Cottage, the elite hotel of one hundred rooms, with an adjoining barn spacious enough to house fifty carriages and one hundred horses. Texans relished the Cottage's iced drinks, made possible by stored ice cut from the Republican River during previous winters.

McCoy had found the Gores at the St. Nicholas Hotel in St. Louis, where J. W. Gore was working as a steward. Lou was a natural-born hotelier, a friend to all cowmen, rich or poor, sick or well. The most hardened horse thief would have considered it a disgrace to beat a board bill at Lou Gore's Cottage.

In 1871 a pair of gambling men, Ben Thompson and Phil Coe, came to Abilene and established the Bull's Head Tavern & Gambling Saloon. For an advertisement, a huge and lascivious bull was painted on the outside wall. After some of the more prudish citizens objected to the painting, Wild Bill Hickok ordered the bull removed. Thompson ignored the order. To settle the argument peaceably, Wild Bill obtained a bucket of paint and "materially altered the offending bovine."

When John Wesley Hardin arrived in Abilene in 1871, his reputation had already preceded him. Wild Bill had in his possession a handbill sent up from Texas offering a reward for the arrest of this eighteen-year-old boy who packed a loose six-shooter. Ben Thompson of the Bull's Head Tavern had also heard of the gun prowess of this smiling young Texan with the light blue eyes.

Thompson tried to prejudice Hardin against Hickok. "He's a dam-yankee." said Thompson. "Picks on rebels, especially Texans, to kill."

"If Wild Bill needs killin'," replied John Wesley Hardin, "why don't you kill him yourself?"

Later Hickok and Hardin did have trouble, but no shots were fired. Wild Bill began referring to Hardin as "Little Arkansaw" and they became friendly. Hickok is said to have told Hardin he would not arrest him for any crimes he had committed in Texas, but that if he killed anyone in Abilene he would not get out of town alive.

One night Hardin was in his bed in the American Hotel when a man unlocked the door and slipped into the room. Hardin fired at the intruder and killed him. As Wild Bill drove up to the hotel in a hack to investigate the gunfire, the young Texan slipped out on the roof in such a hurry he left his trousers behind. Wild Bill ran into the hotel, and Hardin jumped down into the hack and drove away. He stole the first saddled pony he saw, and rode off toward Texas minus his trousers. Several miles below Abilene, John Wesley Hardin took a pair of pants from a luckless cowboy at gunpoint, ordering the man on into town in his underdrawers. "Give Wild Bill my love," was Hardin's parting message.

Abilene's saloons bore colorful names, such as Applejack, Old Fruit, and the Pearl. Obviously christened to appeal to Texans was the Alamo, the most resplendent of the drinking houses. The Alamo boasted three sets of double-glass doors, and a bar with carefully polished brass fixtures and rails. All along the walls were huge paintings, nudes done in imitation of the Italian Renaissance painters. Music was furnished the customers continuously from pianos, raucous horns, and bull fiddles.

Wild Bill selected the Alamo as his headquarters. In 1871 a correspondent from the *Daily Kansas State Record* described a scene inside the saloon: "A bartender, with a countenance like a youthful divinity student, fabricates wonderful drinks, while the music of a piano and a violin from a raised recess, enlivens the scene, and 'soothes the savage breasts' of those who retire torn and lacerated from an unfortunate combat with the 'tiger'."

Every trail town had at least one photograph gallery strategically located near a popular saloon. Visiting cowboys enjoyed having their "pictures taken."

When trail towns became subject to too much law and order, suburbs developed immediately outside the legal limits. Abilene's unsavory sin den was called by several names—Texas Town, the Beer Garden, Fisher's Addition, and the Devil's Addition.

It was booming during the 1871 season. "Beer gardens, dance halls, and dancing platforms and saloons galore were there," wrote Theophilus Little, a lumberman of Abilene. "It was called 'The Devil's

Addition' to Abilene, rightly named, for Hell reigned there—Supreme. Hacks were run day and night to this addition. Money and whisky flowed like water down hill, and youth and beauty and womanhood and manhood were wrecked and damned in that Valley of Perdition."

One of the more violent episodes of Abilene's lush period developed around a fair damsel of the dance halls. Her name was Jessie Hazel, admired by Phil Coe of the Bull's Head Tavern. Wild Bill Hickok was a rival for the favors of Jessie Hazel, and the two men became bitter enemies.

When Hickok accused Phil Coe of cheating at cards, the inevitable gun battle followed. Coe was killed. During the confusion, Wild Bill also accidentally killed one of his deputies, Mike Williams. In bloody anger, Wild Bill chased all the cowboys out of town and began patrolling Texas Street with a sawed-off shotgun loaded with buckshot.

That year, 1871, was Abilene's last big season. During its five-year reign as king of the cowtowns, small farmers—or nesters as the cowmen called them—had been pushing steadily westward along the Kansas Pacific until most of the free range was gone.

Cattlemen were considered natural enemies, and in February 1872 they were ordered to stay away from Abilene:

We, the undersigned, members of the Farmers' Protective Association, and officers and citizens of Dickinson County, Kansas, most respectfully request all who have contemplated driving Texas cattle to Abilene the coming season to seek some other point for shipment, as the inhabitants of Dickinson will no longer submit to the evils of the trade.

The big boom collapsed immediately. Before the end of 1872, the town's leaders were begging the drivers and shippers to come back, but it was too late. New boomtowns were already in the making.

. . .

Another westward-moving railroad, the Atchison, Topeka & Santa Fe, was preparing to share in the cattle trade. By the spring of 1871, the Santa Fe had reached Newton, sixty-five miles to the south of Abilene. As Newton was closer to Texas, the Santa Fe was soon taking a big share of the cattle trade from the Kansas Pacific.

"The firing of guns in and around the town," said Cal Johnson of

Newton, "was so continuous it reminded me of a Fourth of July celebration from daylight to midnight. There was shooting when I got up
and when I went to bed."

And Newton's glory was as flashing and brief as a Fourth of July
skyrocket. Twenty buildings went up the first month of the town's existence. They were the usual false-front structures, and some bore the
names of their predecessors in Abilene.

Joseph McCoy soon arrived to establish his second stockyard, this
one large enough to hold four thousand cattle. McCoy knew from
experience that booming cowtowns developed rapidly, and he built his
Newton yards a mile and a half from the original business section.

Grass still covered the streets of Newton when the first herds arrived.
Prairie dog colonies were on every side, and wild animals were so
numerous that the city council passed an ordinance prohibiting the
running at large of buffaloes and other animals.

One of the few women to go on a trail drive was Amanda Burks,
who accompanied her husband, W. F. Burks, from Nueces County,
Texas, to Newton in 1871. Amanda Burks drove a buggy most of the
way, experiencing lightning and hail storms, witnessing fights with rustlers and Indians, a prairie fire, and a stampede.

Cattle prices had dropped before the Burkses reached Newton, and
they wintered their herd on Smoky River, a considerable distance north
of the town. After selling their cattle in the spring, they made the return
journey by rail to St. Louis and New Orleans, and then by water to
Corpus Christi. In later years, this rail and water route was frequently
used by wives of coastal cattlemen, who arranged their journeys so as
to meet their traildriving husbands in Kansas.

Gunfire was frequent in Newton, as Cal Johnson truthfully reported,
but there was little bloodshed until late in the 1872 season, when a big
shoot-out exploded in Perry Tuttle's dance house. Instead of a Devil's
Addition, Newton had its "Hide Park," a shambling collection of dance
halls and saloons south of the railroad tracks. Perry Tuttle's establishment in Hide Park was a popular rendezvous for trail drivers.

One night Mike McCluskie, the Newton marshal, was seated at a
gambling table in one corner of Perry Tuttle's place when a Texas trail
driver named Hugh Anderson came in on the prod. McCluskie had
killed a Texan a few days earlier, and the man had been a good friend
of Anderson.

Suddenly Anderson strode across the floor toward the marshal.
"You're a cowardly son of a bitch!" he shouted at McCluskie. "I'm

going to blow the top of your head off." Gunfire followed immediately, friends of both men joining in the shooting.

Within a few seconds, nine men lay dead or wounded on the floor. Marshal Mike McCluskie was among the dead. In Newton, the affair was always referred to as the "General Massacre."

McCluskie's successors were kept busy by Cherokee Dan Hicks, a buffalo hunter, who enjoyed getting drunk and shooting up the town. Cherokee Dan seemed to have a preference for pictorial targets. One day he was standing in front of the Bull's Head Tavern, peppering lead into the picture of a bull on that establishment's fancy signboard. When Marshall Charlie Baumann tried to stop him, Cherokee Dan shot the lawman's right thumb off and wounded him in the thigh. On a later occasion, the buffalo hunter walked into Harry Lovett's saloon and suddenly started shooting at the gaudy nude paintings which lined the walls. Harry Lovett was not a man who would stand idly by while his cherished artworks were being destroyed; he opened fire with his six-shooter, and that was the end of Cherokee Dan Hicks.

For a one-season cowtown, Newton spread as much mustard as any of its longer-lived rivals.

Meanwhile, the Kansas Pacific Railroad had pushed westward to Ellsworth, a town which boasted simultaneously of its iniquity and of its superior cattle-shipping facilities.

Ellsworth lay flat on the treeless banks of Smoky Hill River in the midst of an endless prairie of grama grass. Its Main Street, three blocks of frame structures, ran parallel with the railroad tracks.

From Abilene, Lou and J. W. Gore brought their respectable Drover's Cottage. Parts of this building and some of the saloons were loaded on railroad cars and shipped in sections from Abilene to Ellsworth. The term "hell on wheels" is said to have originated from this rail movement of honky-tonks and gambling hells from one trail town to another. The American House, Beebe's General Store, and Brennan's Saloon were other famed landmarks in the town.

Ellsworth began operating as a cattle-shipping point in 1871, but only a few herds were received in the yards that season. The following year the number increased, several herds coming in after the drivers discovered Abilene was a closed market.

The Kansas Pacific, sensing an alert rival for the cattle trade in the new Santa Fe Railroad, gave considerable financial support to the development of Ellsworth. Under the railroad's direction a new cattle trail was surveyed from Ellsworth southeast to the old Chisholm Trail,

COWTOWN

The general store, the hotel, and the saloon were the hangouts for most cowboys. The sidewalks, if there were any, were most likely made of wood, and the streets were just dirt. (Photograph by Erwin E. Smith. Courtesy of the Library of Congress.)

joining it between the Salt Fork of the Arkansas and Pond Creek. It was called the Ellsworth Cattle Trail. To advertise the new trail and Ellsworth's advantages, the Kansas Pacific published a *Guide Map of the Great Texas Cattle Trail from Red River Crossing to the Old Reliable Kansas Pacific Railway*. Copies were distributed thoughout the ranching country.

The new trail and the advertising paid off in 1873. By the end of May more than 100,000 Longhorns had reached the Ellsworth area, awaiting a rise in prices. Two weeks later, 50,000 more had arrived. It looked like a big season for the cattlemen, but when the financial panic of 1873 struck Kansas in late summer, the cattle market collapsed so suddenly several drivers and shippers were immediately bankrupt.

In the meantime Ellsworth had become a roaring trail town, with the frozen market adding to the supercharged atmosphere. Every night hundreds of idle cowboys ripped through the streets and "hurrahed" the saloons. In June a jail was completed, and the Ellsworth *Reporter* described it as the most comfortable place in town, but warned its readers that too many should not crowd into the building at once.

Ben Thompson, who had lost his partner Phil Coe in Abilene, joined forces in Ellsworth with his brother, Bully Bill Thompson. The Thompsons were English-born and had served in the Confederate army, fighting to the end of the war when they rode with Joe Shelby on his venture into Mexico. The brothers operated a gambling concession and saloon in Arthur Larkin's Grand Central Hotel. To meet competition from the more refined Drover's Cottage, the Thompsons induced Larkin to construct in front of the hostelry the only limestone rock sidewalk west of Kansas City. It was twelve feet wide, was covered with wooden awnings, and was complete with a bench for sidewalk loafers.

The darlings of Ellsworth's dance halls dressed as well as their modish sisters in the East, wearing the latest style of headgear dervied from hats of Western buffalo hunters. Keeping up to date with *Godey's Lady's Book* may have seemed too sedate for a certain lady called Prairie Rose. One night she bet a cowboy fifty dollars she would walk unclothed down the main street of Ellsworth. This she did next morning at five o'clock, a six-gun in each hand, threatening to shoot out any eye that showed. The cowboys must have respected Prairie Rose's marksmanship. At any rate, no shots were fired.

With the assistance of the Texas cowboys, Ben and Bill Thompson "treed" Ellsworth, and for a time practically ran the town to suit themselves. Finally a sheriff, a marshall, and four deputies restored law and order. But one hot August afternoon the Thompson brothers both got drunk and began making trouble for the deputy marshals, whose nicknames were Brocky Jack, Happy Jack, Long Jack, and High Low Jack. In the midst of the fracas, Sheriff Chauncey Whitney appeared and was shot and killed by Bill Thompson.

As the Thompsons were Texans, a small army of trail drivers gathered to protect them. Bill was assisted out of town on a fast horse, while Ben remained in the Grand Central Hotel, armed with a double-barreled shotgun. When the deputy marshals all refused to try to arrest Ben Thompson, the mayor discharged them and arranged a deal with the gambler. Ben agreed to be charged with shooting at Happy Jack, but when Happy Jack declined to press the charge, the case was dismissed.

Meanwhile a posse of indignant citizens had gone in pursuit of Bill Thompson. As the citizens dashed out of town, another Texas gambler, Cad Pierce, offered a thousand dollars for the capture of the posse. The posse did not find Bill, and nobody chased the posse for Cad Pierce's reward money.

Not long afterward, Ben Thompson quietly left town, but his friend Cad Pierce remained too long and was killed in a street duel with a new deputy, Ed Crawford.

Lawless or not, visitors poured into the town. Some amateur actors of the Sixty Cavalry came over from Fort Harker and staged a boisterous drama for the guests of the Drover's Cottage. And one anonymous visitor wrote a piece for the Ellsworth *Reporter*:

"This little border town of Ellsworth is not the most moral one in the world. During the cattle season, which, I am told, only lasts during the summer and fall, it presents a scene seldom witnessed in any other section. Here you see in the streets . . . the tall, long-haired Texas herder, with his heavy jingling spurs and pairs of six-shooters . . . the keen stock buyers; the wealthy Texas drovers; dead beats; 'cappers'; pick-pockets; horse thieves; a cavalry of Texas ponies; and scores of *demimonde*.

"Gambling of every description is carried on without any attempt at privacy. I am told that there are some 75 professional gamblers in town, and every day we hear of some of their sharp tricks. Whisky-selling seems to be the most profitable business. But there are many honorable business men here, who are doing a heavy business."

The temporary collapse of the cattle trade in 1873, however, had marked the end of Ellsworth as the principal trail town. About half of the large herds driven in during the summer had to be winter-quartered in Kansas, or moved to Colorado. Other thousands of cattle were slaughtered for tallow, or were sold at a loss to Indian agencies.

. . .

Once again it was the Santa Fe Railroad's turn to share in the cattle trade. A branch had pushed south from Newton to Wichita, and during the 1873 season Ellsworth's chief rival was this new boomtown on the Arkansas River.

Having seen other trail towns turn conservative and drive the impetuous cowmen and their cattle away, Wichita's backers attempted to convince all comers that the new shipping center would be different. Signs were posted on the trails and outside the town: EVERYTHING GOES IN WICHITA.

By 1874, Wichita was the leading shipping center, with 200,000 cattle and 2,000 cowboys swarming into the area at the height of the season. Ben Thompson came down from Ellsworth and set up his gambling tables at the Keno House. Thompson and the cowboys were soon running Wichita to suit themselves. "Shootin' irons" became the law.

Wichita settlers finally decided they needed some real law and order. One of the men they employed to keep the peace was Deputy Marshal Wyatt Earp. Wyatt Earp had been a stagecoach driver in Arizona, a prizefight referee in Wyoming railroad camps, and a buffalo hunter in Kansas. He had been in Ellsworth briefly, refusing an offer to become marshal there in 1873. But one day in May 1874, he got mixed up in a free-for-all fistfight in Wichita and was arrested. A few minutes after his arrest, a bunch of cowboys started hurrahing the town, and Wyatt Earp offered to help the deputy marshal quiet them down. After the affair was over, the mayor of Wichita offered Wyatt Earp a job as deputy marshal.

"I'll take it," said Earp, and in Wichita he began a career that would lead him into many a frontier town of the developing West.

One of Wyatt Earp's friends caused the deputy marshal considerable trouble. His name was Abel "Shanghai" Pierce, a jovial full-bearded giant whose voice could be heard half a mile. He was six feet four inches tall and weighed 220 pounds. He was one of the first ranchers to send stock up the overland trails, and by 1874 was a leading cattle buyer.

So many legends have been woven around Shanghai Pierce that it is difficult to separate fact from fiction. His nickname is said to have originated one day when he put on a pair of oversized spurs. "Great Day!" he shouted. "Them things make me look just like an old Shanghai rooster!" Pierce's ranch was in the Texas coastland ranching country on Matagorda Bay, and his herds of Matagorda steers were known in all the Kansas trail towns as "Shanghai Pierce's sea lions."

He was proud of those rangy mossyhorns. "They're my sea lions!" he would roar. "They come right out of the Gulf of Mexico!"

In Wichita one evening, Pierce was raising merry hell in Billy Collins's saloon. Earp took away his gun, and told him to get out of town until he was sober. Pierce's reply was that he never took a drink but he obeyed the order. Afterward, twenty of Pierce's cowboys rode into town, gunning for Wyatt. The deputy marshal arrested them, disarmed them, and fined each one of them a hundred dollars. Blithely carrying the first walking cane ever seen in Kansas, Shanghai came back into Wichita, and cheerfully paid the two thousand dollars in fines.

Some years later when Shanghai Pierce became wealthy, he spent ten thousand dollars for a twenty-foot bronze statue of himself, and had it set up on his Rancho Grande on the Tres Palacios. The statue now stands guard over Pierce's grave near Blessing, Texas, a town which he named. For years Pierce had been trying to persuade the railroad to build a station adjoining his ranch. When the railroad finally started constructing the station, Shanghai ordered the workmen to paint the words THANK GOD on its sides. The railroad company prevailed upon him to substitute the word BLESSING for THANK GOD.

A much more important memorial left by Shanghai Pierce is a breed of cattle, the American Brahman. On a tour through the Orient, Pierce conceived the idea of introducing Brahman cattle to the Texas coastlands as a means of combating the prevalent tick fever. Returning home, he bought two Brahmans from a circus, and proved his theory that ticks would not affect them. Although Pierce died before he could import Brahmans from India, his nephew A. P. Borden did so, and conducted the first breeding experiments on the Rancho Grande that led to the development of the present-day American Brahmans.

•   •   •

George Peshaur, a gun-toting pal of Ben Thompson, disapproved of the manner in which Wyatt Earp was taming Wichita. When Peshaur tried to use a young cowboy as a gunman against the marshal, Earp turned on Peshaur and whipped him to a finish in a fistfight, blacking both his eyes and smashing his nose.

One of Peshaur's friends was Mannen Clements, a Texas trail boss. Clements said it was not a fair fight, and with his brothers—Joe, Jim, and Gip—rode into Wichita early one morning in 1874, aiming to "tree" the town and have some fun with Wyatt Earp.

The deputy marshal met the Clements brothers on the Cowskin Creek bridge. "Mannen, put up your gun and take your outfit back to camp," ordered Earp.

"You put up your gun and maybe I will," said Mannen.

Earp slid his gun into his holster. Mannen Clements and his brothers followed suit, then rode on into town. Wyatt Earp was smart enough not to press such matters with the Clements brothers, and they spent a quiet morning. By similar diplomatic actions, he finally persuaded the cowboys to check their guns in racks before they started their drinking in Wichita.

The shantytown adjunct of Wichita was known as Delano. Here Rowdy Joe Lowe and John (Red) Beard operated rival dance halls. Rowdy Joe later became a train robber and was killed while holding up a Union Pacific train near Big Springs, Nebraska.

George Custer's famed Seventh Cavalry was stationed near Wichita in 1873, and during that year there was a pitched battle in Delano between the cavalrymen and the Texans. The fight started in Red Beard's place. A cavalryman tried to move in on a girl who was dancing with a cowboy. Immediately fists began flying, and revolvers began exploding in the low-ceilinged dance hall. One soldier was killed, two others wounded, mirrors and glassware were smashed, but no Texans were hurt. Almost all of the cowboys were Confederate veterans, and they disliked the blue uniforms of the army.

Joseph McCoy, who had deserted the Kansas Pacific for the Santa Fe, built a new stockyard in Wichita. He added a sideline to his business that indeed signified things to come. Foreseeing the end of the open range, McCoy began selling wrought-iron fencing guaranteed not to "rot, burn, blow, or fall down."

Hays City, west of Ellsworth on the Kansas Pacific, succeeded Wichita briefly as the leading cattle-shipping point. "The town," said one of its early inhabitants, "was lively but not moral." Hays City boomed so fast, some visitors had to sleep in the railroad's crew cars. Amidst the confusion, one gentleman misread a street sign, and later recorded his error in the Manhattan (Kansas) *Standard*:

"As we sauntered slowly up the street we noticed on a dilapidated looking building a large sign informing all beholders that 'General Outfitting' could be obtained by inquiring within. Seeing no show window, and no display of goods, and being of an inquiring turn of mind, we entered. Instead of seeing a smiling, polite salesman, anxious to show us his goods, as we expected, we were welcomed by two or three very pretty smiling young ladies. We saw no goods, except feminine. Seeing that we had got into the 'wrong pew,' and being rather bashful, in spite of the fascinating appearance of the aforesaid young ladies, we disappeared."

One of the big events of Hays' trail town period was the visit of Phineas T. Barnum, who came in his fancy railroad car looking for wild men to use in his circus. When the local poker players heard of Barnum's presence, they resolved to make a sucker out of the great showman. Barnum's downfall was so crushing the Topeka *Daily Kansas State Record* reported the event in detail:

"P. T. Barnum, wishing to gratify his taste for curiosities, stopped off at Hays City to see the 'man-eaters' of that town 'eat.' He fell in with several of the more carnal-minded youth of the place, who invited him to be sociable and take a hand at poker. The cards that were dealt to his companions literally 'knocked the spots' off anything Mr. Barnum had ever 'held' in his life, and, when the exercises of the solemn occasion were ended, Phineas mourned the departure of $150 that he will never see, not any more. 'Wooly horses' and 'Feejee mermaids' are nice things to have, but they don't weigh out much playing poker at Hays City. Barnum will probably incorporate his Hays City experience into his famous lecture, 'How to Make Money.'"

For several years, Fort Hays had dominated Hays City, which had been a depot for Santa Fe trade long before the cattle period. The fort's chaplain came to Hays every Sunday to read sermons from a freight platform, but few converts were recorded.

The Seventh Cavalry stationed at the fort had kept things lively around Wichita the previous year, and was now a source of considerable trouble for Hays City. Tom Custer, brother of the famous George, considered himself immune from arrest, and at nightfall would ride through the town shooting wildly in all directions. He delighted in riding into saloons, jumping his horse upon billard tables, and raising hell in general. One night when his horse refused to make the table jump, Custer dismounted and shot the animal there in the billard hall.

When Wild Bill Hickok was marshal of Hays, he once tried to tame

Tom Custer. Wild Bill shot Custer's horse, arrested the officer, and fined him heavily. A short time later, Tom Custer and three soldiers jumped Hickok in a saloon. Wild Bill managed to escape by firing backwards over his shoulder at the man who was forcing him to the floor. Tom Custer retaliated by calling out most of the Seventh Cavalry as avengers, and Wild Bill was forced to leave Hays City hurriedly on an eastbound Kansas Pacific freight train.

HAYS CITY STAGECOACH

Important to any Western city was the stagecoach. A typical stop on a stagecoach run was Hays City, which, for several years, was dominated by Fort Hays, Kansas. Long a depot for Santa Fe trade, during the cattle period Hays City boomed so fast some visitors had to sleep in the Kansas Pacific Railroad's crew cars. (Photograph by F. J. Haynes, courtesy of F. J. Haynes Studios, Bozeman, Montana.)

CHAPTER 14
The Vision of Sitting Bull

▲▲▲▲▲▲▲▲▲▲▲▲▲▲▲▲

SEVEN WINTERS HAD PASSED since the Americans had promised peace with the Sioux "so long as the grass shall grow." The abandoned forts had been beaten by the rains of seven springs, and their charred ruins were fast returning to the soil from which they had sprung.

But now the whites were coming back. The treaty words were lost in the roaring of the new word—*gold!* The fights would have to be made all over again. Soon the frontier towns bordering the Black Hills swarmed with prospectors. With them came soldiers.

In April 1876, Sitting Bull, of the Hunkpapa Sioux, held a great council at Chalk Buttes on the Tongue River. Crazy Horse, with Two Moons and He Dog, suffering from Reynolds's attack on their camp on the Powder River, went to the council. It was the time of the new grass, and the restless Indians from the reservations began, once more, to leave for the buffalo country. They came to the camp of Sitting Bull. Northern Cheyennes and Arapahoes, too, joined the big encampment. Seven great circles of lodges spread over the valley of the Tongue.

The talk was all for war. General Crook ("Three Stars") had been at the Red Cloud agency to recruit young warriors as scouts in the coming campaign. Red Cloud, Red Dog, and Red Leaf had stopped those who would have gone with the soldiers to fight their own people, and Three Stars had gone away, angry. Surely it was a time to fight together, not brother against brother! "The whites want war," Sitting Bull observed, "and we will give it to them."

First, however, there was meat to get. Scouts reported buffalo in the Rosebud country, and the great camp moved to where the hunting was

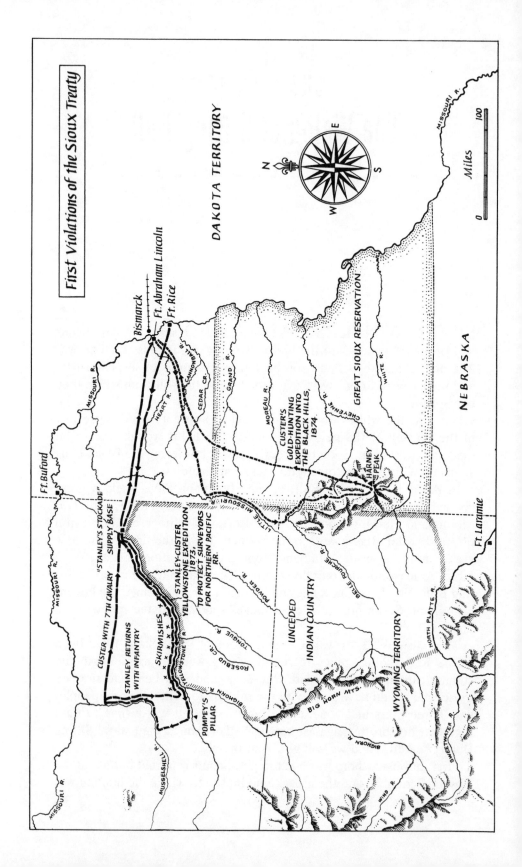

First Violations of the Sioux Treaty

good. As they moved, the Indians were joined by new bands coming in from the agencies and elsewhere. Black Elk and his band came in from the shelter of the reservation, knowing well that war was near. Even the old Santee warrior, Inkpaduta, with a few lodges, joined them. Never before had the warriors gathered in such numbers—Crazy Horse, Big Road, Sitting Bull, Gall, Black Moon, Crow King, Spotted Eagle, Fast Bull, Touch-the-Clouds, Two Moons, Old Bear—all great warriors, chiefs, or medicine men.

It was well that the warriors were many and the chiefs great. On May 17, General Alfred H. Terry with 600 men and horses and 400 infantry started from Fort Abraham Lincoln. General John Gibbon had already left Fort Ellis, Montana, with 450 infantry. He had seen that there were many Indians near the mouth of the Rosebud.

General Crook left Fort Fetterman on May 29, with over a thousand soldiers, and moved toward Tongue River. The soldiers were coming from every direction. General Terry hunted for Sitting Bull on the Little Missouri, and ordered Gibbon to help him. The Indians had not yet been found.

During the second week in June the great Sioux-Cheyenne camp moved from the mouth of the Rosebud to the head of Ash Creek. Here was held the great yearly sun dance, sacred ceremony of the summer solstice.

Sitting Bull was one of those who sought a vision in the sun dance. A hundred small pieces of flesh were cut from his arms with an awl and sharp knife. Bleeding from his wounds, the chief gazed at the sun from dawn to dusk, seeking power, a vision to help his people. Finally he fell, exhausted and unconscious. When he rose again, he spoke to the people. Sitting Bull had seen a vision of many soldiers coming into camp upside down. The people were satisfied. Victory was certain.

A test of Sitting Bull's vision came soon. On June 16, five Cheyenne warriors out on a hunt and horse-stealing expedition spied a column of soldiers in the valley of the Rosebud. They rode back to camp quickly, sounding the wolf howl of danger. Three Stars was only a day's march away! He had Crow and Shoshone scouts with him!

The warriors were hot for a fight, the vision strengthening them. Eagerly they rallied about the chiefs, and it was decided to attack Three Stars where he was, rather than wait for the soldiers to attack the camp. Over a thousand warriors gathered and set out for the valley of the Rosebud. Among them was Sitting Bull, still weak from the sun dance.

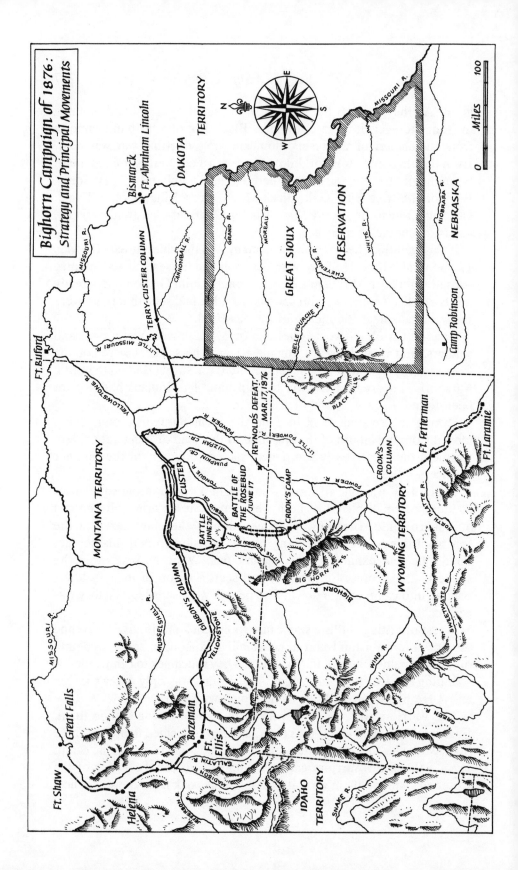

Bighorn Campaign of 1876:
Strategy and Principal Movements

With them, too, was Buffalo Calf Road Woman, sister of Chief Comes-in-Sight. With such warriors defeat was impossible.

Crook's column of cavalry and mule-mounted infantry had come to a halt along the Rosebud at the mouth of a canyon. The great Sioux village was suppposed to be just a little farther down. Soon the "renegades" and "hostiles" would learn how foolish they had been to resist the government.

Rifle shots from scouts in the advance were the first warning of attack. Then came the great war cry, "Lakota, Lakota! Sioux, Sioux!" The warriors, in full fighting array, appeared suddenly in front of the cavalry on the right flank of the column.

Mounted on their small, wiry ponies, a strong rawhide rope drawn tightly just back of the forequarters to serve as saddle, the Indians bent low, shooting from under the necks of their mounts. When a soldier fell, the nearest Indians dashed to his body and struck him with their *coup* sticks—the real glory moment of any fight or hunt.

The Indian attack seemed to be unplanned, but their method of fighting was different. The warriors had learned something from the soldiers. They learned the power of a cavalry charge, and the importance of keeping the detachments of soldiers apart. To that end small bodies of Indians attacked the separated groups of soldiers again and again, preventing them from forming a skirmish line, a single strong front.

Crook sent nine companies of soldiers under Anson Mills toward the narrow canyon, where he believed the Indian village was hidden. But the warriors attacked the remaining force so fiercely that the detachment was recalled.

All day the fight raged. Many brave deeds were done on both sides. The warriors counted fewer *coups*, but their war-making was better. By evening fifty-seven of the soldiers had been killed or wounded, and only eighteen warriors were hurt. It was not a big fight if you counted the number of scalps, but it was enough to show Three Stars that the Indians were strong, and had learned something about fighting. Crook moved back to his wagon train on the Tongue, and licked his wounds. He would hunt the Sioux no longer until he had more men.

The warriors returned in triumph to the big camp on Ash Creek. A four-day scalp dance followed. The keening of the women for the lost ones was not heard for the loudness of the victory songs. The medicine of Sitting Bull was strong.

. . .

While the Sioux-Cheyenne camp was dancing the scalp dance, more
soldiers were gathering for another fight. Terry and Gibbon had given
up hunting for Sitting Bull on the Little Missouri, and had reached the
mouth of the Rosebud on June 21. Here they were met by Major Marcus
A. Reno with most of the Seventh Cavalry, which had been sent on a
reconnaissance up the Powder River to the Rosebud, almost to where
Three Stars lost his fight. Here they had seen a great Indian trail leading
across the divide toward the Little Horn River. The Indians had been
located. Now it was time to make plans.

General Terry divided his forces. The Seventh Cavalry under Colonel
Custer was to march up the Rosebud, find the Indian trail, and follow
it, while Terry would march Gibbon's infantry up the Big Horn, reaching the Little Horn and rejoining Custer on June 26.

The soldiers moved off on their planned march. The great Indian
camp again moved down Ash Creek, this time to the valley of the Little
Horn. It was a grand sight. Five great circles of lodges were strung
along the west side of the river for three miles. Sitting Bull and his
Hunkpapas were farthest up, a little above the mouth of Ash Creek.
Then came the Miniconjous, the Oglalas, and the Sans Arcs. Farthest
down of all was the mighty circle of Cheyenne lodges.

The Indians knew that the soldiers were coming. Box Elder, Cheyenne prophet, proclaimed that they were near at hand. But no one was
afraid. The warriors were strong.

On the evening of June 24, Sitting Bull again offered up a prayer for
strength and victory. That same evening Colonel Custer prayed for
victory for his own peculiar reasons. He told his Ree scouts that he
alone was going to destroy the Sioux nation in one great blow, and that
partly as a reward for his victory, he would someday become the Great
Father in Washington. The scouts were doubtful about both promises.

On the morning of June 25 the Indians proceeded about their work,
as usual. Crazy Horse went down to visit in the Cheyenne camp. Suddenly a great dust was seen in the valley above the Hunkpapa camp.
The soldiers had come! They were coming into the camp as Sitting Bull
had promised!

The warriors rushed from the lower camps, making ready for the
fight. There were only a few soldiers coming toward them, a little over
a hundred. It was easy. Easier than on the Rosebud. These troops,

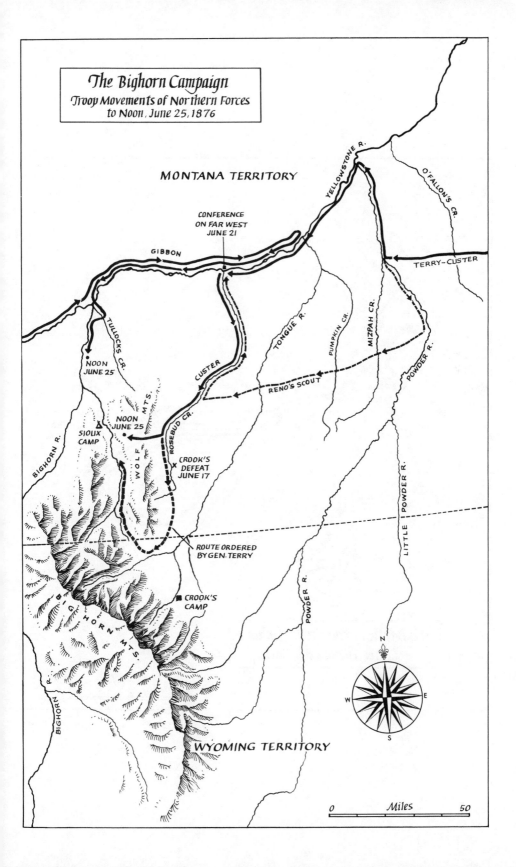

The Bighorn Campaign
Troop Movements of Northern Forces
to Noon, June 25, 1876

MONTANA TERRITORY

CONFERENCE
ON FAR WEST
JUNE 21

YELLOWSTONE R.

O'FALLON'S CR.

GIBBON

TERRY–CUSTER

TULLOCKS CR.

TONGUE R.

PUMPKIN CR.

MIZPAH CR.

POWDER R.

NOON
JUNE 25

CUSTER

RENO'S SCOUT

WOLF MTS.

NOON
JUNE 25

BIGHORN R.

SIOUX
CAMP

ROSEBUD CR.

CROOK'S
DEFEAT
JUNE 17

LITTLE POWDER R.

ROUTE ORDERED
BY GEN. TERRY

CROOK'S
CAMP

POWDER R.

BIGHORN MTS.

BIGHORN R.

N

W   E

S

WYOMING TERRITORY

0   Miles   50

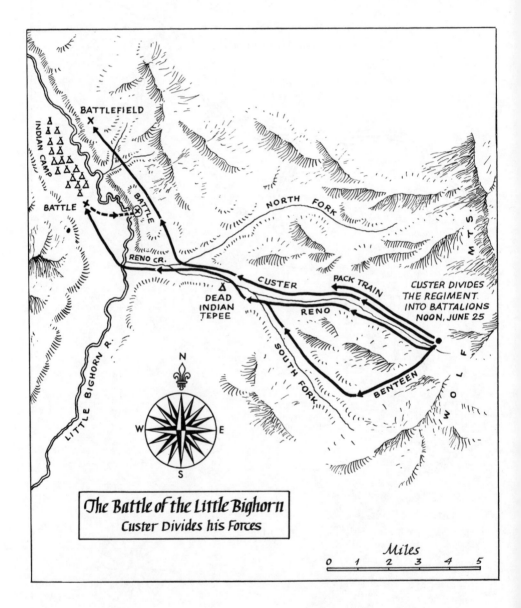

The Battle of the Little Bighorn
Custer Divides his Forces

under Major Reno, had crossed the river about four miles above the camp, and moved toward it at a trot. But they never reached it.

Fierce gunfire from a thousand Indian guns led by Chief Gall, warrior of the Hunkpapa Sioux, wilted the little detachment. In a few minutes twenty-nine soldiers were dead, and many wounded. Those who were able, fled across the river to the safety of bluffs and woods, closely followed by the triumphant warriors. "It was like chasing buffalo," said the warriors afterward, "a great chase."

The pursuit was interrupted by an alarm from the other end of the camp. Soldiers were attacking there, too. The soldier chief on the bluff was left with a few warriors watching him, while the rest of the Indians streamed through the camp to the place of new danger across from the ford by the Miniconjou camp.

Here the soldiers had come down a ravine and threatened to charge across into the camp. But a great deed was done: Four Cheyenne warriors held the soldiers for a few minutes, and waded across the river through the bullet hail. It was enough time for more warriors to come up and drive the soldiers away.

The column turned, and began to move down the east side of the river toward the lower end of the Indian camp, where there was another ford. Some of the soldiers were on a ridge overlooking the river, and others were between the ridges and the river.

Truly the eyes of the soldier chiefs were blinded that day! The Cheyenne and Sioux warriors crossed the Little Horn at the Miniconjou ford, and also at the lower end, by the Cheyenne lodges. The column of soldiers was struck, front and rear. Every rock, bush, and ravine was friendly to the Indians. The soldiers were attacked on every side. When those on the ridge were silenced, the warriors charged up the ridge with a loud shout. *Hoka Hey!* The soldiers between the ridge and the river backed from the charge.

"After that the fight did not last long enough to light a pipe."

It was hard to believe. Never had such a victory been won, so many *coups* counted, so much plunder taken. A few Cheyennes from the south country found that the soldier coats taken from the dead were the same as those seen at the Battle of the Washita years before, and their hearts were glad. But the soldier chief, Custer ("Long Hair"), was not found. Later it was learned that he was among the dead, but his hair was cut short, and he looked like any other man.

The soldiers on the bluff across from the opposite end of camp tried to move away while the fight was raging away from them, but the

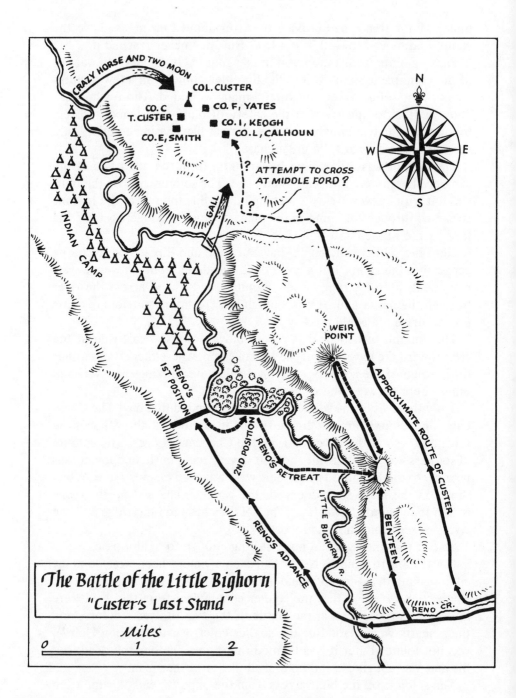

CRAZY HORSE AND TWO MOON

COL. CUSTER

CO. C
T. CUSTER

CO. F, YATES

CO. I, KEOGH

CO. E, SMITH

CO. L, CALHOUN

? ATTEMPT TO CROSS
AT MIDDLE FORD ?

?

?

?

GALL

INDIAN CAMP

N

W E

S

RENO'S
1ST POSITION

WEIR
POINT

APPROXIMATE ROUTE OF CUSTER

2ND POSITION

RENO'S RETREAT

RENO'S ADVANCE

LITTLE BIGHORN R.

BENTEEN

RENO CR.

The Battle of the Little Bighorn
"Custer's Last Stand"

Miles

0   1   2

warriors returned quickly, and drove them back into their holes. All night the warriors besieged the soldiers, and the next morning tried to drive them out to where they could be killed. But the hill was a good place to fight. These few soldiers were not worth the trouble of a big charge, and so the Indians left them. The victory could not be made greater.

Besides, more soldiers were coming up the Big Horn. The Indians went back to their village about noon on June 26, and began to strike their lodges. The grass in the valley was fired, and behind the screen of smoke the Sioux and Cheyennes slowly moved away toward the Big Horn Mountains. The Battle of the Little Horn was over. Two hundred sixty-six soldiers had been killed or mortally wounded. Fifty-four were wounded and recovered. Indeed, many soldiers had fallen into camp upside down.

Among the warriors fighting that day were Low Dog and Crow King of the Sioux, and Rain-in-the-Face, who had long hated the soldiers and was now satisfied. He had been present when Fetterman and his soldiers had been wiped out. He had suffered in prison, arrested by Tom Custer, and was said to have promised to "cut the heart out of Tom Custer and eat it." A wound received this day lamed Rain-in-the-Face for life, but did not dim his victory song. He lived to sing it a long time.

News of the Indian victory was brought to the whites by Curley, a Crow scout employed by Custer who saw what was happening and escaped before the end of the fight. He reached the steamer *Far West* at the mouth of the Little Horn and, by signs, told the unbelieving soldiers of the disaster that had struck the Seventh Cavalry.

White-Man-Runs-Him, another Crow scout employed by Custer, had already led Lieutenant James Bradley of Terry's command to the battlefield where Custer and his men lay dead.

The dead were buried, and identified when possible. The battlefield of Little Horn is still a cemetery today.

After the great victory on the Little Horn the Sioux and Cheyennes went to the Big Horn Mountains to cut lodge poles. The council fires were filled with much talk about the big fights. There was much dancing and feasting that summer. The soldier chiefs had come, and had been defeated. No others had come to take their places. It was a good time. Perhaps the treaty would be kept now, and the Black Hills saved. So, at least, thought the hopeful ones.

In the fall the Indians began their eastward movement, as usual,

CURLEY

News of the Sioux and Cheyenne victory was brought by Curley, a Crow scout, who saw what was happening and escaped before the end of the fight. He reached the steamer *Far West* at the mouth of the Little Horn and, by signs, told the unbelieving soldiers of the disaster that had struck the Seventh Cavalry. He later became somewhat of a celebrity. (Photograph by W. H. Jackson, courtesy of the Smithsonian Institution.)

toward the agencies, to hole up for the winter. But news from the reservations was not good. Indians who went in had their guns and horses taken from them. The friendly Indians were again urged to give up the sacred Hills. The whites prayed over the reservation Indians and then threatened to starve them if they did not agree.

Many of the warriors did not go back. Many of them joined Crazy Horse on the Powder, wintering with the buffalo. Others attached themselves to Sitting Bull, north of the Yellowstone.

CUSTER'S LAST RALLY

The Sioux and Cheyenne crossed the river and attacked the soldiers from both ends. "After that," they said, "the fight did not last long enough to light a pipe." Not a soldier was left alive. Sitting Bull's vision had been strong. (Painting by John Mulvany, courtesy of the Library of Congress.)

CHAPTER 15
The Warriors Come In

▲▲▲▲▲▲▲▲▲▲▲▲▲▲▲▲

DURING THE AFTERNOON of Sunday, June 25, 1876, Captain Anson Mills, Third Cavalry, restless from long waiting, made a scouting trip from the camp of General George Crook on Goose Creek, Wyoming Territory. Far to the northwest the captain saw a great column of smoke or dust in the air. He called the attention of his fellow officers to the column, and they agreed that either some Indians were setting fire to the grass, or perhaps there was a forest fire in the mountains.

Their guess was correct. There was smoke in the air, but it was the smoke of battle rising above the death of the Seventh Cavalry on the Little Horn.

General Crook's command remained in the general area of Goose Creek after the defeat on the Rosebud. No move was made toward a junction with Terry, who was supposed to be moving south from the Yellowstone. There had been no news from Terry for a long time, and no one knew how the other commands of the Yellowstone expedition were faring. Crook had suffered much on the Rosebud, and was in no mood to make a march until orders and reinforcements arrived.

Rumor, the harbinger of truth, began to circulate in Crook's camp. Among the Shoshone and Ute allies it was said that many pony soldiers had been killed in a big fight to the north. Truth, however, did not arrive until July 10, fifteen days after Custer fell. On that day Ben Arnold and Louis Richaud came into camp with news of the massacre. For once rumor had been less than truth. Here was another, greater disaster to add to the toll of the Rosebud fight. The Sioux and Cheyennes were really making war this summer.

General Crook ("Three Stars") was building up his strength to fight the Indians on at least equal terms. On August 3, the command was joined by Colonel Wesley Merritt with ten companies of the Fifth Cavalry and seventy-six recruits. The command now numbered over two thousand men. Merritt brought with him Buffalo Bill Cody, who had hurried from "theatrical engagements" in the East to participate in the late phases of the campaign. Only a few days before, Cody had added a famous chapter to his exploits by his supposed hand-to-hand encounter with Chief Yellow Hand of the Cheyennes at the fight on War Bonnet Creek.

Crook was now ready to move. He separated his command from its wagon train, and arranged to operate with mule train alone, discarding all but the most essential equipment, rations, and ammunition. Traveling light, he believed, was the only way to catch Indians if they fled. Crook hoped that the Sioux, emboldened by two victories, would make a third attempt. If they did, they would fail.

The warriors of Sitting Bull, Crazy Horse, and their Cheyenne allies had no intention of making another big fight. Enough for one season had been accomplished in June. July was spent hunting and feasting along the base of the Big Horns, and then the Indian bands separated. Sitting Bull went beyond the Yellowstone, and Crazy Horse to the Bear Butte country on the Little Missouri.

When on August 10 Crook and Terry finally met, thirty miles below the Yellowstone, they found no Indians between them. The combined commands returned to the junction of the Powder and Yellowstone and then parted, Terry going north on the trail of Sitting Bull, and Crook southeast toward the Black Hills on the trail of the other Indian bands. The Utes and Shoshones, who had served as scouts for the Yellowstone expedition, went back to their tribes disgusted with such poor warmaking. Buffalo Bill went east to his clamoring audiences.

Of those who were left with Three Stars, only Frank Grouard knew something of the country, and could guide the command to the Black Hills. The way was rough, there was almost constant rain, and no firewood. There were no Indians to fight, either. The mud was deep, and the expedition slogged its heavy way toward the end of a fruitless campaign.

Besides the ordinary hardships of the march, the command began to suffer from short rations. Three Stars had not counted on such a long march. He had hoped to find an Indian village full of dried meat to subsist the soldiers. But all the Indians were in front, and they kept their villages out of the way.

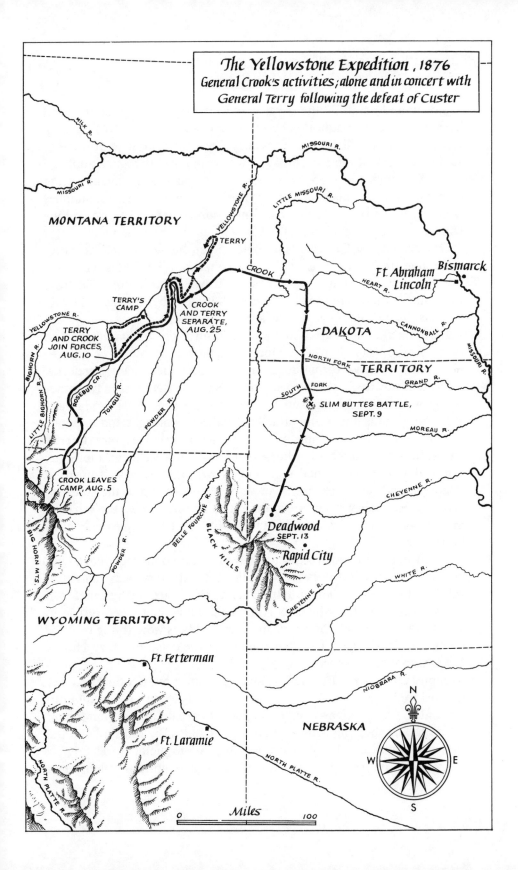

The Yellowstone Expedition, 1876
General Crook's activities; alone and in concert with
General Terry following the defeat of Custer

MILK R.

MISSOURI R.

MONTANA TERRITORY

MISSOURI R.

YELLOWSTONE R.

TERRY

CROOK

MISSOURI R.

LITTLE MISSOURI R.

HEART R.

Ft. Abraham Lincoln

Bismarck

CANNONBALL R.

DAKOTA

TERRY'S CAMP

YELLOWSTONE R.

CROOK AND TERRY SEPARATE, AUG. 25

TERRY AND CROOK JOIN FORCES, AUG. 10

BIGHORN R.

ROSEBUD CR.

TONGUE R.

POWDER R.

NORTH FORK

SOUTH FORK

TERRITORY

GRAND R.

MISSOURI R.

X SLIM BUTTES BATTLE, SEPT. 9

MOREAU R.

LITTLE BIGHORN R.

CROOK LEAVES CAMP, AUG. 5

POWDER R.

BELLE FOURCHE R.

BLACK HILLS

CHEYENNE R.

Deadwood
SEPT. 13

Rapid City

WHITE R.

BIG HORN MTS.

CHEYENNE R.

WYOMING TERRITORY

Ft. Fetterman

NIOBRARA R.

N

NEBRASKA

W   E

Ft. Laramie

NORTH PLATTE R.

S

NORTH PLATTE R.

0   Miles   100

Slowly and painfully the cavalry and infantry plodded along. Food became so scarce that horses had to be killed and eaten. "If we march long enough we will eat up the cavalry," was the grim joke of the foot soldiers. Some of the men broke down, weeping with exhaustion.

On September 8, General Crook sent Captain Mills ahead of the command with 150 men and the best horses. They were to bring supplies from the Black Hills settlements. Tom Moore, chief packer, went along with the strongest pack mules. Frank Grouard went as guide.

During the day Grouard saw some Indian hunters in the distance, and found fresh pony tracks along a stream near Slim Buttes. He knew that there was an Indian camp nearby. It would be full of meat from the summer hunts, and there would be buffalo robes for the cold, wet soldiers. The captain decided to attack the village.

Early on the morning of September 9, after the Indian village had been located, Captain Mills divided his detachment into three groups. The first, twenty-five mounted men under Lieutenant Frederick Schwatka, was to charge the camp and stampede the horses. The other two groups, under Lieutenants Emmet Crawford and A. H. Von Leutt-witz, were to dismount and attack the village from right and left.

It was a cold, wet morning, and the strings of the lodges were slippery and stiff. When stampeding horses and rifle shots wakened the Sioux camp, the warriors opened their lodges with knives, picked up their weapons, and ran across the river, leaving their camp to the soldiers. From across the river, and from the bluffs on three sides, the warriors fought back at the invaders. Captain Mills sent back messengers to Crook, asking for help.

When the main body of troops arrived about noon, the village with its forty lodges was still held by soldiers. The hungry ones ran about wildly, filling their bellies with dried meat. The Sioux, led by Chief Iron Plume, known to the whites as American Horse, had taken refuge in a small ravine beyond the river, and some soldiers were trying to force them out. The Indians had sent runners to the camp of Crazy Horse, nearby, and were expecting help.

Baptiste Pourier, "Big Bat," guide and interpreter, who knew the Indians well, spoke to them during a lull in the fight, asking them to surrender. Eleven squaws and six papooses were delivered from the pit of death, and then the fight raged on. Once more Big Bat spoke to the warriors, promising that no harm would come to them.

This time the old chief and his warriors gave up. Iron Plume had been shot in the belly. With his hands he pressed in his intestines. He bit on a piece of wood to help bear the pain of his wound. Doctor V. T. McGillycuddy examined the chief and told him he would die. The old warrior held himself proudly to the end.

When the plundering of the lodges was at its height, the promised help from Crazy Horse and about six hundred of his warriors arrived. They appeared on the bluffs around the camp, and began pouring carbine fire on the command. The plundering stopped, and a new fight raged. The soldiers formed a great ring around the village, and moved in rushes toward the bluffs. Even up the bluffs they went, their rifles driving the Sioux out of range. The warriors, outnumbered and outshot, their war spirit no longer burning as it had three months before, drew away. The soldiers of the Yellowstone expedition had one victory, small though it was.

The fight cost the Indians ten killed, while three soldiers had died and twenty were wounded. The dead were buried and the wounded carried on travois. The victory added these last men to the terrible price paid for the expedition of 1876.

General Crook and the "horse-meat marchers" reached the Belle Fourche River on September 12, where rations from Deadwood met the command. After a few days at Deadwood, the general went to Fort Laramie for a conference with Sheridan. The rest of the command stayed in the Hills, recuperating from a fruitless campaign.

• • •

Bloodshed and scalp dances on the Little Horn did not lessen the greed of the whites for the Black Hills. The stream of fortune hunters flowed ever wider, and the heart of the Sacred Hills was burrowed into as if by so many prairie dogs. The claims of the Indians were brushed away with one hand while the other dipped the gold pan.

The government in Washington, too, decided that the Hills must be had at any price. In August 1876, another commission was sent to the Sioux. George W. Manypenny, Bishop H. B. Whipple, and A. S. Gaylord were among those charged with the task of stealing the Black Hills. These treaty makers did not ask the Indians what they wanted; they told them what they would get. Bishop Whipple prayed to the Great Spirit to give wisdom to the Indian chiefs, and asked that the commission might "help the poor and perishing."

Judge Gaylord spoke another language. He informed the Sioux that they would either sign or starve, for the treaty was part of the law appropriating money for Indian rations.

Red Cloud, Spotted Tail, and the other reservation Indians knew the truth of the harsh words, but they raised their voices in final protest. The fight at the Little Horn had not been their doing. "Rub it out," said Red Cloud. "Tell the people that this is not an Indian war; it is a white man's war. A great many widows and orphans have been made on both sides. It is displeasing to the Great Spirit."

The cheeks of the commissioners were red with shame, but they had been sent to get the Hills, and could do nothing else.

Not only were the Sioux to give up their sacred Hills, but they were to move again; this time to Indian Territory, if they chose, or to the old place on the Missouri. Neither place was welcome to the Indians. It was a case of move or starve, explained Judge Gaylord. The Indians had better sign.

Standing Elk had heard enough. He had kept a count, and this was the tenth time he had been asked to sign the treaty papers of the whites. "My friend," he told the judge, "your speech is as if a man had knocked me on the head with a stick. By your speech you have put great fear upon us. Whatever the white people say to us, wherever I go, we all say yes to them—yes, yes, yes. Whenever we don't agree to anything that is said in council they give us the same reply, 'You won't get any food! You won't get any food!'"

But the Indians signed. Red Cloud, Fast Bear, and Red Leaf of the Oglalas, Spotted Tail and Standing Elk of the Brulés, Iron Nation for the Lower Brulés, Standing Bear of the Miniconjous, White Ghost of the Yanctons, and a few others. Little Wound, of the Bear People, an Oglala society, made his mark, and John Grass of the Blackfeet also "touched the pen." His tribe had been a symbol of terror to trespassing whites all over the northwestern frontier. But John Grass knew that the old days were gone; he would have to learn to walk the new road. He later signed other papers and lost more land.

It was true that the treaty of 1868 had promised that no new treaty could be made without the agreement of three-fourths of the adult males, but the officials said that this new treaty was only an "agreement." By this "agreement" the Indians lost the Black Hills, the unceded territory where the buffalo were, and were forced to choose a new home on the Missouri or in Indian Territory. The victories of the summer of 1876 counted as nothing.

Red Cloud sulked, and talked war. He would not stay at the agency, but moved about forty miles away on Chadron Creek. He did not like the soldier chiefs who had taken over the agency in July. His friend Red Leaf moved with him. The soldiers, who were getting ready for another campaign, decided to bring in these two chiefs. On October 24, Pawnee scouts surrounded and captured the two camps, took all the arms and horses, and led the chiefs back to the agencies. General Crook, who was angry at Red Cloud's "obstinacy," deposed him, and declared Spotted Tail chief of all the reservation Sioux.

· · ·

While the treaty makers were taking the Black Hills from the Sioux and Cheyennes, more soldiers were hurried from the east to fight the warriors who had killed so many soldiers during the summer. There were enough soldiers to replace all those killed on the Little Horn, and many, many more. The soldier chiefs believed now that it would take more than a "little force" to make the Indians walk their road.

Among the soldiers sent to the fight was General Nelson A. Miles, called "Bear Coat." In October 1876, Miles went to the cantonment at the mouth of the Tongue River, later known as Fort Keogh, and much equipment and supplies came with him.

Sitting Bull was in the country, too, and knew that either he or the soldiers would have to move. He asked the fugitive Johnny Brughiere, his half-breed interpreter and adviser, to write a note to Miles. The note was posted on a cleft stick on the road to the fort:

> I want to know what you are doing on this road. You scare all the buffalo away. I want to hunt in this place. I want you to turn back from here. If you don't, I will fight you again. I want you to leave what you have got here, and turn back from here. I am your friend,
> > Sitting Bull
>
> I mean all the rations you have got, and some powder. Wish you would write as soon as you can.

But the sun dance vision that had fired the warriors in June had faded and grown cold. The soldiers laughed over the note, and kept on coming through the buffalo country.

On October 21, 1876, Sitting Bull had a council with Bear Coat north of the Yellowstone. The warriors had stolen a few mules, and attacked a supply train. Miles was after them. Sitting Bull knew of the betrayal of the reservation chiefs in August. He knew that the old days were gone, and that the land had been given away. But he asked for an old-fashioned peace, one which would let him trade for powder and ammunition, and allow him to stay in the north to hunt buffalo.

The council lasted two days, and ended in a fight. The soldiers were too strong. They had many guns, even quick-firing Gatlings. The warriors were driven back. Most of them, including Red Shirt, finally asked for peace, but Sitting Bull, Gall, High Bear, and 109 lodges of Sioux moved up to the Grandmother Land, Canada, crossing the line in February 1877.

The Sioux and Cheyennes who had gone to the Bear Butte country on the Little Missouri in the fall of 1876 were ready for a quiet winter. They had killed their buffalo, dried the meat, and repaired their lodges. It was not time to fight. Summer—when the days were long and a warrior could fight without freezing to death—that was the time for war-making.

The whites felt otherwise. To them war-making was simply another way of getting pay. Winter was as good a time to fight as any. In fact it was a better time to fight Indians, because they would be separated into small camps, not all gathered together as they had been on the Little Horn.

With these things in mind, General Crook went out on another campaign known as the Big Horn expedition. With him were eleven companies of infantry, eleven of cavalry, and four of artillery. Many Indians joined as scouts: Pawnees, Sioux, Arapahoes, Shoshones, Bannocks, and a few Cheyennes. There were 168 wagons, 7 ambulances, and 400 pack mules. The expedition, starting from Fort Fetterman on November 14, 1876, numbered over 2,000. Crook had learned something at the Rosebud.

The soldiers were looking for the camp of Crazy Horse, supposed to be near the old Rosebud battleground. When the command reached the Crazy Woman fork of the Powder River, an agency Cheyenne came in and reported a large Cheyenne village, under Dull Knife, in the Big Horns near the head of Crazy Woman Creek. Crook sent Colonel Ranald Mackenzie with the Indian scouts and all the cavalry to find and capture the village. The detachment started off November 24.

The Cheyennes, a camp of 150 lodges, knew that the soldiers were coming. Four scouts—Hail, Crow Necklace, Two Moons, and High

Wolf—had been spying on the troops. They reported many soldiers on the Powder, and Indian scouts with them speaking four languages. "If they reach this camp, I think there will be a fight," said Two Moons.

Some of the Cheyennes wanted to move, and join the Sioux camp not far away. But Last Bull, chief of the Fox Society, would not listen. "No one shall leave the camp. We will stay up all night and dance." It was the night of November 24, 1876.

Early the next morning, when the sky was getting a little light, and the dance was ended, the words of Two Moons came to pass. The soldiers and Indian scouts swept into the valley from the north, charging through the camp, driving the Cheyennes from their lodges into the freezing dawn.

It was much like Reynolds's fight on the Powder, except that the soldiers fought better. The warriors retreated south and west, fighting at long range all day, slipping away during the night. They marched through the Big Horn Mountains to the camp of Crazy Horse, where they found food and shelter.

The Cheyennes in Dull Knife's village had lost almost everything. Their lodges were in ashes, their horses taken, their meat and robes gone. Even their sacred medicine things, and the trophies from the fight on the Little Horn, were lost. Over forty warriors died in the defense of the camp. The whites wanted the land, and blood would not stop them.

.   .   .

When the Cheyennes fled to the village of Crazy Horse after Mackenzie's raid, it was but another sign that the time of Indian resistance to the whites was coming to an end. No longer could the Sioux and Cheyennes set up their lodges in peace on the Powder or the Tongue. Most of the buffalo in the southland had already disappeared, and in the north they were fast becoming silent heaps for the bone wagons.

There was no new place to go. The Black Hills were taken away, the last hunting grounds were a pathway for the new iron road. The Grandmother Land, Canada, whence Sitting Bull had fled, was poor refuge. The soldiers in that country did not want raids across the border. They even scolded when the Indians went south after the few buffalo that were left.

Crazy Horse and his chiefs held a council over these things. Their hearts were heavy. The war spirit was low. Cartridges were hard to get, and the soldiers were coming in ever greater numbers. Perhaps the time had come to get things by peace talk rather than war talk.

News from the agencies spoke for peace. Three Stars let it be said that if the warriors came in and made peace they would be allowed to come back to the buffalo country to a reservation there. They would not have to go south to Indian Territory or to the place on the Missouri.

But the tongue of the white man had been crooked so often that the chiefs could not believe what was promised. Perhaps it would be better to go to the fort at the mouth of the Tongue and surrender to Bear Coat, who also spoke for peace.

Late in December 1876, eight chiefs from the camp of Crazy Horse went to the fort to talk peace. When they neared the stockade, Crow scouts, pay soldiers for the whites, came out at them, shooting. Five of the peace talkers were killed. Crazy Horse had enough of that kind of peace talk, and moved his camp away.

Miles now dropped all pretense of peace, and went out with his soldiers after Crazy Horse and the Cheyennes. On January 1 and 3 the troops had little fights with the warriors of the rear guard, while the main Indian camp moved slowly up the Tongue. On the morning of January 8 the soldiers caught up with the main camp, and a big fight followed. A blizzard blew up and hid the camp from view, and the Indians moved away once again. The warriors stayed, and held off the soldiers all day. Bear Coat had enough fighting for that winter, and moved back to the fort.

The winter passed, cold and dreary. Hunger and a heavy heart darkened the days. In February, Spotted Tail came out from the agency, talking peace to his people. He brought new promises from Three Stars about a place to live in the buffalo country. Crazy Horse listened to the promise. He knew that the time had come. the people would go in.

On the morning of May 6, 1877, Crazy Horse and his followers, 1,100 in all, moved through the hills a few miles from Camp Robinson. This time the warriors came in peace. When Lieutenant W. P. Clark rode up to go with the chief into camp, Crazy Horse offered his left hand to the solider, saying, "Friend, I shake with this hand because my heart is on this side; I want this peace to last forever." He Dog took his scalp shirt and put it on Clark to show that all war between them was done.

A little after noon, the procession of Indians wound out of the hills to the agency. First came Red Cloud at the head of the Indian soldier-guards. Then Crazy Horse, Little Big Man, Little Hawk, He Dog, Old Hawk, and Big Road. Behind the warriors, for two miles, moved the rest of the people with their ponies, dogs, and lodges. Everyone was quiet until the warriors struck up the peace chant. The people joined in, holding their heads high, though their hearts were heavy. It was a victory march, not a surrender.

Then came the hard part—horses and guns were all taken away. Over 2,400 ponies were taken that day, and 117 guns. Little Hawk was wearing a silver medal given by the whites to his father at a peace conference on the Platte sixty years before. He was allowed to keep it.

Crazy Horse was restless on the "white man's island." The promise of a reservation in the buffalo country was never kept. The soldiers and Indian scouts watched every move the chief made, and reported it. Crazy Horse was a prisoner.

In September the chief went up to the Spotted Tail agency. The whites were afraid that he was planning to go north with his people, so they arrested him, and tried to put him in the guard house at Camp Robinson. Crazy Horse resisted, and was stabbed to death in the fight. His arms were held by Little Big Man, one of his own chiefs.

The death of Crazy Horse marked the end of all war-making by the Sioux. From this time on they walked the whites' road unless the whites pushed them off.

Red Cloud and Spotted Tail were finally forced to live on the Missouri, the old land where they did not want to be. After a short stay in this hated place they again moved, in the spring of 1878. Red Cloud went to Pine Ridge, and Spotted Tail, with his people, to the Rosebud.

In July 1881, Sitting Bull, whose followers had left him, came south from Canada and gave himself up at Fort Buford. He was sent to Standing Rock agency, where he lived on Grand River, near his birthplace.

When he surrendered, Sitting Bull knew the old life was gone forever. He sang a new song:

> *A warrior*
> *I have been.*
> *Now*
> *It is all over.*
> *A hard time*
> *I have.*

CHAPTER 16
Dull Knife Marches Home

▲ ▲ ▲ ▲ ▲ ▲ ▲ ▲ ▲ ▲ ▲ ▲ ▲ ▲ ▲ ▲ ▲

THE FIGHTS OF THE WINTER of 1876–77, followed by peace talks from the agencies, brought in both Sioux and Cheyennes. On April 22, 1877, a band of Cheyennes led by Two Moons, White Bull, Crazy Head, and other chiefs surrendered to General Nelson Miles at Fort Keogh on the Tongue River. The soldiers were glad to see them come in. There had been much fighting and killing. Peace was better. Thirty of the warriors enlisted as scouts under Miles—they were to fight their relatives who would not come in to the reservations.

Dull Knife and his people, who had wintered with Crazy Horse after Mackenzie's raid, surrendered in the spring of 1877 at Camp Robinson. General Crook held a council with the Cheyennes, telling them they could either go to Indian Territory, go to the agency at Fort Washakie, Wyoming, or stay at Camp Robinson for a year to decide.

It was plain, however, that Crook and the other soldiers wanted the Cheyennes to go south. The Indians decided to stay at Camp Robinson, but Standing Elk, who spoke for them in council, said they would follow the wishes of the whites and go to Indian Territory.

On May 1, 1877, 960 northern Cheyennes, accompanied by a few soldiers, began the long road south to Fort Reno, Indian Territory, the home of their relatives, the southern Cheyennes and the Arapahoes. Ninety days they traveled, moving through the land quietly, and reported to Fort Reno on August 5.

The new home of the northern Cheyennes was different in every way from their old hunting grounds. Here the buffalo were almost gone, and other game was equally scarce. The Indians had to depend on tough Texas steers for meat. Sickness in the form of malarial diseases rode through the land, which was barren and windswept, hot and dusty.

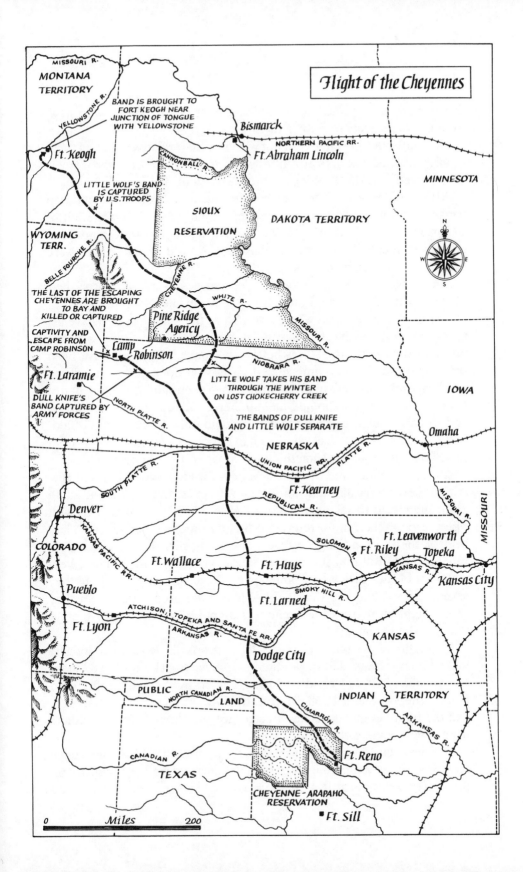

Flight of the Cheyennes

MONTANA TERRITORY

MISSOURI R.

YELLOWSTONE R.

BAND IS BROUGHT TO
FORT KEOGH NEAR
JUNCTION OF TONGUE
WITH YELLOWSTONE

Bismarck

NORTHERN PACIFIC RR.

Ft. Keogh

Ft. Abraham Lincoln

CANNONBALL R.

MINNESOTA

LITTLE WOLF'S BAND
IS CAPTURED
BY U.S. TROOPS

SIOUX
RESERVATION

DAKOTA TERRITORY

WYOMING
TERR.

BELLE FOURCHE R.

CHEYENNE R.

WHITE R.

THE LAST OF THE ESCAPING
CHEYENNES ARE BROUGHT
TO BAY AND
KILLED OR CAPTURED

Pine Ridge
Agency

MISSOURI R.

CAPTIVITY AND
ESCAPE FROM
CAMP ROBINSON

Camp
Robinson

IOWA

Ft. Laramie

DULL KNIFE'S
BAND CAPTURED BY
ARMY FORCES

NORTH PLATTE R.

NIOBRARA R.

LITTLE WOLF TAKES HIS BAND
THROUGH THE WINTER
ON LOST CHOKECHERRY CREEK

THE BANDS OF DULL KNIFE
AND LITTLE WOLF SEPARATE

NEBRASKA

Omaha

MISSOURI R.

SOUTH PLATTE R.

UNION PACIFIC RR.

PLATTE R.

Ft. Kearney

Denver

REPUBLICAN R.

COLORADO

KANSAS PACIFIC RR.

Ft. Wallace

SOLOMON R.

Ft. Leavenworth
Ft. Riley
Topeka

Ft. Hays

KANSAS R.

MISSOURI

Pueblo

SMOKY HILL R.

Kansas City

Ft. Lyon

ATCHISON, TOPEKA AND SANTA FE RR.

Ft. Larned

KANSAS

ARKANSAS R.

Dodge City

PUBLIC
LAND

NORTH CANADIAN R.

CIMARRON R.

INDIAN   TERRITORY

ARKANSAS R.

CANADIAN R.

Ft. Reno

TEXAS

CHEYENNE-ARAPAHO
RESERVATION

Ft. Sill

0   Miles   200

Tepees had to be protected by barricades of brush. There were new, troublesome insects to bother them.

The southern Cheyennes did not welcome their relatives, calling them "fools" and "Sioux." As a result the two tribes did not camp together. "They lived," said the agent at Fort Reno, "but that was about all."

Wild Hog reported, "Very soon after our arrival there the children began to get sick and to die. Between the fall of 1877 and the fall of 1878 we lost fifty children by sickness." The agency doctor did not have enough medicine for the sick Indians, and even if he had, there were five thousand Indians for one doctor.

But the greatest sickness of the Cheyennes was a longing for their old land. Little Chief, who came from the north later, wanted to return, "Because that is the land where I was born, the land that God gave us; and because it was better than this in every way; everything is better up there than here, the soil is better, the water is better. I have been sick a great deal of the time since I have been down here—homesick and heartsick, and sick in every way. I have been thinking of my native country, and the good home I had up there, where I was never hungry, and when I wanted anything to eat could go out and hunt the buffalo. It does not make me feel good to hang about an agency and to have to ask a white man for something to eat when I get hungry."

About three hundred of the Cheyennes decided they would not stay at their new reservation any longer. In July 1878, Little Wolf and some of his men went to see agent John D. Miles. They communicated with Miles through their interpreter, half-breed Edmond Guerrier (who had been warned, when the grievances were great, that the more excitable Indians might kill him for his association with the whites). The Cheyennes told Miles they were going north. There was only one thing they asked. Little Wolf said that if the soldiers were sent after them they should fight away from the agency. "I do not want the agency ground bloody," he explained.

The night of September 9 the Cheyennes took down their lodges, loaded their travois, and began their march north. There were 89 men, 112 women, and 134 children. Their leaders were Dull Knife, Wild Hog, Little Wolf, and Tangle Hair. Little Wolf was head of the warriors, and the fugitives moved as he directed, for they knew that the soldiers would soon come after them.

Two days the Cheyennes moved north, to the Little Medicine Lodge River, where they camped. Here Indian police and white soldiers found them. There was a little talk about coming back, some threats, and then a fight. The shooting was started by the soldiers, for Little Wolf had told his warriors that the Cheyennes would only defend themselves, not attack. There were few bullets in the camp, and few guns. Besides, if they went north without attacking they might be allowed to stay. Three soldiers were killed in this first fight, and five Cheyennes were wounded. The soldiers then went away; the Indians moved north once more.

There were several small fights during the next few days, but the soldiers were always too few, and Little Wolf always picked strong places to make a fight. Just south of the Arkansas River the warriors found a party of buffalo hunters. From these hide hunters they took eighteen buffalo, many guns, and a good supply of ammunition.

The Indians crossed the Arkansas on September 23, and moved north quickly. Five days later, on Punished Woman's Fork of the Smoky Hill River, many soldiers came up, and there was a big fight. Little Wolf had again found a good place. The leader of the soldiers, Colonel William H. Lewis, was killed, and several of his men were wounded. Only one warrior was killed. The soldiers again went away.

The Cheyennes did not stop for scalp dances, or to mourn their dead. They wanted to reach their old home as quickly as possible. Nothing was to stop them. Settlers who got in their way were killed. Fresh horses were stolen, and cattle was taken for meat. Some of the young warriors went wild and took many scalps. They could not help remembering that all this land had once been theirs, and the whites had taken it all away, giving nothing in return.

Across the Kansas Pacific Railroad the Cheyennes fled, over the South Platte River near Ogalalla, over the Union Pacific line east of Sidney, Nebraska, and finally over the North Platte near the mouth of White Clay Creek. Troops were sent after them from every direction, from Laramie, Robinson, Sidney, Fort Dodge, and Fort Wallace, but the Indians succeeded in slipping past the marching columns. The Cheyennes were not looking for scalps, but for the good grass, good water, and the good hunting.

Beyond the North Platte the fugitives separated. Little Wolf with most of the warriors went north toward the old land on the Powder. Dull Knife and 148 followers went toward the place where the old Red Cloud agency had been.

On October 23, in the Sand Hills of Nebraska, Dull Knife and his people suddenly came face-to-face with two troops of the Third Cavalry under Captain J. B. Johnson. A heavy snow prevented **both** Indians and soldiers from finding each other sooner. The Cheyennes surrendered to Captain Johnson without a fight, asking to be taken to Camp Robinson or Sheridan.

For two days the captain held council with the Indians to decide where they should go. By that time more soldiers had come up, and Captain Johnson felt safe enough to tell the Indians that they would have to go to Camp Robinson.

Their guns were taken from them—at least all that the soldiers could find. Some guns were hidden away. The wife of Black Bear later explained, "I had a carbine hanging down my back." Other guns were taken apart, and the big parts hidden on the squaws, the small pieces worn as ornaments by the children.

The Cheyenne captives were housed in an unused barracks at Camp Robinson while the soldiers waited for official word as to what should be done with them. It was not a bad life at the camp. The Indians were allowed to wander away from the post during the day for a little hunting, but they had to come back at night to be counted. There were dances at the post, and the soldiers were very friendly.

There was much talk, however, about going south. The whites always told the Indians that they would probably be sent back to Indian Territory. The answer always came, "We will die first." But none of the soldiers really believed that.

On January 3, 1879, the Cheyennes were finally told that the government had decided that they must return to Fort Reno. "It would upset the entire reservation system" if they were allowed to return to their old land.

Again the chiefs refused. "I am here on my own ground," Dull Knife said, "and I will never go back. You may kill me here, but you cannot make me go back." Besides, it was the middle of winter, and the Indians were in rags.

The soldiers were no longer friendly. They threatened, and locked up the Indians in the old barracks. Still the Cheyennes would not submit. Their food was cut off; they would not change their minds. Water was kept from them; they would not go south. Four days they were without food, and two without water. They were ready to die.

The commanding officer, Captain H. W. Wessells, then took the warrior Wild Hog from the barracks and put him in irons. Old Crow, who had been a scout against the Sioux in 1876, came out with Wild Hog. They put him in irons too, along with Left Hand.

The starving captives then decided that if they must die, it was better to die as warriors. The concealed guns were brought out and assembled. A pile of saddles and parfleches was set by a window, making it easy to climb out. The Cheyennes then said goodbye to each other, and were ready to go.

Shortly after dark on January 9, the Indians, led by Tangle Hair and Porcupine with several other warriors, broke out of the barracks and ran toward the bluffs across White River, west of the post. They fled across the bridge near the sawmill. Five warriors stayed behind with guns, and held the soldiers off until the others had escaped.

There was much shooting on that cold, moonlit night. The five warriors who stayed behind were soon dead, and the soldiers started after the others who had escaped across the river. When daylight came, sixty-five captives, some wounded, had been brought back to the post. Fifty dead, frozen in the snow, were piled into wagons and brought in. Some of the wounded would not be taken. Big Antelope stabbed his wife and then killed himself.

The hunt then began for those who had escaped. They had fled eighteen miles northwest, and were found hidden on a knoll. These few Cheyennes drove the soldiers off, and fled farther. Once more they were discovered. Each time they were found a soldier paid with his life for the finding.

Captain Wessells sent for help, and on January 18 he was joined by two companies of soldiers from Fort Laramie. Finally the troops surrounded the Indians in a hole on top of a bluff above Hat Creek. There were thirty-two Indians in the hole, and after the soldiers were done shooting, only three squaws were alive, and one of them was wounded. One of the dead squaws had stabbed her child and then herself.

After the prisoners had all been brought in, and the dead counted, it was found that eleven soldiers had been killed, and ten wounded. Of the Cheyennes, seventy-eight were captured and sixty-four were dead—they at least would never go south. Seven Indians were unaccounted for. "These last seven," said the report, "are women and children, and are supposed to have died on the bluffs."

General Crook, who had hoped for peace and wanted the Cheyennes to have a home in the north, wrote to the president in sorrow and anger. "Among these Cheyenne were some of the bravest and most efficient of the auxiliaries who had acted under General Mackenzie and myself in the campaign against the hostile Sioux in 1876 and 1877, and I still preserve a grateful remembrance of their distinguished services, which the government seems to have forgotten."

Dull Knife with his family escaped by hiding in a cave. He reached Pine Ridge agency after wandering in the cold for eighteen days. He lived there, and died about 1883.

The warriors under Little Wolf reached the hunting grounds on the Powder in March, but were met there by soldiers under White Hat, Lieutenant W. P. Clark, and surrendered to him. Permitted to stay on their old land, they were taken to Fort Keogh, and enlisted as scouts under General Nelson Miles. A few years later they were given a reservation on the Tongue River. Though they were not as free as of old, they had come home.

CHAPTER 17
Captain Jack and the Modocs

▲ ▲ ▲ ▲ ▲ ▲ ▲ ▲ ▲ ▲ ▲ ▲ ▲ ▲ ▲

LONG BEFORE THE WESTWARD expansion of the United States, the Indians of the southern Pacific coast had been living under the Spanish rulers of California. In many sections they had adopted the customs of the whites, and by the middle of the nineteenth century conflict between the races was almost unknown.

When gold was discovered in 1848, however, new trails were opened into California and Oregon from the northern routes. Coastal Indians who had never seen whites now saw them for the first time. The Modocs, who lived along the shores of Tule Lake on the California-Oregon border, were so startled when they saw their first emigrant train that they ran for the hills. They thought the Great Spirit had sent evil messengers to punish them. Later when they lost their fear the Modocs were friendly, but a series of unfortunate incidents soon turned this small and peaceful tribe into as fierce a band of killers as ever fought in the West.

After a party of Shastan Indians had ambushed a wagon train near Alturas in 1853, the miners sent a posse scouring the countryside. These volunteers were out to kill every Indian they could find. Since the guilty Shastans were hiding and the innocent Modocs were expecting no trouble, the latter were slain like rabbits in their camps.

For weeks after this raid, the Modocs held councils in the mountains, in the Lava Bed caves, and among the thick tules (bulrushes) of the nearby marshes. Some of the chiefs wanted to fight a war of revenge. "If we run every time we see the white people, they will chase us from mountain to valley, and kill us all. They will hunt us like we hunt the deer and antelope."

Keintpoos, the young son of Chief Combutwaush, listened to this talk. He listened to his father say that he was going to kill the whites before they could kill him. Then Keintpoos stood up in the council ring and spoke: "I am a Modoc," he said. "I am not afraid to die, but that is not it. We have not killed any white people yet, so let us not kill any. No one told the white men who fired on us that it was the Shastans and not the Modocs who made the attack on their wagons. I see that the white people are many. We are few. If we value our lives or love our country, we must not fight the white men."

The words of Keintpoos were echoed by some of the Modoc leaders, but a few days later when an emigrant train came near the Lava Beds, the Indians attacked it. "The Massacre of Bloody Point," the white people called the affair, and a group of Oregon settlers led by Ben Wright volunteered to hunt down the guilty Indians. By pretending that they were still friends of the Modocs, the volunteers lured old Chief Combutwaush into a trap and killed him with many of his warriors. Keintpoos was now the leader of his father's peole, and he convinced some of the Modocs that they must make a peace with the whites if they hoped to survive. A few recalcitrants, however, listened to a sub-chief, Schonchin, and his son, Schonchin John, who believed they should fight the invaders.

For two years, young Keintpoos sought the aid of friendly white settlers in Oregon and in northern California. Finally he received promises that the Modocs would not be harmed if they would remain in their Lost River country and not roam too widely afield. Elisha Steele, a lawyer of Yreka, California, proved to be their best friend. It was Steele who first gave Keintpoos the name of "Captain Jack," a name which was quickly adopted by both the settlers and the Indians.

By the summer of 1864, however, the Lost River valley was becoming so thickly settled that the government issued an order to the Oregon superintendent of Indian affairs, instructing him to negotiate a treaty which would remove all the Indians in the Klamath and Modoc areas to a reservation. In the councils which followed, Captain Jack resisted all efforts of the commissioners to force the Modocs off their land. The clever government agents then refused to recognize Captain Jack as Modoc chief, and old Schonchin was declared the legal head of the tribe. Schonchin of course signed the agreement immediately. To avoid violence, Captain Jack reluctantly added his signature.

From the beginning the reservation plan was a failure, largely because the Modocs were forced to live with their traditional enemies, the Klamaths. As the reservation was on land which had always been Klamath territory, the Klamaths refused to allow the Modocs to cut timber or hunt game. Life soon became unbearable for the Lost River Indians. On a dark moonless night in the spring of 1870, Captain Jack led about seventy of his braves and their families back to their old village on Lost River, just above Tule Lake. Another group under a subchief, Hooker Jim, followed and camped on the opposite side of the river.

Settlers who now claimed all the land formerly occupied by the Modocs complained at once to the government authorities. The usual conferences, reports, and postponements of action followed until the autumn of 1872, when the Indian agent at Fort Klamath received a telegram ordering him to proceed to Lost River and return the Modoc Indians to the Klamath reservation.

A final council was held on November 27, 1872, but Captain Jack refused to discuss returning to the reservation. He insisted that the Modocs be given a reservation in their own country, and he was sustained in his plea by Brigadier-General Edward R. S. Canby, who was then commanding the U. S. Army's Department of the Pacific. The general was overruled by higher authority, however, and at dawn on November 29, 1872, Major James Jackson led a cavalry detachment of thirty-six men into the Modoc camp with orders to force the Modocs to return to Klamath.

The Indians' dogs were barking loudly as the soldiers rode directly up to the chief's lodge, halted, and dismounted. Captain Jack's head man, Scarface Charley, was ordered to bring the chief outside. When Jack appeared from his lodge, he was carrying his gun, and from out of the darkness his braves appeared, also well armed.

Major Jackson informed the Modocs that he had been sent to take them back to the reservation. "I will go," Captain Jack replied, "but why do you come to my camp when it is dark?"

The cavalry commander assured Jack that he did not seek to do harm to his people. Then he added, pointing to a bunch of sagebrush: "Lay your gun down over there."

"What for?" asked Jack.

"You are the chief. You lay your gun down, all your men do the same."

After considering the order for a few moments, Captain Jack signaled to his men to disarm themselves. But when Scarface Charley refused to give up his pistol, an argument followed. In a few seconds, Indians and soldiers were firing at each other. Eight soldiers and fifteen of the Modocs were killed in the close-range action.

Though he had repeatedly said he had not wanted a war with the whites, Captain Jack knew that he now had one on his hands. He certainly must have considered the possibility of a war, and had planned a strategy to meet it. The Modocs moved swiftly to the Lava Beds south of Tule Lake. They could have selected no better defensive position anywhere than among the caves and rocks and secret passages of this jagged volcanic mass. And when Jack and his band reached the Lava Beds, they were reinforced by Hooker Jim and his followers, who had been attacked by civilian volunteers on their side of the river. In retaliation, Hooker Jim's Modocs had slain several settlers on the flight to the Lava Beds.

The war was on in earnest, and volunteer companies were organized as rapidly as the news spread through Oregon and California. But it was mid-January before the First Cavalry, the Twenty-first Infantry, and the volunteers were ready to attack the formidable defenses of the Lava Beds. They numbered 400 men; the Modocs had 75 warriors and 150 women and children.

Under the cover of a dense morning fog an attack was launched on January 17, 1873. The combatants could not see each other, could only fire blindly at orange-colored flashes of gunfire. The voices of the Indians echoing mockingly and the fog curling over the wet fantastic shapes of the rocks added to the weirdness of the battle. Although the troops brought up a howitzer battery and fired all through the day, they were forced to retire at nightfall. Sixteen men were dead, fifty-three wounded. The Modocs had not lost a man.

General Canby now took personal command, bringing in reinforcements, raising his strength to a thousand men. He was striving vainly to reach the Modocs with mortars when the U. S. government suddenly ordered a halt to the costly fighting, and arrangements were begun for a peace parley.

Through Princess Winema, a cousin of Captain Jack, the government authorities were able to approach the besieged Modocs. Winema had married Frank Riddle, a miner from Kentucky, and she had adopted her husband's civilization, even changing her name to Tobey Riddle. But she hoped to save her people from extermination and persuaded the Modocs to meet with the government representatives. The Riddles offered their services as intermediaries to General Canby, and on February 28 they went with Elisha Steele and two other old friends of Captain Jack to arrange a parley.

Although the Modocs were split into two factions, Hooker Jim and

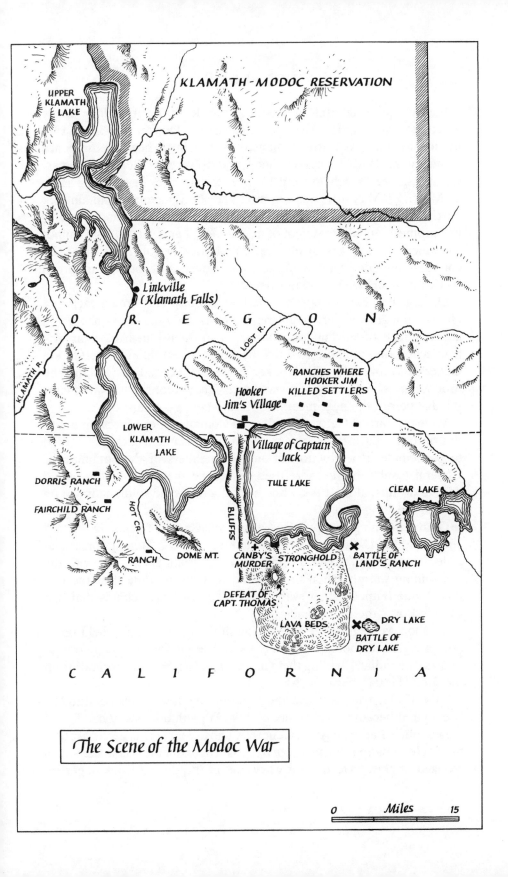

The Scene of the Modoc War

Schonchin John insisting on a war to the death, Captain Jack finally agreed to a discussion. Alfred B. Meacham, a Quaker who had a reputation for fairness to the Indians, was appointed head of the peace commission. With General Canby and Reverend Eleazer Thomas, Commissioner Meacham went to meet the Modocs in the Lava Beds on March 27. Very little was accomplished at this meeting. Captain Jack parried most of their remarks by continually referring to previous broken promises and ill treatment of his people. "I am sorry to say I cannot trust these men that wear blue cloth and brass buttons," he said. The council was ended with handshakes, however, and Jack promised to talk with them again at a later date.

During the next two weeks, the breach between Captain Jack and Hooker Jim grew wider. Schonchin John insisted on a war council, and accused Jack of having less courage than "a fish-hearted woman." Schonchin John then bragged that he would take it upon himself to kill General Canby, and with Hooker Jim he succeeded in working the Modocs up to the frenzy of a war dance. They were singing war chants the day before the next meeting with the peace commission.

Winema warned General Canby and Commissioner Meacham not to return to the Lava Beds. She had heard that Captain Jack had agreed to participate in a plot to kill all the members of the commission. General Canby, however, refused to believe that the Modocs would dare to do this, at least not while he had a thousand soldiers drawn up around the Lava Beds.

On the morning of April 11, Canby, Meacham, Thomas, Frank and Tobey Riddle, L. S. Dyer, the Klamath agent, all mounted horses and rode off for Captain Jack's camp. It was a bright spring day with the sun shining warmly when they started, but by the time they reached the Modoc outpost, snow was flurrying out of heavy clouds that had gathered over the rocky landscape.

As soon as he reached Jack's campfire, General Canby held out a box of cigars to the chief and his men. The gifts were accepted with thanks, the Indians lighting them immediately with burning brands from the fire. The talk began slowly.

"My Modoc friends," said the general, "my heart feels good today. I feel good because you are my friends. We will do good today."

Jack puffed at his cigar. "General Canby, your law is as crooked as this." He held up a sagebrush twig. "The agreements you make are as crooked as this." He drew a wavy line in the dirt with his fingertip.

"Take away your soldiers. Take away your big guns, and then we can talk peace."

Canby glanced at Meacham, and the commissioner spoke up quickly: "General Canby can't take the soldiers away without permission of the Great Father in Washington. If you will come out of the rocks and go with us, we promise to find a new home for the Modocs." As he was talking, Meacham noticed that Hooker Jim, who had been pacing nervously back and forth, had walked up to the commissioner's horse, had taken the overcoat from the saddle, and was putting it on. Suddenly Hooker Jim turned toward the council circle, buttoning up the huge overcoat. "Me Old Man Meacham now," he said, beating his breast and grinning.

Meacham, Canby, and the others laughed. The commissioner took off his hat and handed it to Hooker Jim. "You'd better take my hat, too, Jim," he said.

"No hurry," Hooker Jim replied slyly. "Will get hat by-n-by."

Captain Jack, meanwhile, had not even smiled. He was scratching designs in the hard earth with the sagebrush twig. "Tell me what you will do," he said to General Canby. "I am tired waiting for you to speak."

Meacham now realized that the situation was becoming dangerous. "Promise him something," he said in an undertone to the general. But before Canby could speak, Captain Jack jumped up and started walking away. Schonchin John glowered after his chief, then stepped into his place before the council fire. "You take away soldiers, you give us back land," he shouted. "We tired talking. We talk no more!"

As Schonchin John shouted out these words, Captain Jack swung around and cried in Modoc: "*Ot-we-kau-tux-e* (Let us do it, or All ready)!"

The circle of Indians around the white men closed in quickly, revolvers and rifles ready. Canby stared at Captain Jack, who was pointing a pistol directly at him. The hammer clicked on a dead cartridge. A second later, the trigger clicked again and this time Canby was hit. A Modoc named Boston Charley had shot Eleazer Thomas at almost the same moment. Winema, meanwhile, had saved Meacham's life by knocking Schonchin John's pistol to one side. Meacham was wounded, and Boston Charley tried to scalp him, but Winema interceded and was able to get the commissioner to safety. Frank Riddle and Dyer also escaped.

Thus ended all hopes for peace. The commander of the Department of the Columbia, Colonel J. C. Davis, replaced Canby, and after days of terrific artillery bombardments the Modocs surrendered. Hooker Jim quit first, hoping to escape punishment for his part in the war. After a wild footrace across the rocks and through a thicket, Captain Jack was captured alone on May 31.

He came out of the brush, brazenly wearing General Canby's blue uniform, now dirty and in tatters. "Jack's legs gave out," he said. "I am ready to die." This was the end of the "most costly war in which the U. S. ever engaged, considering the number of opponents," the end of what Hubert H. Bancroft called "a brave and stubborn fight for native land and liberty—a war in some respects the most remarkable that ever occurred in the history of aboriginal extermination."

The Modoc leaders were taken to Klamath reservation and placed in jail. In October, Captain Jack, Schonchin John, Black Jim, and Boston Charley were hanged. During his last moments, a minister came to comfort Captain Jack. The chief received the visitor politely. "You say, Mr. Preacher, that the place I am going to is a nice place. Do you like this place you call Heaven?"

The minister replied that Heaven was a beautiful place.

"Well," Jack continued, without a change of tone or expression, "I tell you what I will do. I give you twenty-five head of ponies if you take my place today, as you say Heaven is such a nice place. Because I do not like to go right now."

The visitor declined Captain Jack's offer. The Modoc chief was hanged, his body preserved, and taken on a tour of the East where it was put on public exhibition, admission ten cents. The remnants of his Modoc band were exiled to Indian Territory.

CHAPTER 18
Joseph of the Nez Percés

▲ ▲ ▲ ▲ ▲ ▲ ▲ ▲ ▲ ▲ ▲ ▲ ▲ ▲ ▲

FAR TO THE NORTH OF THE MODOCS and north-west of the fighting Sioux lived one of the most sophisticated tribes of Indians in North America—the Nez Percés. In the beautiful valleys between the Blue and the Bitterroot mountains, the Nez Percés had developed a culture that was beyond the usual nomadic level of other tribes in the West. They fished for salmon, kept herds of horses, and gathered roots and berries in season. They were a people of superior intelligence; they loved peace; and most of all they loved their land.

In 1805, Lewis and Clark had found the Nez Percés to be friends. Later explorers, missionaries, and then the settlers were also treated as friends. When artist Jacob Miller visited the Nez Percés in 1839, he observed: "These Indians are anti-belligerent and have some other qualities that are rare and commendable." He added prophetically: "All these Indians seem to bear the impress of a doomed race."

At the time of Miller's visit, Dr. Marcus Whitman and the Reverend Henry Spalding were having great success in their efforts to found missions among the Nez Percés. From the numerous small bands of the tribe, three leaders—Kalkalshuatash, Tamason, and Tuekakas—were converted, changing their names, respectively, to Jason, Timothy, and Joseph.

Within a few years, however, Joseph left the mission at Lapwai and led his band back to their old home in the Wallowa valley, the Valley of Winding Waters. He did not like the talk of the people who came with the missionaries, the settlers who wanted to buy the land of the Nez Percés.

"The earth is our mother," said Joseph. "We cannot sell you our mother."

About the year 1850, a religious prophet arose among the Nez Percés, called Smohalla the prophet. He preached that the Indians must cling to their own mode of life, must refuse the teachings and things of the whites and be guided by the will of God as revealed to him in dreams. As the settlers became more insistent about buying the Nez Percé lands, Joseph's band adopted the philosophy of Smohalla.

Old Joseph's son, Young Joseph, also followed the teachings of Smohalla, and the second Joseph became the greatest of the Nez Percés, if not the greatest of all American Indians. As a young man, he had been for a time a student in one of the white schools. He had listened to his father, Old Joseph, plead with the whites, and he had seen many promises broken by them.

In 1855 when the invaders had demanded that Old Joseph move his tribe out of the Wallowa valley, the chief had refused. He had not only refused to mvoe, but he insisted that a definite line of demarcation between white territory and Nez Percé territory be drawn on the council map across the top of the Blue Mountains. The gold-seekers and the land-seekers, however, desired the Valley of Winding Waters for their exclusive use. Old Joseph was summoned to another council in 1859.

"The line was made as I wanted it," he told the commissioners this time. "Not for me, but for my children that will follow me. There is where I live, and there is where I want to leave my body. The land on the other side of the line," he concluded significantly, "is what we gave to the Great Father. Can you not leave us in peace in our valley?"

Young Joseph heard his father's remarks on this occasion and remembered them until the day he died. Was it possible that the whites wanted the Valley of Winding Waters in addition to all the other land the Indians had given them? He could scarcely believe this. But not long after Young Joseph became chief, his father warned him: "When you go into council with the white man, always remember your country. Do not give it away. The white man will cheat you out of your home. I have taken no pay from the United States. I have never sold our land."

In 1863, Young Joseph attended his first council as a chief. The Indian commissioners, acting under pressure from the settlers, had drawn up a treaty which removed to a reservation all the Nez Percés, including Joseph's band in the Wallowa valley. Joseph, of course, refused to sign. He went back to his land, and warned all whites to keep out.

To avoid trouble, the government took no action against him, but cattle ranchers began grazing their herds over Joseph's land, using pastures which the Nez Percés needed for their own cattle and ponies.

JOSEPH

Chief Joseph, son of Tuekakas the original Joseph, became the great leader of the Nez Percés. As a young man he attended many treaty councils with his father, and learned how the whites broke their promises. Refusing to move his people from the Wallowa valley, the Valley of Winding Waters, he ended up fighting the U.S. Army over the course of almost 1,000 miles before finally surrendering, stating, "I will fight no more forever." (Photograph by W. H. Jackson, courtesy of the Smithsonian Institution.)

More gold also had been discovered at Orofino, and the miners were coming in droves.

In 1868 Timothy and Jason, with other leaders who wanted to follow the white way, traveled to Washington to sign a treaty. As heads of the Nez Percés they agreed to withdraw the entire tribe to a reservation. Chief Joseph, however, did not go to Washington, signed no treaty, and ignored all orders to move from Wallowa valley. The Office of Indian Affairs finally sent an agent to interview Joseph in 1873, and as a result of this meeting the Secretary of the Interior decided that the Wallowa valley was rightfully the property of the Nez Percés. On June 16, 1873, President Ulysses S. Grant issued an order:

"It is hereby ordered that the tract of country described be withheld from entry and settlement as public lands, and that the same be set apart as a reservation for the roaming Nez Percés, as recommended by the Secretary of Interior and the Commissioner of Indian Affairs."

This turn of events brought joy to the hearts of Joseph and his people; at last the U. S. government had recognized their claim. The settlers, however, so resented the government's action that they threatened openly to exterminate all the Nez Percés in the valley. Telegraph wires across the continent hummed with indignant demands. Joseph wisely began gathering as many allies as he could: his brother Alikut; an influential disciple of Smohalla, Tu-hul-hil-sote; and two chieftains, White Bird and Looking Glass. While he was doing this, the army was sending troops into the neighboring areas.

The tension lasted for almost two years. Then the Nez Percés were dismayed to learn that President Grant had suddenly reversed his order. All their beautiful valley was to be opened to white settlers! In the spring of 1875, General O. O. Howard, commander of the Department of the Columbia, met Joseph near Pendleton, Oregon. Howard reported back to Washington: "I think it is a great mistake to take from Joseph and his band of Nez Percés Indians that valley. Possibly Congress can be induced to let these really peaceable Indians have this poor valley for their own." But the government took no further action. Violent incidents began to occur here and there in the valley, and General Howard sent more troops to keep the peace.

Joseph and the general met for the second time in 1876. An Indian commission was present, and once again they asked Joseph why he refused to move to the Lapwai reservation in Idaho with the other Nez Percés.

"I have not come to talk about my land," he replied. "For many years my father and I have talked about our land to the whites. They will not listen. It is still our land, but the whites will not stay off it."

General Howard asked him another question: "Suppose several thousand men should come from Oregon with arms, what would you do?"

Joseph was silent for a moment, then spoke as if choosing his words carefully: The white settlers are bad enough. Your soldiers are worse. We have seen them paraded around this whole country. Three or four times they have come into the Wallowa as if to tell us they would make war at any time. We always lived at peace until the white man came. We have not made any war on the white man. But they have pushed over the limits my father set up. They have come over the limits Governor Stevens set up. Now, if soldiers come, what will we do? We will not sell the land. We love the land; it is our home."

The commission's reply was direct: "Unless they come to Lapwai and settle in a reasonable time, they are to be placed by force upon the reservation." Joseph was formally notified that he had until April 1, 1877, to come on the reservation peaceably. When the Nez Percés ignored the order, General Howard went to see Joseph. All the allied chiefs came to the council, Tu-hul-hil-sote, Looking Glass, and White Bird. After long discussions, Joseph and his fellow chieftains decided they would have to bow to the power of the whites.

Yet in June when they started the long march to Lapwai from the Wallowa, White Bird, Tu-hul-hil-sote, and Joseph's brother Alikut began to speak for war. Joseph told them it was "better to live at peace than to begin a war and lie dead." The others called him a coward. One night a few irresponsible braves, unknown to Joseph, went on a raid. Within a few days, death was riding in the valleys of the Salmon and the Snake. Eleven white men and thirty-three Nez Percés were killed the first week. In spite of Joseph's efforts, the war he had feared for so long had now begun.

Though he had opposed the war, now that it had come Joseph was regarded by all as the leader. Without hesitation he began preparing his defenses. The lodges of the Nez Percés were struck and the seven hundred men, women, and children moved up to the comparative safety of White Bird Creek. Joseph's wife was expecting a child, and after the custom of the tribe he pitched their tepee to one side of the camp. Pickets were posted at the entrance of White Bird Canyon, and the Nez Percés waited the coming of the soldiers.

The troops of the First Cavalry under Colonel David Perry entered the canyon at dawn on June 17. Through the narrow passage, the sol-

Chief Joseph's Retreat

CANADA

WASHINGTON

OREGON

IDAHO

MONTANA

WYOMING

Miles 0 100

THE LAST BATTLE
SURRENDER OF CHIEF JOSEPH
BEAR PAW MTS.
ROUTE OF COL. MILES
ROUTE OF COL. STURGIS AND 7TH CAVALRY
7TH CAVALRY
CANYON CREEK BATTLE
Ft. Shaw
Helena
Stevensville
Ft. Missoula
Ft. Fizzle
LOLO PASS
BATTLE OF CLEARWATER, WHITE BIRD BATTLE
NEZ PERCE RESERVATION
Lewiston
Lapwai
CHIEF JOSEPH'S COUNTRY
Bozeman
Ft. Ellis
Virginia City
BATTLE OF THE BIG HOLE
BITTERROOT MTS.
BATTLE OF CAMAS MEADOWS
YELLOWSTONE PARK
BIG HORN MTS.

Rivers: MISSOURI R., YELLOWSTONE R., POWDER R., LITTLE POWDER R., POWDER R., MIZPAH CR., PUMPKIN CR., TONGUE R., ROSEBUD CR., BIGHORN R., LITTLE BIGHORN R., BIGHORN R., WIND R., SHOSHONE R., CLARK'S FORK, SNAKE R., TETON R., SNAKE R., SALMON R., GRANDE RONDE R., POTTS R., SNAKE R., COLUMBIA R., CLARK FORK, MUSSELSHELL R., SUN R., TETON R., MARIAS R., MILK R., MISSOURI R., BIG HOLE, BIG HOLE R., JEFFERSON R., MADISON R., GALLATIN R., YELLOWSTONE R.

N E W S

diers could see the white gleam of the Salmon River. As the darkness lifted, two columns of smoke were visible above the Indian encampment. Perry thought he had trapped Joseph, but he did not know that he was dealing with a master strategist.

While the cavalrymen were approaching along the winding floor of the canyon, Joseph sent White Bird with a large force into concealment along one side of the defile. When the troops reached the opening into the valley, Joseph and his warriors sprang up and began a fierce attack, distracting the soldiers until White Bird could swing down from the left and turn Perry's flank. In a few minutes the cavalrymen were routed, cut into indefensible pockets. A third of the troops were killed before they could escape in disorder through the canyon's mouth. Even after they had reformed, they could not make a stand. Joseph drove the soldiers almost to the town of Mt. Idaho, then ordered his warriors back to the safety of the camp. "Take weapons and ammunition," he said, "but no scalps."

When he returned to his tepee, he found that his wife had given birth to a girl. He wondered how long it would be until the whites came again.

Ten days later, his scouts brought the news that General Howard was marching from Lapwai with very large forces. With the cunning of a fox, Joseph waited until the general was almost into the Salmon valley. Then he crossed the mountains, forcing Howard to divide his army. In a succession of masterful moves, Chief Joseph completely outmaneuvered the veteran military commander, almost wiped out one of the pursuing detachments, and raced to the Clearwater where Looking Glass was waiting with a new force of warriors.

Now that he had almost three hundred warriors armed with rifles, Joseph decided to attack Howard boldly as soon as the four hundred soldiers were in striking range. Incredible as it may seem, Joseph was again successful, outflanking the general and cutting his communications. If cavalry reinforcements had not come up from Lapwai, this might have been Howard's last battle.

Withdrawing beyond the Clearwater, Joseph called a council of the chiefs—White Bird, Looking Glass, and Alikut. They all knew that they could never hope to return again to their beloved valley. They were already outnumbered eight to one, and more soldiers would be coming from the east. Sitting Bull of the Sioux had escaped to Canada and the soldiers dared not go there to capture him. If the Nez Percés could reach the Lolo Trail and cross the Bitterroot mountains, perhaps they might be able to reach the northern country.

And so began the long tragic flight of the Nez Percés. They could not follow the example of other tribes and retreat westward. There was no longer any "west." There was no place to go except north toward Canada.

Although Howard guessed what the chiefs were planning and sent a detachment to block the Lolo Trail, the Indians cleverly outwitted the small force and crossed successfully into Montana. Here Joseph faced his greatest problem. He could not risk crossing the open plains of Montana, which were dotted with military posts. And the northern route was blocked by Howard's troops.

To escape to Canada, he was forced to turn south along the chain of mountains, hoping to shake off his pursuers. His uncanny knowledge of the georgraphy of this vast area amazed the officers who were trying vainly to trap him.

Not until they reached the Big Hole did the Nez Percés meet trouble. Here General Gibbon, coming in from Montana on the night of August 9, caught the weary Indians asleep in camp. More women and children than warriors were slain in this dawn attack. After the first shock of the assult, Joseph rallied his fighting men and they drove Gibbon back, capturing one of his howitzers and two thousand rounds of ammunition. But Looking Glass, Joseph's ablest lieutenant, had died early in the battle.

Howard had now almost overtaken the fleeing tribe. After a brief skirmish at Camas Meadows, however, the Nez Percés escaped again, by cutting across the Yellowstone. Hopefully they turned north into Montana—only to face a new disaster. A fresh force of Seventh Cavalry troops under Colonel Samuel Sturgis from Fort Keogh blocked them at Canyon Creek.

It was September now, and the nights were bitter cold. Canada was still many miles away. Desperately, Joseph once again ordered his thinning line of warriors into battle. After two days' fighting, Sturgis's forces were completely scattered, but there were not many fighting braves left alive.

The survivors had one more chance. They moved swiftly northward. General Nelson Miles with a large force of cavalry was racing to cut them off. Only thirty miles from the Canadian border, in the Bear Paw Mountains, the last battle was joined. Snow was falling when Miles attacked on September 30, but the Indians fought back with desperate fury.

Surrounding Joseph's camp, Miles demanded unconditional surrender. The Nez Percés held out until October 5, when a second blizzard swept across the mountains. "I could not bear to see my wounded men and women suffer any longer," Joseph said afterward. When he rode out to meet General Howard, who had joined Miles, Joseph was holding his rifle loosely across his thighs, both hands clasped on his saddle pommel. He dismounted from his horse with dignity, handing his gun to the general.

"I am tired of fighting," he said. "Our chiefs are killed. Looking Glass is dead. Tu-hul-hil-sote is dead. The old men are all dead. He who led on the young men, Alikut, is dead. It is cold and we have no blankets. The little children are freezing to death. My people, some of them, have run away to the hills, and have no blankets, no food; no one knows where they are—perhaps freezing to death. I want to have time to look for my children and see how many of them I can find. Maybe I shall find them among the dead. Hear me, my chiefs. I am tired; my heart is sick and sad. From where the sun now stands I will fight no more forever."

The long journey was ended. After a thousand miles of fighting, only eighty-seven warriors were now alive, and half of them were wounded. Joseph's wife was dead, his older daughter had escaped to Canada with White Bird, and only the girl papoose born on the flight was left to him. But he hoped that the remnants of his tribe would now be left in peace on the Lapwai reservation.

This was not to be, however. Orders came from Washington to remove the Nez Percés to Fort Leavenworth, Kansas. Joseph's protests went unheeded. He and his people were floated on flatboats down the Missouri River to a malarious bottomland where they were cooped up during the winter of 1877–78. Accustomed to mountain water and air, one-fourth of the Nez Percés sickened and died in this new country.

In the heat of the following summer, those who survived were crowded into railroad freight cars and transported to the hot plains of Indian Territory. Suffering from desert heat and ill with nostalgia for the clean winds of the Valley of Winding Waters, they died one by one.

Bureaucrats and Christian gentlemen visited Joseph at intervals during the following years, interviewing him and making endless reports to their various organizations. Joseph was even allowed to visit Washington, but government officials by this time were bored by touring chiefs, and scarcely any attention was paid to his pleas. Finally, a small group of "good" Nez Percés was permitted to return to Lapwai. Then in 1885, Joseph was transferred to Nespelem on the Colville reservation in the territory of Washington.

Although he was back in the Northwest, he was still an exile from the valley of his fathers. When he fell suddenly dead one autumn day in 1904, his friends said that he had died of a broken heart.

CHAPTER 19
The Peace Seekers

▲ ▲ ▲ ▲ ▲ ▲ ▲ ▲ ▲ ▲ ▲ ▲ ▲ ▲ ▲ ▲

DURING THE FLOW OF MIGRATION westward to the Pacific coast, some of the Indian tribes escaped conflict with the settlers through the skillful efforts of their leaders. Such were the Paiutes, the Utes, and the Shoshones, whose leaders were Chief Winnemucca and his granddaughter Sarah Winnemucca, Ouray the Arrow, and Washakie.

Old Chief Winnemucca was the outstanding chieftain among the Paiute bands that made their homes around Pyramid Lake in Nevada. Peaceable and friendly, the Paiutes—both men and women—wore colorfully decorated clothing. They lived in wickiups, small rounded huts of tule rushes fastened over frameworks of poles, with the ground for a floor and a fire in the center. For food they ate meat, and cakes made from the flour of piñon nuts and other seeds. When John C. Frémont journeyed through this section of the country in 1845, he and Winnemucca became good friends. The chief agreed to accompany the exploring party as a guide across the mountains to California.

Winnemucca liked the whites' country along the coast, and when he returned to Pyramid Lake and found that he had become a grandfather, he resolved to have the girl educated in the California schools. And so before he died in 1859, the old chief arranged for his granddaughter, Tocmetone, to attend a mission school at San Jose. This was the beginning of her career as a peacemaker between the Paiutes and the whites.

As soon as she learned to speak and write English, Tocmetone changed her name to Sarah Winnemucca, a name which was to become more famed than that of her grandfather.

During the 1860s there were frequent clashes between the Nevada tribes and the new settlers. Apparently the younger Winnemucca lacked the qualities of leadership that his father had possessed. He was a chief in name only, and was having difficulty restraining his angry warriors from going on the warpath when Sarah Winnemucca returned from California filled with a desire to help her father's people adjust to their changing environment.

As she was able to speak both English and Paiute, Sarah became an interpreter. By winning the friendship of Nevada's governor, James W. Nye, she also won many concessions for her people. But inevitably, the pressure from the miners, the settlers, and the overland stage companies forced the authorities to transfer the Paiutes north to the state of Oregon where they were quartered on Malheur reservation.

Sarah Winnemucca meanwhile had married a Lieutenant Bartlett, who had been stationed at Fort McDermit, Nevada. When Bartlett was dismissed from the service and departed for the East, Sarah followed her father's band of Paiutes to Malheur and became a schoolteacher there.

For several years she worked earnestly to improve the condition of the Indians, but the corruption of the agency officials finally led her to plan a visit to Washington where she hoped to present her case before the highest authorities. She had traveled as far as Camp Lyon, Idaho, when she received news that the Paiutes had suddenly left Malheur reservation to join the Bannocks.

The Bannock Indians, led by Buffalo Horn, had in 1878 departed their reservation and returned to the Camas Prairie of southern Idaho, where they were holding war dances and collecting stolen horses and weapons to drive out the settlers. Seeking allies among the tribes in nearby reservations, Buffalo Horn had found willing listeners among the Paiutes at Malheur. In spite of the younger Winnemucca's protests, the braves of his band went to join the Bannocks, forcing their unwilling chief to go with them.

Realizing that her people were doomed to destruction as soon as General O. O. Howard could gather his armies, Sarah Winnemucca hurried to Silver City, where she found Captain Reuben F. Bernard in charge of Howard's first attacking force. She persuaded Captain Bernard to hold off his fight with the Bannocks until she had made an attempt to bring the Paiutes out of Buffalo Horn's camp. "The people of Winnemucca do not wish to fight the soldiers," she declared.

Under cover of darkness, she approached the Bannock encampment, and by chance met one of her brothers, Lee Winnemucca. He agreed with Sarah that the Paiutes should withdraw from their alliance with the bellicose Bannocks. He suggested that she exchange her usual neat dress for a squaw's blanket, and together they crept into the camp, found their father, and led most of the Paiute warriors away before the Bannocks knew what was happening.

"Princess" Sarah Winnemucca remained with General Howard's staff for the remainder of the Bannock campaign, serving as a scout and interpreter. Afterward she and her father traveled in the East where she lectured and wrote articles and a book about her people. She was married for the second time in 1882, to a Lieutenant Hopkins. When he became ill of tuberculosis, she took him back to Nevada where she bought a tract of land near Lovelock and opened a school for Indian children.

When Hopkins died in 1886, Sarah Winnemucca abandoned her school and her career, and finished out her life penuriously near the village of Monida, Montana.

●   ●   ●

Ouray the Arrow was the chief of the Uncompahgre Utes of Colorado, a chief by virtue of inheritance rather than by prowess in battle. Ouray preferred talking to fighting. He liked to talk so well that he learned both English and Spanish, and would sit for hours conversing with any traveler who might stop to listen. After Ouray joined the Methodist Church he discontinued using profanity along with hard liquor and tobacco, but even under these self-imposed handicaps to loquacity he was known far and wide as an accomplished conversationalist.

Ouray's dislike for battle may have arisen as the result of an encounter with the Sioux about 1860. In this fight he lost his only son. Thereafter he was a man of peace.

In 1862 he settled down on Los Piños agency, earning what was then a comfortable salary of five hundred dollars per year as an official government interpreter. The Utes meanwhile were scattering all over Colorado, and were being blamed for most of the Indian trouble in the Rocky Mountain region.

To bring these wandering bands together, the government officials recognized Ouray as chief of all the Utes, drew up a treaty at Conejos on October 7, 1863, and assigned land and hunting ground boundaries to the tribe. The garrulous chief thus suddenly became a man of power and affluence. The Utes lost most of their deer-hunting grounds, but some of the more enterprising turned to raising goats instead of hunting deer.

The Utes had long been friends of Kit Carson, and when the old scout came to Colorado after the Sand Creek Massacre of 1864, he and Ouray became inseparable companions. The massacre of Black Kettle's Cheyennes in 1868 had created a dangerous situation in the gold country, and Carson's unofficial assignment was to act as a peacemaker and molder of treaties.

Ouray, who looked upon Carson as something of a god, was of considerable assistance to the scout in helping to quiet the rebellious Indians. In turn, when Ouray wanted to suppress an uprising led by a subchief, Kaniatse, Carson volunteered to assist in the action. Afterward they went to Washington together on a treaty junket, a journey which must have been a continual round of tale spinning, as Kit Carson was as magnificent a talker as Ouray.

The chief's prestige among his people was lowered in 1872, however, when an attempt was made by the government to recover a large portion of the land given to the Utes in the treaty of 1863. Resisting at first, Ouray suddenly changed his mind and signed away the territory. As soon as the Utes discovered that Ouray had received a thousand dollars per year for life and a fine farm and a house in exchange for giving away their hunting grounds, they accused him of betraying his deer-hunting brothers.

An indirect result of this disillusionment was the Ute War of 1879. When hostilities flared up on the White River reservation, Ouray commanded the warriors to come in and surrender their arms. Instead of obeying, the angry Utes attacked a troop of cavalry and killed Major Thomas Thornburgh and a number of his command. They then swarmed upon the buildings of the agency to massacre agent Nathan C. Meeker and his men and to carry off Mrs. Meeker and her daughter.

The fury of the Utes had been aroused by the policies of Meeker, an eccentric experimentalist who had come out to Colorado some years earlier to found a cooperative community at Greeley. He developed a set of theories on how to "civilize" the Indians, and had found an opportunity to test his ideas in 1878 when he was appointed agent at the White River reservation. "I propose to cut every Indian to bare starvation point if he will not work," announced Meeker enthusiastically. The Utes, who had been feeding and clothing themseles on the products of their hunting trips, did not find it easy to obey the strong-willed Meeker, who ordered them to move into log cabins and plow the fields and raise crops. When Meeker started playing off two chiefs, Jack and Douglas, one against the other, he was setting his own death trap.

It was Douglas who led the massacre. Meeker was shot down in his living room, dragged into the courtyard, and staked to the ground with an iron tent pole.

Ouray, the peacemaker, was powerless to stop the war (though Mrs. Meeker and her daughter were later released through the intercession of Ouray). The Utes were driven back to the stronghold of the Roan Mountains of Utah. It was here in a desolate wasteland that the deer hunters finally were locked upon a reservation named for their chief.

But Ouray did not go there to join his people. He who preferred talking to fighting stayed on his comfortable Colorado farm with his wife, Chipeta, until he died like a white man in 1880.

. . .

Since the days of the Lewis and Clark expedition, the Shoshones had always been proud of their friendship with the whites. Sacajawea, the legendary Shoshone woman, had accompanied the explorers westward from Fort Mandan on the Missouri to her people's country beyond the Rockies.

In the same winter of 1804–05 that Sacajawea joined Lewis and Clark, there was born among the eastern Shoshones of Montana a boy called Shoots Straight. When he was old enough to kill his first buffalo, Shoots Straight made from the skin of that animal's pate a rattle filled with stones which he kept as a charm. And from that time his people called him Washakie, "the Rattler."

As a young man, Washakie was a great warrior, leading the braves of his band in many battles against the Blackfeet and the Crows. By 1840 he was well known among the trappers, and the Hudson's Bay Company employed him seasonally as a guide in the Green River country of Wyoming. He was tall and handsome, a man of dignity.

During the peak of overland emigration following the opening of the Oregon Trail, Washakie ordered his followers to become friends with the whites. There are numerous accounts of amicable meetings between the travelers and the Shoshones, who went out of their way to help the wagon trains safely across fords. Though the migrants' straying livestock often ruined the Indians' root and herding grounds, animals captured by any of Washakie's band were always dutifully returned to the rightful owners.

But by the spring of 1862, the Bannocks who lived in the same area were beginning to raid the smaller emigrant trains. Seeing the plunder that the Bannocks were obtaining with such ease, some of the Shoshones joined in the attacks. Washakie warned them, "You are all fools. You are blind and cannot see. You have no ears, for you do not hear. You are fools, for you do not understand. We can make a bow and arrows, but the white man's mind is strong and light."

Taking his loyal followers to Fort Bridger, Washakie waited until General Patrick E. Connor had defeated the marauding Bannocks and Shoshones at Bear River. When the contrite survivors of this affair came in to Washakie's camp, the chief met them with cold dignity. He asked one of them: "Who are you?" The beaten Indian replied: "I am a Shoshone." Washakie shook his head and declared: "You have been whipped. Shoshones are never whipped. You are no Shoshone." The penitents, however, were taken back into the fold, Washakie believing that they had learned their lesson.

Not long afterward the Shoshones were given a reservation near Fort Bridger, and after the Sand Creek Massacre of 1864, Washakie agreed to take in the fleeing Arapahoes and Cheyennes. His Green River country was becoming a peaceful refuge.

But the whites' trails and telegraph lines and finally the hated railroads were swiftly ruining the once lush hunting grounds. Fearful of what his people might do if pressed too far, Washakie went to agent Luther Mann at Fort Bridger and asked for a new reservation, off the routes of the western travelers. His reputation for peace and loyalty won for the Shoshones one of the most beautiful sections in Wyoming, the Wind River valley.

In 1868, the treaty was completed. When informed of its approval, the chief declared: "I am laughing because I am happy, because my heart is good. Now I see my friends are around me, and it is pleasant to meet and shake hands with them. You have heard what I want. The Wind River country is the one for me. I want for my home the valley of the Wind River and lands on its tributaries as far east as the Popoagie, and want the privilege of going over the mountains to hunt where I please."

Before the move was made, however, the chief chanced to overhear some of his younger braves arguing about his prowess as a warrior. Some of them said he was too old to remain as the chief of the mighty Shoshones. "He is too old to win victories in battle. He is an old woman who will not even scalp his victims. War blood no longer flows in his veins."

This talk angered Washakie, but he said nothing to the young braves. He quietly disappeared for two moons, reappearing suddenly at the campfire one evening with seven scalps in his possession. He may have talked of peace with the white men, but the Blackfeet and the Crows were still his mortal enemies. "Let him who can do a greater feat than this claim the chieftainship," he said, lifting the scalps above the heads of the young braves. "Let him who would take my place count as many scalps," His abilities as a warrior were never questioned again.

After he became the undisputed ruler of the great Wind River reservation, Washakie's policy was to treat all Indians who warred against the whites as his enemies. The U. S. Army showed its appreciation by changing the name of the fort on the reservation from Fort Frederick H. Brown to Fort Washakie.

Although Wind River and Fort Washakie were far off the main trails, many travelers made the long journey by stagecoach from Rawlins to visit the Shoshones' beautiful country. The Shoshones would stage dances for visitors and soldiers.

In the late spring of 1876, when General George Crook was preparing for the battle of the Rosebud, Washakie sent eighty-six of his best scouts to assist the bluecoats. Three weeks later he arrived himself, leading two hundred warriors. When he arrived at Crook's headquarters, he was wearing a giant headdress of eagle feathers sweeping far along the ground behind his pony's tail. The government, he said, had been generous to him. He would now show that the Shoshones never forgot a kindness given.

As the years went by he became a nationally known figure, a patriarch among the Indians of the West. He never allowed horse thieves or vagabonds to find refuge among his tribe. He became a devout Episcopalian, and tried to set what he thought was a correct moral example for his people.

When Washakie died in 1900, the adjutant-general of the U.S. Army ordered that he be given a military funeral, the first ever given to an Indian. The procession is said to have been the largest in the history of Wyoming, a mile and a half long, the mounted Indian police, the agency employees, the soldiers and officers of the U.S. Army, and all the Shoshones and Arapahoes of the reservation following behind the flag-draped casket.

In the granite of his monument were chiseled these words: "Always Loyal to the Government and to His White Brothers."

CHAPTER 20
The Saga of Dodge City

▲ ▲ ▲ ▲ ▲ ▲ ▲ ▲ ▲ ▲ ▲ ▲ ▲ ▲ ▲

ON THE WESTERN FRINGES of the shifting trail towns, the camps of the white buffalo hunters were becoming more numerous. Small trading centers, established for the hunters, soon were mushrooming into towns.

For centuries the buffalo had served as a source of food, clothing, and shelter for the plains Indians. When the whites first pushed westward, and for many years afterward, they considered buffalo unworthy of exploitation. Finally, when the fur trappers had practically exterminated the beaver and other animals, they turned to the buffalo for skins.

One of the great hunters was William F. Cody, who won his legendary name, Buffalo Bill, during this time. After the Kansas Pacific Railroad reached Hays City, the contracting firm needed a good buffalo hunter to supply meat for the railroad laborers. Cody was recommended by Wild Bill Hickok, and the contractors offered him five hundred dollars a month if he could supply enough buffalo meat to feed the hungry men. Buffalo Bill worked for the company for seventeen months, and by his own count killed 4,280 buffalo during that time. The railroad workers are said to have given Cody the name that stayed with him the remainder of his life.

Many of the famed peace officers of the trail towns also began their careers as buffalo hunters, including Wyatt Earp, Jack Bridges, Pat Garrett, and William Barclay (Bat) Masterson.

Experienced buffalo hunters knew how to fire so as to keep a herd milling, bringing a new target into place after each shot. Favorite weapons of the hunters were Springfield "needle guns" and the Sharps rifle, which were sometimes used with telescopic sights and placed on tripods because the barrels became so hot from continuous firing. Needle guns received their name from the long firing pins which plunged through paper cartridges to strike the primers. Buffalo Bill used a Springfield which he called *Lucretia Borgia*, and he preferred firing from horseback. He would ride to the head of the herd and turn the leaders until he had the buffaloes revolving in a circle. Then he shot the animals which broke off in a straight line. A good hunter could average between fifty and a hundred buffalo killed per day.

When it was discovered that buffalo hides made excellent machine belting, demand and prices increased sharply. The railroads extending across the plains made possible economical shipments to the Eastern markets, and cattlemen welcomed and assisted in the obliteration of the buffalo herds which supported the Indians and also interefered with their cattle.

The railroads had split the buffalo into two great herds. In 1870, four million buffalo roamed south of the Platte; a half million were on the northern plains. Between 1871 and 1875 practically all of the southern buffalo were slain. The slaughter not only wiped out the buffalo, it also ended the civilization of the plains Indians. But it was a boon to the cattlemen.

During the period of greatest slaughter, a bill was proposed in the Texas legislature to protect the buffalo from the hunters. General Phil Sheridan, who wanted to destroy the buffalo herds in order to subdue the Indians, appeared before the legislature to oppose the bill. He predicted that the passing of the buffalo would herald the greatest era of the cattle trade. "Your prairies can be covered with cattle, and the cowboy will follow the hunter as a second forerunner of an advanced civilization." Sheridan's prediction proved true. Even before the last of the buffalo had vanished, cattle herds began moving into the millions of acres of grassy buffalo range.

In the early days of the slaughter, buffalo skinning was considered an ignominious trade, but as wages increased skinning became more respectable. In a hunting party only one or two men used rifles, the others being skinners. Skillful skinners could "peel" a large buffalo in five minutes.

After a buffalo skin was removed, it was pegged to the ground and left in the sun to dry. In his autobiography, John R. Cook tells of having at one time two thousand hides stacked up and drying; "890 of them I had skinned and was so credited," he says.

The spirit of the buffalo hunters' camp is expressed in these lyrics of "The Buffalo Skinners":

> . . .*buffalo hump and iron wedge bread,*
> *All we had to sleep on was a buffalo robe for a bed.*

On the Santa Fe Trail five miles west of Fort Dodge, Kansas, a sod house was erected in 1871 to serve the buffalo hunters of that area. The place was known as Buffalo City. When the Santa Fe Railroad's construction gangs arrived in 1872, they found beside the old Santa Fe Trail a general store, three dance halls, and six saloons. On all sides were huge piles of buffalo bones, not then considered to be of value.

The town now bore the name of Dodge City, after Fort Dodge. Dodge, the old-timers called it, and they fondly hailed the place as "the cowboy capital." Dodge was also the last and longest lived of all the Kansas trail towns.

Wright & Rath were the largest shippers of buffalo hides in Dodge, sending out 200,000 hides to Eastern markets the first winter the Santa Fe Railroad reached Dodge City.

Dodge was a ready-made trail town. Two veteran buffalo hunters, Ed Jones and Joe Plummer, had hauled buffalo hides north from Texas, and their trace was soon converted into a route for cattle herds. Originally known as the Jones and Plummer Trail, it soon became the Dodge City Trail, and later the Western Trail. Before its glory was ended the great Western Trail ran all the way from Bandera, Texas, through Dodge City to Ogallala, Nebraska, and on across the Sioux reservations in the Dakotas to Calgary, Canada.

In the Texas buffalo-hunting grounds where Jones and Plummer operated, another hide trading center developed around Fort Griffin. At this supply base, F. E. Conrad's general merchandise store sometimes averaged sales of $2,500 daily in guns and ammunition to buffalo hunters.

"The town of Griffin," wrote a reporter for the Galveston *News*, "is supported by buffalo hunters and is their general rendezvous in this section. The number of hunters on the ranges this season is estimated at 1,500. We saw at Griffin a plat of ground of about four acres covered with buffalo hides spread out to dry, besides a large quantity piled up for shipment. These hides are worth in this place from $1.00 to $1.60 each. The generally accepted idea of the exciting chase in buffalo hunting is not the plan pursued by the men who make it a regular business. They use the needle gun with telescope, buy powder by the keg, their lead in bulks and the shells, and make their own cartridges."

Early cattle drivers on the Dodge City Trail usually funneled their cattle north through Fort Griffin, seeking protection from marauding bands of Comanches. Below the hill where the fort stood was "the Flat," a small cluster of adobes and frame shacks on the Clear Fork of the Brazos.

Nearby were the Tonkawas, friendly Indians, who evidently believed the cattle herds were replacements for the buffalo killed by the white hunters. It was said that more beeves were lost to the friendly Tonkawas than to the unfriendly Comanches.

Few cattle drivers passed Fort Griffin without stopping over at the Bee Hive Saloon, which had on its front a honeysuckle-bordered sign:

Within this hive we're all alive
Good whiskey makes us funny,
So if you're dry come up and try
The flavor of our honey.

Gambling was the favorite relaxation for drivers and buffalo hunters, and faro was the popular game.

During its heyday, Fort Griffin's "Flat" boasted some remarkable characters, including the ubiquitous John "Doc" Holliday and his strong-willed inamorata, Big Nose Kate Fisher. Doc Holliday was originally a Georgia dentist, a thin, haggard-faced man with deep-set blue eyes and a neatly trimmed mustache. He had come west to Texas in hopes of improving his tubercular condition, opened an office in Dallas, and then turned to gambling. Wyatt Earp said that he once saw him bet ten thousand dollars on the turn of a card.

In Fort Griffin, Doc Holliday teamed up with Big Nose Kate Fisher, who in spite of her name was a rather attractive although fiery-tempered dance hall girl. One night in January 1878, Holliday killed Ed Bailey in a fight over a poker game, and the Fort Griffin marshal, for lack of a jail, imprisoned the gambler in a hotel room. Learning that Bailey's friends were planning a lynching party for Holliday, Big Nose Kate packed their belongings in a bag, secretly obtained two fast-footed horses, and then set fire to the rear end of the hotel in which her lover was imprisoned.

As soon as everybody in Fort Griffin ran to fight the flames, Big

Nose Kate went to Holliday's room, threw down on the surprised guard with her six-shooter, disarmed him, gave Holliday the gun, and then hurried him out to the waiting horses. By the time the fire was out, the redoubtable pair was miles away.

The most mysterious inhabitant of Fort Griffin was Lottie Deno, a good-looking, red-haired gambling woman. She lived in a cottage alone, and received no visitors. The cattlemen, who called her "Mystic Maude," learned to respect the lady's gambling abilities. But she remains a mystery, vanishing completely when she left Fort Griffin.

With its continual cattle traffic, Fort Griffin became a boomtown. As the buffalo disappeared, many of the hunters turned to outlawry. To combat them, masked vigilantes were organized. Horse thievery was considered so heinous a crime that the vigilantes discontinued placarding the dead with their names. Instead they labeled the victims "Horse Thief No. 5," "Horse Thief No. 6," etc., and left them to swing anonymously from the trees along the Clear Fork.

From Fort Griffin the drovers headed north, striking Red River at a place which came to be known as Doan's Crossing. At this point, Judge C. F. Doan and his nephew, Corwin Doan, opened a large store, selling whisky, guns, ammunition, saddles, and blankets. It was a favorite stopping place for Texas cattlemen throughout the lifetime of the Western Trail.

The Bar X Ranch, owned by English investors, was near Doan's Crossing. One day in 1887 a company emissary, Arthur James Balfour, arrived unannounced on the mail stage. He stepped off the stage, a faultlessly dressed Britisher, and walked into Doan's Store. After purchasing a pair of duck overalls, a big hat, boots, and a red bandanna, Balfour retired to a back room and changed costumes. When he arrived at the Bar X Ranch, he asked for a job as cowhand and got it.

During the next ten days, Balfour learned why the ranch was earning no profits for his colleagues. Returning to Doan's Store, he changed back to his English gentleman's costume, summoned the manager of the ranch, fired him, and cabled information to England which saved his company a considerable fortune.

North from Doan's Crossing, the next base on the Western Trail was Camp Supply in Indian Territory. From this army center, used by George Custer during his operations against the southern Cheyennes, the remainder of the route to Dodge was over a well-traveled wagon trail, worn deep across the rolling prairie.

One of the first cattlemen to make the long drive over this trail from

Texas through Dodge City and beyond to the Sioux country was James H. Cook. In 1876, while still a young cow waddy, Cook helped drive a herd from the Nueces River deep in southeast Texas all the way to the Dakotas. It was the first great herd of cattle to be driven through western Nebraska. The cattle were to be used to supply reservation Indians.

While camped on the Niobrara River, Cook and his companions were caught in the backwash of the Custer defeat on the Little Horn. A party of Sioux warriors swarmed down on the cowboys and charged their camp, "a yelling, screeching line of riders, beautifully painted and nearly naked. Some had rifles and pistols, but the greater part were armed with bows and arrows. Most of our little band felt, I think, that our time on earth would soon be ended; but, as the Indians did not shoot, none of us pulled a gun. They were all riding bareback, and they certainly made an impressive picture. Their impetuous rush soon brought them upon us, and they formed a complete circle about us. One old warrior with a badly scarred face dashed up almost to my feet, where he pulled his horse to a sudden stop."

The warrior wanted to know what the cowboys were doing in his country. Cook, who had learned a few words of Sioux, told him that he and his companions had just driven a herd of cattle to the Indians on the Missouri River. "My Lacota [Sioux] friends have bad hearts," said Cook. "But they must not kill the cowboys who bring the cattle which the Great Father sends to them, or the soldiers will come in great numbers and with many big guns and wipe out the Sioux nation."

Immediately the Indian turned to his war party and explained what the white men were doing. "Yells of 'How! how!' came back to him from every direction. Packing our camp outfit on our ponies, we started in to round up our saddle horses and drive them across the river, the entire band of Indians helping us. Their mood had changed, and there were many 'How's!' exchanged as we parted on the south side of the Niobrara."

·   ·   ·

In addition to seeing new country and experiencing new adventures, trail drivers on the Western Trail were also handling a new breed of cattle. The scrawny Longhorns were still plentiful, but they were gradually being displaced by a crossbreed of rangy Durhams, later known as Shorthorns. Texas cattlemen were also importing Hereford bulls from Kentucky where Henry Clay had introduced them in 1817. A crossing of Herefords with Longhorns added as much as three hundred pounds to the weight of the steers, and "Whitefaces" instead of "Longhorns" would soon become the symbol of trail cattle.

Trading center and "capital city" of the trail was of course Dodge City, a fabulous town of innumerable legends for a golden decade. Its sprawling collection of false-front wooden buildings was a familiar sight to thousands of cowboys throughout the West. Its saloons and gambling dens and theaters—Beatty and Kelley's Alhambra Saloon, the Dodge Opera House, Delmonico's Restaurant, the Alamo, the Long Branch, the Comique, the Lady Gay—were known from the Rio Grande to the Canadian border.

The legendary Long Branch Saloon was owned by Chalk Beeson and Bill Harris, with Luke Short running the gambling concessions. Under its ornate chandeliers, Doc Holliday once saved Wyatt Earp's life; in its entranceway, Clay Allison and Earp once threw down on each other to begin a bloodless feud; and over one of its gaming tables, a celebrated faro dealer, Cockeyed Frank Loving, killed a gambler in a quick gunfight.

It was in the Long Branch that Luke Short employed the first female pianist to perform in a Dodge saloon. Naturally she drew all the cowboys from the other saloons, including the Alamo, which was owned by the mayor, Ab Webster. Mayor Webster had his council pass an ordinance prohibiting female piano players in Dodge saloons, and as soon as Luke Short discharged the young lady, the mayor had the law repealed and gave her a job in the Alamo.

By the late 1870s, Dodge was the center of the cattle trade. Its reputation was international, with half a million cattle moving through its shipping yards every year. And, as a veteran trail driver once declared: "Dodge was a town with the hair on!" One of the hotels, borrowing from Mark Twain, posted the following rules:

This house will be considered strictly intemperate.
None but the brave deserve the fare.
Persons owing bills for board will be bored by bills.
Sheets will be nightly changed once in six months—oftener if necessary.

Boarders are expected to pull off their boots if they can conveniently do so.

During Dodge's first big season, twenty-four men were killed in gun battles. Its famed cemetery, Boot Hill, was founded in 1872 as a burial place for slow-triggered gentlemen and satin-slippered ladies. Among the interments recorded are such personages as Horse Thief Pete, Broad Mamie, Pecos Kid, and Toothless Nell.

Boot Hill was a rocky elevation northeast of Dodge. Other towns had their Boot Hills, but Dodge claims credit for first use of this term. According to Paul Wellman, the phrase "Red Light District" also originated in Dodge, red glass being used in the entrance of one of the favorite honky-tonks, the old Red Light House south of the tracks. Other words still surviving in the American language which can be traced to Dodge are *stinker, stiff,* and *joint* (in the sense of a place). *Stinker* was first applied to buffalo hunters for their odor after handling partially rotted buffalo hides. *Stiff* was used to describe the frequently seen dead men lying on the streets. And the Dodge City *Times* originated the word *joint* in referring to the numerous saloons in the town.

To stop the practice of "killing a man for breakfast every morning," Dodge's solid citizens imported veteran peace officers from other trail towns. Wyatt Earp was town marshal for a time, and William Barclay (Bat) Masterson was sheriff of the county. The riding of animals into stores, saloons, and dance halls was expressly forbidden.

But Dodge's reputation for wildness did not die easily. Newspapers in former trail towns fanned the legend with tall stories. The Dodge City *Times* itself reported: "Miss Frankie Bell who wears the belt for superiority in point of muscular ability, heaped epithets upon the unoffending head of Mr. Wyatt Earp to such an extent as to provoke a slap from the ex-officer, besides creating a disturbance of the quiet and dignity of the city, for which she received a night's lodging in the dog house and reception at the police court next morning, the expense of which was about $20. Wyatt Earp was assessed the lowest limit of the law, $1."

Floyd B. Streeter has told the story of the drunken cowboy who boarded the Santa Fe train at Newton. When the conductor asked for the fare, the cowboy handed him a fistful of money.

"Where do you want to go?" asked the conductor.

"To Hell," replied the cowboy.

"Well, give me $2.50 and get off at Dodge."

．　　　．　　　．

Some of the law dogs who finally tamed Dodge City were Mysterious Dave Mather, Bill Tilghman, Pat Sughrue, Frank McLean, Charlie Bassett, Bat Masterson, and his brother, Ed Masterson.

Bat Masterson was Dodge's favorite, a calm, well-dressed, blue-eyed man, a veteran buffalo hunter and an artist with a Colt forty-five. Before he came to Dodge, Bat was a civilian scout with the army. In a dance hall at Mobeetie, Texas, a jealous army sergeant shot and killed the girl with whom Bat was dancing, wounding Masterson in the leg. As he hit the floor, Bat pulled his gun and shot the sergeant through the heart. When the soldier's friends tried to mob Masterson, Ben Thompson came to his rescue. During his Dodge City days, Bat repaid Ben Thompson for the favor by rescuing his brother Bill Thompson from the wrathful citizens of Ogallala, Nebraska. Bill had been badly wounded, and the Ogallala citizens were waiting for him to recover so that they could hang him. Slipping into town secretly, Masterson engineered a sham battle in a dance hall just as a passenger train was pulling into Ogallala. During the commotion, Bat smuggled Bill out of his hotel bed and carried him to the train. Next morning they were in North Platte, where they stopped over at Buffalo Bill Cody's home until a team and stage could be commandeered into Dodge. It was a masterful escape.

On another occasion, Bat Masterson was called upon to protect a minor rascal, a certain Dr. Meredith who came to Dodge to lecture on phrenology and miscellaneous diseases. Having had rough experiences with cowboys in other trail towns, Dr. Meredith persuaded Bat to act as a sort of bodyguard during the lecture. The Lady Gay Theater was rented for the evening, and Bat introduced the speaker to a large audience.

The good doctor began: "Ladies and gentlemen, I have been asked to—"

"You lie!" shouted a voice from the audience.

The doctor turned, glancing appealingly toward Sheriff Masterson. Bat stood up. "I'll shoot the first man that interrupts this gentleman again," he cried.

As soon as quiet was restored, the doctor began: "Several prominent citizens of Dodge—"

"You lie!" shouted the voice again.

Bat jumped up. "I meant what I said," he shouted. "The next time this gentleman is interrupted, I'll begin shooting."

Once again, Dr. Meredith started his speech. And a third time he was interrupted by the cry of the dubious listener.

Instantly Bat drew his revolver and shot out the lights. A crash sounded as a window was smashed. The Lady Gay was filled with yells, and other shots were fired. When the pandemonium ceased, Bat lighted a lamp. The Lady Gay was empty, except for Dr. Meredith, who was crouching under the speaker's stand. Some chroniclers of this event have implied that the entire affair was prearranged by Bat and the man in the audience. At any rate, Dr. Meredith's lecture was good for many a joke around the saloons of Dodge for the remainder of that shipping season.

Long after his tour of duty as sheriff, Bat Masterson became a friend of President Theodore Roosevelt, was appointed deputy United States marshal in New York City, and ended his days as a sportswriter on the *Morning Telegraph*.

Drawn to Dodge City by the romance of its living legend was Edward Fitzgerald, a New York stage comedian. Adopting the name of Eddie Foy, he first angered, then captivated the rugged but sentimental cowboys.

As Eddie Foy was arriving in Dodge City with his partner, Jim Thompson, he noted from the train window the enormous piles of buffalo bones. He thought the gunmen were killing people in Dodge faster than the bodies could be buried.

At first the cowboys resented Eddie's fancy clothing, his strut, and his jokes about them. In typical frontier fashion they roped and hauled him from the stage of the Comique (always pronounced *Com-ee-cue* in Dodge). Then they tied him to a horse and threatened to hang him from a tree. If he was frightened, Eddie Foy showed no evidence of it, continuing his jokes all the while. The cowboys liked his spirit, and for many months afterward they packed the Comique Theater, begging for encores of Foy's specialty, "Kalamazoo in Michigan."

Shows usually began at eight o'clock and lasted until after midnight. At one end of the hall, you could hear throughout the performances the noise of the inveterate gamblers—the click and clatter of poker chips, balls, cards, dice, and wheels.

"All around the room," said Eddie Foy, describing the Comique, "up above, a sort of mezzanine, ran a row of private boxes—and they were boxes, indeed! As plain as a packing case!—where one might sit and drink and watch the show. When the various stage performances were over, there was dancing which might last until four A.M. or daybreak."

Another Easterner who came to Dodge about this time, seeking fortune and fame of another kind, was Edward Z. C. Judson, who wrote blood-and-thunder fiction under the name of Ned Buntline. His dime novels about Buffalo Bill were winning a small fortune for both writer and subject.

Buntline sought out Wyatt Earp as a possible successor to the great Cody. Earp proved to be such a rich source of material that Buntline expressed his gratitude by presenting the marshal and his deputies with forty-five-caliber six-guns fitted with barrels twelve inches long. "Buntline Specials" they were called, with the word "Ned" carved in the handles.

Wyatt Earp once had to use his Buntline Special to tame Clay Allison of the Washita. Allison, credited with twenty-one killings, rode into Dodge purposely to smoke up the town, and to take Wyatt down a notch. Clay Allison had quite a reputation, too. In Canadian, Texas, he once stripped naked except for his holster and belt, then rode whooping through the main street. Allison was a Tennessean who never forgot that he fought on the Confederate side in the Civil War. He was six feet six inches tall, quick as a cat, wore his wavy black hair long, had dark blue eyes, and kept his short beard and mustache neatly trimmed. Fastidious in his dress, he affected contrasting blacks and whites, and usually rode either a white or a jet black horse.

When the dashing gunman rode into Dodge, he found Wyatt Earp standing in the entrance of the Long Branch Saloon. The two men exchanged fewer than a dozen words. Allison had his fingers around his revolver and had drawn it out of its holster, when he felt Earp's Buntline Special pressing into his ribs. It was just about a tie draw.

Earp backed slowly away.

"Reckon I'll be going," said Allison.

"Go ahead," replied Earp. "And don't come back."

But Clay Allison did come back a few days later, to prove he wasn't afraid of a Yankee peace officer. He transacted his cattle business in short order, and was not often a visitor to Dodge again.

Another Dodge City celebrity was John H. (Doc) Holliday. After he and Big Nose Kate Fisher had run afoul of the law and fled from Fort Griffin, Texas, they came to Dodge, which was just beginning its boom period as a trail town. Wyatt Earp took a liking to the gaunt, pale-faced Holliday, and in 1878 the gambler saved the marshal's life. When a band of cattle rustlers tried to gang up on Earp in the Long Branch Saloon, Holliday coolly stepped to the gun rack, removed his revolver, and broke up the party by shooting one of the rustlers in the shoulder. He then helped herd the outlaws across the street to the jail. Earp never forgot that incident. When he later went to Tombstone, Arizona, he took the sad-faced gambler with him, and there they fought together in one of the Southwest's bloodiest gun battles.

Dodge's mayor during its toughest years was a retired army sergeant, James H. Kelley, a former orderly of Colonel George Custer, who for some reason became known as "Hound" Kelley in Hays City. When he moved to Dodge, he established with P. L. Beatty the Alhambra Saloon and Gambling House, and also operated the Dodge City Opera House and a dance hall. In Dodge, he was known as "Dog" Kelley.

One of Mayor Kelley's good friends was Dora Hand, an actress whose real name was probably Fannie Keenan. Dora Hand sang with Eddie Foy on the stage of the Comique, and in several bars and honky-tonks. More than one legend exists as to her identity. Some said she was from an old Boston family. Others said she had sung in European opera. She was popular with both townsfolk and visiting cowmen, and frequently was invited to sing at weddings and funerals.

Dora Hand was living in a house owned by Dog Kelley when a feud between Kelley and Jim (Spike) Kennedy resulted in her tragic death in 1878. Believing Kelley to be asleep in the house, Kennedy fired into the actress's room, killing her instantly.

Dora's funeral was the most magnificent in Dodge's history. Instead of being buried on ignominious Boot Hill, her coffin was carried to Prairie Grove. Practically every dance hall girl, gambler, cowboy, gunman, businessman, and rancher in the vicinity followed the hearse to the cemetery.

Wyatt Earp and Bat Masterson chased Spike Kennedy for a hundred miles, captured him, and brought him back to Dodge for trial. Kennedy was freed, however, after he proved to the satisfaction of the judge that Dora Hand was not the person he had intended to kill.

CHAPTER 21
The Beef Bonanza

▲ ▲ ▲ ▲ ▲ ▲ ▲ ▲ ▲ ▲ ▲ ▲ ▲ ▲ ▲ ▲

ONE REASON FOR THE LONG REIGN of Dodge
City as the cowboy capital was the development of a great new grazing
area in the Texas Panhandle during the 1870s.

Texas ranchers had known for a long time that this short-grass country
was ideal for cattle. With the passing of the great buffalo herds and the
removal of the Comanches, a vast ocean of tufted velvet grass suddenly
became open for ranching. In 1875, Fort Elliott was established on
Sweetwater Creek as a deterrent to Indian raids from the north. That
same year a rancher left Colorado and started driving remnants of his
herd south to Texas. He was a victim of the Panic of 1873, and his name
was Charles Goodnight.

Charles Goodnight's career as a cattleman had begun long before
the Civil War. As a boy of eleven he rode a horse bareback from Illinois
to Texas, and by 1857 was running a herd on the Palo Pinto range along
the Brazos. When other Texans began driving their cattle north in 1866,
Charles Goodnight decided to try the western market. He knew beef
was scarce and brought high prices in New Mexico, where there were
many soldiers on army posts and many Indians on reservations.

Forming a partnership with Oliver Loving, he gathered a mixed herd
of two thousand cows and steers. In June 1866, the two partners and
eighteen cowpunchers started their historic drive over the abandoned
route of Butterfield's Overland Mail.

For this hazardous journey, Charles Goodnight constructed what was
probably the first chuckwagon. He bought the gear of an old army
wagon, and had it rebuilt with the toughest wood he knew, a wood
used by the Indians for fashioning their bows—Osage orange or *bois
d'arc*. The wooden axles were replaced with iron, and for lubrication

a can of tallow replaced the usual army tar bucket. Instead of horses
he selected alternate teams of sturdy oxen to draw the wagon. At the
rear of the bed he built a chuckbox with a hinged lid which dropped
to form a cook's work table. Duplicates of Goodnight's chuckwagon
were soon seen on all the ranges and along the cattle trails. (Over the
years the wagon changed very little, still carrying the chuckbox with its
hinged lid and compartments, and up front the cowboy's bedrolls and
the simple tools needed on the range.)

Driving south to avoid the Comanches, Goodnight and Loving forced
their Longhorns for three days over eighty miles of the waterless Staked
Plains to the Horsehead Crossing on the Pecos. When the thirsty herd
smelled the river they became unmanageable. Several were drowned
in the stampede, and so many dashed into the Pecos at once that the
flow of the waters was blocked for a time.

After resting for three days, the herd swung north along the Pecos,
fording the stream at Pope's Crossing, and then trailed on north to Fort
Sumner, New Mexico. The gamble on the western drive paid off better
than either Goodnight or Loving had expected. Although the government contractor at Fort Sumner would not take the eight hundred
stocker cattle in the herd, he paid eight cents a pound on the hoof for
the steers, a fabulous price in those days. The beef was needed to feed
several thousand starving Navajos, recently placed in the government's
keeping at Fort Sumner by the famous scout Kit Carson.

While Goodnight hastily returned to Texas with twelve thousand
dollars in gold to buy more cattle, Oliver Loving continued toward
Denver, herding the unsold cows and calves. When Loving drove into
the Raton Pass, he was stopped by a tollgate chain. The tollgate was
guarded by a sly old scout named Richard Lacy Wootten, generally
known as "Uncle Dick." Wootten had constructed a crude road through
the pass and put up a tollgate and roadhouse. To Loving's chagrin,
Uncle Dick demanded ten cents toll on each head of cattle. Loving
probably got his money back, however, when he sold the herd for
stocking to John W. Iliff of Colorado. The following year, while Charles
Goodnight was driving another herd to Colorado, he had to pay the
same toll. But in 1868 Goodnight outfoxed Uncle Dick by scouting a
new route through Trincheras Pass.

The routes used by Goodnight and Loving soon became standard
cattle trails to New Mexico and Colorado, and were known as the
Horsehead Route and the Goodnight-Loving Trail.

The partnership of Oliver Loving and Charles Goodnight ended in

1867 after a tragic occurrence on the trail they had opened to New Mexico. Comanches attacked their herd near the Horsehead Crossing, stampeding most of the cattle. To further complicate matters, a thunderstorm broke suddenly. After a night of danger and confusion the trail drivers found the herd split into two sections, with Comanches on all sides.

Because of delays in rounding up the scattered Longhorns, Oliver Loving and "One-Armed Bill" Wilson rode toward Fort Sumner to notify the government contractor that the cattle would come through later than promised.

Riding only at night and hiding in the brush during the day, Loving and Wilson made fair progress for two days. At noon on the third day, Loving suggested that they continue without waiting for darkness. They had seen no Indians along the route, and no evidence of any recent raiding parties. But they had traveled only about ten miles when they saw a band of Comanches swarming down from the Guadalupe Mountains. Spurring their horses, the two men made a dash for the Pecos, and took cover in a brush-bordered ditch. They were armed with six-shooters and rifles, and carried considerable ammunition, but there were almost a hundred Indians in the party.

After surrounding Loving and Wilson, the Comanches began firing. Then as darkness fell, one of the Indians called out in Spanish, proposing surrender terms. The trapped white men decided to talk. While Loving covered the rear, One-Armed Bill moved up into view of the enemy. Immediately a bullet crashed into Loving's hand and side. Wilson dropped back into the ditch cover, firing at the charging Indians until they retreated.

Loving took care of his wounds as best he could, but as night fell he grew too weak to help defend their position. Meanwhile the Comanches began dropping arrows perpendicularly into the ditch, at the same time showering the men with stones.

Believing that he was dying, Loving finally convinced Wilson that he should make an attempt to escape under cover of darkness. The escape of Wilson is one of the classics of Western adventure. One-Armed Bill, carrying his long Henry rifle, crawled down the ditch to the river, where he saw mounted Comanches in the shallow stream waiting for him. Three times he attempted to pass them submerged; three times he withdrew, once because of the slight movement of a horse, twice because a cunning Comanche rider kept thrusting his foot down into the stream. Finally Wilson crawled under some overhanging brush along the bank and drifted in the mud until he was safe in the current beyond the watching Indians.

Through rocky, cactus-studded country, under a burning sun, he walked on foot for miles, always wary, until finally he met Charles Goodnight and the herd. Wilson's eyes were swollen, his feet cracked and bloody, and but for his one arm, Goodnight would not have recognized him.

A relief party was formed immediately, and with Goodnight leading rode hastily back to the scene of the fight on the Pecos. But when they reached the ditch where Wilson had left Loving, they found nothing but hundreds of arrow shafts and piles of stones hurled by the Comanches. Rainfall had obliterated all footprints. One-Armed Bill Wilson believed that Loving had shot himself and that his body had been thrown into the river by the Comanches. Everyone gave him up as dead.

But Oliver Loving was not dead. For two days he had held out against the Comanches, against the pain and fever of his wounds, against the gnawing pangs of hunger. The Indians showered him continually with stones and arrows, and even attempted to tunnel through the sand bank into his position. Finally on the third night of his stand, half-crazed with fever, he crawled down to the river as Wilson had done, and miraculously escaped. For three more days he wandered. Once he stopped and tried to cook his buckskin gloves for food. He was in a stupor when a German immigrant boy and three Mexicans found him.

They took Loving to Fort Sumner, where several days later Charles Goodnight found him, standing inside the fort with one arm in a sling, watching the trail drivers come riding in. The pleasures of reunion, however, ended shortly afterward. Gangrene affected Loving's arm, and the only doctor in Sumner was called upon to amputate it.

After the operation, Goodnight did not like the looks of the severed artery. He sent a man on relays of horses all the way to Las Vegas for a trained surgeon. But nothing could save Oliver Loving. He died after securing a promise from his partner to have his body removed to Texas.

Goodnight kept his word. He ordered the cowboys to gather empty oil cans from the fort's dumping ground, and had them flattened and soldered together to form a tin coffin. In this crude casket, Oliver Loving went home to Texas over the trail he had helped to blaze. For more than sixty years, Charles Goodnight kept Loving's photograph on his ranch house wall.

With Oliver Loving gone, Charles Goodnight continued his cattle drives to Colorado. In 1868 he made a drive to Cheyenne, selling his herd to John W. Iliff. He ranged cattle in New Mexico on the Bosque Grande, an area later taken over by John Chisum, a man to be linked later with the name of Billy the Kid. The two men were friends, and Goodnight trailed thousands of Chisum's cattle northward.

During the winter of 1869, Goodnight selected a sheltered valley in Colorado on the Arkansas River above Pueblo, and decided to locate his home ranch there. The next year he married Mary Ann Dyer, and for three years prospered as a rancher, irrigation promoter, and banker. But the Panic of 1873, in Goodnight's words, "wiped me off the face of the earth." He spent two years trying to recover, then turned back to Texas for the greatest venture of his life.

He remembered the unbroken miles of grass on the Staked Plains, recalled canyons, springs, and small streams he had seen at scattered intervals. He knew that most of the buffalo were gone, and that the danger of the Comanches was now practically ended.

After assembling a herd of about two thousand cattle in the autumn of 1875, he accepted as volunteer assistant on the drive James T. Hughes, an Englishman who had come to the United States to learn the business of ranching. He was the son of Thomas Hughes, author of *Tom Brown's Schooldays.* Another partner was J. C. Johnston, a Scot, later director of the Matador Land and Cattle Company. Hughes and Johnston were the pioneers of a small army of British adventurers who would in the next few years assume dominant roles in the development of the cattle trade.

During Goodnight's drive south toward the Texas Panhandle, James Hughes proved to be an excellent cowpuncher, and he found time to keep a diary of the journey.

The army was operating extensively across their path, and loose bands of Indians were everywhere. Goodnight decided to make winter camp near Fort Bascom in New Mexico. He was not certain of his exact destination, and needed plenty of time. He knew he wanted to locate his new ranch somewhere on the Staked Plains south of the Canadian River, but was not sure of the best place.

In the spring of 1876, he started the herd drifting slowly down the Canadian. They moved into the Panhandle, and near Tascosa crossed the river. Here a Mexican trader, Nicolas Martinez, helped Goodnight decide on his ranch site. Martinez had wandered into the cow camp, and during a conversation with Goodnight chanced to speak of the Palo Duro Canyon, an enormous grassy valley where Chief Lone Wolf had once made a stand against the cavalry. Goodnight employed the Mexican as a guide, and they went ahead to see the Palo Duro. As soon as the two men rode up to the edge of the canyon, Goodnight knew it was the place he had been seeking.

Buffalo grass carpeted the valley of the canyon, but to reach the grazing area from the plain the cattle had to be driven single file down an old Indian trail. Goodnight's cherished chuckwagon was taken apart and lowered by lariats.

In the canyon, they found ten thousand buffalo feeding upon the luxuriant grass. Goodnight and his men chased them out, but a guard had to be maintained at the entrance of the canyon to keep the buffalo from returning to this choice feeding ground.

Probably nowhere else could have been found such a natural location for a ranch. No fencing was needed, water was plentiful, the grass was like a velvety green sea. Goodnight named it the Old Home Ranch. It was the first in the Panhandle.

When Goodnight returned to Colorado for his wife, he met John G. Adair, a wealthy Irishman. Adair offered to finance the cattleman in a mammoth venture, and the million-acre ranch which resulted became the famed JA, after Adair's initials.

After the splendid ranch buildings were completed in the Palo Duro Canyon, the Adairs occasionally came to Texas for inspections. Cornelia Wadsworth Adair usually brought a trainload of personal baggage, dozens of maids and butlers, and all the luxuries of the East. What Charles Goodnight thought of these early attempts at dude ranching is not recorded. Perhaps he was not surprised when Mrs. Adair, after her husband's death, became one of the best ranch managers in Texas.

The JA flourished from its beginnings. Goodnight introduced Durhams, the early Shorthorns, but they were unsuited to that country. Herefords proved to be so successful, however, they were given a special brand, the JJ. In five years, the Goodnight-Adair partnership realized a profit of over half a million dollars.

But after eleven years, Charles Goodnight withdrew from the JA. He was ready to finance his own ranch now. Sixty miles from the Old Home Ranch, he selected a ranging area along the Fort Worth & Denver City Railroad. The town which developed near his headquarters was named Goodnight.

One of the experiments he conducted on this ranch was the cross-breeding of buffaloes and cattle. The calves were named cattaloes, but they were unsuccessful as meat producers. He also found time to design a saddle for Western women. In those days no lady straddled a horse; she rode sidesaddle on a piece of Eastern gear strictly unsuited for lively range ponies. After witnessing an accident, Goodnight decided to design a safe sidesaddle, and he persuaded his favorite saddle maker, S. C. Gallup of Pueblo, Colorado, to manufacture a few for sale. The Goodnight sidesaddle was popular immediately, and came into general use in the West.

As he grew older, Charles Goodnight insisted on strict rules for his men. Card playing and liquor drinking were taboo. He particularly disliked mumblepeg, a harmless but time-consuming game popular with the cowboys. Determined to break up mumblepeg, Goodnight asked the Panhandle Cattlemen's Association to forbid the game on all ranches.

Goodnight's punchers either loved him or hated him; they all worked hard to please him. His drives to Dodge City were leisurely marches, so well organized that his steers gained weight on the trail. When range fencing began in the 1880s, he purchased the best equipment on the market, and insisted that each post be set like a rock.

On a diet consisting chiefly of meat and black coffee, and sometimes a box of cigars per day, Charles Goodnight lived to be ninety-three, one of the last of the giants of the old cattle trails. He died in 1929.

Charles Goodnight had pioneered the development of the Panhandle, but a cavalry soldier named James S. Brisbin probably had more influence in generating the beef bonanza of the 1880s than any other single human being.

Before the Civil War, James Brisbin was a Pennsylvania schoolmaster and country newspaper editor. He joined up with the Union army in 1861 at the age of twenty-four, and four years later he was a brevet-general. Brisbin liked army life, and after the war he went west with the Indian-fighting cavalry. During his movements from post to post on the plains, he got a firsthand view of the rapidly expanding cattle trade. He saw fortunes made in a single season, and after years of army service for scanty pay, he was tremendously impressed by the cattlemen who could drive a herd into a reservation and depart the next day with a bagful of money.

General Brisbin figured all the angles, on paper. He sent enthusiastic reports to *Wilkes's Spirit of the Times,* a widely circulated sporting journal. Finally he wrote a book, *The Beef Bonanza, or How to Get Rich on the Plains,* published in 1881. The book had a good sale in this country, and a phenomenal sale in Britain.

To say that Brisbin's prose fascinated his British readers would be an understatement. They were hypnotized by such passages as the following:

> The West! The mighty West! That land where the buffalo still roams and the wild savage dwells: where the broad rivers flow and the boundless prairie stretches away for thousands of miles; where new States are every year carved out and myriads of people find homes and wealth . . . where there are lands for the landless, money for the moneyless. . . .
>
> If $250,000 were invested in ten ranches and ranges, placing 2,000 head on each range, by selling the beeves as fast as they mature, and all the cows as soon as they were too old to breed well, and investing the receipts in young cattle, at the end of five years there would be at least 45,000 head on the ten ranges, worth at least $18 per head, or $810,000. . . . I have no doubt but a company properly managed would declare an annual dividend of at least 25 per cent. . . .

It seemed that every Briton with money to invest was reading Brisbin's book. Several of them had already visited the American West to shoot buffalo, and had seen the possibilities of ranching. Brisbin's *Beef Bonanza* met an unusually receptive public.

One of the first British companies to be formed was the Prairie Cattle Company, Ltd., and it opened the era of big-money ranching in the Panhandle in 1882 with the purchase of Thomas Bugbee's Quarter Circle T for the startling price of $350,000.

Shortly after the establishment of the JA in Palo Duro Canyon, Thomas Bugbee and his wife, Molly, had driven a small herd down from Kansas, moving into a dugout near Adobe Walls on the Canadian. It was the first headquarters of the Quarter Circle T. Molly Bugbee had insisted on bringing along a wooden door, and they used buffalo robes for carpeting the earthen floor. Six years later, the Bugbees sold out to the Prairie Cattle Company for that unbelievable sum of $350,000.

In 1877, a year after the Bugbees settled on the Canadian, Major George W. Littlefield sent a large herd up the trail from central Texas to Dodge City, but the market was glutted that season. Littlefield's trail boss drifted the unsold herd back into the open range of the Panhandle, setting up winter headquarters near Tascosa.

Here was established the LIT, one of the largest "squatter" ranches in Texas. Littlefield never claimed any land rights, but four years later he sold his equipment and stock to the British-financed Prairie Cattle company for more than $125,000.

"That outfit owns all outdoors," Texas cattlemen were now saying of the Prairie Cattle Company. It seemed the British had no end of money. In 1885 they offered Henry W. Creswell one and a half million dollars for his Bar CC, north of the Canadian. They bought up the Cross L's and the JJ Ranch in New Mexico. Within three years, the Prairie Cattle Company had acquired an unbroken range from the Canadian River in Texas to the Arkansas River in Colorado.

Other British investors were also coming into the Panhandle. On 500,000 acres in Dickens, Kent, Crosby, and Garza counties, the Spur Ranch was founded for the express purpose of resale to British capitalists, who were so eager to invest in the beef bonanza. As grazing areas became scarce, the Scotch and English promoters seemed to become more avid than ever. The fad was "to buy at once and repent at leisure." So, in 1882, a group of smart stockmen headed by Colonel A. M. Britton of Colorado organized the Spur, and sold it two years later to a London syndicate at more profit than the absentee owners earned over the next two decades.

And in 1883 the Rocking Chair Ranche Company was formed, a remarkable organization. Principal shareholders were James Gordon, the Earl of Aberdeen, and Edward Marjoribanks, Baron Tweedmouth. "Little England" was soon established in the Panhandle, between the North and Salt Forks of Red River. Headquarters was known as Aberdeen. The Britishers called their punchers "cow servants." The cowboys dubbed the place "Nobility Ranch," and in a few months every outfit in the neighborhood was mavericking cattle from the inefficient Rocking Chair.

Archibald John Marjoribanks, a young relative of Baron Tweedmouth, arrived from London to set things in order. He brought over some English horses, and the cowboys immediately dubbed them "peckernecks." When young Marjoribanks ordered the punchers to address him as Sir Archibald, they rebelled. They took to hiding out on the range where they would wait for Marjoribanks to come galloping by on his English saddle with his scissors-tail coat flying; then the cowboys would charge him, firing off their pistols and whooping like Indians.

One day, as later happened on the Bar X Ranch, Aberdeen and Tweedmouth arrived incognito to find out why the ranch was earning no profits. Although Tweedmouth personally supervised the cattle count, his manager tricked the nobleman by driving the same herd past him several times.

Rustling from the Rocking Chair grew so common that the Englishmen's bloodhounds had to be pressed into service to round up the few cattle left on the sprawling range. When the owners finally sold out, their books showed fourteen thousand head belonging to the ranch. But the final roundup produced only three hundred.

Another ranch that was big and rich from its beginnings was the LX. D. T. Beals and W. H. Bates of Boston pooled their resources and soon had the added backing of a wealthy Scotch-English company for a 200,000-acre range near Tascosa. Charlie Siringo was a cowhand on the LX, and helped drive thousands of fat cattle up the trail to Dodge every season. Siringo later became a range detective, and after his retirement he wrote several books about his adventures, including *A Texas Cowboy,* one of the great classics of the American West.

When Billy the Kid rustled some steers off the LX, Charlie Siringo and a group of punchers from neighboring ranches went into New Mexico in hot pursuit. They recovered some of the cattle, but the elusive Kid got away as usual. William C. (Bill) Moore was the first LX foreman, and he also helped chase Billy the Kid away from the ranch. But later, Moore was suspected of mavericking from the LX himself. In three years he built up a herd which he sold for $70,000, a large sum for a man on top hand's wages. Moore left the LX hastily and disappeared. Many years afterward Charlie Siringo saw him in Juneau, Alaska, but Bill Moore refused to admit his identity.

One of the mail drivers on the stage route from Tascosa to Dodge City was a young man named Cape Willingham. He had learned to punch cattle under Charles Goodnight, and had served for a while as a cowboy detective on the LX when Bill Moore was under suspicion for rustling. Later he became sheriff of the county dominated by Tascosa.

When the Hansford Land and Cattle Company established the huge Turkey Track Ranch near historic Adobe Walls in 1883, Cape Willingham was chosen to boss the outfit. For twenty years he was also the "boss" of that section of the Panhandle, carrying a sawed-off shotgun that stood for law and order. He built for his wife the first frame house in Hutchinson County from lumber hauled all the way from Dodge City. He liked to play poker with his cowboys, and was fond of horse racing. Willingham was once tried for murder as the result of the shooting of a "nester" believed to be a cattle thief, but he received a quick and complete acquittal.

.   .   .

One night in 1878, Henry H. Campbell was attending a banquet in Chicago. He had just sold a herd of cattle at twenty-three dollars a head, cattle that had cost him nine dollars in Texas. By the time his story got around the banquet table, a new cattle company was being formed. H. H. Campbell went back to Texas with $50,000 to found the Matador Ranch in the southern Panhandle.

Campbell bought up a ranging area southeast of the JA headquarters below the Prairie Dog Fork of Red River. His first ranch house was a dugout; his first cattle came from John Chisum's New Mexico range. As soon as the Matador was well organized, Campbell and his wife gave a Christmas ball, inviting all the ranchers and cowboys within a hundred miles. For years, the Matador's Christmas ball was an annual event in the lower Panhandle.

Not long after the ranch was established, Scotch financiers backed an expansion program, and soon the Matador was spreading over the entire Panhandle, even into Montana. Thanks to the efficient management of Henry H. Campbell and his successors, Murdo Mackenzie, Frank Mitchell, and other great cattlemen, the Matador survived droughts, blizzards, and depressions. It was operated by its original owners longer than any other ranch in the Panhandle.

Long before the Panhandle was opened for ranching, a farmer in De Kalb, Illinois, was trying to invent a method for manufacturing barbed wire. The farmer's name was Joseph F. Glidden, and finally in 1874, using an old coffee grinder, Glidden manufactured the first coil barb. The effect of this invention on the Panhandle and all open ranges was such that in a very few years the entire cattle trade was transformed. Barbed wire meant the end of free grass forever.

At first Glidden could not sell his barbed wire to cattlemen, who feared that it would harm their stock. Such influential ranchers as Shanghai Pierce were determined to have nothing to do with it; they said the barbed wire would cut up their cattle and the injured animals would all die of screw worms. When the Texas legislature threatened to make the wire illegal, two extraordinary salesmen, Henry B. Sanborn and John (Bet-a-Million) Gates, were sent as missionaries into the ranching country.

A barbed-wire corral was built in the main plaza of San Antonio, and a bunch of Longhorns were placed inside it. The Texas cowmen were soon convinced the wire would hold cattle satisfactorily and without injury. To prove further the advantages of barbed wire, Glidden and Sanborn established the first barbed-wire enclosed ranch in the Panhandle, on Tecoras Creek in Potter County. Their brand was designed as a panhandle, but to cowboys the design looked more like a frying pan. From the Frying Pan's activities developed the town of Amarillo, now the largest city in the Panhandle.

On Glidden's first visit to the ranch, he was asked: "What do you think of our country, Mr. Glidden?"

"Country's all right," said he, "but there's not enough grass to feed a goose." He did not know that the short yellow-gray, sun-cured grass of the Panhandle was as good forage for beef cattle as the green grass of his Illinois farmland.

When a brisk Texas wind swept off Glidden's high-topped silk hat, a cowboy had to retrieve it with a lariat. Glidden soon returned to De Kalb where his partner, Isaac Elwood, was having troubles with their barbed-wire patents.

Strangely enough, the burning of the Texas state capitol in 1881 started a chain of events which led to the greatest barbed-wire fencing project in history. Texans demanded that their new capitol be the biggest in the United States, with a dome at least one foot higher than that of the national Capitol in Washington. To get it they traded three million acres of Panhandle land to a Chicago group of contractors and financiers.

The Texas legislators who made the swap thought they had the better of the bargain until John and Charles Farwell of a Chicago syndicate formed the Capitol Freehold Land and Investment Company. The Farwells proceeded to wind eight hundred miles of barbed wire around their holdings and soon had the biggest ranch going in the Panhandle.

The ranch was called the XIT, supposedly meaning "ten in Texas" for the ten counties from which the land had been surveyed. Actually there were only nine counties, and Ab Blocker, who designed the brand, said he picked XIT because "it looked good, sounded good, and was easy to put on." Blocker, a veteran trail driver, never worked for the XIT, but when he brought in the first cattle to the ranch on July 1, 1885, the resident manager, B. H. (Barbecue) Campbell, asked him to help design a suitable brand. With his boot heel, Blocker slowly marked off the letters XIT on the ground. While trying out the design on a couple steers, Blocker was informed that the old method of throwing cattle to the ground before branding was frowned on by the ranch owners. They wanted all their stock chute-branded.

Next day, Barbecue Campbell offered Blocker a job on the XIT, but the trail driver declined immediately. "I don't want to work for a ranch that don't know how to brand cattle," said Blocker.

When Barbecue Campbell resigned, following a dispute over policies with the XIT owners, A. G. Boyce became general ranch manager. The XIT soon became so large it was cut into eight divisions, each with a foreman and each designed for a specific function—some for breeding, some for young stock, some for top-grade cattle, and so forth.

Boyce ruled the enormous area for eighteen years, controlling politics in several counties, enforcing the company's unpopular rules against drinking, gambling, and the carrying of firearms. Even the traditional hospitality of the range was forbidden. Travelers crossing the XIT holdings, or riders from other outfits visiting an XIT chuckwagon, were charged for their meals. A. G. Boyce knew that the Panhandle disapproved of XIT policies, but he had his orders and he carried them out to the letter. He was happiest organizing long drives to the XIT pastures in Montana, each year sending about twelve thousand cattle up the Montana Trail through eastern Colorado and Wyoming to Miles City. These were the last great cattle drives from Texas.

XIT cowboys fared better than the average. One division foreman always supplied his men on range and trail duty with ham, eggs, and even butter, a chuckwagon diet undreamed of before the coming of the XIT.

At the peak of its operations, the great ranch was running cattle on a two-hundred-mile range in Texas, on a two-hundred-mile range in Montana, and was trailing them over the twelve hundred miles of the Montana Trail. No other ranch ever equaled this geographic record. Its stockholders, however, never received a penny in dividends from ranching operations. At the turn of the century, the company began selling its acreage to small ranchers and to farmers, and the XIT was no more.

·   ·   ·

A favorite haunt for off-duty cowboys in the Panhandle was old Tascosa, where Charles Goodnight had crossed the Canadian on his pioneering venture in 1876. Tascosa developed rapidly after the coming of the ranches. The town lay in a shady cottonwood grove above the river, and during roundup seasons it became a little "Dodge City," with its Frog Lip Sadies, Rowdy Kates, Panhandle Nans, Midnight Roses, and Box Car Janes.

Billy the Kid made Tascosa his temporary headquarters on several occasions. During one visit, the Kid, Bat Masterson, and Temple Houston, son of the great Sam Houston, engaged in a polite target-shooting match before a large crowd of spectators. For the glory of Texas, Temple Houston won the match and the Kid's congratulations. The Kid was usually on his best behavior while in Tascosa. He used the town as a sort of hideout after stirring up hornet's nests in New Mexico.

But other outlaws were not so well behaved. Toscosa's Boot Hill filled up rapidly in the early 1880s. The town's bloodiest gun battle occurred one night in March 1886, when four LS cowboys rode into Tascosa looking for fun and pleasure. One of them became involved in a quarrel over a dance hall girl and was killed on the street. His three companions pulled their guns, and in a few seconds two of them and one Tascosa resident were dead. Tascosans had a big burying in Boot Hill next day.

The XIT, which had begun to dominate Tascosa, disapproved of such violent practices, and the growth of that businesslike ranch had also doomed the colorful trading town. The XIT fence across 260 miles of land to the north and west of Tascosa soon cut off free access from New Mexico, and the rough-riding punchers from those parts would come no more to h'ist the tarantula juice and lay the dust in their throats.

Tascosa's principal rival in the Panhandle was Mobeetie, a hundred miles to the east on Sweetwater Creek. Mobeetie grew up beside Fort Elliott in the early days of the cattle trade, and its citizens claimed they could raise more hell any day of the week than the inhabitants of Tascosa.

Clarendon, on the other hand, was a highly moral town. No saloons were permitted, but thanks to the paternal protection of Charles Goodnight and other ranchers who liked to keep their cowboys sober, Clarendon prospered. The punchers called it "Saint's Roost." The extreme penalty of the Tascosa court was the sentence ordering offenders "to spend a week in Clarendon."

For a short time after the closing of the range in the Panhandle, Clayton, New Mexico, just west of the Texas line, served as a trail driving point on the new Denver & Fort Worth Railroad. But Clayton's career as a trail town was short-lived. Range fencing recognized no state lines.

. . .

Meanwhile, Dodge City had grown prosperous catering to the Texans, prosperous and perhaps "dandified" as some of the old-timers charged. There was less violence, more concern with cattle prices. In July 1884, some of the early settlers tried to revive the old spirit by staging the first bullfight in the United States.

But Dodge was sophisticated now. A fancy cowboy band was organized to play for the cattlemen's conventions. The band toured in the East, marching in President Benjamin Harrison's inaugural parade. When a newspaper reporter asked J. W. Eastman, the director, why he carried a six-shooter, Eastman replied: "It's my baton."

"Is it loaded?" asked the reporter. "Yes," said Eastman. "What for?" continued the reporter. "To kill the first man who strikes a false note," replied Eastman.

Symptoms of the great cowtown's waning glory were already apparent. Land office business was booming. The "fool hoe men" were on every side. And instead of herding cattle, these new settlers were rounding up jackrabbits.

As early as 1879, Wyatt Earp decided that Dodge was too tame for him. At the end of the season that year, he and Doc Holliday and Big Nose Kate Fisher left for Tombstone, Arizona.

In 1884, cattlemen from the range country suddenly became so concerned over the rapid extension of fences and the growing power of the grangers that they gathered for a convention in St. Louis. Trail drivers everywhere had discovered there were no more open trails to market. They called their meeting the First National Cattle Growers Convention. Ranchers from Texas and the Southwest demanded a National Livestock Trail, to be established by law, extending from Red River in Texas to the Canadian border. It was to be three miles wide, with grazing areas at intervals, and was to be fenced all the way.

The National Livestock Trail died in St. Louis. A Texas congressman introduced a bill in the House of Representatives, but the grangers and the railroads opposed it firmly, and the northwestern cattlemen gave it no support.

The day of the Texas trail driver was coming to an end.

With the closing of the trails, Dodge City's golden splendor declined rapidly. Even during its best years, cattlemen had occasionally driven herds past Dodge's shipping yards to Ogallala, Nebraska, on the Union

Pacific Railroad; and now as Dodge declined, Ogallala boomed. The trainloads of beef from this little town on the Platte were soon creating a new packing center in Omaha.

But Ogallala was only a transition point, a brief moment in the great swing of open-range cattle ranching from southwest to northwest. The beef bonanza which had transformed the Panhandle had also been developing the great plains of Wyoming and Montana.

The last great trail drives from the Southwest were not drives to markets, but emigrations from a closed range to the last great open range in the United States. Thousands of picked young cattle had been going north to flood the grasslands of Wyoming and Montana, the sacred hunting grounds lost by the fighting Sioux and Cheyennes in the late 1870s. Here, like the Indians, the free-range cattlemen would make their last stand.

CHAPTER 22
Billy the Kid

▲▲▲▲▲▲▲▲▲▲▲▲▲▲▲▲▲

BEFORE THE OPEN-RANGE cattlemen made their last stand in the Northwest, a classic tragedy played out its action on the dry ranges of New Mexico, creating an immortal American legend. Chief actor in this drama was William H. Bonney, better known as Billy the Kid.

The story of Billy the Kid and the Lincoln County War begins properly with John Simpson Chisum, feudal lord of the Bosque Grande, a range 150 miles long with 100,000 cattle carrying his Long Rail brand and jingle-bob ear mark. John Chisum was the king of the Pecos. Beside a gushing spring of clear sparkling water, he built a magnificent ranch house, a rambling Spanish adobe with verandas, surrounded by irrigated fields of green alfalfa, blooming fruit trees, and towering cottonwoods—all watered by this priceless spring in the heart of a desert.

Chisum was a veteran of the cattle country. During the Civil War, he had made drives to Shreveport on Red River, and after the war he ventured into a packing business in Fort Smith, Arkansas. He formed a business association with Charles Goodnight, while the latter was driving Longhorns on the Goodnight-Loving Trail.

Gradually Chisum built up his empire, and then brought his brothers, Jess, Pittser, and James, from Texas to help run the vast range operation. In 1875, brother James's daughter, Sallie Chisum, came to manage the busy household of the Jingle-Bob Ranch.

"I knew Billy the Kid during the Lincoln County War," she said years later, after she married her uncle's bookkeeper, William Robert, and became Sallie Chisum Robert. The Kid and his followers had taken refuge on the Jingle-Bob during the bloody fighting of July 1878. "Look out, Miss Sallie, take cover!" the Kid shouted. A bullet just missed her head, drilling a hole through a wash pot in which she was doing her laundry.

In the late 1870s, John Chisum's troubles began multiplying as rapidly as his cattle were increasing in numbers. Rustlers raided his far-flung herds. And as more settlers came into New Mexico, the Long Rail and Jingle-Bob became the target of land-hungry owners of small ranches on its borders.

In 1875 a former army officer, Major L. G. Murphy, established a general store in Lincoln, New Mexico, the trading center for the ranching country. Murphy became leader of the anti-Chisum forces. In a short time he was also operating a flour mill and hotel and, most important of all, a small ranch adjacent to Chisum's.

The Long Rail cowboys were alert. When they suspected Murphy's riders of rustling their cattle, they passed the word along to John Chisum, who went directly to Lincoln and accused Murphy of planning the thievery. Instead of drawing his gun, Murphy laughed at Chisum. After all, he controlled the town of Lincoln, he had elected the Lincoln County sheriff, and for legal insurance he had just retained a brilliant young lawyer, Alexander McSween.

Young Alexander McSween and his wife had recently arrived in Lincoln from Atchison, Kansas. He was a religious man who always carried a Bible in his saddlebags, and was probably the only adult male in the county who did not pack a gun. With Major Murphy as his client, McSween was soon prospering.

When John Chisum caught some rustlers red-handed on his range and brought them into Lincoln for trial, Murphy called on McSween to defend them. The mild-mannered lawyer investigated the circumstances, then refused politely but firmly to have anything to do with the defense. Naturally, he lost his lucrative job as Murphy's attorney, at the same time arousing the bitter enmity of the major.

Murphy's anger turned to rage when John Chisum soon afterward retained the honest lawyer to handle his side of the case.

Into this turbulent setting now came an energetic British character, John H. Tunstall, wearing fancy riding breeches and a checked sporting cap. "The belted earl," the cowboys called him, after his English hunting jacket. Tunstall was fascinated by the New Mexico ranching country, and immediately purchased a spread about thirty miles from Lincoln on the Rio Feliz. He and Alexander McSween soon became close friends.

The two men pooled their resources and built a rival trading store in Lincoln, and they were soon making heavy inroads on Murphy's business. When John Chisum established a bank in the McSween-Tunstall building, Major Murphy knew he would soon have to fight to hold his power in Lincoln County.

Bitterness increased even more when the major accused McSween and Tunstall of embezzling an estate involving a former partner of Murphy. Murphy claimed that the assets of the estate were legally his, and threatened to seize the partners' personal property if they did not turn the money over to him. When McSween and Tunstall refused to budge, Murphy decided to take direct action. Through the sheriff's office, which he controlled, Murphy finally sent twenty armed deputies riding one morning in February 1878 with orders to take possession of the cattle on Tunstall's ranch.

On this day, young William H. Bonney, the Kid, rode headlong into the dispute to begin a period of bloody action that would end his life and at the same time bring into being the cattle country's most romantic legend.

Billy the Kid began his short life in New York City, in the Bowery in 1859, his parents moving west during the Civil War into the violence of border-state Kansas. After his father died in Coffeyville, his mother went to Colorado, there marrying a man named Antrim. They followed the mining camps into New Mexico.

According to the legend, Billy killed his first man at the age of twelve:

> *When Billy the Kid was a very young lad*
> *In old Silver City he went to the bad;*
> *Way out in the West with a gun in his hand*
> *At the age of twelve years he killed his first man.*

A Silver City blacksmith is said to have made a slighting remark about the boy's mother, and Billy killed the man with a knife. After bidding his mother goodbye, he fled to Arizona, drifting into Fort Bowie, where he lived by doing odd jobs around the post. He also became adept at the art of gambling.

Blacksmiths seemed to fare badly at the hands of the Kid. Pat Garrett, who later killed Billy, said that the boy's second victim was a soldier blacksmith at Fort Bowie. This blacksmith was trying to cheat him in a card game.

Fleeing with a gun-packing partner named Jesse Evans, Billy went south into Mexico, and for several months the two lived by their wits and by their guns. They worked out a system of stealing from Mexicans and fleeing north to safety in New Mexico. Then they would rustle a few cattle from the New Mexican ranchers and jump the border back into Chihuahua.

In the autumn of 1877, as the feud between the McSween-Tunstall-Chisum alliance and the Murphy partisans began to wax hot, Billy the Kid rode into the Pecos valley. He was weary of running back and forth across the border, and was looking for a place to settle down for the winter. The Kid never claimed to be a cowboy, but he had trailed so many stolen steers over rough Southwestern trails that he probably felt he could qualify as an accomplished range hand. Just how he met the Englishman John Tunstall is not clear, but it is evident from what followed that Tunstall liked the eighteen-year-old Billy. He gave him a job on his ranch, treated him kindly, and quickly won a loyal friend.

On the chill February morning when Murphy's hired posse swept into Tunstall's ranch and began rounding up the Englishman's cattle, Billy the Kid appears to have been absent from the ranch house. Several versions of the death of Tunstall exist: His men may have deserted him; he may have fired first as Murphy's deputies claimed; or he may have been shot in the back as Pat Garrett later declared.

At any rate, Billy learned of his friend's death before nightfall. In a cold rage he rode into Lincoln to inform Alexander McSween. The lawyer immediately sent some Mexicans out to the ranch, and at dawn they returned to the front of McSween's store with Tunstall's body strapped to a burro.

While Tunstall was being buried, Billy is said to have stood by the grave, clenching his fists and swearing an oath of vengeance: "I'll shoot down like a dog every man who had a hand in this murder."

By noon that day, Lincoln County became a potential battleground. Fifty cattlemen rode in from far distant ranches to rally around Mc-Sween. The bold act of the Murphy faction had crystallized them into forming an alliance. They feared that what had happened to Tunstall might happen to them. Meanwhile, Murphy was supported by several of the small ranch owners, by his political henchmen, and undoubtedly by a sizable group of hired gunmen. A small war was in the making.

Violent action followed swiftly. As Murphy controlled the sheriff's office, McSween and the cattlemen decided to elect Tunstall's foreman, Dick Brewer, a special constable, empowering him to raise a posse to search out and arrest Tunstall's murderers. Billy the Kid of course joined the posse. They captured two of the Murphy men, holding them at the Chisum ranch overnight. On the way back to Lincoln for trial, the two men were killed while attempting to escape. Just how hard they tried to escape will never be known, but they were both shot by Billy the Kid.

On April 1, for a grim Fool's Day trick, Billy got two more of Tunstall's enemies. He hid out behind an adobe wall in Lincoln until four of Murphy's men strolled into his gun-sights. One of them was Murphy's sheriff, William Brady. The Kid took him with his first shot, and then killed one of the remaining three while they were running for cover. Two weeks later, the Murphy forces struck back. Buckshot Roberts, a Murphy gunman, killed McSween's constable, Dick Brewer. Roberts died in the duel, but McSween had to find another posse leader. The job went to Billy the Kid.

Through the summer of 1878, the war continued. A bloody fight broke out in Lincoln in July, almost at the moment a small Murphy army was trying to smoke Alexander McSween and Billy the Kid out of John Chisum's South Springs ranch house. Chisum's cowboys rode in from a distant roundup just in time to break up the siege, and when the Kid heard what was happening in Lincoln he led his posse into town. But they were too late to join in the battle. He and his men barricaded themselves in McSween's big twelve-room house to wait for morning.

At dawn the Murphy forces had the McSween house surrounded, but before an attack could be launched, McSween arrived with thirty-five men to rescue Billy. A few shots were exchanged, then McSween begged for a parley. He wanted to settle the war before any more blood was shed.

McSween got nowhere with his pleas for peace. Shooting broke out again, and the lawyer's house became a fortress. Although there were few casualties, the battle raged for three days. On the evening of the third day, a distant bugle call cut across the rattle of gunfire.

Echoes of the Lincoln County War had finally reached Fort Stanton, and Colonel Nathan A. M. Dudley came riding into town with a company of infantry, a troop of cavalry, a Gatling gun, and a twelve-pounder cannon. Ignoring the combatants, he drew his soldiers up in front of the McSween residence. Both sides ceased firing, and except for the clinking of harness chains and the snorting of the sweated horses, the town was silent after its three days of gunfire.

In his loudest parade-ground voice, Colonel Dudley shouted toward the house: "Mister McSween!"

McSween stepped out in full view of fifty men who would have shot him dead instantly had the cavalrymen not been there. "This fighting must stop at once," the colonel told McSween.

"I have tried to stop it," replied McSween, "but with no effect."

"You can cease your fire."

"The besiegers started this fight," answered the lawyer. "I am being attacked in my own home. My friends and I are fighting for our lives."

The colonel then explained that he could offer no protection to McSween and his men. Murphy's new sheriff, George Peppin, who was leading the attack, had been legally appointed. In the eyes of the army, McSween was outside the law.

"My orders to you," concluded Colonel Dudley tersely, "are to cease firing. If you do not do so, you must suffer the consequences. My troops cannot interfere with the law."

While this conversation was taking place, some of the Murphy men had crept to the rear of the McSween home and set fire to the back porch. By the time Colonel Dudley had moved his troops away, the back room was blazing.

In a vain attempt to stop the flames, the trapped men used their two barrels of drinking water. But the fire had gained too much headway; the walls and roof of the back room were already collapsing.

Darkness was falling as the flames licked into the center of the big twelve-room house. Two men tried an escape. They were dead before they hit the front steps.

McSween decided to surrender himself to the besiegers, hoping that such an act might save the lives of his friends. Taking his Bible in his right hand, he held it up like a talisman of peace. He stepped outside the front door, the bright flames behind him silhouetting his figure for the waiting gunmen. "Here I am, gentlemen," he called. "I am Mc-Sween!" A dozen rifles cracked, and Alexander McSween was dead on the ground.

One by one, the others began dashing out of doors and windows, running madly for the protecting cover of darkness. The roof of the McSween home became a solid mass of orange flame.

Billy the Kid was the last to depart. He loaded and cocked both pistols, noting carefully the positions of the dead lying on the porch, calculating the distance from the door to the back wall of the yard, and then charged out through a choking cloud of smoke.

His pistols were firing continuously. "Here comes the Kid!" somebody yelled, and he was gone, over the wall in one leap and down into the dark brush-grown canyon and the safety of the hills beyond.

The Lincoln County War was now officially ended. McSween was dead. Major L. G. Murphy also was dead, peacefully in bed in Santa Fe where he had gone for medical care shortly before the three-day battle began. With Murphy gone, John Chisum no longer had any interest in the feud. But to Billy the Kid, after the disastrous fight in the burning home of his friend McSween, the score seemed more uneven than ever. He became an avenging spirit, attracting supporters almost as deadly as himself. He determined to search out and destroy every man who had taken part in the siege of the McSween home.

Billy the Kid's private war spread to the cattle ranges. Lonely line riders were dry-gulched, and rustlers were killed in return. The ranch owners, still distrusting the local government, finally called on President Rutherford B. Hayes in Washington to stop the bloodshed. Hayes responded by appointing a new territorial governor in August 1878. The new governor was General Lew Wallace, soldier and novelist.

With the same thoroughness that he was then devoting to the writing of his novel, *Ben-Hur,* Lew Wallace applied himself to studying what he termed the "Lincoln County Insurrection." He took statements from McSween's widow, from Sheriff Peppin, and called in John Chisum for an interview. Finally he decided to have a talk with Billy the Kid, and announced publicly that he would be in Lincoln at a certain time and would grant the young outlaw immunity if he would come in to see him.

Billy the Kid arrived in Lincoln on the governor's appointed hour, packing a rifle across his saddle and a forty-four in his belt. He had dressed for the occasion, wearing a new hat and a fresh bandanna. He stared calmly at Wallace's pince-nez glasses, neat gray mustache, and pointed beard.

"So you are Billy the Kid," said Wallace.

"I am," replied Billy, and they shook hands.

They talked for several minutes, the governor attempting to persuade the outlaw either to give up his arms or to leave New Mexico Territory.

"If I walked through Lincoln without my guns," said the Kid, "I'd be killed so quick I wouldn't know what happened to me. And I'm not leaving. This is my country and I'm staying here."

For all Wallace's efforts, the feud continued. To end it, a tall, soft-drawling buffalo hunter from Texas, Patrick F. Garrett, was named sheriff. Garrett had known Billy in Texas and had always liked him, but he realized as well as the governor that the time had come to stop the killings. The Kid had already slain nineteen men.

Garrett selected a posse of the best deputies in the Southwest, and for months he tracked the Kid like a bloodhound. Finally Billy was cornered in an abandoned stone hut near Stinking Spring. A gun battle followed, but the Kid surrendered and was taken into Mesilla for trial.

His fate was sealed in the grim faces of the jurors. The judge received the verdict, and began intoning the ritual of the sentence: "You are sentenced to be hanged by the neck until you are dead, dead, dead."

The Kid gave the judge one of his impudent cherubic grins, and replied in a high piping voice: "And you can go to hell, hell, hell."

Under heavy guard he was taken to Lincoln and locked in a room above the late Major Murphy's old general store. Taking no chances, Pat Garrett kept him in handcuffs and leg irons.

But on the very day that Garrett left town to arrange the final details of the hanging, Billy made his escape. He persuaded one of the deputies, Johnny Bell, to play a game of monte with him. During the game he pretended to drop a card, leaned forward as if to pick it up from the floor, grabbed Bell's pistol instead, and shot the deputy dead. Crawling to the window, he saw the other guard, Bob Ollinger, running forward across the street. The Kid fired, and Ollinger was dead before he reached cover. The Kid then forced a terrified jail cook to loose the chain binding his leg irons, stole a horse from the county clerk, and rode out of Lincoln at an easy gallop. He had killed his twenty-first and last man on an April evening in 1881.

Once more Pat Garrett took up the chase. He gathered a new posse, and sent riders off to every town in the area to organize other local posses. Eight weeks passed before Garrett smelled out his quarry near Fort Sumner, where Billy had gone to see the "only girl he ever loved."

Garrett set his trap, waiting in the darkness of a bedroom. The Kid stepped inside the doorway, halting quickly as he sensed someone's presence. *"Quien es?"* he whispered.

"He raised his pistol quickly," Garrett says in his account of the final scene. "Retreating rapidly across the room he repeated: *'Quien es? Quien es?'* All this occurred in a moment. Quickly as possible I drew my revolver and fired, threw my body aside, and fired again. The second shot was useless. The Kid fell dead. He never spoke. A struggle or two, a little strangling sound as he gasped for breath and the Kid was with his many victims.''

The day was July 14, 1881.

Six weeks later *The True Life of Billy the Kid* was being sold on the streets of New York. The legend was on its way. Billy may have been only a part-time cowboy, but folklore has made him the foremost range-riding Robin Hood of the American West.

CHAPTER 23
Free Grass in the Northwest

▲ ▲ ▲ ▲ ▲ ▲ ▲ ▲ ▲ ▲ ▲ ▲ ▲ ▲ ▲ ▲

WHILE BILLY THE KID WAS RIDING to his doom in the cattle country of New Mexico, the Indians and their buffalo were being swept from the ranges of Wyoming and Montana, and the sacred hunting grounds were filling rapidly with herds of cattle.

The first overland drive from the Texas cattle country to Montana had come as early as 1866, but after that single venture a number of years passed before Texas cattle again crossed the waters of the Yellowstone River.

Hero of the 1866 drive was Nelson Story. His journey, while not as long in distance as Tom Ponting's eastern drive from Texas to Illinois in 1852, was all overland, and was certainly more fraught with perils, suspense, and high drama.

Nelson Story, born in Ohio in 1838, had gone west to Denver during the Pike's Peak gold rush. When the Colorado boom collapsed, he moved on to Alder Gulch, Montana, and finally struck pay dirt to the amount of thirty thousand dollars. By this time, Story was weary of washing gold, and after converting his diggings into greenbacks, he sewed ten thousand dollars into the linings of his clothes and went south to Texas. He believed the cattle business might be just as profitable and probably more interesting than searching for the elusive yellow metal.

Arriving in Fort Worth, he sank most of his ten thousand dollars in a herd of about one thousand Longhorns, hired a crew of cowboys, and in 1866 became one of that army of hopefuls moving north toward the barricade at Baxter Springs, Kansas. Instead of digging in and battling the Jayhawkers, Story detoured. He remembered how hungry he had been for beef when he was digging gold in Montana, and he was certain he could obtain premium prices for every steer he could deliver to the Northwestern mining camps. He also must have known it was a foolhardy chance he was taking, but he went boldly ahead with his plans.

At Fort Leavenworth, Kansas, he made thorough preparation for the drive, buying an ox-drawn wagon train and loading it with groceries. His little army of cowboys and bullwhackers moved leisurely along the old Oregon Trail across Kansas and Nebraska to Fort Laramie, Wyoming. At Laramie, the army officers tried to persuade him to abandon his plans for going on to Montana. The Sioux and Cheyenne were swarming all over central Wyoming, attacking everything that moved along the Bozeman Trail. The efforts of the army to keep the trail open by building three forts had served only to arouse the tribes and to weld them into a single fighting force led by a wily leader, Chief Red Cloud.

"Red Cloud will stampede all your cattle and probably take your scalps, to boot," the Laramie officers informed Nelson Story.

Story calmly inspected his twenty-seven cowboys and bullwhackers, examined their arms and ammunition, equipped each man with one of the new Remington rapid-fire breech-loaders, and started north.

Near Fort Reno, they met their first Sioux, a war party that boiled up suddenly over a hill. The Indians' hit-and-run punch left two trail drivers badly hurt with arrows. They also cut away a good slice of the herd, leaving the remainder of the Longhorns in a state of stampede.

As soon as Nelson Story and his men had quieted the cattle and taken care of the wounded, they organized a war party of their own to pursue the raiding Sioux. Dusk was falling rapidly, but just before darkness ended the chase, Story and his seasoned trail men tracked the Sioux into their camp. The Indians had the Longhorns bedded down in the center of an arc of tepees.

One of the drivers present on this occasion later said: "We surprised them in their camp and they weren't in shape to protest much against our taking back the cattle." Story also told his son some years afterward that he had never killed an Indian before that night attack. "We had to wipe out the entire group to recover our Longhorns," he said.

When the herd was reassembled, the drivers pushed them north across the Powder River. The summer was waning and Story wanted to move his Longhorns into Montana before snow fell.

At Fort Phil Kearny where the army was centering its sparse forces for an expected autumn attack from the Sioux, Colonel Henry B. Carrington solemnly advised Story to halt his trail drive if he wished to remain alive. All through the summer, Carrington had been losing men, one or two at a time, and he had acquired a high respect for the cunning of Red Cloud's warriors.

When Nelson Story indicated that he would be moving on north despite the colonel's warning, Carrington ordered him to halt the herd and wait for permission to leave the vicinity of the fort.

Story was fuming with impatience, but not wishing to tangle with the army, he started his men to building a temporary corral adjoining the fort. Carrington immediately ordered the corral moved three miles from the stockade. When Story pointed out that this distance would give his men and cattle no protection from the fort in case of an attack, Carrington replied that all the grass near the fort was reserved for his cavalry mounts.

For a few hours, Story brooded over this impasse. The date was October 22, and blizzards could be raging in a matter of days. If he intended to act, he must do so quickly. That evening, after he heard the bugler blow taps inside the fort, he called his men together.

"If we stay here," he said, "the Indians are going to rush our camp some morning and have us all scalped before the soldiers over at the fort know what's happening. If we go ahead up the trail, they may take our scalps, but I don't think they will. All in favor of moving out tonight say 'Aye.' Opposed say 'No.' "

One driver named George Dow said: "No!"

As soon as the word was out of Dow's mouth, Nelson Story had the man covered with his six-gun. "We'll have to tie you up, George, until we're one day gone."

In the darkness, Story and his men hitched their oxen to the wagons, moved the cattle out of the corral, and slipped away north toward the Montana goldfields. Next day, Dow was released and informed that he could return to Fort Phil Kearny. He decided to stay with the drive.

Later events proved Story had been wise in making his unauthorized departure from the fort. Exactly two months after that October evening, Red Cloud's combined Sioux and Cheyenne warriors wiped out a good part of Colonel Carrington's garrison in the historic Fetterman Massacre.

The trail herd made such good progress on the night it left Fort Phil Kearny that Nelson Story decided to finish the journey by night movements, resting by daylight. Before the herd reached the Yellowstone, the Sioux attacked twice, but only one man was killed. The Remington repeaters which Story had purchased at Fort Laramie were too much for the Indians.

On December 9, 1866, Nelson Story reached Virginia City. Near Livingston, on the Yellowstone, he built a permanent corral, and Montana ranching with Texas cattle was begun.

The drive had been a phenomenal success, but Story had made it just in time. For the next decade, the trail south to Texas was effectively sealed behind him. During that time, northern Wyoming was the battleground for the last great wars of the Indians, culminating in the Custer Massacre on the Little Big Horn, and ending with the capitulation of the chiefs and the retirement of the tribes to the reservations in 1878.

.   .   .

While the wars were being fought to a conclusion, Montana ranching developed slowly, the ranch houses scattered widely across the vast territory. The ranges were being stocked with cattle driven eastward from Oregon. The Oregon herds came, of course, from the breeding stock driven west over the Oregon Trail a quarter of a century earlier. Most of the cattle were Durhams, gradually being improved by the introduction of thoroughbred Shorthorn bulls, brought either overland from the East or by boat around Cape Horn. The Montana ranchers found good markets for beef in the goldfield boomtowns such as Last Chance Gulch, which later changed its name to Helena and became the state's capital.

The great flood of Oregon cattle did not come into Montana and Wyoming until the bonanza years of the 1880s. What is probably the earliest diary of a trail drive from Oregon was recorded in 1876 by a seventeen-year-old boy, William Emsley Jackson, who rode that year with a herd from La Grande, Oregon, to Cheyenne, Wyoming. The route followed was to the Fort Hall Indian agency, southeastward to Bear Lake, then eastward to a point on the Union Pacific Railroad near Granger, on over the Continental Divide at Bridger's Pass, and across Wyoming by way of Rawlins and Laramie to Cheyenne.

Jackson left La Grande on May 23, "to go with Lang and Shadley's cattle to Cheyenne. Overtook the herds on Clover Creek and went driving with Lang's herd May 24, for $30.00 a month."

On June 23 for an unexplained reason he was made cook for the outfit, and when they passed near Shoshone Falls he reports regretfully:

"Was within seven miles of the Falls and was greatly disappointed at not getting to see them. The cook could not leave."

Mosquitoes bothered the drivers and the cattle all through the Snake River valley. On July 10, two weeks after the Custer Massacre in Montana, they first heard news of that disaster from a party of Oregon-bound emigrants. Jackson immediately became Indian wary, and the next day after the herd passed through a narrow gap near the American Falls, he commented: "It is said that this was once a favorite place of attack for Indians, and there are about 75 graves there."

On Medicine Bow River they passed a trail herd which had been driven east from Idaho, bound for Laramie. On the Laramie Plain, Jackson stopped his cook wagon at a miners' camp store. "They have for sale a few canned fruits, baking powder, oysters, and some '49' butter, also one jumper, two overshirts, and a pair of overalls, by selling which they seem to expect to get rich, judging from the prices that they ask for them."

Near Laramie, he reported a number of grazing cattle scattered over the plains. It was September now, and all the drivers were complaining of the cold nights. To keep warm they built "rousing old fires" from pitch pine. As they neared Cheyenne, they also complained bitterly of the vast sheep herds which had devoured most of the grass along the route.

At the end of the drive, the Oregon cowboys did not gallop their horses wildly into Cheyenne. Instead they boarded a train at a water-tank stop near the cattle camp, and rode to town in style.

If the Wyoming cow capital of 1876 bore any resemblance to the Kansas trail towns, young William Jackson does not reveal it. "Took a square meal at Ocean Wave restaurant for .25 cents, after which took a shave, a shampoo and a bath, and put on some clean clothes. I left my watch at a jewelers and wandered around through town the balance of the day, looking at the curiosities and works of art. Cheyenne is quite a large flourishing town of probably 8,000 population and is the most convenient shipping point for the Black Hills."

• • •

Ten years before William Jackson made his drive from Oregon, cattlemen were establishing ranches in southern Wyoming and in Colorado. As has been recorded in Chapter 21, Oliver Loving and Charles Goodnight drove Longhorns from Texas to Colorado in 1866 and 1867, and

Goodnight in 1868 sold them to John W. Iliff as stocker herds. Goodnight himself owned for a few years a ranch near Pueblo.

It was John Iliff, however, who became the first "cattle king of the plains." Iliff was an Ohio college man who joined the Colorado gold rush in 1859. He became a trader to the miners, and soon found that the demand for beef in Colorado was much greater than the supply. In a few years he was running herds on practically all the grazing lands in northeastern Colorado. Iliff was one of the first cattlemen to recognize the value of water rights, and by filing strategic claims in the names of all his friends and cowhands, he controlled about a hundred miles along the Platte. Julesburg was Iliff's headquarters. With stocker cattle moved up by the thousands over the Goodnight-Loving Trail, he made a fortune after fattening them on his extensive range by selling the beef to the miners, to workers in railroad camps, and to the government for distribution on the Indian reservations. His cowboys lived in dugouts, scattered up and down the Platte. The earthen floors were fine for playing a favorite game, mumblepeg.

Iliff probably never owned more than 40,000 cattle at any one time; he believed in the quick turnover of his stock. John Hittson, a Texan who came to Colorado during this early period, ran his holdings up to 100,000 head of cattle. But Hittson suffered continually from wholesale rustling, and once had to lead an expedition into New Mexico to recover thousands of his stolen cattle.

John Iliff was one of the first cattlemen to recognize the possibilities of ranching in Wyoming. He is credited with being the second man— Nelson Story was the first—to trail Texas cattle across the Wyoming border. In February 1868, he brought a slaughter herd into Cheyenne, sold part of the beef to local merchants, and shipped the remainder already butchered to Chicago.

In October of the same year, the first Wyoming range herd was established outside Fort Laramie. Two Indian traders, W. G. Bullock and B. B. Mills, purchased this herd in Kansas and Missouri. Their experiences set the pattern of Wyoming ranching for a decade. Indians searching vainly for the vanishing buffalo began raiding the ranchers' cattle, forcing them to establish fortified camps. Until the power of the Indians was broken in 1878, all Wyoming ranches operating north of the Union Pacific Railroad had to be built like small forts.

As the years passed and the Indians began to retreat to the north or to the reservations, the cattlemen pressed forward to the Powder River valley and to the basin of the Big Horns. The winter of 1877–78 finally

saw the breaking of the dam. By 1879 there were enough ranches along
the Powder to organize Johnson County, and thousands of cattle were
being trailed into the watered ranges of the Tongue, the Belle Fourche,
the Greybull, and the Shoshone.

The beef bonanza, which has already been described, was developing
in Wyoming just as it had in Texas. Most of the ranchers moving into
the lush grasslands of the Indians' sacred buffalo country were people
of wealth, or were experienced agents employed by financial syndicates.

Several of the larger Texas companies either moved their holdings
into Wyoming and Montana or established subsidiary ranches. The
brands of the XIT and the Matador came to be as well known in the
Northwest as they had been in the Southwest. The XIT leased two
million acres between the Yellowstone and the Missouri, driving herds
of ten thousand young steers from the Panhandle to Montana for pasture
finishing.

As the bonanza period developed, Wyoming became the mecca for
wealthy and adventurous people from all over the world. English and
Scottish noblemen, German barons and French counts, Harvard, Yale,
and Princeton graduates—all were riding the ranges with the drawling
Texans who also came in large numbers.

It was not unusual to find polo ponies in corrals adjoining cow ponies,
and "postage-stamp" English riding saddles hanging next to lariated
Spanish saddles. The term "remittance man" came from the practice
of ne'er-do-well sons of wealthy Britishers spending all their money and
then awaiting remittances from home. Everything was done on a grand
scale: They brought valets and chefs; they built expensive ranch houses
furnished with imported rugs and chairs; they laid in huge stocks of
fine wines and whiskys. Dress suits were worn to ranch parties, and
one of the many stories still told about that period concerns a young
British nobleman invited to a Christmas dinner by a neighboring
rancher thirty miles away. He went in a dress suit, through a howling
blizzard, and on arrival had to be lifted from his horse frozen like a
sitting statue.

John Clay, a Scot who managed one of the pioneer Wyoming cattle
companies, has left a colorful record of these days in *My Life on the
Range*. The British companies, he says, "were mostly floated in Scotland
and it is simply marvelous how freely the Scottish investors loaded up
with securities of this character."

But somehow the routine tasks of raising cattle were performed, the
everyday work on the range being quite similar to the pattern set in

the Southwest. The clothing and the working gear differed slightly; the terminology of the cowboys sometimes differed considerably. Woolly angora chaps and Cheyenne wing chaps were the fashion in the Northwest. The hats were not only creased differently, they were usually called hats and not sombreros. The Texas "remuda" had become a "cavvy." It was common in both locations for a man to wear a bandanna and opened vest, with a yellow slicker folded behind the saddle in case of rain. Chute branding was more frequently used than in Texas. And instead of single-ranch roundups, several ranchers would combine operations into a general "pool roundup."

But the line riding, the herding, the cutting out, the river crossings, and the drives to market were performed in the usual manner, requiring plenty of muscle, sweat, and hard skillful riding. The trail drives, of course, were much shorter than the old Texas-to-Kansas drives. The Union Pacific and the Northern Pacific Railroads were only a few days away at the most, and the celebrations at the ends of the drives were mild affairs. In the Northwest, the cowhands did most of their town celebrating on customary holidays, such as Christmas and New Year's Day.

By 1880, the Wyoming cattle boom was well under way. Cheyenne, which had become almost a cosmopolitan city, was the center of operations, and the luxurious Cheyenne Club was the headquarters for all the wealthy cattlemen.

The cattlemen's lives fell into a set ritual, geared to spring and autumn roundups. Just before the spring roundups, it was the custom for the ranch owners to gather in Cheyenne for a week of celebrating at the club, then off they rode for a month or so on the ranges. Most of their summers also were spent in Cheyenne, where the club provided practically all the facilities that could be found in any similar London establishment. The management was very proud of the fact that the Cheyenne was the first club in the United States to replace the old gas lamps with electric lights. On its walls hung Albert Bierstadt's *In the Heart of the Big Horns,* and a realistic painting of a huge bull by Paul Porter. The latter had been pierced by a bullet from a critical cattleman's six-shooter. As the club frowned on such exhibitions of exuberance, the wounded bull was retired to a back room.

The Cheyenne Club's exterior was not particularly pretentious, but in the summer its broad veranda would be filled with cattlemen in dinner clothes sipping cool drinks from tall glasses, and probably reading the London *Times.*

Tennis matches, dances, and banquets filled out the summer season. Then, early in the autumn, the cattlemen all disappeared, riding off to their ranches like young medieval knights to lead the roundups. When the cattle counts and the antelope hunts were ended, they came back to Cheyenne, but stopped only briefly this time, just long enough to make arrangements for winter departures to the East, to England, and to the Continent.

The cattle business had come a long way since those first perilous drives from Texas in 1866, across Red River and through the Indian nations to old Abilene town.

. . .

Big-time ranching was also developing rapidly on the western Dakota ranges, where the last dwindling herds of buffalo had retreated to die from the bullets of wealthy sportsmen, who came out on special railroad excursions for the hunts.

A French nobleman, Count Fitz-James, who accompanied one of these hunting parties in 1882, returned to France and related such glowing stories of the Dakota country to his cousin, the Marquis de Mores, that the latter decided to pay a visit to the Badlands and see them for himself.

And so one day in April 1883, the private railroad car of Antoine de Vallombrosa, the Marquis de Mores, was shuttled off on a side track in the town of Little Missouri. Railroad men on the Northern Pacific called Little Missouri the "toughest town on the line." But as succeeding events proved, the Marquis was a fair match for any of the gamblers, trappers, buffalo hunters, and cattle rustlers who ruled the dives of Little Missouri.

A few months earlier in Cannes, the Marquis, a debonair Frenchman, had met and wedded Medora von Hoffman, daughter of a millionaire New York banker. The dowry was said to have been three million dollars, and as soon as he saw the miles of unclaimed buffalo grass awaiting herds of cattle, the Marquis was prepared to invest it all in the Badlands.

He went into action immediately. He was friendly even to the most hostile of the citizens of Little Missouri, and quickly adopted the dress of the country, wearing the widest hats and the most flamboyant bandannas obtainable. He also adopted Western weapons. If the local citizens judged the "crazy Frenchman" to be another foreign tenderfoot, they soon discovered their error. The Marquis had heard of water rights, and by careful placement of claims along the Little Missouri River, he became owner of 45,000 acres which effectively controlled several hundred thousand acres of grazing lands. For this feudal empire, he expended only $32,000. He was soon buying trail herds wholesale, as fast as they could be moved into the Badlands.

The Marquis won no local friends by this action, and when he discovered that Little Missouri disapproved of his plans to build a meat-packing plant as an adjunct to his ranch, he decided to create a new town east of the river. The town was named Medora after his wife, and he immediately began construction of a chateau on an elevation overlooking the stream. The chateau was a frame structure of twenty-eight rooms, lavishly furnished with Oriental rugs and imported Sheraton furniture. To keep the decorations partly indigenous, he included some hand-hewn cottonwood furniture and a few bearskin rugs.

When his wife arrived to manage the chateau, the town discovered that the Marquise de Mores was as dynamic as her husband. The Frenchman's cowboys were soon calling her "the Queen of the Bad Lands." The chateau had a butler, a coachman, a gardener, a laundress, and several chambermaids and cooks.

In Chicago about this time, meat packer Gustavus Franklin Swift was proving that refrigerated freight cars could be used for shipping meat over long distances. The Marquis became interested when he heard the Chicago packer referred to as "that crazy man Swift who believes he can ship fresh meat to local markets." Swift's plan was to slaughter cattle at their points of origin, and save enough in shipping costs to undersell his competitors. If Swift could do it, reasoned the Marquis, then so could he. He would go even farther and eliminate the meat-packing middleman by selling direct from the range to the consumer.

After convincing his wealthy father-in-law and a few Western financiers that his scheme was practical, de Mores organized a ten-million-dollar company which he called the Northern Pacific Refrigerator Car Company. Railroad cars using the latest refrigerating equipment were ordered constructed, and through the summer of 1883 trainloads of building materials rolled into Medora. By autumn the Marquis had his packing plant in operation. It had the most modern machinery available, even a new blood-drying machine which cost him ten thousand dollars. He planned to use the fertilizer by-products in growing fifty thousand cabbages in individual pots under glass, rushing them to early markets for premium prices.

This was only the beginning. He built a large hotel, the De Mores, as well as a theater and a clubhouse equipped with billiard tables and bowling alleys for the use of his cowboys and butchers. Just for a hobby, he established a two-hundred-mile stage line to Deadwood. This transportation project finally won him some grudging support from the Badlands citizens. To operate the coaches, the Marquis employed the local newspaper editor, A. T. Packard, who was a graduate and star baseball player of the University of Michigan. Young Packard was a comparative newcomer also, but the frank reporting in his newspaper, the *Bad Lands Cow Boy,* had won the hearts of his six hundred subscribers in western Dakota.

When de Mores asked Packard to take charge of the line, the newspaper editor protested: "But I never saw a stage or stageline. I don't know anything about stagecoaches." The Marquis replied that he would rather have an honest manager than an experienced one, and Packard accepted the job. Four fancy coaches were ordered, application was made for a mail contract, and fast horses were selected. The coaches were christened "Kittie," "Medora," "Dakota," and "Deadwood," and had "United States Mail" emblazoned upon their sides—although the mail contract was never awarded. Packard succeeded in getting the line into smooth operation, but most of its business was lost in a few months when Deadwood began to decline and rival lines started operations to Miles City. The gaily painted coaches were finally sold to Buffalo Bill Cody, who rechristened all four of them "Deadwood," and wore them out, one by one, in his Wild West Show.

Meanwhile, to assure control of all the major Western markets for meat, de Mores had begun establishing branch slaughterhouses at Miles City and Billings, and took his company right into the center of the big meat-packing competition by building cold storage plants in New York, Chicago, Milwaukee, and other cities.

Just what motivated the Marquis in his grand design is not clear. Legend has it that he was in line for the throne of France and planned to use the wealth gained from his huge cattle operations to finance a revolution and reestablish the monarchy with himself as king.

In the midst of the Frenchman's whirl of activity, violence intruded suddenly when he became involved in a quarrel with three buffalo hunters, Riley Luffsey, Frank O'Donald, and Dutch Wannigan. The disagreement started when de Mores fenced part of his land. In the free-range country, fencing of any kind was considered a public offense, a crime almost as heinous as horse stealing. It was a "nester trick," abhorred by both hunters and cattlemen. But the Marquis wanted his breeding herds fenced in, and the wire was strung across an old trail where the hunters were accustomed to trail their pack horses.

A few days after the work was completed, the fence was cut. The Marquis rode out, inspected the damage, and ordered the holes mended. But the wire snippers immediately went to work again. After repairing the damage once more, de Mores set an ambush for the hunters. As soon as they rode up to his fence, he opened fire, and Riley Luffsey was killed. O'Donald and Wannigan wounded. Feelings ran high against the Marquis in the community. He was arrested, jailed, and then released. The trial dragged on for weeks, during which time the Marquis added twelve thousand sheep to his range, a move which made him more unpopular than ever among the cattlemen. But he was finally acquitted of the murder charge.

The Marquis's mushrooming empire was beginning to totter even before the Great Blizzard of 1887 practically wiped out his herds. His meat business was running a loss of over a million dollars a year, and his alarmed father-in-law, from whose pockets the money was coming, had journeyed to Medora to advise suspension of operations. The Marquis did not capitulate, however, before announcing through the *Bad Lands Cow Boy* one more magnificent scheme for recovering his losses:

Marquis de Mores has completed contracts with the French government to supply its soldiers with a newly invented soup. He intends to visit Europe soon to make contracts with western range cattle companies who have their headquarters there, for the slaughtering of their herds.

But in the spring of 1887, the Marquis with his family and entourage boarded his private railroad car in Medora and departed forever. The chateau and its contents were left almost intact—the twenty-eight rooms of costly furniture, the children's toys, and numerous leather trunks packed with the personal belongings of the charming Marquise.

After returning to France, the Marquis became involved in the Alfred Dreyfus affair, went to India to hunt lions, started a railroad in China, and finally was killed in a battle with Arabs in Africa.

Today his chateau still stands in the midst of the Badlands, a curiosity for tourists. And facing defiantly down the main street of Medora, the town he built, is a bronze statue of Antoine de Vallombrosa, the Marquis de Mores, dressed in the costume of an American cowboy.

．　．　．

A close neighbor but not a close friend of the Marquis de Mores was another man of action, a young New Yorker who was destined to become one of the United States' most colorful presidents—Theodore Roosevelt. A pale, slender, shy young man in his twenties, Roosevelt arrived in Medora in September 1883, about the time the Marquis was building his chateau. He came for a short hunting trip, but stayed for four years. During this period he operated two ranches, wrote several books, and developed his philosophy of self-reliance and direct action.

Although there was some similarity in the natures and tastes of the dynamic Frenchman and the energetic New Yorker, they exchanged visits only occasionally, and toward the end of the Marquis's dizzy whirl across Dakota, he and Roosevelt almost met in a duel. Roosevelt chose to go his own way in the West. He spent most of his spare time writing hunting books and biographies. He preferred the quiet life of the ranch to the hullabaloo of Medora, and soon found that his rough cowboys could discuss books and politics much more picturesquely and quite as entertainingly as the cultured Frenchman.

Only a few days after Roosevelt's arrival in the Badlands, he made up his mind to become a ranch owner. Aware that he knew nothing of the problems involved, he established a partnership with two of his hunting companions, Bill Merrifield and Sylvane Ferris, who already owned a small ranch.

Known as the Maltese Cross, the Roosevelt ranch began operations on a small scale, with about three hundred cattle the first year, increasing to a thousand head in the spring of 1884. As was the practice in the open-range country, the partners owned no land, but filed a claim for grazing rights along a section of the Northern Pacific Railroad.

From Sylvane Ferris, Theodore Roosevelt learned how to saddle a cow pony, and in a short time conquered his intense fear of bucking horses. When he found it necessary to visit Medora he always called on editor A. T. Packard at the *Bad Lands Cow Boy* office. Around a potbellied coal stove in this building, young Roosevelt listened and talked, learning the grassroots politics that would help carry him to the White House a few years later. But he was remarkably slow at learning the terminology of the range country. One of the stories told about him during his first year in the Badlands concerns a phrase he used in ordering a cowboy to head off a steer. Rising in his stirrups, Roosevelt

TEDDY ROOSEVELT

A close neighbor of the Marquis de Mores was another man of action, Theodore Roosevelt. Young Roosevelt arrived in Medora in September 1883 for a short hunting trip, but he stayed for four years. A few days after his arrival, he made up his mind to become a cattleman. (Teddy Roosevelt Collection, Harvard College.)

shouted in his correct Harvard accent: "Hasten forward quickly there!" All the cowhands in hearing distance burst out laughing. They immediately adopted the words as their own, and "Hasten forward quickly there" could be heard ringing on the Maltese range for weeks afterward.

As were all Easterners come to the West, Roosevelt was considered a dude at first, just another tenderfoot. The huge round eyeglasses which he wore soon won him the nickname of "Four Eyes."

It was during his second year in the Badlands that the nickname was altered. On a bitter cold day, Roosevelt had been trailing some strayed horses, and night fell before he could ride back to the ranch house. Because of the weather, he decided to stop in Mingusville, a railroad station which boasted a single combination hotel and saloon.

As he approached the saloon entrance, two shots suddenly exploded inside. A bearded man, obviously drunk, was shambling up and down the floor, carrying two cocked pistols in his hands. He had just shot two holes in the clock above the bar. Most of the men inside were sheep herders, busily pretending they did not know the gunman existed.

"Four Eyes!" cried the drunk as soon as he saw Roosevelt. "Four Eyes is going to set up drinks!"

Roosevelt calmly ignored him, and moved directly toward the stove to warm his hands. "Four Eyes is going to treat us," the gunman began chanting drunkenly. He waved his guns recklessly toward Roosevelt, becoming more voluble and profane by the second.

Roosevelt was unarmed. He finished warming his hands, turned around slowly, and then suddenly delivered a blow that would have pleased John L. Sullivan. Both guns roared, but the bullets went wild. The gunman dropped senseless to the floor.

In a matter of hours, news of the affair was all over the Badlands. It seemed that everyone who heard it delighted in repeating the story. "Four Eyes" became known affectionately as "Old Four Eyes." Theodore Roosevelt was now "one of the boys."

In a few more months he had become "Mister Roosevelt," and some of the Dakota newspapers began booming him as a possible candidate for Congress. Temporarily, however, Roosevelt had had enough of politics back in New York. He let it be known that while he was in the Badlands he was more interested in ranching than in politics.

Selecting an excellent grazing area in the Elkhorn bottoms, he established his second headquarters, the Elkhorn Ranch, and began buying more cattle. Like the Marquis de Mores, he loved the costume of the cowboys. He wore dashing wide-brimmed hats with flat tops, bandannas of fine silk, fringed buckskin shirts, sealskin chaps, and alligator-hide boots. After the affair in the Mingusville saloon, he added two pearl-handled revolvers.

In the spring of 1885, he decided to perfect his knowledge of ranching by participating as an ordinary cowhand in a roundup. He delighted in breakfasting in the cold at three o'clock in the morning, and in riding fifty miles a day. He invented his own lullaby to sing to the cattle when riding night herd. The other cowhands finally forgave him his daily practice of shaving and brushing his teeth. At the end of the roundup, one of them commented: "That four-eyed maverick has got sand in his craw a-plenty."

It was during the time of the Marquis de Mores's legal troubles over the shooting of Riley Luffsey that Roosevelt and the Frenchman almost came to dueling. The indictment of de Mores had been brought about largely through the efforts of Dutch Wannigan, who had been wounded by the Marquis at the time Luffsey was killed. Wannigan was employed on Roosevelt's ranch, and the Frenchman believed that Roosevelt had assisted the cowhand in arranging the murder charge. The Marquis had also been brooding over his meat-packing losses, and he had hinted that Roosevelt might be in league with his enemies, the big packing companies and the railroads.

De Mores finally wrote a threatening letter to Roosevelt, using a phrase intimating that he would like to fight a duel. When Roosevelt replied that he would fight with rifles, the Marquis immediately apologized, claiming he had been misunderstood.

The two men had no more trouble after this. In fact they made their peace and joined forces in one of the Northwest's greatest campaigns against stock thieving, a manhunt which originated in the Montana rangelands.

*   *   *

In the early 1880s, Montana ranchers were suffering heavy losses from cattle rustlers and horse thieves. Horse stealing was even worse than cattle rustling, good horses being scarce in the new range country, and for a time they were better legal tender than gold dust. This situation arose when a multitude of whisky traders swarmed into Montana to sell their potent beverages to the reservation Indians. As the Indians had no money, the liquor traders had to use the barter system, with horses placed high on the list of desirable property for trading. When the Indians had traded in all their own mounts, they began making quick raids on the isolated ranches, chasing off horses faster than the ranchers could replace them. In his diary, Granville Stuart reports a raid in 1881 by Canadian Indians. Twenty-five horses were stolen.

Finally the losses became so severe the cattlemen requested aid from the military posts in the range country. The cavalrymen went into action, chased down the raiding Indians, and recovered a few horses. Stricter reservation policies were then adopted, and the Indians found it more difficult to get out of bounds.

But as soon as the Indians were under control, gangs of white outlaws began operating on a big scale, rustling cattle and horses together. Brand blotching was common in Montana, and intricate designs were invented to circumvent the thieves. Yet at the end of one of the bigger pool roundups in western Montana, the ranchers discovered that three thousand of their cattle had been stolen in one season. As a result of this lawlessness, the ranchers organized the Montana Stock Growers' Association to protect their property. They met in Miles City in April 1883, held a parade, and then settled down to serious business.

Leader of the association was a soft-spoken gentleman from Virginia, Granville Stuart, who had made the first gold strike in Montana in 1858. In the summer of 1879, Stuart organized a cattle-ranching firm in Helena, and after several months of touring through the Yellowstone River valley, he selected a range on what had been one of the Indians' choicest hunting grounds, east of the Judith Basin.

Some years earlier, Stuart had helped wipe out organized stagecoach robbers in western Montana, but he hated unnecessary killings. He proposed to employ stock detectives, one for each county in western Montana, use them to gather evidence, and attempt to convict the thieves in the courts. But after a year's trial, he saw that this plan would not stop the rustling. The legal machinery in Montana in those days was ineffectual, and the cattle thieves began scattering their bases of operation, spreading into Wyoming and the Dakotas, making it more difficult than ever to find them and their stolen cattle. In the lawless country of the Badlands, the thieves began to fatten off the unprotected herds of such men as the Marquis de Mores and Theodore Roosevelt.

One day in the spring of 1884, Roosevelt and the Marquis boarded a train in Medora and rode to Miles City to attend the second annual meeting of the Montana Stock Growers' Association. Recognizing that the problem of stock thieving had spread beyond territorial boundaries,

Granville Stuart had invited them and several other cattlemen from beyond the Montana line.

The first order of business was a demand that a small army of cowboys be organized to search out the rustlers in their hidden cabins and fight them down in open warfare. Roosevelt and de Mores both joined in this demand, but Stuart and some of the older cattlemen blocked the proposal. Stuart pointed out that the rustlers were well armed, and all were desperadoes and dead shots; many cowboys would lose their lives, and those who survived would have to stand trial in the Montana courts for the murder of any rustlers they might kill. Although he did not say so publicly in the stockmen's meeting, the soft-talking Virginian had another plan.

When he returned to his ranch, Stuart found that in his absence the emboldened thieves had stolen his best stallion and thirty-five of his prized steers. As soon as the spring roundup was ended, he called a meeting of fourteen of the most close-mouthed cattlemen in the Northwest. They met secretly at his ranch, and called themselves the Vigilance Committee.

In a few weeks they were known as Stuart's Stranglers. The Stranglers worked methodically. When a stock thief became known, he was tracked down, captured, and quietly hanged. A simple placard labeled "Horse Thief" or "Cattle Thief" was always left fastened to each victim's clothes. The Northwestern newspapers, aware of what was happening, kept almost as silent as the Stranglers. The *Mineral Argus* of Maiden, Montana, commented laconically: "Eastern Montana is rapidly reducing the number of horse thieves."

The Stranglers became so deadly in their efficiency that on some occasions they permitted the names and dates of the hangings of their next victims to be known in advance. A. T. Packard, editor of the *Bad Lands Cow Boy,* once learned that two horse thieves well known in Medora were scheduled to be hanged on a certain Thursday. As that was his press day, he decided to print the news of their executions, being rather confident that the Stranglers would keep their appointed date.

That afternoon as he was putting his mail shipment of the newspaper on the railroad train, the young editor saw the two desperadoes step off the passenger car, very much alive. Packard was more than mildly shocked. He stood there, wondering if the hardened pair intended to stop in Medora, and if so, would they read the current edition of the

Bad Lands Cow Boy? When the train began to move out, the two men stepped back aboard. Packard was immensely relieved. And before the next sunrise, the two horse thieves were dead, as scheduled.

By the autumn of 1884, the Montana and Dakota ranges had been swept clean of stock thieves. No one can say for certain how many men were hanged. Estimates run as high as seventy-five, but hundreds more fled the Northwest, a few, including Butch Cassidy, retreating south to the Hole-in-the-Wall country of Wyoming. A few years later, the ranchers of Wyoming would come to know them as the Hole-in-the-Wall Gang, or the Wild Bunch.

THE LAST SPIKE

Final conquest of the Western plains and mountains was made by the railroads. In 1869 the Union Pacific celebrated its meeting with the Central Pacific at Promontory Point, Utah. The country was now united overland by the first transcontinental railroad, and it would change the West forever. Thousands and thousands of Chinese and Irish had been used to build the railroads. On September 8, 1883, the Northern Pacific, the nation's second overland railroad, had its "last spike" ceremony between Garrison and Gold Creek, Montana. Present at the celebration was Henry Villard. The Crow Indians held solemn council on the spot because, unfortunately for them, the iron horse had come to stay. (Photograph by F. J. Haynes, courtesy of F. J. Haynes Studios, Bozeman, Montana.)

CHAPTER 24
Big Blizzards and Little Wars

▲ ▲ ▲ ▲ ▲ ▲ ▲ ▲ ▲ ▲ ▲ ▲ ▲ ▲ ▲ ▲

AT SUMMER'S END OF THE YEAR 1886, a soft blue haze spread over most of the range country. It had been a dry season; the smokes of many grass fires lay over the land from the Yellowstone River valley to the Big Horns and across the Colorado high plains, eastward down the Platte and south to Dodge City. Over the Texas Panhandle and New Mexico's Llano Estacado, the golden sun burned hot into October. Except for the chill nights, dry warm temperatures kept the cowboys in their shirtsleeves, and autumn came to Indian summer with no break of frost.

In Cheyenne, the Northwestern cattlemen were boarding trains for New York, Boston, and New Orleans. They were gayer than ever. Big ranches and little ranches showed good profits, not the 100 percent profit of the early bonanza days, but money was plentiful enough. The beef market had sagged a little, but almost everyone had added more cattle to cover the price drops, and the grass was still free. The winter of 1885–86 had been a bad one; the range was drier than it should be for top-weight steers. But every year could not be a perfect year. Some of the older cattlemen were making worried talk about overstocking the ranges, but there was still plenty of grassland unclaimed.

The weather was too fine for a person to worry—the days sundrenched, the air pure and crisp and tangy against the colorful splendor of autumn in the West.

But along the upper branches of the Missouri River in Montana, the wild geese and ducks and the songbirds were starting south earlier than usual. For the first time since ranching had started in Montana, white Artic owls appeared on the ranges. When the older Indians saw these strange white birds, they drew their blankets closer and shivered, remembering a winter many moons gone.

The muskrats were building their houses taller and thicker along the creeks; the beavers were working day and night cutting willow brush. In late October the blue haze lifted to high altitudes, creating by day a subdued and unnatural light and by night a ghostly moonlight. The air was dead and still.

Fires burned so much grass on the Montana ranges that Conrad Kohrs, one of Montana's first and greatest ranchers, knew his cattle could not survive the winter. He had established a pioneer herd from cattle collected along the old California and Oregon trails, and operated ranches on the Sun River range and the Tongue River. He asked the Canadian government for permission to move his herds across the line into Canada for grazing. Droughts in Wyoming's Powder River valley brought herds north into Montana, and these in turned moved across the Canadian border.

On November 16, the thermometer fell below zero over the Rockies; a northwest wind broke the long silence of the earth and sky, drifting six inches of fine hard snow across the dry ranges. Native stock stood the storm well, but cattle recently brought up from Texas wandered aimlessly in circles.

Three weeks later, a second blizzard was howling across the Yellowstone country. Stagecoach travel was halted for three days. Then the sun reappeared; Christmas was bright and cheery. The cattlemen who had stayed on their ranches for the winter were optimistic over their New Year's toddies.

But now it was January, the Moon of Cold-Exploding-Trees. For sixteen hours on the ninth day of January, a north wind spewed out an inch of snow an hour; the storm continued for ten days. By January 15, the thermometer was forty-six below zero, and the world was white.

On January 28, the Great Blizzard struck again. For seventy-two hours, it seemed as if all the world's ice from time's beginnings had come on a wind that howled and screamed with the fury of demons. It was a tornado of white frozen dust. When the storm ended, millions of open-range cattle were scattered for miles, dead or dying, heaped against the barbed-wire fences of homesteaders, frozen stiff as statues in solid drifts, drowned in the air pockets of snow-blanketed rivers. The gulches and the coulees were filled with snow to depths of a hundred feet or more, leveling with the land. Ranch houses were completely drifted over.

The cowboys stumbled through snow up to their shoulders, rode floundering cow ponies to drifts where they dug out surviving steers. The men wore all the clothing they could fasten around their bodies; they blacked their faces with burned matches to fight the snow glare; but many a cowboy died in the aftermath of the Great Blizzard.

In Great Falls, Montana, five thousand hunger-mad cattle stormed into the streets, uprooted hundreds of recently planted trees to devour the branches and roots, then they fought each other for bits of garbage thrown into the snow. Eastward in Dakota, hundreds of gaunt and bony steers drifted into Medora, eating tar paper from the sides of the shacks until they dropped and died. Wolves and coyotes roamed the frozen range in packs, howling until their bellies were filled from the easy kills.

On February 11, the Bismarck *County Settler* reported "an appalling loss of human lives in Montana and Western Dakota." All life and movement were suspended. Trains were blocked. Towns were isolated for weeks. Whole families were found frozen to death in their thin-walled cabins; those in dugouts fared better.

On Wyoming's plains the great herds of the cattle syndicates searched desperately for shelter in canyons and under rimrocks, but thousands drifted against homesteaders' fences and died there in frozen masses. The survivors had a chance until a chinook blew warm and melting for one day early in February, then vanished before an Arctic blast that froze the melted snow into an impenetrable sheet over the precious grass.

In western Kansas, 5,000 of a herd of 5,500 cattle died in the storm. The Dodge City *Daily Globe* reported in January: "Within a few miles of here, no less than five hundred cattle have drifted to the river, where they perished in attempting to cross, or drifted up to fences, where they remained until frozen to death. A gentleman from a ranch south of here reports seeing cattle on his way up that were still standing on their feet frozen to death."

Finally in March the sun burned through the cold gray haze. For the first time in weeks over the Northwest ranges, the sky was blue again. A chinook poured warmth down over the mountains, and trickles of melted ice flowed down the slopes, uncovering the brown grass. In a few days the Little Missouri was in flood, rushing out of its banks, its huge ice cakes smashing tall trees in the bottom lands. The river was filled with the frozen carcasses of cattle, rolling over and over in the churning current, bobbing up and down on the crests of the flood waters.

As the snow retreated, the cattlemen could count their losses. Coulees and wooded areas were packed with dead cattle; occasionally a grotesquely frozen steer was found high in a tree's crotch, where it had struggled over drifts to gnaw at the bark and then die.

In Montana, Granville Stuart rode over his range and decided he wanted no more of the cattle business: "I never wanted to own again an animal that I couldn't feed or shelter."

Charles M. Russell, the Northwest's cowboy artist, was managing a herd of five thousand cattle in the Judith Basin during that winter. The ranch owner, who lived in Helena, wrote Russell for a report on the herd's condition. Unable to find words to describe the situation, Russell drew on a postcard a sketch of one skeletal cow, with these words: " 'Waiting for a Chinook,' or, 'The Last of Five Thousand'."

Not until they held their spring roundups did the cattlemen know the real truth, and then "it was only mentioned in a whisper." The roundups were dismal affairs, no joking, no singing, not much talk. No one could take pleasure in cutting out and roping the gaunt survivors of what had once been the greatest range herds in the world.

Through the spring and summer one after another of the great cattle firms closed out or went bankrupt. "From southern Colorado to the Canadian line, from the 100th Meridian almost to the Pacific slope it was a catastrophe," said John Clay. "The cowmen of the west and northwest were flat broke. Many of them never recovered. Most of the eastern men and the Bristishers said 'enough' and went away. The big guns toppled over; the small ones had as much chance as a fly in molasses." The gay young men of Cheyenne lost their zest for cattle raising and departed the country. Banks failed, stockyards closed.

And over this lost land of the buffalo herds reappeared that ghoulish army of a decade past, the old buffalo bone-pickers of the plains, now come to gather all that remained of the great cattle herds. The once flourishing ranges had been transformed into a boneyard for the fertilizer factories.

·   ·   ·

After the winter of the Great Blizzard, only "the men with the bark on" came back to stay on the Northwest ranges. A few of the big cattlemen survived, but in the years immediately following the disaster the grazing lands were rapidly fenced by hundreds of small ranchers homesteading claims. Many of the homesteaders were former cowboys who had lost their jobs with the bankrupt syndicates; others were Eastern farmers who had moved farther west; some were outlaws, such as those driven out of Montana by Granville Stuart and the Stranglers.

Between the Big Horn Mountains and Powder River in Wyoming, the homesteaders soon became a political power, controlling Johnson County, with their headquarters in the county seat of Buffalo. South of Johnson County, the larger companies still ran thousands of cattle, the owners controlling Cheyenne and much of the political power of the state. Through the Wyoming Stock Growers' Association, which had been formed in Cheyenne in 1873, the cattlemen acted to keep the ranges open and to protect their property.

By 1890, friction between homesteaders and stockmen had reached a state of undeclared warfare. The stockmen believed they were entirely within their rights. They had come back after the Great Blizzard; by shrewd management and by risking borrowed capital they had rebuilt their herds. And now, they claimed, these herds were being rapidly decimated by their neighbors, the small ranchers, who seemed to delight in rustling and branding the big companies' stock in wholesale numbers.

The homesteaders, on the other hand, declared that the Cheyenne cattle kings were illegally using the best grasslands, and were invading their homesteads by force with patrols of gunmen.

In the preliminary skirmishes, the stockmen developed a new profession, that of the range detective, or range inspector. The range detectives led lives as dangerous as international spies, and spies they were in effect; most of them were former peace officers or hard-bitten gunmen imported from the declining trail towns of the Southwest. Posing as ordinary cowhands, they secretly watched the homesteaders, reporting any evidences of stock thieving to their employers. At first, charges of rustling were taken to the courts for settlement. To prove brand alterations, the detectives often removed hides from stolen cattle. The inner side of a hide would reveal the original owner's brand, which a clever blotcher with a running iron might have changed and concealed on the outside.

In spite of the best efforts of the range detectives, rustling increased all over Wyoming. Edgar Wilson (Bill) Nye, the nineteenth-century humorist who was editing the Laramie *Boomerang* in the early 1880s, summed up the situation in a single sentence: "Three years ago a guileless tenderfoot came to Wyoming, leading a single Texas steer and carrying a branding iron; now he is the opulent possessor of six hundred head of fine cattle—the ostensible progeny of that one steer."

Modeling a campaign after that of Granville Stuart and his Montana Stranglers, the Wyoming cattlemen arranged a few sporadic hangings. One of them involved a woman named Ella Watson who operated a small saloon in the Sweetwater River country.

Ella, the "Queen of the Sweetwater," was a buxom, good-natured blond. Her business partner was Jim Averill, a pale-faced, scholarly man, who was supposedly a graduate of Cornell University. Jim liked to write letters to the Casper *Weekly Mail,* denouncing the cattle barons of Cheyenne in the libelous language that editors dared to print in those days. As their saloon business prospered, Ella changed her name to Kate Maxwell and purchased a small ranch nearby the saloon. From the evidence of both friends and enemies, it appears that she stocked it with mavericked steers traded to her by cowboys in exchange for her favors.

Cattle Kate's herd increased at such a rapid rate that range detectives were soon swarming around the Sweetwater saloon. Both Kate and Jim Averill were warned to leave the country, but they refused. One night in July 1889, they were seized in their saloon and taken to Spring Creek Gulch, and hanged from a tree, their bodies left dangling over the gulch.

All northern Wyoming was immediately aroused. The Casper *Weekly Mail* reported the loss of its scholarly correspondent in headlines: JIM AVERILL, AN OLD RESIDENT OF SWEETWATER, HANGED TO A TREE. ELLA WATSON MEETS A SIMILAR FATE. CORONER'S JURY FINDS THAT PROMINENT LAND OWNERS ON SWEETWATER COMMIT THE ATROCIOUS DEED.

Six men were accused of the hangings, but no indictments were ever returned; one witness died and the others disappeared mysteriously before they could testify.

Violence spread across the ranges. Hanging followed hanging. In Buffalo, political stronghold of the homesteaders, Frank Canton, a former sheriff who had taken a job with the Wyoming Stock Growers' Association as a range inspector, found himself a virtual prisoner within the town. The homesteaders suspected him of being responsible for several of the hangings. With the aid of four armed friends, Canton finally escaped and fled to Chicago.

To protect their property, the stockmen secured passage of new laws which set definite dates for all roundups, with state inspectors required to be present to oversee the branding. The homesteaders, however, were suspicious of the honesty of the state brand inspectors, and in the spring of 1892 decided to circumvent plans of the stockmen by ignoring the law and holding an early pool roundup in northern Wyoming.

This action was reported to the stockmen, and the Cheyenne Club began buzzing with wild rumors and secret meetings. Within a few days, some of the extremists among the cattlemen formed a society of Regulators, and drew up plans for a military invasion of Johnson County. As their leader, the Regulators selected a former army officer, Major Frank Wolcott, a hot-blooded Kentuckian who owned a large ranch on Deer Creek near the Platte. Wolcott was a stocky, domineering martinet, a master of the quick retort. At dinner one day he offered a visiting Texas cowboy some carrots. The Texan sniffed at Wolcott, and drawled: "We feed carrots to hogs down where I come from." "So do we," said Wolcott. "Have some."

Wolcott's chief lieutenant was Frank Canton, hastily summoned to Cheyenne from Chicago. Canton knew Johnson County better than any of the members of the Regulators, and he was offered a handsome price for his services.

Wolcott and Canton made quick trips to Colorado and the Southwest to hire an army of gunmen, the best that could be found at a salary of five dollars a day and expenses, plus fifty dollars bonus for every homesteader they might kill during the invasion. In Denver, Wolcott rented a special train from the Union Pacific—an engine, one passenger car, one baggage car, and three freight cars. When the train reached Cheyenne on April 6, several stock cars filled with horses were added. During that day, guns, ammunition, dynamite, tents, blankets, and wagons were quietly moved into the freight cars.

Shortly after nightfall, fifty-two men armed with six-guns and rifles boarded the train. Several were well-known citizens of Wyoming; twenty-four were hired gunmen imported from the Southwest. Dr. Charles Penrose signed on as official surgeon. The city editor of the Cheyenne *Sun* and a Chicago journalist went along as war correspondents.

At three o'clock in the morning on April 7, 1892, the little army arrived in Casper, end of the rail line. Telegraph wires to Buffalo were immediately cut, and scouts were sent ahead on fast horses.

Major Wolcott had prepared an exact military timetable, and supposedly a list of seventy homesteaders and rustlers, all of whom were scheduled to die before the "war" was to be declared ended. The timetable called for the army to arrive in Buffalo on April 9, where they would capture and publicly hang the sheriff, William H. (Red) Angus.

As they rode north from Casper under a gray blizzardy sky, what few travelers they met were immediately captured and forced to accompany the expedition, to prevent any news of the invasion being carried ahead of the advance. When they reached the Tisdale Ranch, on the border of Johnson County, Major Wolcott ordered a halt. Bob Tisdale, owner of the ranch, was accompanying the party, and the ranch stop was on Wolcott's timetable.

A short time later, Mike Shonsey, who had been scouting for the Regulators in Johnson County, arrived at the Tisdale Ranch with some interesting information. On the border of the Hole-in-the-Wall country, where homesteaders had established small ranches adjoining the big cattle companies' ranges, Shonsey had discovered two "rustlers" living at the K C Ranch. He said they were Nick Ray and Nate Champion.

Wolcott checked his list of seventy names. They were both there, Ray and Champion. The major held a war council. A side stop at the K C Ranch was not on his timetable and might delay the scheduled arrival in Buffalo. But Nate Champion was an important leader of the homesteaders; he would have to be tracked down sooner or later. Wolcott decided to ride.

Ordering three of his best gunmen to act as guards for the drivers of the slow commissary wagons, he led the remainder of the expedition on a fast dash north to the Powder.

Meanwhile in the K C Ranch house, Nick Ray and Nate Champion were playing hosts to two trappers, Bill Walker and Ben Jones, who had stopped over to spend the night. Champion was a friendly, powerfully built Texan, blue-eyed, sandy-haired, who had trailed Longhorns up the Goodnight-Loving route. Nick Ray was also a former cowboy. The partners had recently leased the K C Ranch, and like most of their neighbors had probably mavericked a few steers from the open ranges south of their spread.

After supper that evening, Champion got out a gallon jug of "snake juice," and trapper Bill Walker unpacked his old fiddle. The four men sat up late—singing, drinking, swapping stories, and looking through a new Montgomery Ward catalog.

Early the next morning, Champion started the breakfast fire and asked Ben Jones to fetch up a pail of fresh water from the river. Jones went out with the pail, but several minutes passed and he did not return. "Maybe you'd better go and hurry old Ben up," Champion said to Bill Walker. "I need water for coffee right now."

Walker strolled down the trail toward the river. He saw a man crouched among the willows near the bank, then noticed that the horses in the corral had their heads up, ears pointed. Walker swung toward the barn.

"Hold it, pardner!"

Five rifle barrels bristled at him from the barn door. He stood in his tracks, astounded, until one of the gunmen brusquely ordered him to come inside, out of sight of the house.

Bill Walker had stepped right into the middle of Major Wolcott's army; they had already captured Ben Jones. And there was nothing the two trappers could do to warn Ray and Champion.

When Ray came outside a minute or two later, he was wounded by a volley from the Regulators' guns, but Champion managed to drag his partner back inside to temporary safety.

Champion was an excellent shot. In the middle of the afternoon he was still holding out against more than forty men. But Nick Ray was dead.

Shortly after three o'clock, Black Jack Flagg, a homesteader and editor from Buffalo, came riding by on horseback, trailing his stepson who was driving a light wagon. Flagg was puzzled over the firing, but not for long. When the Regulators began firing at him, he shouted to his stepson to jump on one of the team horses, then cut the harness, and the two galloped away, heading for Buffalo to sound the alarm. As all telegraph wires had been cut by the invading cattlemen, the Cheyenne and Denver newspapers could print only the wildest of rumors.

Wolcott knew he would have to act fast now if he expected to keep the element of surprise in his timetable. He ordered an old wagon piled high with hay and pitchpine. After setting fire to the hay, four men rushed the wagon against the ranch house. Champion stayed inside as long as he could, then kicked off part of the burning roof and came crawling over the wall, with both his six-guns in action. When he tried to run for cover in a nearby draw, fire from twenty rifles burst upon him.

They found a short diary in one of Nate Champion's pockets, a record which he had kept during lulls in the fighting. He had included the names of some of his besiegers. But before the diary was replaced in the dead man's pocket, these names were cut out with a sharp penknife.

After pinning a placard, "CATTLE THIEVES BEWARE," to Nate Champion's coat, the Regulators rode away behind Major Wolcott, who was shouting: "On to Buffalo!"

At that moment in Buffalo, however, another army was rapidly forming. Rumors of the invasion had reached Sheriff Red Angus before noon, and he had ordered posses formed. When Jack Flagg arrived to substantiate the rumors, the town was quickly transformed into a military base.

Bob Foote, the owner of Buffalo's largest general store, donned a theatrical black cape and mounted a stallion. Foote was a tall elderly man with white curly hair. He rode through the town, his long white beard flowing in the wind, exhorting the citizens to arise. "Come to my store," he shouted, "and get whatever you need for this battle. Fall in line!" He led a parade back to his store, opened it up, and began passing out guns and ammunition. Reverend M. A. Rader, a Buffalo minister, gathered a troop of forty armed churchmen. Arapaho Brown, a veteran Indian fighter, and E. U. Snider, a former sheriff, rode off to summon the outlying homesteaders.

Within a few hours, Sheriff Angus had an army of several hundred men, mounted and armed. The sheriff spent the night trying to get aid from the state militia and from regular army troops stationed at nearby Fort McKinney. But no assistance was offered him.

At dawn on the tenth day of April, Johnson County's army began moving south, as strange an army as ever went to war: the sheriff's regular posse leading the advance, the volunteer homesteaders following.

About the same time, Major Wolcott's Regulators, the Cheyenne stockmen, were preparing to march north into Buffalo. They had spent the night in the T A ranch house on Crazy Woman Creek, fourteen miles south of the town. Advance scouts, however, saw the homesteader army moving toward them, and the Regulators retreated rapidly back to the T A Ranch. In the short time left to them, Wolcott and his men prepared barricades and deployed for a siege.

The battle lasted for two days. Toward the end of the second day, Arapaho Brown began preparing a "go-devil" to finish off the Regulators. He chose a method similar to that used by Wolcott to smoke out Nate Champion. Dynamite surrounded by bales of hay was mounted on a wagon. But just as the homesteaders were moving their crude bomb slowly toward the T A ranch house, a bugle sounded from far up the trail to Buffalo.

No dime novel author ever contrived a more dramatic arrival of the United States cavalry. During the previous night, Wolcott had sneaked one of his best scouts out through the homesteaders' lines; the man had reached Fort McKinney, and now three troops of cavalry came riding to the rescue of the apparently doomed stockmen. The Johnson County invasion ended abruptly.

The United States cavalry had wanted no part of the war, but on orders from Washington, Colonel J. J. Van Horn, commanding the Fort McKinney troops, now had in his custody all the participants on one side of the conflict. Colonel Van Horn refused to turn his prisoners over to the Johnson County authorities; he knew well enough that if he did so, about fifty hangings would follow within a few hours.

The Regulators were taken to Fort D. A. Russell, and held for several weeks awaiting trial. All expenses for guards and food were charged against Johnson County until that county's treasury was exhausted. An application for a change of venue was then made, and the men were transferred to Cheyenne. Here their imprisonment became a farce, the prisoners employing their own guards, moving freely about town during the day and returning dutifully to their imposed jail at night. When the time for their trial came in January 1893, no jurors acceptable to both sides could be found. Finally the case was dismissed, and so ended the Johnson County War.

*　　*　　*

Peace came slowly to the Wyoming ranges after 1893. It was obvious now to everyone that the day of the open range was almost over. Theodore Roosevelt had seen the end in 1888, when he wrote: "In its present form stock-raising on the plains is doomed, and can hardly outlast the century. The great free ranches, with their barbarous, picturesque, and curiously fascinating surroundings, mark a primitive stage of existence as surely as do the great tracts of primeval forests, and like the latter must pass away before the onward march of our people; and we who have felt the charm of the life, and have exulted in its abounding vigor and its bold, restless freedom, will not only regret its passing for our own sakes, but must also feel real sorrow that those who come after us are not to see, as we have seen, what is perhaps the pleasantest, healthiest, and most exciting phase of American existence."

But before the barbed-wire fences sealed off the last of the northwestern trails, one more dramatic actor was to play out a significant role. His name was Tom Horn, and his passing definitely marked the end of the free range.

Tom Horn may have been a member of the Johnson County invasion force, escaping before the showdown at the T A Ranch. Bill Walker, one of the trappers captured at Nate Champion's ranch, later claimed that he saw Horn there, but the statement has never been proved. It is certain, however, that Horn did play a part in preparations for the invasion.

In 1890, after a remarkable and sometimes heroic career as an army scout in the Apache country of the Southwest, Tom Horn had joined the Pinkerton Detective Agency in Denver. Two years later, when the Cheyenne Regulators were planning their raid against the northern homesteaders, he was selected to go to Arizona and employ a few desperadoes to join the invasion army. He also may have gone to Idaho on a similar mission.

In 1893, Horn's reputation for efficiency won him a job as a range detective with the Swan Land and Cattle Company, at that time managed by John Clay. On the company's books, Horn was listed as a cowhand employed to break horses. "I never fathomed his character," said Clay, who told how Horn would come into the ranch office without making a sound, and then after passing the time of day would roll a cigarette, light it, and sit silent for long periods of time, braiding ropes of fine horsehair.

For the next few years, Tom Horn roamed the ranges of several of the big cattle companies as a cowpuncher, covering almost half of Wyoming. Whenever a cattleman suspected rustling, he quietly summoned this tall sunburned man with drooping, sharp-pointed mustaches. "Killing is my business," Horn remarked on several occasions. He operated alone, making his kills with a rifle, leaving two stones under the heads of his victims as a sort of signature. He worked for a flat fee of six hundred dollars. After each killing, it was his habit to drift into Cheyenne or Denver, and go on a big drunk. A silent man while sober, he became unusually loquacious during these periods. While Tom Horn was drunk he talked wildly, bragging of his skill as a killer.

When the Spanish-American War came along in 1898, Horn went to

Cuba as master of a pack train. Many of his old army friends of the Apache campaigns were there, and for him the war was a long lively holiday.

In the spring of 1902, he returned to Wyoming and took a job with John Coble, a wealthy cattleman who operated a ranch north of Laramie near Iron Mountain. Coble suspected that some of the homesteaders who had claims adjoining his ranch were rustling from his stock, and he knew that Horn was the man who could put a sudden stop to the thieving.

Tom Horn took his time, scouting around and studying the neighbors. One day he rode casually up to the farmhouse of Victor Miller and got himself invited to supper. The Millers had a boarder, the Iron Mountain schoolteacher, Glendolene Kimmel, who had recently come west from Missouri. To Miss Kimmel, Tom Horn was a knight in shining armor, the Western horseman she had dreamed of meeting when she accepted her schoolteaching contract.

But the tall killer was wary of schoolteachers. He shied away from Glendolene Kimmel, and concentrated carefully on the Millers, feeling them out about the cattleman John Coble. Although the Millers had heard of Tom Horn's reputation, they spoke freely. They disliked Coble, and considered his big ranch an intrusion. But if they disliked the wealthy stockman, then their feelings for a neighboring homesteader, Kels P. Nickell, were pure hatred by comparison. Nickell and Miller had quarreled over land boundaries, the quarrel finally resulting in a fight in which Nickell had attacked Miller with a knife, wounding him seriously. After he recovered, Miller began carrying a loaded shotgun for protection. One day the shotgun slipped from its position on the wagon seat, went off accidently, and killed one of Miller's sons. Miller told Tom Horn that Nickell was indirectly responsible for his boy's death, and that the score would not be even until one of Nickell's sons had been killed.

Horn listened quietly to Victor Miller's violent talk. He made several return visits, and became more friendly with Glendolene Kimmel. But he was also watching and listening to the Nickell family.

On July 18, Nickell's thirteen-year-old son, Willie, prepared to ride over to the family's sheep camp to spend the night. He told his mother goodbye at the door of the house. Twenty minutes later, two shots from a rifle killed thirteen-year-old Willie Nickell.

They found his body the next day. Two men were immediately suspected of the murder, Tom Horn and Victor Miller. Horn produced an alibi that he had been on a train between Laramie and Cheyenne on the day the boy was murderd. And the Miller family, supported by Glendolene Kimmel, swore that Victor Miller was at home the day of the killing. When she realized that Tom Horn might be endangered because of her testimony, Miss Kimmel immediately reversed her statement, and swore that Victor Miller had been absent from the house. No arrests were made.

Meanwhile the county and state had posted a thousand-dollar reward for the capture of the murderer. A short, plump, mild-mannered marshal named Joe Lefors appeared at Iron Mountain, questioned everybody concerned, and soon made up his mind as to the identity of the killer. He immediately set to work to prove his case. He had known Tom Horn quite well, and did not believe the range detective would deliberately kill a small boy. When Kels Nickell was shot and wounded a short time later, Lefors guessed that Horn had killed Willie Nickell by mistake.

While Lefors was quietly gathering evidence, Tom Horn was in Denver on a big drunk. He finally woke up in a hospital with a broken jaw, the result of a barroom brawl. Some time later he returned to Cheyenne and found awaiting him there a letter from Glendolene Kimmel warning him to beware of Joe Lefors.

Lefors soon found Horn, got him to drinking, then persuaded him to come up to his office to swap some talk in private. The marshal had two deputies concealed behind a thin partition, and while Tom Horn drank and talked out what seemed to be a confession of the Willie Nickell shooting, his words were being secretly recorded in shorthand.

The next morning Tom Horn was arrested. John Coble and other stockmen rallied to his aid; they employed a battery of lawyers to defend him and arranged a trial delay to October, 1902.

On October 12, Cheyenne was crowded with cattlemen and homesteaders from all over the state, come to see Tom Horn's trial. Glendolene Kimmel arrived at the courthouse wearing a red tam-o'-shanter. John Coble was there, and Kels Nickell. Every important newspaper in the West had representatives present.

The trial lasted for two weeks, with sensational front-page news stories every day. Joe Lefors's shorthand record of Tom Horn's conversation clinched the argument for the prosecution. The jury found him guilty of murder in the first degree.

Horn shrugged off the judge's sentence "to be hanged by the neck until you are dead." He was confident his friends would obtain a new trial for him. He sat in his cell braiding intricately designed horsehair ropes. He wrote the story of his life on five hundred large-sized letter pages.

A new trial was denied, but the execution date was postponed. His friends then arranged for a young cowboy to be arrested and confined for a few days in the jail. Through this boy, Tom Horn was to reveal a detailed plan of escape. He wrote the plan on pieces of toilet paper, rolling them into pellets and dropping them into the cowboy's cell.

But at the last moment, the youthful accomplice lost his nerve, and when he was freed he ran to a Cheyenne newspaperman and revealed the plot. The newspaper scooped not only its rivals but also the county sheriff.

Horn decided to escape anyhow. August 9, 1903, working with another prisoner, he overpowered the guards, but before he could get outside the jail, a deputy spread an alarm. When Tom Horn dashed into the streets of Cheyenne, almost all the bells and whistles in town were jangling of shrieking. The veteran of a dozen Apache raids was ignominiously captured by a bluecoated policeman.

On November 15, 1903, Tom Horn's jailer informed him that he would hang five days later. No more postponements had been ordered. But Horn had received rumors that John Coble and an army of cowboys were in Cheyenne, and that Butch Cassidy and the Hole-in-the-Wall Gang had been hired to pull him out of the jail.

The Cheyenne authorities heard the same rumors. The governor ordered a troop of soldiers to patrol the courthouse square. A November blizzard had just swept across eastern Wyoming, leaving temperatures of forty below, but hundreds of spectators came to watch the patrolling soldiers and to see what would happen if the cowpunchers and Butch Cassidy's outlaws came swarming toward the jail.

On November 18, Tom Horn received a secret message that he would be freed on the nineteenth, one day before the scheduled execution. When he awoke on the morning of the nineteenth and looked out of his cell window, he saw three words marked in the snow: *Keep Your Nerve.* But all day long as he sat waiting he could hear the sheriff and his deputies at work on the gallows.

Glendolene Kimmel, with a pack of statements swearing to the innocence of her hero, went to see the governor that day, but the governor refused to read them. And throughout that night, Cheyenne's saloons stayed open, the gamblers giving odds that Tom Horn would be freed before morning.

But the man who had survived attacks from deadly Apaches, from sure-shot train robbers, and from a hundred skulking enemies on the cattle ranges was officially hanged on schedule the morning of November 20, 1903.

Before nightfall, rumors were all over Laramie County that Tom Horn had not really been hanged. And in parts of Wyoming for decades, old-timers would solemnly swear a last-minute switch was made, and that in some lonely place up a remote canyon somewhere one might find a white-haired old man hiding out in a cabin, braiding intricate horsehair riatas to pass the time away.

.   .   .

In the fifteen years following the Great Blizzard, changes had come so rapidly on the Western rangelands that the old trail drivers could scarcely realize what had happened: deep wells dug for water, windmills, pasture planting and hay mowing, cattle dehorned to keep down losses from goring, fences stretched, and sheep—whole herds of sheep running on the same ranges with cattle! Ranch life had certainly changed.

One old cowhand summed it up for the Sidney (Texas) *Independent:* "Cowboys don't have as soft a time as they did eight or ten years ago," he said. "I remember when we set around the fire the winter through and didn't do a lick of work for five or six months of the year, except to chop a little wood to build a fire to keep warm by. Now we go to the general roundup, then the calf roundup, then comes haying—something that the old-time cowboy never dreamed of—then the beef roundup and fall calf roundup, and gathering bulls and weak cows, and after all this a winter of feeding hay. I tell you times have changed. You didn't hear the sound of a mowing machine in this country ten years ago. We didn't have any hay, and the man who thinks he is going to strike a soft job now in a cow camp is woefully left."

Civilization was intruding with all its superfluous comforts, and the dude ranch was not far away when working cowboys began packing mattresses on the roundups. The old chuckwagon drivers cursed the extra loads of gear—but the trail driving days were gone forever.

All that was left were the names strewn across the land—Sweetgrass and Ogallala, Tensleep and Powder River, Boot Hill and Turkey Track, Abilene and Bitterroot, Rawhide Creek and Sweetwater, Texas Street and Horse Thief Creek, Medicine Bow and Chisholm Trail, Red River and Hat Creek, the Chugwater and the Pecos, Whoopup and Box Elder, Kaycee and Badwater, the Palo Duro and Dodge City.

These and a hundred other evocative and musical names will forever remain, symbols of the long-gone, golden days of the old trail driving cattlemen.

CHAPTER 25
Jollification

▲▲▲▲▲▲▲▲▲▲▲▲▲▲▲▲▲

ACCOUNTS OF FRONTIER LIFE suggest that the pi-
oneer marched into the western wilds with a rifle in one hand, and a
fiddle in the other. A violin seems to have been available in almost
every circumstance, no matter how remote or desperate. Dances were
held on the slightest provocation, or on none at all. In frontier society
where women were scarce, men organized stag dances, either with
designated partners or on a solo basis. River raftsmen were noted for
their fiddling and prancing. The exploring expedition of Meriwether
Lewis and William Clark included Jean Cruzat, who played "extreemly
well" on the violin. To the fiddling of Cruzat, the men of the expedition
danced for their pleasure and the amazement of the Indians.

The violin and dance has, since that early day, been part of Western
social situations. There were fiddles and dances in the wagon trains, in
mining towns, at weddings, and at barn raisings. At Florence, Idaho,
in 1862, according to one young gold-seeker, it was "easier to make a
stake with my violin than by hard work in the diggings."

Dances were part of most celebrations, holidays, or jollifications.
They were a form of entertainment that required little planning, few
talents, a minimum of equipment, and much energy—an ideal combination for a frontier environment. Formally know as "hops," social
dances often lasted from "early candle lightin' " until "the rooster
warned us it was time to go home."

Occasionally it was more than a rooster that broke up a sociable
dance. One account tells of the "Cole's Valley boys," who, filled with
fifty-cent whisky and social rivalry, "decided to break up a dance."
Two sets had been formed for a quadrille, when "Sol Culver reached
the ballroom, drew his heavy pistol, and hit George Bennet a terrific

CHEYENNE CLUB

Popularized in American Western mythology and movies, the Cheyenne Club was a popular spot with wealthy cattlemen in a booming, cosmopolitan city. (Photograph courtesy of Wyoming State Museum.)

blow across the nose with the barrel of the gun. It smashed Bennet's nose flat, disfiguring him for life. The fight now became general. The women crowded out on the porch. Sol Culver had pretty much his own way till he came to Ash Clayton, one of the musicians. Ash hit Sol over the head with a violin, and followed after with his knife. Culver soon had enough, and left for parts unknown."

Church bans on social dances were not effective in early frontier days. When "Methodist feet" became a byword, the Kansas newspapers staged a mock debate over "which was the least harmful at church socials—dancing or kissing games." The question may have been economic rather than spiritual, for the "hug social" was not uncommon as a fund-raising device. At one such affair, prices varied from ten cents to "hug anyone from fifteen to twenty," to "old maids, two for a nickel." It cost one dollar to hug another man's wife, while "female lecturers were free, with a chromo thrown in."

Settlers in search of entertainment were noted for "just visiting." The welcome phrase "Light and tie, the latch string's out" was a sincere expression of the anxiety of the isolated pioneer for fresh news, exchange of gossip, or simply a break in the daily routine. Visits in the thinly settled plains country were more than casual affairs. "We used to stay all night," said one old lady, "or as long as two or three days."

Hospitality sometimes reached extremes, as described in the experience of one visitor who protested, "We can't stay here, there is but one bed."

"We'll put you in that."

"And what will the family do?"

"They will sleep on the floor."

"And what will you do?"

"Oh, I will lean up against the house outside."

The Fourth of July was the only holiday observed on the frontier with organized community jollification. It was the major public holiday on the American calendar. The day even lent its name to one of the physical landmarks of the Western trail, Independence Rock.

Under primitive conditions, the Glorious Fourth was celebrated by joy-shooting, and diligent application to firewater. Under more settled conditions, "the day we celebrate" was organized into a pattern. "Up early, fired cannon in town 10 or 12 times & played fife and drum. I blew on clarionet and flute. Shot revolver, rifle and shotgun. All formed in procession, all on ground. Button prayed long and loud. Declaration read, then Jack Thompson got up and read his awfully sublime speech of 24 pages. Very tedious. A fat Rev. spoke a few minutes. Then to table. A ball at Puckets.''

The parade was the big whoop-up event of the day. Patriotic and military organizations dominated, but decorated floats sponsored by merchants, fraternal organizations, or churches provided opportunity for all to participate.

Independence Day was littered with fragments of firecrackers and political oratory. One young man observed of July 4, 1863, ''The day was chock-full of patriotism, pie-ty, roast beef and cakes. I partook of the good things, and saw a great variety of slim-legged girls.''

Variations on the usual program were sometimes exciting. In one frontier town, while the ''band discoursed eloquent music through the streets,'' an Indian attacked a white man in revenge for alleged wife stealing. On July 4, 1871, in ''a row of saloons on the Kansas-Pacific railway, called Hays City, the soiled doves [fancy women] joined in the druken carnival. Strange to say, nobody was killed; this fact will be deemed a mistake by all old residenters.''

When baseball became popular after the Civil War, Fourth of July festivities usually included an afternoon game between local teams. In the 1880s it took seven bad pitches to walk a man, and the batter could call for a high or low pitch, as he pleased. For speedier base running, the players took off their shoes.

Competition in occupational skills provided a means of entertainment on July 4th and on other days of jollification. Volunteer firemen were proud of the speed of their companies, and challenged other outfits to contests. Tournaments between towns, and even between states, decided champions. The eastern Oregon and Washington firemen's tournament held in 1896 was a major event. The 220-yard dash over the dirt streets of Pendleton, Oregon, was won in 24⅕ seconds.

Firemen's tournaments included tests of speed with equipment. The hook and ladder company pulled its gear from a standing start to a given point, usually one hundred yards away, raised the ladder to maximum height, and placed a man on the top rung. In one tournament the Pendleton lads performed the operation in 28⅗ seconds.

In mining districts where hardrock work and blasting were necessary skills, miners staged rock drilling contests. Cooperation between the man with the sledge and the one with the drill required an acute sense of timing, and mutual trust.

Contests were also held in the logging camps. Of the many skills required of the logger, most spectacular was his ability to ride logs

PENDLETON & ARLINGTON BASE BALL, M
1888.   No 190

PLAY BALL!

When baseball became popular after the Civil War, Fourth of July festivities usually included an afternoon game between local teams. In the
1880s it took seven bad pitches to walk a man, and the batter could call
for a high or low pitch, as he pleased. The Pendleton and Arlington teams
of 1886 were recruited from the wheatfields of eastern Oregon. For speedier base running, they took off their shoes. (Photograph by W. S. Bow-
man, courtesy of the University of Oregon Library.)

through swift water and handle himself on a slippery stick. Contests were based on the ability to balance on a floating log and spinning it with one's feet, while throwing off an opponent (a skill known as birling, or logrolling). In some regions, birling contests were advertised as an annual attraction, and drew contestants out of the woods from surrounding states. Such affairs ended in celebrations of mutual friendship at which water was notably absent.

The bicycle also provided recreation for townspeople. The first bicycle was introduced in America in 1876. In four years the sport had become so popular that a League of American Wheelmen was formed, "to promote the general interests of bicycling, to ascertain, protect, and defend the rights of wheelmen, and to encourage and facilitate touring." The League also established rules for racing. It decided that racers "must wear shirts that shall not bare the shoulders, and breeches that must reach the knee." Clothed in official decorum, cyclists competed at various distances, and in trick riding. The ladies, too, in proper wheeling habit, were encouraged to cycle for reasons of health.

The condition of most Western roads made bicycling difficult. Horse racing did not require smooth courses, and was a sport that appealed in a country where almost everyone owned or could borrow a mount. In the absence of a track, horse races were run down Main Street. Much money changed hands at such events, especially when a local favorite was left behind by a trained runner introduced by gypsy horse traffickers.

Wealthy ranchers interested in horse racing built their own tracks, established local rules, and in general took the sport seriously. The enclosed mile track at the Daly ranch near Helena, Montana, was a headquarters for local horse fanciers. Both ranch ponies and racing stock provided entertainment.

Among the earliest Western sports were the "sliding clubs," formed about 1864 in the mountain towns of Idaho. Such contests, "unobjectionable from a moral standpoint," involved racing with cutters down snow-covered hills. Stakes for a grand race between towns ran as high as $2,500. Ski clubs, too, were formed in mountain states. Called "snowshoers," the clubs engaged in cross-country jaunts, rather than downhill races.

The household arts were also pressed into service for frontier fun, usually referred to as "bees." The settlers were ready to participate in any one of a whole swarm of bees—apple paring, corn husking, quilting, and house or barn raising. "One inexorable rule," recalled a Kansas frontiersman, "if Smith built a house, the whole community insisted on the right to have it dedicated by a dance before he should move into it, and everybody—that is most everybody—attended; and those who could not, or would not dance, and of such there were very few, spent the night in visiting, playing games, or settling questions of social and political importance. It was nothing unusual to meet at those dances families who resided twelve to fifteen miles away."

Frontier amusements were not necessarily related to the useful arts. "Game," reported one frontier newspaper, "is abundant just now. Buffalo, draw poker, antelope, old sledge, venison, faro, quails, billiards, rabbits, euchre, elk, and keno are the prevailing varieties." A man could lose his pile over these or even on a wager concerning the exact arrival time of the next stage. Gambling houses were constant targets of moral objection. In 1861 the Denver city council outlawed three-card monte, but conveniently neglected to ban other games of skill.

Few pastimes were simpler, more congenial, and, to some, more profitable than a card game. In a land where money was often scarce, stakes in a game sometimes consisted of land, gold dust, mining claims, or livestock. The cowboys, noted for gambling, in lieu of formal saloon equipment would just spread a blanket on the prairie and shoot craps. Horse and saddle could be lost in a few throws.

Mining towns were, by nature, the most profitable locations for organized gambling establishments. One mining town is supposed to have been located on a particular spot because the pack mules carrying the billiard tables for the saloon broke down there.

Associated with the gambling houses were the fancy women. They, too, moved west as an accompaniment of civilization, and afforded amusement of a special quality to certain elements on the frontier. Railroad, mining, and military post towns were especially noted for their sporting houses, for there was cash and a floating male population on hand. Lieutenant Sylvester Mowry, writing from a Utah army post in 1855, was pleased to report that "every officer except the Colonel has got a woman. The doctor has three—a mother and two daughters. The mother cooks for him . . ."

Weddings offered frontier folks special opportunities for jollification of a rowdy variety. "Belling and fussing" were carried to extremes. One crowd followed a pair of newlyweds to their home, shot through the windows, broke down the door, dragged the couple out, cut open the feather beds, and tore up the floor. "It requires backbone to get married out this way," said the local paper.

More benign, though perhaps less picturesque, were the "socials" involving candy-pulling, tableaux, and kissing. Strawberry festivals were a familiar entertainment among town and country folk alike. Everyone enjoyed the eating, and the festival advertised the agricultural qualities of a community. One such was the festival at Glenwood, Colorado, sponsored by the Midland Railroad, which was interested in attracting settlers.

The Sunday school picnic was an approved form of entertainment. Held annually, it offered plenty of food, lemonade, unexceptional atmosphere, and sports of the jolly sort, including sack races. The singing school was also regarded as improving for the young. "We think our young folks employ their evenings well in attending singing school," said an 1854 editorial. Better-informed sources referred to the singing school as a "sparking school." The real activity of the evening commenced when couples strolled quietly home after an evening of music and song. The singing school was, according to one observer, "remanded to oblivion by the piano epidemic of the late 1850s."

Séance socials were, in some Western regions, as popular and informal as whist and bridge parties in a later day. The young people, fascinated by the new spiritualism, gathered for sessions of ghostly conversation. "Formed a little circle, and had over an hundred bright spirits present, and no dark ones. Among those that gave their names were Thomas Paine, D. Webster, Geo. Washington, Fr. Marion, H. Clay, B. Franklin, A. Hamilton, M. Luther, Montezuma, Cortez, Eck, Leo X, Josephus, Mary the Mother of Jesus, and Paul the Apostle. I say present, though they communicated at the distance of twenty miles."

Once the rough edges had been knocked off the frontier environment, tourism became a popular form of recreation. Tourists had long been a part of the Western scene. The "traveling Englishman," who often published accounts of his adventures, was a frontier byword. The tale of Jim Bridger discussing Shakespeare with Lord Gore has been embalmed in frontier literature in several forms. In 1872, another foreigner, the Grand Duke Alexis of Russia, hunted buffalo in Nebraska, under the guidance of General Sheridan, George Custer, and Buffalo Bill.

Westerners were quick to realize the attractions of the "wild and wooly" for adventure-hunting Easterners, and the opportunity for commercial exploitation of "adventure" was particularly favorable in the border states. Advertisements were circulated urging "health and pleasure seekers" to join expeditions "over the wild prairie for buffalo and antelope." The hardships of such sport were considerably mitigated by railroad accommodations to the hunting grounds.

The settlers themselves began to find time for vacations, and discovered the experience was pleasing. "There is quite a stir now in this warm weather for the Soda Springs, or what we call Saratoga. There are some there all the time, and some camp out and stay a week at a time, rusticating."

An outing in the mountains or at the beach became fashionable for those emigrants who now found recreation in "roughing it." Some of the overland trail landmarks were preempted by enterprising parties, and fashioned into resorts.

The new Western tourist was given the best of care in palatial hotels, established where only flea houses had flourished before. Hot springs, in particular, were enclosed, and their waters advertised as healing. The Broadwater Hotel in Helena, Montana, greeted tourists in 1890. Attached to the hotel was a hot-springs bath, elegantly camouflaged as a "Natatorium." The railroads, too, early realized the profitable possibilities of resort hotels or historic sites.

It was the Western interest in tourism, in amateur exploring for the fun of it, that among other factors led to the full discovery and establishment of Yellowstone National Park, the nation's first national park, in 1872.

With the development of the resort hotel, the vacation camping ground, and the beach cottage, the pioneer story had run full circle. The settlers had left civilization to make a place for themselves on the new land, and now they left their new homes to find pleasure and amusement in the wilds. The once-dreaded Indian had become an object of tourist curiosity, the landmarks and scenic spots on the overland trail were dotted with picnic tables, and the mountain meadows were graded into golf links.

CHAPTER 26
Geronimo and the Chiricahuas

▲▲▲▲▲▲▲▲▲▲▲▲▲▲▲

THE APACHE INDIANS, subdued and settled on reservations by General George Crook in 1873, had not been allowed to live in the ways of their conquerors. No sooner did they lay down their rifles and pick up a hoe than the whites began to forget their promises. The "Indian agents who had sought cover before came out, brave as sheep, and took charge of the agencies, and commenced their game of plundering."

One young agent, John P. Clum, tried subduing the warriors with kindness, but his methods were unpopular on the frontier. He believed the Apaches could learn to like their new captivity, and reported his portion of the tribe "obedient, law-abiding . . . making strenuous efforts toward self-support and civilization," But other agents were not so optimistic, and Clum was almost as much disliked as his Indian wards.

The greed of the whites for the spoils of Indian bounty, and the greed of the settlers for the richest land, brought about the removal of the Apaches from the area that had been marked off for them. Most of the tribes were herded together and forced to live on the hot, dry flats of Arizona's San Carlos River. The trading post, rather than the hunt, now supplied the Apaches with meat. They who had once taken what they wanted now had to ask.

Not all the Apaches moved to the new reservation. Many of them, especially the Chiricahua and Warm Springs bands, crossed the border into Mexico, into the mountains of Chihuahua and Sonora. Later, others from the reservation fled south and joined them.

The boldest and wildest of the warriors could not abide the new life. They had lived free too long to submit to every indignity. These warriors, once led by Cochise and Mangas Coloradas, had lost none of

GERONIMO

This is the famous Apache warrior Geronimo, in a photo taken around
1884. (Photograph by A. Frank Randall, courtesy of the American Research Museum of New Mexico.)

their fighting qualities. Under new chiefs—Victorio and Nana of the Warm Springs band, Nachez (who was second son of the great Cochise) and Chato of the Chiricahuas—they terrorized New Mexico and Arizona. They raided Mexican cattle herds, and supplied themselves with ammunition from Arizona and New Mexico citizens. They boasted of their killings, saying they fought Mexicans with rocks, not bullets.

In September 1882, General Crook, whom the Apaches well remembered as the "Gray Wolf," was recalled to Arizona to take charge of his old wards and to see what could be done. He went about the territory with a guide and interpreter, talking with his old friends, finding out for himself what was wrong.

Alchise, a reservation chief, told him: "When you left, there were no bad Indians out. We were all content; everything was peace. The officers you had were all taken away, and new ones came in—a different kind. The good ones must all have been taken away, and the bad ones sent in their places. I have always been true, and obeyed orders. When the Indians broke out at San Carlos, when Major Randall was here, I helped him to go fight them. When Major Randall was here we were all happy, and we think of him yet. Oh, where is my friend Randall— the captain with the big mustache which he always pulled? He was my brother, and I think of him all the time."

The burden of complaint was the same from all the Apaches—Chalipun, Navatane, Santos, Chiquito, Eskiminzin. All complained that the new soldiers and agents who had come to Arizona were not friends, and did not understand the Apaches. They had been forced away from their homes, had been mistreated, and were not able to make a living at the San Carlos.

General Crook made a number of quick changes after his council with the Indians. The Apaches at San Carlos were permitted to scatter from the agency headquarters and settle on land of their own choosing on the reservation, by the creeks and springs, where they could raise crops and become self-supporting. They would wear identification tags, so that they could be recognized as reservation Indians, not renegades.

The assurance of peace on the reservation was coupled with preparations for war against the Apaches who had left. The pack trains were reorganized under Tom Moore. Friendly Apaches were recruited as scouts to help bring in their people, and old guides and interpreters were rehired. Al Sieber and Archie MacIntosh showed up again.

In March 1883, the Apaches in Mexico set out on another raid. One band, under Geronimo, raided in Sonora for stock, while the other, led by Chato, swept through southern and central Arizona looking for ammunition. Chato's band traveled four hundred miles in six days, killing twenty-six persons, and taking what ammunition they could pick up. One of Chato's party was a White Mountain Apache called Tsoe, married to a Chiricahua woman. (He was known as "Peaches" by the soldiers because of his light complexion.) Tsoe deserted and surrendered himself at San Carlos. He offered to guide General Crook to the hiding place of the Chiricahuas.

Final preparations were made for the campaign. An agreement had been arranged with the Mexican government permitting U.S. troops to cross the border when they were in pursuit of Indians, and this was what Crook intended to do—follow the renegades to their home *rancherias*.

The expedition, with Crook in command, set out on May 1, 1883, with 193 Apache scouts under Captain Emmet Crawford, and one company of the Sixth Cavalry, comprising forty-two enlisted men and two officers. There were field rations for sixty days, and 150 rounds of ammunition per man; 350 pack mules carried the load. Before starting, the Apache scouts killed a couple of mules and sat to a feast of roast mule meat, a great treat.

By May 8 the command was in the heart of the wild Sierra Madre. Travel was done at night under the guidance of Tsoe. The trail was rough, and several of the mules were lost over the cliffs.

One Apache camp was found, deserted. By this time the command was so close to the *rancherias* that the pack train was left behind while the scouts and troops moved forward on foot. On the fifteenth day, the advance, Indian scouts under Crawford, surprised a camp belonging to Bonito and Chato. There was a short, sharp fight. Nine warriors were killed, and five Apache children captured. The rest of the Chiricahuas scattered into the wilderness.

The Apaches were tired of their mountain life. They were tired of being hunted; it was impossible to rest, for fear of surprise. They sent word into Crook's camp, offering to surrender and return to the reservation. Crook suggested that he did not care whether they surrendered or not—he would just as soon kill them all and be rid of them for good. Hearing this, the hostiles begged for peace, and it was granted. All the chiefs gave themselves up: Geronimo, Chato, Loco, Nachez the son of Cochise, and Kan-ti-no. Only Juh was missing. He had fled south, far up the Yaqui.

On May 24 the prisoners arrived at San Carlos, 52 men and 273 women and children. Geronimo came in late. He stayed in the mountains with a few followers, stealing stock from the Mexicans, so that he should not return poor. He finally came in, in June 1883, escorted by Lieutenant Britton Davis.

General Crook then arranged to have full control over the Apaches on the reservation. With a firm hand he helped them learn the ways of the whites. For two years there was no Indian trouble in Arizona or New Mexico. The Apaches, even the warlike Chiricahuas, policed by their own people, farmed their *rancherias* and killed no one. Chato and Geronimo had the best farms on the reservation.

.   .   .

Two years of peace made the agents brave again. The old troubles sprang up anew. There was quarreling and bickering between the soldiers and the agents over control of the Indians.

The Apaches were quick to see the friction between their two masters. Some of the chiefs were happy over it, for they knew a chance had come to regain some of their old power. Their medicine was stronger in the mountains of Sonora than in the cornfields of San Carlos. The Apaches had lived so long on plunder and theft that it took more than a couple of years to forget. It was irksome to have to give up some of their old habits, such as *tiswin* drunks and wife-beating. Besides, had not this whole land once belonged to the Apaches? They had been free, then, to go and do as they pleased.

The threatened outbreak of the restless ones occurred on May 17, 1885. Nachez, Geronimo, Chihuahua, Mangas (son of Mangas Coloradas), and 140 followers fled the reservation. They traveled 120 miles without rest or food, and took refuge in the Black Range in New Mexico.

The soldiers followed immediately, helped by Indian scouts, but it was soon evident that a major campaign would have to be organized, especially after the runaways crossed the border, back to their old fortress of the Sierra Madre. On September 5, the commands in the file were recalled. General Crook established headquarters at Fort Bowie, Arizona, and began refitting his outfits for a new campaign.

By the end of November, two new commands under Britton Davis and Emmet Crawford had set out to hunt down the Apaches wherever they might be. Chato, rival of Nachez and Geronimo and once a feared and hunted warrior, was now a trusted scout with Crawford. He was made a sergeant of scouts.

On January 10, 1886, Crrawford and his scouts attacked the main camp of the Chiricahuas about ninety miles below Nacori, Sonora. The entire camp with all its plunder was taken, though none of the Apaches was captured.

The loss of their camp and equipment was enough to demoralize the Chiricahuas, so that Nachez, Chihuahua, and Geronimo asked for a peace talk with Crawford. Before the talk took place, Crawford's camp of Indian scouts was attacked by Mexican troops, who thought all Apaches were fair game, peaceful or hostile.

Captain Crawford, attempting to stop the fight, was killed by a shot through the brain. Before the Mexicans could be made to understand that they were attacking United States troops, the commander of the Mexican force and fifteen of his soldiers had been killed. Lieutenant Marion P. Maus, aided by interpreter Tom Horn, finally stopped the fight.

The Chiricahuas, camped on a hill across from the scene of the fight, were "interested spectators." Later they had a council with Lieutenant Maus, and agreed to meet General Crook in "two moons," the exact time and place to be settled later, at their pleasure.

On March 16, Lieutenant Maus informed Crook that the Apaches were ready to talk peace. The general, with Captain John Bourke, Cyrus S. Roberts, and Roberts's young boy, Charlie, left Bowie for the council. An enterprising photographer from Tombstone, C. S. Fly, came along with his assistant and some equipment.

The Chiricahuas, fully rearmed and reequipped after their fight with Crawford, had chosen a good spot for the peace talk, Cañon de los Embudos, Sonora, about twenty miles south of the border, near the Sonora-Chihuahua line.

The council began on March 25, and lasted three days. Geronimo, who did most of the talking, was very nervous, and tried to show that he had left the reservation to escape arrest. General Crook called Geronimo a liar, saying that he had broken his word so often he could not be trusted.

Alchise and Ka-e-ten-a, trusted Apache scouts, were sent to the Chiricahua camp to talk peace and divide opinion. They did their work well, and on March 27 both Nachez and Chihuahua were in favor of peace. Geronimo, seeing how things were going, also decided for peace.

Crook promised that they would be sent east with their families for a few years, and then return to Arizona.

No sooner had Crook started back to Fort Bowie than a white man named Tribolet sold the Chiricahuas some whisky to celebrate the peace. The resulting drunk brought about a change of mind in Geronimo and Nachez. With twenty men and nineteen women and children they broke camp and fled south. Another campaign would be necessary to rout them out. It was for acts of this sort that Geronimo won his reputation as a great chief, though he actually was no chief. He was a good fighter and a daring leader, and attracted other warriors to him.

The result of this final outbreak was the resignation of General Crook from the Department of Arizona. His superiors in the East were not satisfied with the peace terms. They wanted unconditional surrender. They hinted, too, that the Indian scouts had been disloyal. General Crook knew that unconditional surrender would have driven the Chiricahuas back to the Sierra Madre, and he knew also that his scouts were loyal beyond question. But rather than operate with official disapproval, he resigned.

On April 7 the Chiricahuas who had surrendered left Bowie station on their way to exile in Florida. General Crook went to see them off. "There were seventy-seven in all of them—fifteen men, thirty-three women and twenty-nine children," he wrote; "it is a big relief to get rid of them." Four days later he left Arizona himself, and General Nelson A. Miles took command.

When Miles began his campaign, there were seventeen men and nineteen women and children left among the Chiricahuas who had fled. Miles decided to capture them in a new way—he would run them down with cavalry. Accordingly, he dismissed the Indian scouts, and set Captain H. W. Lawton, with cavalry and mounted infantry, after the Apaches south of the border.

The cavalry soon wore out, and became infantry. For three months the commands chased the Chiricahuas in and out of Sonora while the wily warriors raided over wide areas in southern and central Arizona, killing settlers, stealing stock, and escaping all troops sent after them.

Finally, in July 1886, Geronimo and Nachez let it be known that they would consider surrender if granted terms. Lieutenant Charles B. Gatewood, who had served under Crook and was well known to the Chiricahuas, was recalled from his post at Fort Stanton, New Mexico, and sent out to talk peace. After a month of waiting, Geronimo allowed himself to be located, and the council took place. With considerable hesitation, Nachez and Geronimo took the advice of Gatewood and surrendered. The Apache war was over.

Geronimo and Nachez were sent by train, with their entire band, into exile in Florida. Later all of the Chiricahuas, even those like Chato who had served faithfully as scouts, were also sent east. Their reward for services rendered was imprisonment with those whose surrender they had brought about.

Pressure from the Indian Rights Association and interested army people finally effected the removal of the Apaches to Mt. Vernon barracks, Alabama, and later to Fort Sill, Indian Territory. Geronimo lived until 1909, colorful to the end. He appeared at the St. Louis Fair, and rode in the procession in honor of the inauguration of Theodore Roosevelt. He obtained pocket money through the sale of photographs of himself, and by selling brass buttons from his coat.

CHAPTER 27
The Ghost Dance and Wounded Knee

▲▲▲▲▲▲▲▲▲▲▲▲▲▲▲

EVERYWHERE NOW THE INDIANS of the West were locked within the reservations. The great chiefs were shorn of their power. Many of the mighty warriors were dead. Those who lived spent their days in idleness. The buffalo and the antelope had vanished; the old ceremonies of the tribes had become rituals without meaning. The agents doled out food and clothing, and it was not necessary for one to think of the changes of the seasons, the moons of the snow and cold, the moons of greening grass, the moons when the buffalo bulls are fat, the moons of the ripening chokecherries and the falling leaves.

There was nothing to be done. One might trade a few skins for the white man's crazy-water, and then it was possible to dream of the old days, the days of the splendid hunts and the fighting. They would drink the crazy-water and make big talk for a little while. But it was a time without spirit, a time of despair.

And in this time the medicine men became the leaders. Everywhere there were dreamers and swooning men. Most of them were great fakers, but some were sincere in their vagaries and their visions.

Long before the Indians suffered their last great defeats, Smohalla the Prophet had preached his visions to the Nez Percés, and he had won the loyalty of Chief Joseph. When the Great Spirit had decided to make humans on the earth, said Smohalla, he had made the Indians first. Then he had made the other peoples of the earth, but he was fast becoming dissatisfied with these other ones. That was why the Indians must not follow the ways of the whites.

Among the Apaches there had also been great dreamers. In 1881, Nakai-Doklini was teaching his followers in southern Arizona a new dance which he was certain would drive the whites from the land.

In Montana, a Crow medicine man, Sword Bearer, was preaching the same philosophy a few years later. He claimed that he was immune to bullets and weapons, and would soon make the hearts of the whites like water, so that they would go back to their homes in the East.

It was a time of despair, and in such a time new religions are born. Why the religion reached its flower in Nevada and among the Paiutes, no one can say. But here it had begun in a small valley near the Walker River reservation south of Virginia City; here it had begun like the small trickle of a spring in the year 1870.

Tavibo, a minor chief, had made a lone pilgrimage into the mountains, and the divine spirits had made a revelation to him. All the people of the earth were to be swallowed up, he was told, but at the end of three days the Indians would be resurrected in the flesh to live forever. They would enjoy the earth which was rightfully theirs. Once again there would be plenty of game, fish, and piñon nuts. Best of all, the whites would be destroyed forever.

When Tavibo reported his vision to the Mason Valley Paiutes, he attracted few believers. But gradually he added other features to his story, and he went up into the mountains again for further revelations. It was necessary for the Indians to dance, everywhere; to keep on dancing. This would please the Great Spirit, and in the Moon of the Little Grass he would come and destroy the whites and bring back the game as thick as the stars in the Road of the Ghosts, the Milky Way.

Tavibo died shortly after he told of these things, but his son, Wovoka, was considered the natural inheritor of his powers by those Paiutes who believed in the new religion of the dance. Wovoka, who was only fourteen years old at the time of his father's death, was taken into the family of a white farmer, David Wilson, and was given the name Jack Wilson.

But as the years passed, Jack Wilson, or Wovoka, continued to receive revelations as his father had done before him. Once during an eclipse of the sun, he fell asleep and was taken up to the world of the Great Spirit. "When the sun died," he said, "I went up to heaven and saw the Great Spirit and all the people who had died a long time ago. The Great Spirit told me to come back and tell my people they must be good and love one another, and not fight, or steal, or lie. He gave to me a dance to give to my people."

This dance was the ghost dance, and Wovoka believed the Indians must dance it if they wished to bring back the old days of glory, the old days of the buffalo. It would sweep across the mountains and the prairies of the West like a great flow of waters.

The first ghost dance was performed on a dancing ground selected by Wovoka on the Walker Lake reservation in Nevada in January 1889. The ceremony was simple, the Indians forming into a large circle, dancing and chanting as they constricted the circle, the circle widening and constricting again and again. The dancing continued for a day and a night, Wovoka sitting in the middle of the circle before a large fire with his head bowed. He wore a white striped coat, a pair of trousers, and moccasins. On the second day he stopped the dancing and described the visions that the Great Spirit had sent to him. Then the dancing commenced again and lasted for three more days.

When a second dance was held soon afterward, several Utes visited the ceremony out of curiosity. Returning to their reservation, the Utes told the neighboring Bannocks about the ceremony. The Bannocks sent emissaries to the next dance, and so did the Mission and Shastan tribes of California, who had somehow heard of the new messiah.

Within a few weeks many Rocky Mountain tribes were dancing the ghost dance. The Shoshones at Fort Hall reservation saw a ritual staged by the Bannocks, and were so impressed they sent a delegation of five tribesmen to Nevada to learn the new religion from Wovoka's own lips.

When it spread to Washakie's Wind River reservation, the old Shoshone patriarch ordered the dancing stopped. Yet it was from the Wind River Shoshones that the plains tribes learned of the ghost dance religion. Perhaps more than any of the other tribes, the Cheyenne and the Sioux felt the need of a messiah who could lead them back to the days of glory. The story of Wovoka was carried swiftly across the plains.

In the autumn of 1889, a Cheyenne delegate named Porcupine made a journey from Montana to learn more about the ghost dance. Almost at the same time, Short Bull, Kicking Bear, and several other medicine men of the Sioux traveled all the way from the Dakotas.

The Sioux accepted the ghost dance religion with more fervor than any of the Indians. On their return to the Dakota reservations, each delegate tried to outdo the others in describing the wonders of the messiah. He came down from heaven in a cloud, they said. He showed them a vision of all the nations of Indians coming home. The earth would be covered with dust and then a new earth would come upon the old. All the nations of Indians long dead would come back to life. The whites would disappear. The Indians must use the sacred red and white paint and the sacred grass to make the vanished buffalo return in great herds.

In the spring of 1890 the Sioux began dancing the ghost dance at

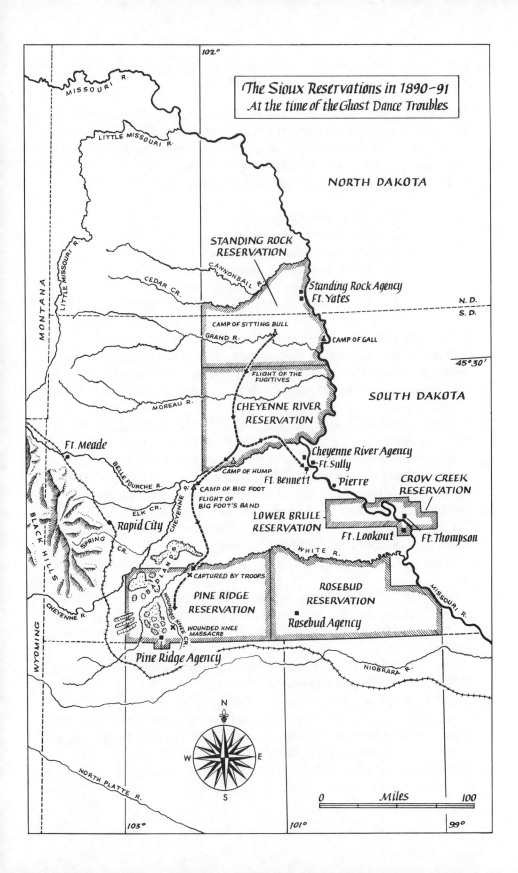

The Sioux Reservations in 1890–91
At the time of the Ghost Dance Troubles

MISSOURI R.

LITTLE MISSOURI R.

NORTH DAKOTA

MONTANA

LITTLE MISSOURI R.

CEDAR CR.

CANNONBALL R.

STANDING ROCK
RESERVATION

Standing Rock Agency
Ft. Yates

N. D.
S. D.

CAMP OF SITTING BULL

GRAND R.

CAMP OF GALL

45°30'

FLIGHT OF THE
FUGITIVES

MOREAU R.

CHEYENNE RIVER
RESERVATION

SOUTH DAKOTA

Ft. Meade

BELLE FOURCHE R.

CHEYENNE R.

Camp of Hump

Cheyenne River Agency
Ft. Sully

CROW CREEK
RESERVATION

CAMP OF BIG FOOT

Ft. Bennett

Pierre

ELK CR.

FLIGHT OF
BIG FOOT'S BAND

Rapid City

SPRING CR.

BLACK HILLS

LOWER BRULE
RESERVATION

Ft. Lookout

Ft. Thompson

MISSOURI R.

WHITE R.

CHEYENNE R.

BADLANDS

CAPTURED BY TROOPS

ROSEBUD
RESERVATION

WOUNDED KNEE CR.

PINE RIDGE
RESERVATION

WOUNDED KNEE
MASSACRE

Rosebud Agency

WYOMING

Pine Ridge Agency

NIOBRARA R.

N
W E
S

NORTH PLATTE R.

0   Miles   100

103°   101°   99°

Pine Ridge, adding new symbols to Wovoka's original ceremony. By June they were wearing ghost shirts made of cotton cloth painted blue around the necks, with bright-colored thunderbirds, bows and arrows, suns, moons, and stars emblazoned upon them.

To accompany the dancing they made ghost songs:

> *The whole world is coming,*
> *A nation is coming, a nation is coming,*
> *The Eagle has brought the message to the tribe.*
> *The father says so, the father says so.*
> *Over the whole earth they are coming,*
> *The buffalo are coming, the buffalo are coming.*

Soon the songs became warlike chants.

It was at this moment of keen excitement that the greatest maker of medicine among the Sioux, Sitting Bull, chose to come forth from his "retirement" near the Standing Rock agency, and join the new religion of the dance.

News of the old war-maker's action soon reached General Nelson Miles, commanding the army's Department of the Missouri. At a chance meeting with Buffalo Bill Cody, the general told the scout about a report he had received from the Pine Ridge agency. "The Ghost Dance craze," said Miles, "has reached such proportions that it's now entirely beyond the control of the Indian agent and the police force."

Cody asked the general if he knew who was behind the movement. Miles guessed that it might be Sitting Bull.

"How about giving me an order for his arrest?" suggested Buffalo Bill.

"Why not? You've known the old rascal for years. He might listen to you, when under the same conditions he'd take a shot at one of my soldiers. But if you think you'll need any help, the army will back you up."

"All I'll need is a wagon load of candy," said Buffalo Bill. "Sitting Bull always did have a weakness for sweets."

Bill Cody proceeded at once to Fort Yates on the Standing Rock reservation, but the military authorities there were opposed to the scout's plans to arrest the Sioux leader. They thought the act might cause more trouble than it would prevent. The officers in command decided to get Buffalo Bill drunk, send a wire to Washington, and have his orders rescinded.

According to Captain A. R. Chapin: "All the officers were requested to assist in drinking Buffalo Bill under the table. But his capacity was such that it took practically all of us in details of two or three at a time to keep him interested and busy throughout the day."

And even though the rugged Cody managed to keep a clear head through all this maneuvering, he had scarcely started out to Sitting Bull's encampment before the order came postponing the arrest. Buffalo Bill returned to Fort Yates, and so ended his part of the affair.

Meanwhile the reservation agent, James McLaughlin, had decided to take Sitting Bull into custody himself, and thus prevent a dangerous disturbance which he feared would result if the military authorities forced the issue and tried to make an arrest. McLaughlin gave the necessary orders to his Indian police, instructing them not to permit the chief to escape under any circumstances.

Just before daybreak on the morning of December 15, 1890, forty-three Indian police surrounded Sitting Bull's log cabin. Lieutenant Bull Head, the Indian policeman in charge of the party, found Sitting Bull asleep on the floor. When he was awakened, the old chieftain stared incredulously at Bull Head. "What do you want here?" he asked.

"You are my prisoner," said Bull Head calmly. "You must go to the agency."

Sitting Bull yawned and sat up. "All right," he said, "I'll dress and go with you." He called one of his wives (his two wives were Seen-by-Her-Nation and Four Times) and sent her to an adjoining cabin for his best clothes, and then asked one of the policemen to saddle his horse for him. While these things were being done, the police began searching for weapons. Two rifles and several knives were seized, and this action evidently angered Sitting Bull, because he began abusing all the police within hearing distance.

About the same time, his ardent followers who had been dancing the ghost dance every night for weeks were gathering around the cabin. They outnumbered the police four to one, and soon had them pressed against the walls. As soon as Sitting Bull was brought outside, he must have sensed the explosive quality of the situation. Suddenly he turned on Lieutenant Bull Head and told him he was not going to Fort Yates. Then with a dramatic gesture of his hands, he called on his followers to rescue him.

Responding immediately, an Indian named Catch-the-Bear fired point-blank at Lieutenant Bull Head, wounding him in the side. As Bull Head fell, he tried to shoot his assailant, but the bullet struck

Sitting Bull instead. Almost simultaneously one of the sergeants, Red Tomahawk, shot Sitting Bull through the head. A wild fight developed almost immediately, with the trained police having difficulty holding their own. Only the timely arrival of a cavalry detachment saved them from total extinction.

.   .   .

The great Sitting Bull was dead! The news spread like a grass fire across the prairies. Most of the frightened followers of the Hunkpapa leader immediately come into Standing Rock agency and surrendered. Others fled west.

Those who were fleeing west knew exactly where they were going. They were seeking to join forces with a ghost dance believer, an old chieftain named Big Foot. Big Foot for some time had been gathering followers at a small village near the mouth of Deep Creek, a few miles below the fork of the Cheyenne River. As the ghost dance craze had increased, so had Big Foot's forces, and even before the fatal shooting of Sitting Bull, a small party of cavalrymen had been assigned to watch his movements.

As soon as the news of Sitting Bull's death reached Big Foot, he began preparations to break camp. The cavalry commander, Colonel E. V. Sumner, accepted Big Foot's explanation that the Indians were preparing to proceed to Standing Rock to go on the reservation for the winter. However, a patrol watch was kept on Big Foot's journey. When the band of Sioux fleeing from Sitting Bull's camp joined the new leader, Colonel Sumner again decided to question Big Foot as to his intentions.

The chief was unusually friendly, and declared that the only reason he had permitted the band from Sitting Bull's camp to join his people was that he felt sorry for them, and wanted them to return to the reservation with him. For the second time, Sumner accepted the explanation. In fact the Indians all seemed so friendly that they were permitted to keep their arms—a decision which was to precipitate the tragedy of Wounded Knee.

Before dawn the next day, December 23, Big Foot and his ever-increasing band were in rapid flight, moving in the opposite direction from the Standing Rock reservation. They were heading for the Badlands.

Perhaps Big Foot did not know that Kicking Bear and Short Bull had withdrawn to the Badlands. But it is a fact that a few days earlier those two leaders, who had once visited the ghost dance messiah in Nevada, were in the Badlands. And they had with them about three thousand fanatical followers, keyed up to a high frenzy as a result of their continual dances.

No matter what Big Foot did or did not know, trouble was certainly brewing now.

Moving swiftly to prevent an escape to the Badlands, the military authorities ordered Major S. M. Whitside of the Seventh Cavalry to intercept the Indians. As soon as these cavalrymen were sighted by Big Foot, he sent out mounted Indians with a white flag to meet them. When Major Whitside insisted on parleying with Big Foot, the chief rode out in a wagon.

As he approached Major Whitside, Big Foot seemed to regard the entire affair as a fine joke. "We parley," he said.

The major shook his head. "No parley," he replied sternly. "Unconditional surrender."

Big Foot considered this abrupt demand for a moment, then nodded acceptance. When Major Whitside gave him orders to lead his people to Wounded Knee Creek and make camp, Big Foot complied to the letter.

During the ensuing march, none of the cavalrymen suspected that anything was amiss; not one could have guessed what the fates were preparing for the following day on the banks of Wounded Knee Creek. The Indians seemed to be in good humor; they talked and laughed with the soldiers, and smoked their cigarettes. But not one of the cavalrymen seemed to have been aware that all of these Indians were wearing sacred ghost shirts, magic shirts with bright-colored thunderbirds and buffaloes emblazoned upon them. The Indians believed that the ghost shirts would protect them from the soldiers' weapons, even from the powerful Hotchkiss guns. And the soldiers seemed to be completely ignorant of the fact that their prisoners were fanatically certain the day of the Indians' return to power was close at hand.

Big Foot had fallen ill from exposure, and rode in his wagon litter. No one paid any particular attention to the chief medicine man, Yellow bird, who all during the march was moving stealthily up and down the line, occasionally blowing on an eagle-bone whistle, and muttering ghost dance chants.

When they reached Wounded Knee, the Indians were assigned an area near the cavalry camp. They were carefully counted—120 men and 230 women and children were present. Rations were issued, and they set up their shelters for the night. For additional cover, Major Whitside gave them several army tents. The troop surgeon, John van R. Hoff, was sent to attend the ailing Big Foot, and a stove was set up in the chief's tent.

Whitside revealed, however, that he did not entirely trust Big Foot's band. He posted a battery of four Hotchkiss guns, training them directly on the Indians' camp.

It was a cold night. Ice was already an inch thick on the tree-bordered creek, and there was a hint of snow in the air.

During the night, Colonel James W. Forsyth of the Seventh Cavalry rode in with additional troops and took command. With Forsyth came a young lieutenant, James D. Mann, who was to witness the opening shots of the approaching battle.

"The next morning," Mann said afterward, "we started to disarm them, the [warriors] being formed in a semi-circle in front of the tents. We went through the tents searching for arms, and while this was going on, everyone seemed to be good-natured, and we had no thought of trouble. The squaws were sitting on bundles concealing guns and other arms. We lifted them as tenderly and treated them as nicely as possible.

"As soon as we had finished this search, the squaws began packing up, which was a suspicious sign.

"While this was going on, the medicine man, who was in the center of the semi-circle of [warriors], had been going through the Ghost Dance, and making a speech, the substance of which was, as told me by an interpreter afterwards, 'I have made medicine of the white man's ammunition. It is good medicine, and his bullets can not harm you, as they will not go through your ghost shirts, while your bullets will kill.'

"It was then that I had a peculiar feeling come over me which I can not describe—some presentiment of trouble—and I told the men to 'be ready: there is going to be trouble.' We were only six or eight feet from the Indians and I ordered my men to fall back.

"In front of me were four [warriors]—three armed with rifles and one with bow and arrows. I drew my revolver and stepped through the line to my place with my detachment. The Indians raised their weapons over their heads to heaven as if in votive offering, then brought them down to bear on us, the one with the bow and arrow aiming directly at me. Then they seemed to wait an instant.

"The medicine man threw a handful of dust in the air, put on his war bonnet, and an instant later a gun was fired. This seemed to be the signal they had been waiting for, and the firing immediately began. I ordered my men to fire, and the reports were almost simultaneous."

Things happened fast after that first volley of shots. The Hotchkiss guns opened fire and began pouring their two-pound explosive shells into the crowd at the rate of nearly fifty per minute, mowing down everything alive. In a few moments, two hundred Indian men, women, and children and sixty soldiers were lying dead or wounded on the ground, the ripped tepees blazing and smoking around them. Some of the surviving Indians fled to a nearby ravine, hiding among the rocks and scrub cedars. Others continued their flight up the slopes to the south.

On the bloody campground, surgeon John van R. Hoff did what he could for the wounded. He disarmed a wounded Indian who was still trying to fire his rifle. The warrior staggered to his feet, and looked down fixedly at the body of Yellow Bird, the medicine man who was responsible for inciting the attack. "If I could be taken to you," the wounded Indian muttered to the dead medicine man, "I would kill you again."

Disillusionment over the failure of the ghost shirts had already affected most of the others. One of the women tore off her brilliantly colored shirt and stamped upon it, while blood flowed from her wounds and trickled down into the dust.

As it was obvious by the end of the day that a blizzard was approaching, the medical staff began gathering the wounded together, and they were carried in to a field hospital at Pine Ridge. One hundred twenty-eight Indians and thirty-one soldiers had died, but the exact totals were not known until several days afterward, for a great snowstorm was blanketing the South Dakota plains.

When the burial party went out to Wounded Knee after the blizzard, they found many of the bodies, including that of Big Foot, frozen grotesquely where they had fallen. All the Indians were buried together in a large pit, and a few days later their tribesmen came and put up a wire fence around the trench and smeared the posts with sacred red medicine paint.

But the vision of the peaceful Paiute dreamer, Wovoka, had come to an end with the Battle of Wounded Knee. And so had all the long and tragic years of Indian resistance of the Western plains.

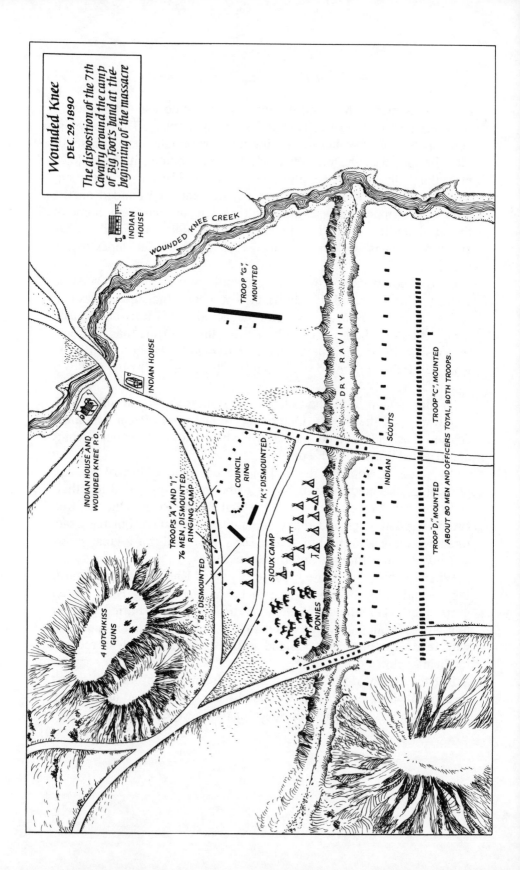

Wounded Knee
DEC. 29, 1890

The disposition of the 7th Cavalry around the camp of Big Foot's band at the beginning of the massacre

INDIAN HOUSE

WOUNDED KNEE CREEK

INDIAN HOUSE

INDIAN HOUSE AND WOUNDED KNEE P.O.

TROOP "G", MOUNTED

DRY RAVINE

SCOUTS

COUNCIL RING

TROOPS "A" AND "I", 76 MEN, DISMOUNTED, RINGING CAMP.

"K" DISMOUNTED

"B", DISMOUNTED

SIOUX CAMP

PONIES

INDIAN

TROOP "D", MOUNTED

TROOP "C", MOUNTED

ABOUT 80 MEN AND OFFICERS TOTAL, BOTH TROOPS.

4 HOTCHKISS GUNS

DEAD CHIEF

Big Foot, the Sioux leader, was found dead, frozen grotesquely where he had fallen. (Photograph by G. E. Trager, courtesy of the Smithsonian Institution.)

YOUNG-MAN-AFRAID-OF-HIS-HORSES

Young-Man-Afraid-of-His-Horses, at the Pine Ridge agency, taken a fortnight after the Wounded Knee Massacre. (Photograph courtesy of the Smithsonian Institution.)

CHAPTER 28
Wild West Shows and Rodeos

▲ ▲ ▲ ▲ ▲ ▲ ▲ ▲ ▲ ▲ ▲ ▲ ▲ ▲ ▲ ▲

IN THEIR SEARCH FOR jollification, Western settlers developed rodeo, an orginal sport probably more indigenous to this continent than baseball. Rodeo had its simple beginnings in the roundup camps of cowboys, but as an organized sport it was nurtured in the old Wild West shows.

The first modern rodeo may have been the rehearsals held at North Platte, Nebraska, in 1883, by Buffalo Bill Cody for his Wild West Show. A born showman, Cody was also a skilled rider and marksman. He had accumulated several thousand dollars touring with a stage show, and now advertised throughout the West that he was organizing a company of "cowboys, Mexican vaqueros, famous riders and expert lasso throwers." So many applied for jobs as "actors" that he arranged a roping and riding competition to select the best. Buffalo Bill's Wild West Show opened at the fair grounds in Omaha on May 17,1883.

Many a Western town and city, however, lays claim to the honor of holding the first rodeo. In 1847, Mayne Reid reported that he witnessed a roping contest at Santa Fe. According to newspaper accounts, Cheyenne had some unorganized cowboy contests in 1872. Colorado's state fair of 1876, held in Denver, featured a race between a cowboy and a horse. Winfield, Kansas, claims the first rodeo was an exhibition held there by the 101 Ranch in 1882.

The same summer that Buffalo Bill's Wild West Show took to the road, 1883, the first roping and riding tournament was held in Texas. Some cowboys got into a friendly argument in a Pecos City saloon as to whether the Hashknife, the Mill Iron, or the Lazy Y had the best bronc riders and steer ropers. To settle the argument, they decided to hold a public contest on July 4th. Using the courthouse yard as a corral

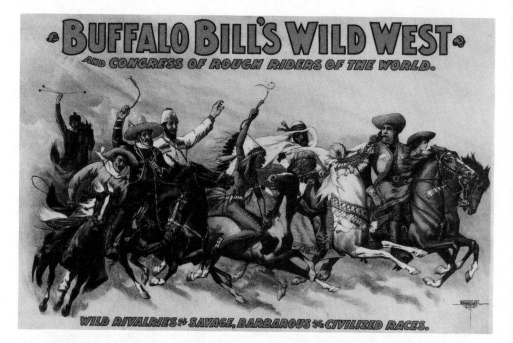

THE WILD WEST SHOW: RODEO'S PROVING GROUND

In their search for amusement, Western settlers developed rodeo, an original sport as American as baseball. Rodeo began in the roundup camps of cowboys, but before becoming an organized sport it was nurtured in the Wild West shows. The first modern rodeo may have been the rehearsals held at North Platte, Nebraska, in 1883 by Buffalo Bill Cody to select "cowboys, Mexican vaqueros, famous riders and expert lasso throwers" for his Wild West Show. (Poster by Courier Lithograph Company, courtesy of the Library of Congress.)

and Pecos City's main street for an arena, the cowboys put on quite a show.

Rodeo's real origins, of course, were in the roundup camps of the cowboys. Even before the great cattle drives up the Chisholm Trail, vaqueros in Mexico were holding tournaments for the best ropers and riders. One of their favorites was throwing the bulls by the tails. It was no accident that the Spanish word for roundup, *rodeo*, came into use early as the name for the most popular sport in the West.

Horse racing was always a favored amusement of Westerners. The larger towns and some big ranches had racetracks, but a track was unnecessary if rival range outfits happened to get together and start boasting of the relative speeds of their cow ponies. They raced right off across the prairie. If a high-spiritied bronc turned up in a horse herd, an informal riding contest was usually arranged on the spot, the spectators placing bets as to how long each competitor could ride bareback, or in the saddle. And whenever two or more cowboys were otherwise unoccupied for a few minutes, more than likely they would compete with each other at rope throwing.

For many years, however, these local contests were purely amateur, and if an expert rider or roper wanted to earn money with his special skills he had to join a Wild West show. The success of Buffalo Bill's "cowboys, riders and expert lasso throwers" soon brought many imitators into the business. Touring circuses added riding and roping acts, and often changed their names to "Wild West Shows." As might have been expected, these shows were quite popular with Western settlers; they would travel long distances to see tent shows if there was plenty of roping and riding and shooting guaranteed with each performance.

Some tamed-down Western towns that had lived with wild cowboys through trail driving days were not entirely happy to see them return with the tent shows—especially if the boys slipped from make-believe back to real old-time wildness. The Cheyenne *Democratic-Leader* of July 22, 1884, commented on a visiting show: "Last night at 12 o'clock, cowboys belonging to Hardwick's Wild West Show made a drunken raid on South Clark street in regular western style. They succeeded in frightening the people from the streets, and were finally captured by the police and locked up. Twelve large navy revolvers and a large knife were secured. The entire party was bailed out this morning, and this afternoon gave the usual exhibition to a crowd of 12,000 people. The cowboys in their raid last night were led by Ben Circkle, for years a celebrated character in the far West."

Meanwhile in the Southwest, riding and roping contests were continuing to gain popularity. During the summer of 1888, cowboys from the Laurel Leaf Ranch organized a two-day celebration in Canadian, Texas. Horse racing and square dancing were on the program, but the main event was a steer-roping contest. From miles around, folks rode into Canadian on horseback and in creaking buckboards. As there were no standard rules for rodeo contests, individual champions were not officially recognized in the early days of the sport. But Ellison Carroll won the roping contest on that day, and, for the next quarter of a century, he was undisputed king of the steer ropers.

On July 4, 1888, Prescott, Arizona, initiated its famous Frontier Days, including in the celebration what was probably the first commercial rodeo, or "first organized rodeo." Winning ropers and riders received small cash prizes, and spectators paid admission fees. For years, Arizonans had been fond of traveling street circuses, *romeriomaras,* which came up from Mexico with clowns and acrobats and trick riders. Arizona also is the only state in the Union which ever supplied camels for a Wild West show—nine camels which had escaped from the old War Department herd imported for desert use before the Civil War. So it is not surprising that Prescott organized the first commercial rodeo.

The hero of that Independence Day of 1888 was a cowboy named Juan Leivas who received a silver trophy inscribed as follows: "Citizens Prize, contested for and won by Juan Leivas over all competitors at the Fourth of July Tournament. Held in Prescott, A. T., 1888. For roping and tieing steer. Time 1:17½, 100 yards start."

In the Northwestern range country, the woolly-chapped ropers and riders kept their contests on an amateur basis until 1893. In that year, E. Farlow of Lander, Wyoming, combined a cowboy tournament with a Wild West show and circus. Farlow borrowed the Frontier Days idea from Arizona, but he added stagecoach holdups and horse-team relay races to the usual bronco-busting and steer-roping events. Lander's first Frontier Days was a grand show, but spectators were few, consisting mostly of participants relaxing between other contests.

After the slow start of Lander's Frontier Days, rodeo languished in the thinly populated Northwest. Contests were held at some of the stockmen's conventions in Montana, and cowboys from some of the larger Wyoming ranches occasionally met for informal rivalry. Then in 1897, Cheyenne staged its first Frontier Days, the first big-time rodeo. Cheyenne still considered itself the "cowboy capital," but even so the rodeo organizers sought aid from local businessmen and the Union

Pacific Railroad to ensure a paying crowd. Special trains brought in thousands of spectators in 1897, and the show was a success, with seats selling at fifteen to thirty-five cents.

Wyoming, the first state to give women the vote, was also the first to admit them to rodeo. The first female contestant was Bertha Kaepernick, who entered both the bucking contest and the wild horse race staged at Cheyenne's premiere Frontier Days. "She rode a wild horse in front of the grandstand," said Warren Richardson, one of the organizers of the celebration, "and she stayed on him all the time. Part of the time he was up in the air on his hind feet; once he fell backward, and the girl deftly slid to one side only to mount him again as he got up. She rode him in the mud to a finish, and the crowd went wild with enthusiasm."

Cheyenne also borrowed the most popular feature of Buffalo Bill's Wild West Show—a stagecoach holdup. It was a "thrilling event," according to the newspapers, but the stunt which truly gave the customers their money's worth was the hanging of a horse thief by a vigilante posse. Bill Root, Laramie newspaperman, played the part of the horse thief up to the moment when the noose came down. Then in the confusion around the scaffolding, Root dodged out of sight, and a dummy was dangled high and riddled with real bullets.

During these early years of rodeo's development, William Frederick Cody continued to win fame and earn fortunes with his Wild West troupe. His programs did not use the word "rodeo," but he selected the best riders and ropers to introduce this new sport of the American West to millions of people across the country.

In the 1890s, Buffalo Bill was at the zenith of his popularity. His Nebraska friends wanted him to run for governor; other admirers backed him for president of the United States. When Chicago's Columbian Exposition, the World's Fair of 1893, barred the Wild West Show from its grounds because it was "too undignified," Cody rented fourteen acres opposite the fairgrounds, set up a grandstand for 18,000 people, and started selling tickets. Every day thousands were turned away for lack of seats, and many a visitor paid his way into the Wild West Show, believing it to be the World's Fair.

Sir Henry Irving attended both, and decided Buffalo Bill had the better show: "Such dare-devil riding was never seen on earth. When the American cowboys sweep like a tornado up the track, forty or fifty strong, every man swinging his hat and every pony at its utmost speed, a roar of wonder and delight breaks from the thousands in the grandstand.''The cowboy band of 1893 was a feature soon to be adopted by many rodeos.

It was inevitable that professional Wild West show performers and rodeo contestants sometime would join forces for a grand extravaganza, and this event occurred at Cheyenne's second Frontier Days, in September 1898. "Buffalo Bill's big outfit added over six hundred to the crowd," reported the Cheyenne *Daily Sun-Leader* of September 6. "Never in the previous history of the town have the streets presented so animated an appearance as they did this morning with crowds of cowboys, Indians of the Sioux, Arapahoe and Shoshone, and thousands of well-dressed people."

As the popularity of rodeo spread across the West and more and more cities began organizing annual shows, a few outstanding performers soon became famous. No official records were kept in the early days of the sport, but Westerners seemed to know who the "champions" were.

Clay McGonigal of Texas was the "World's Champion Roper." He was beaten only once, and that time by Ellison Carroll, the first champion. Like Buffalo Bill's sharp-shooting Annie Oakley, Clay McGonigal's name became a noun in the terminology of Wild West shows and rodeos. To all pioneer rodeo performers, a fast-roping exhibition was a "McGonigal."

Another early champion was Bill Pickett, the first bulldogger. According to rodeo legend, Pickett's method of downing steers originated the term "bulldogging." His technique has been graphically described by Colonel Zack Miller of the 101 Ranch: "He slid off a horse, hooked a steer with both hands on the horns, twisted its neck and then sunk his teeth into the steer's nostrils to bring him down."

After a tour of rodeos, Bill Pickett joined up with Miller Brothers 101 Ranch Show and became a first-rank star. He was one of the few great black rodeo performers. After he was killed in 1932 while roping a bronc, the Cherokee Strip Cowboy Association honored him by erecting a special marker at his grave, and Zack Miller wrote a poem to his memory.

Texas-born Leonard Stroud was the first "All-Around Cowboy Champion." He was a bronc rider, a superb roper and bulldogger, and he introduced trick riding to many rodeos. Trick riders still perform his "Stroud Layout," in which the rider swings his body free from the horse with only one foot in a stirrup, the other balanced against the saddle horn.

TROUPING IN THE "WILD WEST"

Westerners were Buffalo Bill's most loyal customers, and Cody loved trouping in the country where he had begun his colorful career. In 1898, he took his show to Cheyenne for the second Frontier Days celebration. "Buffalo Bill's big outfit added over six hundred to the crowd," reported the Cheyenne *Daily Sun-Leader* of September 6. "Never in the previous history of the town have the streets presented so animated an appearance as they did this morning with crowds of cowboys, Indians of the Sioux, Arapahoe and Shoshone, and thousands of well-dressed people." (Photograph by Lee Moorehouse, courtesy of the University of Oregon Library.)

Among the early cowgirls in rodeo were Prairie Rose Henderson and Prairie Lillie Allen. Prairie Rose started her career at Cheyenne as a bronc rider, and attracted so much attention that other rodeos soon introduced cowgirl bronc-busting contests as regular events. She decided rodeo costumes were too drab, and instead of the usual long divided skirt, Prairie Rose wore a short one of velvet with a brilliantly decorated hem. Her chief rival for the crown of champion cowgirl bronc rider was Prairie Lillie Allen. Prairie Lillie also did stunt riding for some of the early Western movies, and starred in circuses.

Lucille Mulhall was described as "the greatest cowgirl on earth" by Buffalo Bill Cody when he saw her perform. She could rope eight horses with one throw of the lariat. When President Theodore Roosevelt, an irrepressible cowboy himself, visited the Mulhall ranch, Lucille amazed him by roping a coyote from horseback.

The story of Lucille Mulhall's career has all the ingredients of a classic American tragedy. She became a public figure in 1904 with her appearances at the Louisiana Purchase Exposition in St. Louis. Her father, Colonel Zack Mulhall, brought together a lusty troupe of riders for this show; one of his stunts was to have a mounted rider board a ferris wheel. He also advertised a bullfight and sold eight thousand tickets, but the law interfered just before the fight was to begin. The disappointed customers expressed their feelings by setting fire to the canvas-draped arena.

After leaving her father's colorful aggregation, Lucille Mulhall worked with Tom Mix and Will Rogers in rodeo, performing in the first shows at Madison Square Garden. Later she was a queen of the silent Western movies. She made a fortune and lost it. After riding wild horses for years without an accident, she died in an automobile crash. Her old friend, Foghorn Clancy, wrote a poignant description of her funeral: "The day after Christmas she was buried on the last pitiful acres of the once great Mulhall ranch, as a wild and driving rain turned the ground into a quagmire and the horses strained to pull the hearse across the field."

Lucille Mulhall's fellow Oklahomans, Tom Mix and Will Rogers, used their skills to achieve national fame as stage and screen actors; their names are a part of the legend of the American West. Tom Mix was a cowboy on the 101 Ranch and did his first rodeo work with Miller Brothers Wild West Show. Will Rogers also left off punching cattle to join a small Wild West show under the name of the Cherokee Kid. In

1905, they reached New York's Madison Square Garden. A few years later, gum-chewing, rope-twirling Will Rogers was the star of the Ziegfeld Follies, while Tom Mix was Hollywood's king of the silent Western movies.

Another Southwesterner whose name was almost a synonym for rodeo is Foghorn Clancy. Originally christened Frederick Melton Clancy, he lost his first two names while he was a newsboy on the streets of Mineral Wells, Texas. Because his voice sounded "like a foghorn at sea," he became Foghorn Clancy. It is doubtful if any of the thousands of rodeo performers and spectators who knew Foghorn during his half-century career as rodeo announcer, promoter, and handicapper ever suspected that he had any other name.

Foghorn Clancy entered his first roping and riding contest at San Angelo, Texas, in 1898, and was promptly bucked off a bronco. He had scarcely picked himself up out of the dust when he was offered a job calling the succeeding events; the contest manager suspected that Foghorn's voice might be more spectacular than his bronc-busting abilities. The manager was right, and on that summer day in San Angelo, Foghorn Clancy began the long career which carried him to almost every rodeo, roundup, and stampede in North America.

While rodeo was developing these pioneer heroes and heroines, the old Wild West shows were beginning a slow decline. After his great success of the 1890s, Buffalo Bill had fallen on evil days; his health was failing, his family life was breaking apart, his numerous investments used up money faster than he could earn it. One by one his partners deserted him to start shows of their own—"Bill" shows they were called because they all copied the original. Hundreds of tawdry imitations of his exciting program format toured the country, disillusioning the customers.

Gordon William Lillie, Pawnee Bill, had the only Wild West show that rivaled Cody's. After growing up in Oklahoma among the Pawnees, Gordon Lillie had taken a troupe of these Indians into the original Wild West Show of 1883. In later years he split with Cody and formed his own organization—Pawnee Bill's Far East. His wife, Mae Lillie, was the "little sure-shot" of the show. Always an intrepid showman, Pawnee Bill took his performers into places where others never would have dared to go, such as Princeton University, where in 1899 a street brawl developed between Pawnee Bill's parading horsemen and the Princeton students.

In 1908, Pawnee Bill rescued Buffalo Bill from bankruptcy, and the new organization became Buffalo Bill's Wild West and Pawnee Bill's Great Far East Combined.

But even the joint efforts of the two Bills could not save the Wild West Show. Time had passed it by. After two farewell cross-country tours, with the aging Cody appearing in a carriage instead of on horseback, the public stopped buying tickets. A mortgage kept the show going for a few months, but it lost money through one hundred successive performances. Ironically, the Wild West Show made its last stand in Colorado, the heart of the land from which its name had come. There the sheriff's men moved in to foreclose. "The show business," said Cody, "isn't what it used to be." He retired to his Wyoming ranch. And Pawnee Bill went home to Oklahoma to promote rodeo shows.

As the Wild West shows folded their tents forever, rodeo sprang to full growth. Veterans of the big tents moved into the rodeo arenas as pioneers of developing circuits that swung from Texas to California, from Cheyenne to Calgary, from Pendleton, Oregon, to Madison Square Garden in New York.

Rodeo was becoming more and more popular among Westerners. When farmers and ranchers drove their buggies and early model autos to their local county fairs (such as the one at Broken Bow, Nebraska), they expected to see or participate in roping and riding contests. An Iowan recalling his boyhood told of attending a county fair where two cowboys "dressed up in leather britches, red flannel shirts and broad brimmed hats rode into the ring and took after a little herd of horses. After a good deal of galloping and circling around, they roped one of them and threw him down so hard we thought it surely had broken his neck."

As rodeo became a standardized sport, it developed its own stars, who were as well known as the champions of other sports. Many competitors in the first big rodeos were orginally troupers with the old tent shows. Indians, being natural riders, provided both color and an element of menace for the big acts in traveling shows. Later they were among the main attractions of rodeos such as the Pendleton Roundup. One pioneer professional was Jackson Sundown, a nephew of the heroic Chief Joseph of the Nez Percé. He won a riding championship at Pendleton when he was fifty years old and was billed as "the greatest rider of the red race."

The Pendleton Roundup was born the year that Pawnee Bill temporarily rescued Buffalo Bill's show from financial disaster. Pendleton's baseball club that summer was as bankrupt as Buffalo Bill, and to help the team finish out the season, a group of Oregon cowboys staged a small rodeo in the ballpark. They received five dollars each for their efforts—and stole the show from the ball-and-bat boys.

Two years later Pendleton Roundup had become big-time rodeo. As an added feature to the usual program, more than a thousand North-western Indians set up their tepees on the grounds, donned their tribal costumes, paraded on gaily bedecked ponies, and performed war dances—making the Roundup one of the most dazzling rodeos in the West.

The golden boys of early Pendleton competitions were Yakima Canutt and Art Acord. Both were champion riders for a while, but like a number of other outstanding rodeo competitors they soon found themselves before the cranking movie cameras of Hollywood, performing silent epics of the Western range.

Last of the big rodeos to be organized was the Calgary Stampede. Canada's Alberta Province was the last stamping ground of frontier ranching in North America, and amateur roping and riding contests were held in Calgary in 1893. Some years afterward, Tom Mix and Guy Weadick attempted to stage a full-fledged rodeo there, but the first Stampede was not held until 1912. Four Canadian ranchers backed the show, providing the largest money prizes ever before offered rodeo contestants.

"The finest gathering of contestants and ropers ever got together," reported the Calgary *Herald*. The governor-general of Canada came to see the show and partook of a "typical roundup breakfast, prepared and served by men who had been in the country ever since the days of the open range." Participating in the first Calgary Stampede were Bertha Blancett, Lucille Mulhall, and many other rodeo stars from the United States. Bertha Blancett was "champion lady bronco buster of the world." In the winters, when rodeos were inactive, she worked in Hollywood as a stunt rider for the old Bison Moving Picture Company. She could down a galloping horse with the suddenness of a pistol shot.

And so, in the early years of the twentieth century, the old Wild West shows vanished and rodeo came to maturity. Modern rodeo has all the individual spirit of the Western settlers, yet is as stylized as a bullfight or a ballet. The programs follow a classical pattern—grand entry, bronc riding, bulldogging, calf roping, steer riding, steer roping.

The Wild West shows were based on riding and roping; the pageantry of modern rodeo in turn is borrowed from the Wild West shows. The grand entry which opens every rodeo is pure Buffalo Bill with its swirl of brilliant costumes and pennants, patriotic music, swift-paced flashing hooves, hats swept off, and trained ponies bowing to the cheering crowds.

No two bronc riders and no two bucking mounts are alike, yet in a rodeo contest rigid rules must be followed. The rider can use only a plain halter, one rein, and a regulation saddle. He must stay aboard for ten seconds after he and his bronc spring from the chute. During those ten seconds he can be disqualified for changing hands on the rein, pulling leather, blowing a stirrup, or failing to keep his spur active. Both mount and rider are judged by a point system. Yet in the rodeo arena the horse remains the king. No printed regulations forbid a horse to sidewind, corkscrew, skyscrape, sunfish, or high-dive; and all the cowboy and rodeo associations in the world can't keep a rider in the saddle for ten seconds if the horse decides otherwise.

Bulldogging or steer wrestling is a timed event, a series of rapid actions beginning with the dogger leaping from his horse to grasp the steer by the horns. By twisting the horns, he forces the steer down until it lies flat upon the ground. No longer does he bite the steer's nose or lip as did Bill Pickett; instead modern rules protect the animal. For instance, if a dogger lands too far forward and drops the steer's head to the ground in a somersault, the animal must be allowed to gain its footing again before the throw is made.

Steer riding is much like bareback bronc riding. The rider has only a single rope for security and can use only one hand. To qualify, he must stay clear of the ground for eight to ten seconds. Judging is by a point system.

Rodeo rules require that calves be thrown by hand, with three of their feet tied together at the finish. Steers are roped by their heads and should be brought to a halt facing the roper's horse.

Trick riding came to rodeo by way of a troupe of Cossack daredevils imported by the 101 Ranch. Intrigued by the Cossacks' stunts on their galloping horses, Western cowboys soon introduced variations to American rodeo. Colorful costumes seem to be a necessary part of trick riding, and it is quite possible that the outlandish Western garb which has invaded rodeo arenas can be blamed directly on Cossacks and trick riders.

And every rodeo must have its clown, usually the "rube" type who rides a burro when he first appears in the arena. A direct descendant of combined circuses and Wild West shows of the nineteenth century, the rodeo clown is in continual hot water throughout the events. Jake Herman, the famous Sioux clown of pioneer rodeo, commented: "A clown had to be a comic in the old days. Now the bulls have taken over. Now a clown needs to be a clever bullfighter. If a clown gets hooked in the pants the people think it funny. It's more like the olden times when the gladiators fought hungry lions in the Roman arenas. The more risk to life and limb the more laughs from the populace."

Witth the passing of the years, rodeo had become more and more professional, bound by numerous associations and regulations. But the sport remains the favored one of the West. The odds are still on the calf or steer every time a roper takes off across the arena swinging his loop. The spectators still come up cheering when the lariat snaps tight and the critter goes spinning into the dust.

CHAPTER 29
Law, Order, and Politics

▲ ▲ ▲ ▲ ▲ ▲ ▲ ▲ ▲ ▲ ▲ ▲ ▲ ▲ ▲ ▲ ▲

"FORMS AND CEREMONIES are at a discount, and generosity has its home in the pure air of the Rocky Mountains," wrote Thomas Dimsdale, Oxford graduate, singing-school teacher, and editor of the *Montana Post* in 1865. Another Briton, a cowboy named John J. Fox, observed in Wyoming that "democracy was practiced at its best and purest form at this time and place."

Dimsdale and Fox were idealists and probably oversimplified the state of law and order in the Old West. Informal, direct, and democratic, the first Westerners truly were; but they also had an instinct for group organization that began with the Lewis and Clark expedition, developed into complex printed constitutions for the government of overland parties crossing the plains in the gold rush of 1849, and became full blown in the elaborate secret rituals of the Grange and its political successors of the late nineteenth century.

Before the emigrants reached their destination, almost every one of them recognized the power of law in the person of the wagon master or the commander of the overland company:

"The commander shall have entire and complete control. . . .

"There shall be no exemption from any service. . . .

"We do solemnly and mutually pledge to each other, our lives, our fortunes, and our sacred honors."

But the first Western settlements, being under loose territorial control, had neither laws nor officers for enforcement. Petty thieving and crimes of violence were generally unknown in the homesteading country, but the mining settlements and cattle-shipping towns often became so lawless that the only cure was "a short cord and a good drop." When conditions became unbearable, the more respectable citizens would call a meeting to select a justice of the peace. Justices more often than not were elected by voice vote, as was Richard C. Barry of Sonora, a former Texas Ranger turned California gold miner.

One of Dick Barry's decisions:

"N. B. Barber, the lawyer for George Work, insolently told me there were no law for me to rool so. I told him that I didn't care a damn for his book law, that I was the law myself. I fined him $50 and committed him to gaol 5 days for contempt of court in bringing my roolings and dississions into disreputableness and as a warning to unrooly persons not to contradict this court."

Violence fed on violence in the booming polyglot communities of the West—in Onion Valley, Panamint, Tailholt, Skidoo, in Tucson, Dodge City, Rawhide, Abilene, Brewery Gulch, and Bannock. Every mining town had its "hang tree," and every trail town had its "boot hill." Many an outlaw received a "suspended sentence" from the famed old hang tree in Helena's Dry Gulch. In San Francisco, the vigilantes hanged their victims from a wharf derrick on Market Street. In Tombstone, they were left dangling from convenient telegraph poles.

Bad men and good men had no more use for the old-fashioned *code duello* than they had for a formal gallows. "Calling a man a liar, a thief, or a son-of-a-bitch was provocation sufficient to justify instant slaying."

In San Francisco, a group of desperadoes did some organizing on their own, committing robberies, rapes, murders, and arson. Late at night they roamed the streets in bands, barking like dogs at the respectable citizenry, who named them the Hounds. Courts could do nothing with them; as a New England visitor observed, the jurors were as bad as the Hounds, chatting and winking and smirking at the judge, and smoking with the accused.

But by 1861, the West was sufficiently organized to take sides on the issues of the onrushing Civil War. One strong faction wanted to go with the South; another proposed a separate Republic of the Pacific. The Far West, with California in the van, seemed to be moving toward separation from the Union.

On May 11, however, along San Francisco's Market Street—where only a few years earlier vigilantes were hanging men to keep the peace—a group of Union supporters rallied around the bannered words of Daniel Webster: "The Union, the whole Union, and nothing but the Union."

Before the day ended, almost everybody in San Francisco gathered in the muddy street to join the tumultuous meeting. People came on foot, on horseback, in carriages; the crowd blocked the horse-drawn street cars, swarmed over water carts and bread wagons, climbed upon roofs and packing boxes and barrels so that they could see the speakers' stand.

A few days later, California's legislature voted to support the Union, and all the West followed its example. Law, order, and politics were not well established beyond the Mississippi River.

During the wild years when society in the West was without "forms and ceremonies," the women who had crossed the plains and mountains gradually discovered that they were a free gender. At first, only a few realized that law, order, and politics no longer barred them from doing as they pleased. But the others caught on fairly rapidly. "They were treated with a deference and liberality unknown in other climes," commented the observant Thomas Dimsdale in what soon proved to be an understatement. Western women busted loose from centuries of law and order and started a revolution that has spread around the world. Arch-rebel in this Western revolt was Calamity Jane.

Throughout the period of Western settlement, men outnumbered women two to one—in some places thirty to one. But then as now, mere numerical superiority was of no consequence in the war between the sexes.

Britisher John J. Fox noted signs of the revolution in 1885 when he arrived in Carbon, Wyoming, to begin his ranching career. As Fox walked up into the town from the railroad depot, he met a cowboy and a woman "dashing down the street on horses, yelling, the man firing several shots in the air. He was evidently well 'lit up,' and the noisy female rode astride her pony, her long hair streaming behind her. She had on nothing but a chemise. To a very green young man raised in the most conservative little country town in Wessex, this was Life with a capital L. How my eminently respectable Victorian training leapt to meet it!"

A correspondent for the Missouri *Statesman*, visiting the California gold mines, wrote his newspaper that he had seen a woman in a gambling house, "sitting quietly at the monte table, dressed in white pants, blue coat, and cloth cap, curls dangling over her cheeks, cigar in her mouth and a glass of punch at her side. She handled a pile of doubloons with her blue-kid-gloved hands and bet most boldly."

And California women were way ahead of the bloomer craze in the East, according to a San Francisco newspaper of 1851: "The city was taken quite by surprise yesterday afternoon by observing a woman in company with her male companion, crossing the lower side of the Plaza. She was magnificently arrayed in a black satin skirt, very short, with flowing red satin trousers, a splendid yellow crape shawl and a silk turban *a la Turque*. She really looked magnificent and was followed by a large retinue of men and boys, who appeared to be highly pleased with the style."

In Wyoming Territory on December 10, 1869, for the first time on this continent, women were invested with "all the political rights, duties, franchises, and responsibilities of male citizens." A dozen years later, the editor of the *Laramie Weekly Sentinel* was still trying to figure out how it happened. "The motives which prompted the legislature to lay aside its conservatism and take this new departure were, so far as can be judged, an ambition to immortalize themselves and out-Herod Herod." On second thought, he suspected the legislature might have been "influenced by the idea that this act would materially serve to advertise our young territory and bring it into notoriety abroad."

Whatever the reason for this remarkable action on the part of the Wyoming lawmakers in giving women the vote, both major political parties began vying with each other for support from the new voters, providing fine horse carriages to transport them to the polls.

Margaret Thompson Hunter has told of how she voted the first year Wyoming became a state: "When election day rolled around, Mr. Hellman stopped in and asked me to go and vote for him. I was busy making pies and hadn't intended voting, but after all Mr. Hellman was a neighbor and also a very good friend of my husband's. So I pushed my pies aside, removed my apron, and tidied myself up a bit. Then I got into the buggy with Mr. Hellman and he drove me to the polls. Well, I voted and as we turned to leave we came face to face with my husband. When I explained to him that I had just voted for Mr. Hellman, I thought he would have a fit.

"You see, my husband was a staunch Democrat and one of the leaders in his party, and there I had just voted for a Republican. He was never so humiliated in all his life, he told me."

Running for office was a strenuous task in the geographically enormous Western counties and states. Voters were scattered over vast distances, and roads and trails were often impassable. During one campaign, a Wyoming candidate traveled 1,500 miles by buckboard, attending forty-five political rallies—which in Wyoming always ended with dancing well past midnight. Because of their new political power, he felt compelled to dance with every woman present.

In spite of all this, there were candidates aplenty for every office. According to the editor of the Leavenworth (Kansas) *Weekly Herald*, there were often more candidates than voters: "Dr. H_____ tells a good story at the expense of our worthy ex-city marshal. While the latter was endeavoring to rescue the team which broke through the ice on election day, he broke through himself, and came very near drowning. As the ice was giving way, and he about going down, he exclaimed at the top of his voice: 'I have not voted—I have not voted!' Of course he was rescued, as candidates could be found within hearing of every man's voice."

Western politicians wanted everybody to vote, and on occasion even welcomed the poor and voteless Indians. "Yuma was a hell of a place when I first went there in 1870," said Frederic G. Brecht, an old settler of Prescott, Arizona. "The politicians would bring a string of Yuma Indians up to vote. They wore nothing but a breech-cloth and perhaps a stovepipe hat, and held their already marked tickets in their hand. When a clerk would ask an Indian his name he would say 'Sullivan' or 'Malony,' or any other good Irish name he had been drilled in saying."

After the Panic of 1873 and the years immediately following, the Westerners' capacity for ready organization was demonstrated when they rushed by the thousands to form local and state units of the Patrons of Husbandry, or National Grange. The Grange had been started in the East by Oliver Hudson Kelley in 1867, but met with small success until the outraged Western farmers suddenly put all their reckless vigor into it. Settlers beyond the Mississippi were angry over the high prices they had to pay for things they had to buy and the low prices they received for things they had to sell. They were not only disgusted with grasshoppers and droughts, they were fighting mad against the railroad monopoly which raised rates higher and higher until there was no profit in shipping products to Eastern markets.

"Let the public be damned," said Commodore Cornelius Vanderbilt, spokesman for the railroads, and the Westerners began buzzing like angry bees. They welcomed the National Grange with its secret rituals and hopeful expectations. Across the dusty plains of Kansas and Nebraska, and far out into Colorado, Montana and Washington, long processions of buggies were rolling to Grange meetings. In front were the banners and crudely lettered mottoes of the lodges, with sometimes a band playing, and marshals on horseback in red sashes galloping up and down the columns, keeping them moving in orderly fashion.

To eliminate middlemen and keep prices low for the things they had to buy, the Grangers entered into an agreement with a young Chicago drummer who had been traveling through rural areas selling bargain merchandise to farmers. The traveling salesman's name was Montgomery Ward, and in 1872 he issued a single-sheet catalog for members of the Grange. Three years later his catalog had seventy-two pages with illustrations—one of them featuring a "Grange hat."

Montgomery Ward's catalog was particularly welcomed by Granger wives, who, being Western women, had of course become members of the new organization along with their men. Caroline Arabella Hall of Minnesota, niece of the founder, had taken care of this by traveling all the way to Washington to insist on women being admitted. Caroline Hall won her suit against much opposition from some male members, who thought that admitting women to equal membership in a secret society was "going altogether too far."

No longer could the male Western settler leave his wife in a lonely farmhouse while he rode off to town on horseback for an evening of revelry with his lodge brothers. Now he had to hitch a team to the buggy and ride sedately to the schoolhouse, to listen to Grange debates and lectures, and sing songs out of a Grange songbook compiled by Miss Caroline Arabella Hall.

By the late 1870s, many Westerners lost their warm enthusiasm for the Grange movement. They thought its aims were admirable, but the railroads, the banks, and the government paid no attention. And prices for everything the farmers bought kept going up; prices for everything the farmers sold kept going down.

About this time, far out in Lampasas County, Texas, a group of ranchers and farmers organized the Texas Alliance to combat cattle and horse thieves, barbed wire, and land sharks. They had secret signs, grips, and passwords. Like the Grange, they also attempted to eliminate middlemen through cooperative buying and selling. Within a few years the Alliance spread across all of Texas, north into Kansas and Nebraska, and then moved westward.

Unlike the Grange, this new organization was keenly interested in politics and soon attracted thousands of non-farmers into its ranks— preachers, teachers, editors, and country doctors, persons whose livelihood depended upon the prosperity of farmers. "The Grange had been social," said Hamlin Garland, who was just beginning his literary career as a partisan journalist, "but the Farmers' Alliance came as a revolt."

As outstanding leader of the Alliance was Jerry Simpson, a mild-

mannered Kansas farmer with a Scotch burr in his voice. Originally a
Great Lakes sailor, Jerry Simpson had ventured to Kansas in the great
wave of Western land settlement. "I came to Kansas to plant something
in the ground and see it grow and reproduce its kind," he said. Jerry
Simpson also had a yen to be a politician, and he took for his motto:
"I love my fellow man."

"The Grange was full of poetry, the Alliance was full of politics,"
said this natural-born frontier politician.

He changed from an Abraham Lincoln supporter to a Greenbacker;
in succession he was a Granger, a Union Labor man, and a Single Taxer.
He won his colorful nickname in his first campaign for Congress as an
Alliance candidate running against a powerful Republican lawyer from
Wichita. When the Republican press called Jerry Simpson a clown, an
ignoramus, a boor, and a ragamuffin, he retaliated by describing his
opponent as "Prince Hal, a prince of royal blood who travels in his
special car, his dainty person gorgeously bedecked in silk stockings."

William Allen White, then a young reporter, immediately dubbed
Simpson "the Sockless Socrates." Sockless Jerry Simpson he was from
that time on, glorying in the portrait which his opponents made of him
as an ignorant fool. Actually he was an avid reader of Dickens, Carlyle,
Scott, Burns, the Bible, Tom Paine, and the *Congressional Record.*

"It was an era of fervent meetings and fulminating resolutions," said
Hamlin Garland, who was traveling through the rebellious West in 1890
as correspondent for the *Arena.* "I attended barbecues on drab and
dusty fairgrounds, meeting many of the best known leaders in the field."
It was the day of the political picnic, the day of the orator with waving
arms and flapping coattails, of eloquence so emotional that speaker and
audience wept streams of tears.

And women were everywhere in this political revolt. "Farmers' wives
and daughters rose earlier and worked later to gain time to cook the
picnic dinners, to paint the mottoes on the banners, to practice with
the glee clubs, to march in processions . . . in that wonderful picnick-
ing, speech-making Alliance summer of 1890."

Eighteen-ninety was the year that Mary Elizabeth Lease, leading
woman orator in the Western revolt, made her most famous speech at
a political picnic on the fairgrounds of Paola, Kansas: "The people are
at bay. Let the bloodhounds of money who have dogged us thus far
beware. What you farmers need is to *raise less corn and more hell!*"

Mary E. Lease became a legend in her own time. Born in Ireland
of a nonconformist father who had fled to Pennsylvania, she had come

to Kansas in the early 1870s to earn a living by teaching school. She married Charles Lease, and lived the lonely life of a farmer's wife until a mortgage foreclosure forced them to move into Wichita where Lease could earn a little money as a pharmacist. Mary Elizabeth took in washing and read law until she was swept up into the Alliance movement.

Wearing her high-collared black dress, which became a sort of trademark, Mary Lease toured the farming country and made 161 speeches in the campaign of 1890. She was a long-legged, fair-skinned, dark-haired woman with a prominent chin and melancholy blue eyes. She hypnotized herself as well as her audiences with her golden contralto voice. "There were times when I actually made speeches without knowing it, when I was surprised to read in the morning paper that I had spoken the night before. . . . My tongue is loose at both ends and hung on a swivel."

After hearing her for the first time, a Western farmer recorded in his diary: "Went to town to hear Joint discussion between Mrs. Lease & John M. Brumbaugh. Poor Brumbaugh was not in it."

The dynamic Alliance drew into its ranks Grangers, Greenbackers, Single Taxers—all the voices of dissent in the West. "The campaign of 1890," commented the Kansas City *Times,* "was a good deal more than a political campaign . . . it was a religious rivival, a crusade."

Alliance parades moved through the streets of villages and towns. Protesting farmers—men, women, and children—rode on hayrack floats, singing gospel tunes with new words. "The Kingdom of Mammon Shall Fall" was a favorite:

> *There's a grand reformation*
> *Have you heard the welcome tune?*
> *It is sweeping through our nation*
> *'Tis a mighty power grown.*

Torchlight parades were so popular that salesmen toured the plains country selling rubber capes to protect the marchers from sparks. Crudely lettered placards bobbed along the lines of march: WE ARE MORTGAGED, ALL BUT OUR VOTES. SPECIAL PRIVILEGE FOR NONE, EQUAL RIGHTS FOR ALL. DOWN WITH WALL STREET. And there was usually a float crowded with pretty girls knitting socks for Sockless Jerry Simpson.

And when the ballots were counted after the elections of 1890, the nation was startled by the power of the farmers' revolt. In Kansas alone, they elected a senator, four congressmen, and ninety-one state legislators. In Nebraska, their success was almost as great; in Colorado, the Dakotas, and Minnesota, they controlled the balance of power.

The victories of 1890 stimulated agitation for organization of a third political party in the United States. Throughout 1891 and into 1892, conventions were held in various cities, while thousands of unemployed miners in the Far West were swelling the ranks of the rebellious.

At St. Louis in December 1891, delegates went wild when their leaders presented a Populist Manifesto calling for a national convention to nominate a presidential candidate for the new People's Party. "Everyone was upon his feet in an instant and thundering cheers from 10,000 throats greeted these demands as the road to liberty. Hats, papers, handkerchiefs, etc., were thrown into the air; wraps, umbrellas and parasols waved; cheer after cheer thundered and reverberated through the vast hall, reaching the outside of the building where thousands, who had been awaiting the outcome, joined in the applause till for blocks in every direction the exultation made the din indescribable. For fully ten minutes the cheering continued, reminding one of the lashing of the ocean against a rocky beach during a hurricane."

The hurricane lashed across the west to Omaha, where on July 4, 1892, the new People's Party nominated General James B. Weaver of Iowa to run for president against the candidates of the two old parties. Weaver lacked the color of Sockless Jerry Simpson and Mary E. Lease, but as a loyal follower described him, he was a composite of strength and gentleness: "The cannibalism of politics has snapped at him in vain."

The delegates gave Weaver an ovation but reserved their most enthusiastic applause for the reading of the new party's platform, a sacred creed designed to bring back prosperity to the settlers of the Western land. After its reading, the band played "Yankee Doodle" for twenty minutes.

Among Western leaders campaigning for the Populists in that dramatic political year of 1892 was Senator William Alfred Peffer of Kansas. "Formerly the man who lost his farm could go west," he said. "Now there is no longer any west to go to. Now they have to fight for their homes instead of making new." Even in a day when beards were common, the facial adornment of Senator Peffer was so lengthy it attracted national attention. Political cartoonists had a field day with Peffer's beard. One newspaper commented: "Senator Peffer is not obliged to spend money for a Christmas tree. He simply puts glass balls, small candles, strings of pop-corn and cornucopias in his magnificent whiskers and there you are."

In Colorado, Davis Waite launched into a campaign for governor on the Populist ticket, emphasizing the new party's platform proposal for "free and unlimited coinage of silver." Waite was a printer, editor, and lawyer, a headstrong zealot, a master of rich rhetoric. "It is better, infinitely better," he cried, "that blood should flow to the horses' bridles rather than our national liberties should be destroyed."

Known thereafter as "Bloody Bridles" Waite, he terrified conservatives with his threats to coin state money for Colorado, to lead the silver states out of the Union—and if need be, invade the East with an armed body of Populist cavalry. "Mr. Waite comes from a fine New England family," said one of his friends, "but sometimes he has rather peculiar notions." In spite of his "peculiar notions," Waite rode to victory over his old-party opponents.

Another ardent Populist supporter was Hamlin Garland, who had grown to manhood on his father's prairie homestead and had seen the bright promises of the Western horizon turn into poverty and endless toil. Rejecting it all, Garland had fled eastward to Boston where he hoped to earn a living by teaching and writing. Now he returned to his West to join the Populist crusade. He wrote a propaganda novel, *Prairie Folks,* joined the staff of a periodical supporting the cause, and offered his services as a campaign speaker.

"With other eager young reformers, I rode across the odorous prairie swells, journeying from one meeting place to another, feeling as my companions did that something grandly beneficial was about to be enacted into law. In this spirit I spoke at Populist picnics, standing beneath great oaks, surrounded by men and women, workworn like my own father and mother, shadowed by the same cloud of dismay. I smothered in small halls situated over saloons and livery stables, traveling by freight-train at night in order to ride in triumph as 'Orator of the Day' at some county fair, until at last I lost all sense of being the writer and recluse."

The noisy campaigning of the Populists was heard across the nation. Although most contemporary newspapers and periodicals were sympathetic toward the plight of Western farmers, few were friendly toward the new third party, which they believed to be a threat to the American political system. The presidential election of 1892 was an unorthodox affair, with voters crossing party lines in all directions. When it was all over, the Populists were victorious only in the West, while the rest of the country elected Grover Cleveland and a Democratic government.

In Kansas, the Populists had won their most spectacular victories, electing the governor and a large majority of state senators. They also claimed the state House of Representatives, but the Republicans disputed this. Leaders of the third party gathered in Topeka in January 1893 to celebrate the inauguration of the "first People's Party administration on earth," but arguments over control of the House dampened the proceedings.

The Populists and the Republicans each elected a presiding officer for the House, and for several days each side took turns passing laws and making speeches. Finally the Republicans announced that after one more week they would bar from the floor all who refused to recognize their organization as the legally elected House. When the Republicans adjourned for the day, Populists armed with rifles took possession of the legislative halls. Next morning, the Republicans smashed in the doors with sledgehammers, and the governor called out the state militia. "War times in Topeka," a Kansas farmer recorded in his journal; but the Gatling guns which rolled out upon the capitol grounds were harmless; someone had stolen all the cranks necessary to operate them.

A Kansas blizzard interrupted action for several hours, and when the weather cleared the Populists agreed to leave the dispute to the courts. As the courts were controlled by Republicans, this retreat of the Populists amounted to a surrender. From that day the People's Party was on the defensive in Kansas. Some months afterward, the Concordia *Empire* slyly observed: "Pops don't spring up out of the bushes now by the thousands as they did three or four years ago."

In spite of the Populists' victories, more unrest came to the West with the money panic of 1893. Miners, loggers, and workers in the new cities were soon in a worse plight than the mortgaged farmers. Silver prices dropped sharply, forcing mines to close. Banks shut their doors. Thousands of unemployed drifted into Denver, and when Governor "Bloody Bridles" Waite attempted to provide food and shelter, he became involved in a dispute with Denver city officials. Rioting followed, cannons were aimed at the city hall, and federal troops had to be rushed in to restore order. Proposed remedies for the situation across the West were as numerous as the unemployed, but the Free Silver advocates seemed to be winning the most followers; free silver became a popular panacea for relieving the economic plight.

On a summer day in 1893, a huge bearded man, wearing high boots, a sombrero, and a fringed buckskin shirt with buttons made of silver dollars, arrived in Chicago to attend a Free Silver convention. He was Carl Browne of San Francisco, rancher, cartoonist, editor, dreamer, emotional orator, and inventor of flying machines. His friends called him "Old Greasy" because he seldom took time to bathe.

During the convention, Browne made the acquaintance of mild-mannered Jacob Coxey of Ohio and convinced him that an army of a million Westerners was ready to march on Washington to demand action from the government. Coxey thought that perhaps a million Easterners might also join the march, and so he and Browne began the organization of Coxey's Army. Browne was responsible for the slogans, the badges, and other publicity for the Great March, "the petition in boots," as he called it.

Coxey's Army consisted of dozens of armies rather than one, and they all began moving toward Washington in the spring of 1894. Coordination of operations was completely lacking, however, with Browne and Coxey devoting all their energies to the comparatively short march from Massillon, Ohio. The largest armies were formed in the Far West, in California, Washington, Colorado, Idaho, and Montana.

In Butte, a group of unemployed miners and railroad workers kicked up a storm by seizing a Northern Pacific freight train. They ran it to Bozeman, picked up some new recruits and three tons of flour and beef, and continued to Billings. Here they were met by a United States marshal and seventy-five deputies who demanded an unconditional surrender. In the fight which followed, one man was killed and several wounded; the marshal and his deputies beat a hasty retreat.

While the train rolled on to Forsyth to sidetrack for the night, War Department headquarters in Washington, D.C., was ordering six companies of infantry from Fort Keogh and four troops of cavalry from Fort Custer to march out and capture the stolen train. About midnight, while the Coxeyites were asleep in the boxcars, their sentinels saw a train approaching from the east at high speed. Before the sleeping men could be awakened, the oncoming train stopped, and six companies of infantry swarmed out of it. The civilian "army" of 331 men surrendered; they were taken to Helena as prisoners, were tried, and given light sentences. One month later this determined division of Coxey's Army was headed east again, going down the Missouri River in flatboats.

The largest army from the West originated in California, its leader being Charles T. Kelly, a San Francisco printer, a small, soft-spoken man with light blue eyes. Kelly and his 1,500 followers (among whom was Jack London, just beginning his career as a writer) also commandeered trains. The railroads were willing to cooperate by providing a special freight train, but Kelly's men wanted passenger cars. "We are United States citizens, not hogs," said Kelly.

When the army bogged down in Utah for lack of transportation, "Bloody Bridles" Waite, the fiery Populist governor of Colorado, invited them into his state. But the Rio Grande Western Railroad refused to ride them for free. Finally, Kelly's men seized a Union Pacific freight train, which they manned and rode all the way to Omaha with no opposition from the railroad.

But by the time the Western divisions of Coxey's Army reached Washington, they found the first arrivals hungry, disgruntled, and divided into factions. Coxey had already left the city to raise more funds; Carl Browne and sixty of his lieutenants had departed for Atlantic City to bathe in the ocean.

The Westerners stuck it out longer than most of the others, but at last they also admitted the Great March was a failure. "We are going back to our homes," one Californian told a newspaper reporter, "where we will continue the fight for liberty and equality at the ballot box."

Meanwhile in Nebraska, thirty-four-year-old William Jennings Bryan was laying plans to ensure that his name would be on the next presidential ballot as the choice of the rebellious Westerners. Bryan had just lost an election race for United States senator to a Populist, and thereupon decided that what his Democratic Party needed was an infusion of new blood from the dynamic People's Party. Borrowing practically all of the Populists' 1892 platform, with emphasis on free silver, Bryan began his campaign to be nominated for president by the Democrats in 1896.

The Silver Knight, as he was soon to be called, was an odd sort of Westerner. In his black cutaway coat, low-cut vest, string tie, and soft felt hat, he looked like a politician from the deep South. He disliked whisky; as a small boy working the harvests, he refused to carry any alcohol to the threshing hands, insisting they drink water instead. His voice ("clear and silvery as a bell") might have been that of an imploring, Bible Belt evangelist.

But the West's Democrats and the West's Populists backed him from the beginning in the Chicago convention. His "Nebraska boys" wore red bandannas, waving them like provocative flags at the opposition delegates. Bryan's "cross of gold" speech won him the nomination, and shortly afterward the Populist candidate of 1892, General Weaver, gave the Silver Knight his party's blessing.

Bryan campaigned everywhere, day and night. He wore out his staff and the newspapermen assigned to report his tour of the nation. "Bryan's youth and strength," commented one of these reporters, "stand him in good stead for his continual jaunting through the country. An older man could not go through the ordeal and live."

It seemed that everyone wanted to see him. Old ladies in sunbonnets trotted along the tracks beside his train, fifes and drums marched ahead of him in the streets, bands played "See the Conquering Hero Comes," the shrieks of the crowds became delirium. He averaged thirty speeches a day. Millions of Americans heard and saw this wild tornado from the plains.

But, as the campaign progressed, it became evident that he was making enemies as well as friends. He was called a tool of the capitalist silver interests, and anarchist, a blasphemer, an anti-Christ, "a mouthing, slobbering demagogue." At least one attempt was made to poison him.

Bryan did not win the election, but he came very close. Twenty thousand votes more would have taken him into the White House. He missed carrying Kentucky by 281 votes, California by 962, Oregon by 1,000.

Twice again, Bryan was to make his try for the presidency. But the West, along with the rest of the country, was entering upon a period of prosperity and organized protests were no longer popular. There would be no more Western political uprisings for another generation.

While Western politicians were making history—if not winning elections—the appointed keepers of the law had been busy combatting horse thieves, train robbers, stagecoach bandits, and other rugged individualists. The sheriff—lonely, proud, corrupt, deadly, cowardly, or brave—has been well preserved in the annals of the American West. In actuality, Western sheriffs spent as much time riding swivel chairs behind rolltop desks as they did on horses leading posses.

One of the lawmen was Judge Roy Bean of west Texas. In 1882, at the urgent request of the Texas Rangers, Bean was appointed justice of the peace, charged with maintaining law and order in the railroad construction camps along the Southern Pacific. After the railroad was completed, Roy Bean held on to his office, and for twenty years he was the law west of the Pecos (a four-hundred-mile stretch of wild outlaw

country). He was a huge, gray-bearded man with a beer paunch strain-
ing over his belt. He liked Mexican sombreros, and in most of his
photographs (one shows him dispensing beer and justice to a horse thief
on the porch of his combination courtroom and saloon) he is seen with
his shirttail hanging out, a wilted bandanna knotted around his neck,
and a heavy gold watch chain running across a vest which is never
buttoned except at the top. The Pecos was waterless country, so naturally Judge Bean drank a considerable amount of liquor and bathed
only upon special occasions.

The only written law he knew was what he got out of a copy of the
Revised Statutes of Texas, 1879 edition. He practically memorized that
volume and had no use for later editions. "They sent me a new book
every year or so," he once recalled, "but I used them to light fires
with."

But Roy Bean gave cold-blooded killers, cattle rustlers, and horse
thieves no mercy. "Court's in session," he would announce, and then
delivered his sentence without pausing: "To be hanged by the neck until
dead." As each trial ended, he would serve up cold beer all around;
his courtroom was also his saloon.

Roy Bean may have been a great fraud in his later years, but in the
early days when he was the only law west of the Pecos, he was a fair
representative of the strong-willed folks who brought law and order to
the West.

Continuous rough treatment from the forces of law finally discouraged most Western bad men from engaging in serious crimes. Down
in the Southwest, however, after the male lawbreakers were fairly well
thinned out, a sizable group of gunwomen arose to take the men's
places. These irrepressible women expressed themselves as freely in
outlawry as other Western women did in gambling and politics.

Among the more efficient of these armed females were Belle Starr,
Pearl Hart, Rose of the Cimarron, Poker Alice, Cattle Annie, and Little
Britches. Annie McDougal (Cattle Annie) and Jennie Metcalf (Little
Britches) started their careers in their teens by selling whisky illegally
to Indians in the Osage nation. Soon they broadened their operations
to include horse thieving and cattle rustling. Occasionally they helped
Bill Doolin's Wild Bunch rob a bank. A pair of U.S. marshals finally
trapped the young ladies, but Little Britches scratched her captors' faces
with her long fingernails, escaped, and had to be caught again. One of
the marshals shot her horse from under her.

Cattle Annie and Little Britches were sent away to a government reform school in Massachusetts. After serving her sentence, Little Britches turned to religion and died shortly afterward in a New York slum. Cattle Annie returned to Oklahoma and took up respectability.

According to legend, Rose of the Cimarron became an outlaw in order to be with her sweetheart, George (Bitter Creek) Newcombe. Newcombe robbed banks and trains with the Dalton and Doolin gangs, and Rose went along for love and excitement. The dramatic moment of her career occurred the day a posse trapped Doolin's Wild Bunch at Ingalls, Oklahoma. Rose was on the second floor of the town's only hotel when the shooting started. Realizing that her lover, Bitter Creek, was across the street without his rifle and ammunition belt, she decided to try to take them to him. But both back and front exits of the hotel were full of flying lead from the posse's guns.

Always resourceful, Rose improvised a rope from stripped bedsheets and slid to the ground through a side window. Trusting the chivalrous Western marshals would not shoot an apparently unarmed woman, she concealed the rifle and belt beneath her flowing skirts and rushed across to the building where Bitter Creek was waiting. Thanks to Rose, he escaped this bloody battle, but was killed two years later in another gunfight.

Like many frontier characters, Rose of the Cimarron may be more folklore than fact. Her real identity has never been satisfactorily established; some chroniclers have identified her as Rosa Dunn and Rose O'Leary, others claim she never existed at all. One of her outlaw friends revealed only that she was "a Texan born and raised," who ended her public career by marrying a homesteader and becoming the respectable mother of three children.

As the female outlaws retreated before law and order, banditry languished in the West. Cattle and horses were secure behind barbed wire; the banks kept their money in safety vaults; the trains moved too fast for robbers; and stagecoaches had all but disappeared.

But in the Teton valley below Yellowstone Park lived an amiable fellow who had always had a yen to hold up a stagecoach. His name was Ed Trafton, and he had done time for cattle rustling in the 1880s. After his release from jail, his friends found him a job as U.S. mail carrier to keep him out of mischief.

Ed Trafton kept his eye on the fancy yellow stagecoaches rolling around Yellowstone Park. Automobiles were banned from the park in those days, and the stagecoaches were always filled with well-dressed tourists. These sight-seeing coaches usually moved around the park in a caravan, spaced about ten minutes apart.

On July 20, 1914, Ed Trafton and an accomplice stationed themselves near Shoshone Point and started holding up stagecoaches. They were confident nobody would shoot at them because firearms, like automobiles, were banned from Yellowstone. Wearing a fancy black mask and armed with a Winchester rifle, Trafton stopped thirty-five stagecoaches between ten in the morning and early afternoon. He would order the passengers out of each coach, line them up on the road, and then his assistant would drive the empty coach off out of sight behind a big rock outcropping.

"Cash only," Ed said politely to the tourists, and passed a big sack along each new line of victims. By the time he was finished with one group, another coach would roll around the bend, and he would hold it up. During the midst of the proceedings, one of the victims asked permission to take Kodak snapshots of the next holdup. "Sure," Ed replied gallantly. He thought it was a splendid idea to have his picture taken in his black mask holding up a stagecoach.

Ed Trafton took $3,000 from 165 tourists, and then decided it was time to ride away. With a friendly bow to his long line of victims, he mounted his horse and with his assistant galloped off to the north. As they rode out of the park, they cut the telegraph and telephone lines.

But law and order caught up with Ed Trafton four days later, and he served some more time in jail. His was the last stagecoach holdup in the history of the West, and it was also probably the biggest on record.

Old Ed Trafton lived until 1924. He died with his boots on, while eating an ice cream cone in a Los Angeles drugstore.

An uncommon outlaw was the Indian, but when one of these native Westerners joined the fraternity, he was a rough customer. A protégé of army scout Al Sieber, the Apache Kid was a highly respected first sergeant in the Apache government scouts until he left the San Carlos agency one day to murder an Indian who had killed his father. When Al Sieber attempted to arrest him, the Kid shot his old friend in the leg and fled the reservation.

For the next several years, the Apache Kid robbed wagon trains, rustled horses and cattle, and tortured and murdered an occasional rancher who got in his way. When he wanted female compaionship, he would steal a woman from a reservation and then leave her stranded in the desert. His name was as much feared as that of old Geronimo in Indian-fighting days.

Sheriff Glen Reynolds and a deputy as last captured the Kid with five other wanted Apaches, but en route to jail, the outlaw suddenly threw his handcuffed wrists over Reynolds's head and pinioned the sheriff's arms. While Reynolds was struggling to escape, one of the other Apaches knocked out the deputy with a pair of heavy iron handcuffs, seized his rifle, and shot the sheriff to death.

Posses were soon combing the rugged mountains and deserts of the Apache country. They caught the outlaw's five companions, but the impassive, cold-blooded Kid vanished and was never seen by the whites again.

Unlike the Apache Kid, most reservation Indians were law-abiding. Some of them, like old Red Cloud, the fighting Sioux leader, adopted the dress, manners, and speech of their conquerors and were more interested in making laws than breaking them. Wearing a cowboy hat, stiff white collar, and long-tailed coat, Red Cloud sometimes traveled in the East as a sort of lobbyist for laws to improve the conditions of his people.

Hundreds of civilian army scouts found themselves without employment in a West of law and order. After years of danger and excitement, the chase had ended. Scouts despised farming as heartily as did most Indians, and many of them wasted out their lives around army posts and reservations. Many grew fat and lazy, occasionally earning a few pennies posing for traveling stereophotographers.

Western cavalrymen who had conquered the Indians also found life tedious in a pacified West. Petty garrison duties, continual drilling, and intricate reviews for visiting generals replaced the exciting chases and battle marches. Old campaigners like General George Crook who rarely ever wore a full regulation uniform could never accustom themselves to the spit-and-polish of the West's peacetime army. One day, during a review held in his honor at a camp named for him in Nebraska, General Crook's dress trousers refused to keep company with his shoe tops, and his drawer string broke loose, to the vast amusement of the assembled troop. "He was rather a funny spectacle, galloping down the lines on a strange and not imposing horse at the head of his staff, escort and orderlies, numbering perhaps a hundred."

In 1898, however, with the beginning of the Spanish-American War, the dormant Western cavalry came to life again. But the show was stolen from the regulars by a regiment of volunteers—the First United States Volunteer Cavalry, known as the Rough Riders. Organized by Theodore Roosevelt, the Rough Riders' regiment was made up of one thousand "good shots and good riders"—cowboys, army scouts, and former Indian fighters predominating. Roosevelt armed his men with six-shooters instead of sabers, trained them hard in San Antonio, and then led them to glory at San Juan Hill in Cuba. A few months later he was president, the first cowboy to reach the White House.

The last organized threat to peace and order in the West at this time came out of Mexico when Pancho Villa and his wild-riding revolutionists crossed the border and raided Columbus, New Mexico, just before dawn on March 9, 1916. Several hundred Villistas wearing their high-crowned sombreros galloped into Columbus under cover of darkness, firing carbines and shouting, "Viva Mexico!" and "Viva Villa!" Two hundred and fifty American cavalrymen stationed in the town rolled out of their blankets and began firing back, but the only targets were sudden flashes of carbine fire. "The raiders burned up thousands of rounds of ammunition," a cavalry lieutenant said afterward. "Then a hotel was set afire, and this lit up the terrain so effectively that we were able to see our targets very plainly." At dawn, the raiders beat a hasty retreat, but they had killed seven American soldiers and eight civilians and left the town burning behind them.

Villa's purpose in raiding Columbus was to provoke an American cavalry pursuit into Mexico, an action which he hoped would cause the fall of the Mexican government and give the Villistas a chance to seize power. The first part of his plan worked perfectly. A troop of cavalry was mounted and hot on the trail of the raiders before they could recross the border. Under General John J. Pershing, three cavalry columns—including the famed Seventh Regiment—marched four hundred miles into Mexico in pursuit of Villa. They marched over the same type of rugged cactus-studded desert country where an earlier generation of Western cavalrymen had pursued the Apaches Geronimo, Cochise, and Victorio. They failed to capture Pancho Villa, but they dispersed his armies, broke his power and prestige, and restored law and order in the Southwestern border country.

As the cavalry marched southward, eight thunderbird airplanes strange to Western skies flew above the dust-clouded columns, their fragile wings and struts bending and stretching, their chattering little motors breaking the silences of the hot desert land. These eight machines comprised the entire fighting air force of the United States, the

First Aero Squadron, Signal Corps. By the end of the Punitive Expedition, all the planes had crashed but one, and it was so badly damaged it had to be condemned.

But the thunderbirds had made their mark on history over those unfriendly deserts of the West. General Pershing commented laconically: "One airplane is equal to a regiment of cavalry."

And there in the Apache country—where many a blue-clad soldier had fought hard to win this Western land for settlement—was ended forever the old cavalry. No more would the bugle sound stable call or the charge. No more would the sergeants order "mount" or "dismount." No more would the columns go swinging away to the strains of "Garryowen" and "The Girl I Left Behind Me." The thunderbirds had erased time and space, the mysterious unknown that lay beyond the horseman's horizon. The old West of the rider on horseback was gone forever; the big rolling land was now the settlers' West.

·   ·   ·

The story of the American West never really comes to an ending. Like the sparkling waterfalls and perpetual springs of Western parks, the stories flow continuously, changing with passing time. Each generation looks back upon the land and its legends with fresh viewpoints, perceiving a past that their predecessors overlooked or saw without perspective because they were too close to the events.

Folk cultures brought to the Old West by emigrants from distant lands have grown pale or are being absorbed by the symbols and heroes of the frontier. Even the first Native Americans are developing new mythologies around their old oral traditions, with tales of heroic happenings during the period of the Indian Wars. Out of all this ferment, innovative art, music, and an enriched literature are being created.

One of the remarkable phenomena of the enduring and endless story of the Old West is its expanding reach around the earth. Human beings in many a faraway nation often know the story better than they know their own legends. They organize Wild West clubs, cowboy clubs, American Indian clubs. In various languages they study the costumes, weapons, habitations, daily lives, and the histories. From Katmandu to Singapore, from Casablanca to Calcutta, in Valencia, Naples, Paris, Dresden, Kraków, or Shanghai, the names and faces of George Custer and Sitting Bull, of Calamity Jane and Little Sure Shot Annie Oakley are becoming as well known as they are in El Paso or Cheyenne.

With images in words and photographs this volume is a view of the Old West as seen from the last half of the twentieth century. Already a coming generation is beginning to see it through different prisms. Most of the legends will survive, some fading, some being brought into sharper focus. Good surely will prevail over evil. As in a serial story, this magically unending saga of the American West is always "To Be Continued."

A Selected Chronology of Events in the West

▲ ▲ ▲ ▲ ▲ ▲ ▲ ▲ ▲ ▲ ▲ ▲ ▲ ▲ ▲ ▲

All dates and events contained in this table are not necessarily mentioned within the text of this book, but are for placing the related events within the context of the larger picture that is American history.

1803 President Thomas Jefferson concludes the Louisiana Purchase for $15 million, and doubles the size of the United States.

1803–06 Captain Meriwether Lewis and Captain William Clark explore the west country, obtained by the United States during the Louisiana Purchase.

1806 Lieutenant Zebulon M. Pike discovers 18,000-foot peak in the Rocky Mountains of Colorado.

1809–11 Chief Tecumseh of the Shawnee launches campaign to unite the Native American nations west of the Mississippi River. He and his brother, the Prophet, advocate Indian independence from whites. General William Henry Harrison defeats Tecumseh at Tippecanoe, in the Indiana Territory, and crushes the Shawnee.

1813–14 In what is now Alabama, the Creek Wars take their toll on both Native Americans and white settlers in the Mississippi Territory.

1817–18 Seminoles are brutally removed from the Florida Territory by General Andrew Jackson.

1819 The United States acquires all of Spanish Florida after General Jackson's unauthorized conquest of Spanish settlements there. The price tag is $5 million.

1825 The Creek nation cedes the rest of its lands to Georgia, in a controversial agreement reached with William MacIntosh, a Georgia Indian commissioner. Large bribes are said to have been given to the chiefs who signed the papers, instead of putting the treaty to a vote among the nation's members, which is both custom and law.

1827 In Prairie du Chien, which is part of the Michigan Territory, Chief Red Bird of the Winnebago nation is defeated.

1828 Cherokee nation cedes its lands in the Arkansas Territory, and agrees to migrate west of the Mississippi.

1828 Andrew Jackson is elected president. He will win reelection in 1832.

1832 All territory west of the Mississippi River is declared by Congress as Indian country.

1835 Samuel Colt, of Hartford, Connecticut, patents gun with revolving chambers.

1836 Martin Van Buren is elected president.

1836 The American Home Mission Society sends a group of settlers to establish a mission for the conversion of Indians to Christianity in the Oregon country.

1836 Arkansas is admitted to the Union, June 15, 1836.

1837 Osceola, chief of the Seminoles, and other Indian leaders are imprisoned after arriving in St. Augustine under a white flag to pursue a treaty. General Zachary Taylor defeats the Seminole nation sometime later in the Battle of Lake Okeechobee.

1837 Michigan is admitted to the Union, January 26, 1837.

1838 The Trail of Tears takes place, as more than 18,000 Cherokees are driven from their homelands in Georgia to a place west of the Mississippi River.

1840 William Henry Harrison is elected president on the slogan "Tippecanoe and Tyler too."

1840 John Tyler becomes president upon the death of President Harrison.

1842 The Oregon Trail is begun. A pioneer route to the Pacific Northwest, it is two thousand miles from Independence, Missouri, to Fort Vancouver, Washington. The Oregon Trail will continue to be the most heavily used westward route until 1860, and the outbreak of the Civil War.

1844 James K. Polk is elected president.

1844 The telegraph is invented by Samuel F. B. Morse.

1845 John L. O'Sullivan, editor of the *United States Magazine* and *Democratic Review,* coins the idea of "Manifest Destiny," explaining it is God's will that the United States should control and dominate North America.

1845 Florida is admitted to the Union, March 3, 1845.

1845 Texas is admitted to the Union, November 29, 1845.

1846 Utah is admitted to the Union, January 4, 1846.

1846 Iowa is admitted to the Union, December 28, 1846.

1846–48 The United States declares war on Mexico. General Winfield Scott captures Vera Cruz and Mexico City. Mexico's formal surrender includes concessions of land in Texas and California. The United States grows 33 percent larger.

1846 The Bear Flag Revolt, led by John Frémont, establishes the United

States as the sovereign of California, which had been previously controlled by Spain, and then Mexico.

1847 Brigham Young and the Mormons settle in the Great Salt Lake area, Utah.

1848 Zachary Taylor is elected president.

1849 Gold found in California the year before creates the great gold rush of 1849, and the term "forty-niner" is coined.

1849 Wisconsin is admitted to the Union, May 29, 1849.

1850 California is admitted to the Union, September 9, 1850.

1850 The U.S. census includes four states west of the Mississippi River, including Arkansas, California, Iowa, and Texas.

1850 Millard Fillmore becomes president upon the death of President Taylor.

1852 Franklin Pierce is elected president.

1856 James Buchanan is elected president.

1858 Minnesota is admitted to the Union, May 11, 1858.

1859 Oregon is admitted to the Union, February 14, 1859.

1860 Abraham Lincoln is elected president.

1860–65 The Civil War between the North and the South plunges the United States into a bitter and costly war over states' rights and slavery. Many troops on the frontier are drawn from their forts to be enjoined in the great cataclysm.

1861 Kansas is admitted to the Union, January 29, 1861.

1862 The Homestead Act is passed, offering 160-acre parcels of land for five years of improvement, establishing thousands of small farms across the United States, especially on the Great Plains.

1863 West Virginia is admitted to the Union, June 20, 1863.

1864 Nevada is admitted to the Union, November 31, 1864.

1865 Abraham Lincoln is assassinated, and Andrew Johnson becomes president.

1866 Retaliating for a trespass onto treaty lands by the U.S. Army, members of the Sioux nation, led by Chief Red Cloud, ambush and kill eighty soldiers near Fort Phil Kearny. The action will be called the Fetterman Massacre, named for the ambitious captain who led the army unit.

1867 The United States purchases Alaska for $7 million. The purchase is ridiculed by many and named "Seward's Folly," for the secretary of state who pursued the agreement recklessly.

1867 Nebraska is admitted to the Union, March 1, 1867.

1867 The great cattle drives from Texas to Abilene begin. Abilene, a sleepy little Kansas town, is turned upside down by promoter-entrepreneur Joseph McCoy.

1868 Red Cloud agrees to peace with General William Tecumseh Sherman, in exchange for the army's abandonment of forts along the Bozeman Trail.

1868 Colonel George Armstrong Custer and his Seventh Cavalry wipe out an entire Cheyenne village, now known as the Battle of the Washita Massacre.

1868 Ulysses Simpson Grant is elected president. He will be reelected in 1872.

1869 The joining of the Union Pacific and the Central Pacific opens up transcontinental travel overland across the United States.

1875–76 The Sioux and the miners, with the help of the U.S. Army, continue to wage war, trying to force passage through Indian Territory, to get to the Montana goldfields. The Seventh Cavalry Regiment, led by the overambitious Colonel Custer, moved against the Indians at the Little Big Horn, in the Dakota Territory. They were met by Chiefs Sitting Bull and Crazy Horse and were decimated, beginning the legend now known as "Custer's Last Stand."

1876 Colorado is admitted to the Union, August 1, 1876.

1876 Centennial Exhibition held in Philadelphia.

1876 James Butler "Wild Bill" Hickok dies.

1876 Rutherford B. Hayes wins a hotly debated election against Samuel J. Tilden. This election symbolizes the end of Reconstruction.

1877 A victor at both White Bird Canyon, Idaho, and Big Hole River, Montana, Chief Joseph of the Nez Percés surrenders, after fighting and attempting to flee to Canada over a 1,000-mile-long trail. He says upon surrender, "I will fight no more forever."

1880 James A. Garfield is elected president.

1881 President Garfield is assassinated and Chester A. Arthur becomes president.

1881 Chief Sitting Bull, victor at Little Big Horn, long in hiding, surrenders to the U.S. Army.

1881 Deputy Marshal Wyatt Earp, his two brothers Virgil and Morgan Earp, and "Doc" Holliday win the gunfight at the O.K. Corral, where they duel with members of the Clanton family.

1881 Billy the Kid is killed near Fort Sumner, New Mexico, by Pat Garrett.

1882 Jesse James, longtime bank and train robber, dies after being shot by his cousin, who wishes to claim the $10,000 reward placed on James.

1883 Buffalo Bill begins his series of entertainments, called the Wild West Show, featuring a buffalo roundup, a stagecoach chase, and other rodeo spectacles.

1883 Northern Pacific completes second transcontinental railroad.

1884 Grover Cleveland is elected president.

1885 Permanent National Cattle Trail is established by an act of Congress but is proved impractical and unenforceable.

1886 General Nelson A. Miles accepts the surrender of Geronimo, a by now famous and mythic Apache warrior, and his followers. He has been at war with the United States for more than fifteen years.

1887 The Dawes General Allotment Act is passed to help solve the "Indian problem."

1888 Benjamin Harrison is elected president; he is the grandson of William Henry Harrison.

1889 The remaining land inside what was the Indian Territory, now Oklahoma, is given up in claims on one great day, April 22. Those who tried to sneak through before the gunshot sounded at noon were called "Sooners."

1889 North Dakota is admitted to the Union, November 2, 1889.

1889 South Dakota is admitted to the Union, November 2, 1889.

1889 Washington is admitted to the Union, November 4, 1889.

1889 Montana is admitted to the Union, November 8, 1889.

1889–90 The ghost dance, a rite which will restore the earth to the days before the white man, begins to sweep through many Native American communities. It is begun through a vision by a Paiute warrior, Wovoka.

1890 Sitting Bull is killed, while being arrested by order of government officials, who are afraid of growing unrest among Native Americans brought on by the ghost dance. Chief Big Foot attempts to move his group of more than 350 followers to Pine Ridge reservation to avoid military retaliation. At Wounded Knee Creek on the reservation, on December 29, 1890, the United States Seventh Cavalry, five hundred strong, moves to intercept the fleeing Sioux. After insisting on surrender, shots ring out— 153 Sioux are murdered, more than half of them women and children.

1890 Idaho is admitted to the Union, July 3, 1890.

1890 Wyoming is admitted to the Union, July 10, 1890.

1891 Colorado gold and silver rush at Cripple Creek draws huge numbers of miners, speculators, and settlers to the small Colorado town.

1891 General William Tecumseh Sherman dies.

1892 Historian Frederick Jackson Turner, at a meeting of the American Historical Association, delivers his paper "The Significance of the Frontier in American History," wherein he declares that the American frontier, after four hundred years, is finally closed, "and with it has closed the first period of American history."

1892 Grover Cleveland is elected president for a second, nonconsecutive term.

1896 William McKinley is elected president. He will be reelected in 1900.

1900 President McKinley is assassinated. Theodore Roosevelt becomes president, and will win reelection in 1904.

1900 Chief Washakie of the Shoshones dies.

1900 The U.S. census now includes seventeen states west of the Mississippi River.

1904 Chief Joseph of the Nez Percés dies.

1907 Oklahoma is admitted to the Union November 16, 1907.

1909 Geronimo, Apache warrior, dies.

1917 William Frederick "Buffalo Bill" Cody dies.

1929 Wyatt Earp dies.

1929 Charles Goodnight of Goodnight-Loving Trail fame, as well as many other trails, dies. He is ninety-three.

Bibliography

▲ ▲ ▲ ▲ ▲ ▲ ▲ ▲ ▲ ▲ ▲ ▲ ▲ ▲ ▲ ▲

1. BOOKS AND FULL-LENGTH MANUSCRIPTS

Abbott, Edward C., and Helena H. Smith. *We Pointed Them North: Recollections of a Cowpuncher.* New York: Farrar & Rinehart, 1939.

Adair, Cornelia. *My Diary.* Bath, England, 1918.

Adams, Andy. *Cattle Brands.* Boston: Houghton, 1906.

———. *Log of a Cowboy.* Boston: Houghton, 1927.

Adams, Ramon F. *Western Words: A Dictionary of the Range, Cow Camp and Trail.* Norman: University of Oklahoma Press, 1945.

Aldridge, Reginald. *Life on a Ranch: Ranch Notes in Kansas, Colorado, the Indian Territory and Northern Texas.* New York: Appleton, 1884.

Allen, Albert H. *Dakota Imprints, 1858–1889.* New York: R. R. Bowker Co., 1947.

Allen, Jules V. *Cowboy Lore.* San Antonio: Naylor, 1933.

Allen, Lewis F. *American Cattle: Their History, Breeding and Management.* New York: Taintor Bros., 1881.

Allsopp, Fred W. *History of the Arkansas Press.* Little Rock: Parke-Harper, 1922.

Angell, George T. *Cattle Transportation in the United States.* Boston, 1872.

Applegate, Jesse. *A Day with the Cow Column in 1843.* Chicago: Caxton, 1934.

Applegate, Oliver C. Papers, 1847–1870. Manuscript, University of Oregon Library.

Armour, J. Ogden. *The Packers, the Private Car Lines & the People.* Philadelphia: Altemus, 1906.

Armour, Philip D. *The Present Condition of the Live Cattle and Beef Markets in the United States.* Chicago: Legal News Co., 1889.

Arnold, Oren. *Hot Irons: Heraldry of the Range.* New York: Macmillan, 1940.

Arnold, R. Ross. *Indian Wars of Idaho.* Caldwell, Idaho, 1932.

Artrip, Louise, and Fullen Artrip. *Memoirs of Daniel Fore (Jim) Chisholm and the Chisholm Trail.* Booneville, Ark.: Artrip Publications, 1949.

Atchison, Topeka and Santa Fe Railroads. Documents Relating to . . . Boston, 1890–93. 3 vols.

Babbitt, A. T., and others. *Cattle Brands Owned by Members of the Wyoming Stock Growers' Association.* Chicago, 1882.

Baber, D. F. *The Longest Rope, the Truth about the Johnson County Cattle War.* Caldwell, Idaho: Caxton, 1940.

Baillie-Grohman, William A. *Camps in the Rockies.* New York: Scribners, 1882.

Bakarich, Sarah Grace. *Gun Smoke.* Tombstone, Ariz., 1947.

Ballinger, R. H. *Does It Pay?* Larned, Kansas: Chronoscope Job Print, 1883.

Bancroft, Hubert H. *History of Arizona and New Mexico.* San Francisco, 1889.

———. *History of Nevada, Colorado and Wyoming.* San Francisco, 1890.

———. *History of Washington, Idaho, and Montana.* San Francisco, 1890.

Barnes, William C. *Western Grazing Grounds and Forest Ranges: A History of the Livestock Industry as Conducted on the Open Ranges of the Arid West.* Chicago: Breeders' Gazette, 1913.

———. *Tales from the X-Bar Horse Camp.* Chicago: Breeders' Gazette, 1920.

———. *Story of the Range.* Washington, D.C.: U.S. Department of Agriculture, 1926.

———. *Apaches and Longhorns.* Los Angeles: Ward Ritchie, 1941.

Beadle, John H. *The Undeveloped West, or Five Years in the Territories.* Philadelphia: National Publishing Co., 1873.

Bechdolt, Frederick R. *Tales of the Old Timers.* New York: Century, 1924.

Bell, J. G. *Log of the Texas-California Trail, 1854.* Edited by J. Evatts Haley. Austin, Texas, 1932.

Bennett, Estelline. *Old Deadwood Days.* New York, 1928.

Bennett, Russell H. *The Compleat Rancher.* New York: Rinehart, 1946.

Benton, Frank. *Cowboy Life on the Sidetrack.* Denver: Western Stories Syndicate, 1903.

Beverly, Bob. *Hobo of the Rangeland.* Lovington, N. Mex., n.d.

Biggers, Don H. *From Cattle Range to Cotton Patch.* Bandera, Texas, 1944.

Binns, Archie. *Northwest Gateway.* New York: Doubleday, Doran, 1941.

Black, A.P. *The End of the Longhorn Trail.* Selfridge, N. Dak.: Selfridge Journal, n.d.

Bourke, John G. *An Apache Campaign in the Sierra Madre.* New York, 1886.

———. *Mackenzie's Last Fight with the Cheyennes.* Governor's Island, N.Y., 1890.

———. *On the Border with Crook.* New York, 1891.

Bowles, Samuel. *Our New West.* Hartford, Conn.: Hartford Publishing Company, 1869.

Branch, Edgar M. *The Literary Apprenticeship of Mark Twain.* Urbana: University of Illinois Press, 1950.

Branch, Edward Douglas. *The Cowboy and His Interpreters.* New York: Appleton, 1926.

Bratt, John. *Trails of Yesterday.* Lincoln, Nebr.: University Publishing Co., 1921.

Breakenridge, William M. *Helldorado.* Boston: Houghton, 1928.

Briggs, Harold E. *Frontiers of the Northwest.* New York: Appleton-Century, 1940.

Brill, Charles J. *Conquest of the Southern Plains.* Oklahoma City, 1938.

Brininstool, Earl A. *Trail Dust of a Maverick.* New York: Dodd Mead, 1914.

———. *Fighting Red Cloud's Warriors.* Columbus, Ohio, 1926.

Brisbin, James S. *The Beef Bonanza.* Philadelphia: Lippincott, 1881.

Britton, Wiley. *Pioneer Life in Southwest Missouri.* Kansas City, Mo.: Smith-Grieves Co., 1929.

Bronson, Edgar Beecher. *Cowboy Life on the Western Plains.* New York: Grosset and Dunlap, 1910.

———. *The Red-Blooded.* Chicago: McClurg, 1910.

———. *Reminiscences of a Ranchman.* Chicago: McClurg, 1910.

Brown, John Henry. *History of Texas.* St. Louis: L. E. Daniell, 1892–93.

Brush, Wilmot Proviso. *Brandbook Containing the Brands of the Cherokee Strip.* Kansas City, Mo.: Moore, 1882.

Buck, Solon J. *The Agrarian Crusade, a Chronicle of the Farmer in Politics.* New Haven: Yale University Press, 1921.

Burdick, Usher L. *Marquis de Mores at War in the Bad Lands.* Fargo, N. Dak.: 1929.

Burney, John H. *Memoirs of a Cow Pony as Told by Himself.* Boston: Eastern Publishing Co., 1906.

Burns, Walter Noble. *The Saga of Billy the Kid.* Garden City, N.Y.: Doubleday, 1926.

Burt, Maxwell Struthers. *Powder River.* New York: Farrar & Rinehart, 1938.

Burton, Harley True. *History of the J A Ranch.* Austin, Texas: Von Boeckmann-Jones Co., 1928.

Canton, Frank M. *Frontier Trails: The Autobiography of Frank M. Canton.* Edited by Edward Everett Dale. Boston: Houghton, 1930.

Carr, Robert V. *Cowboy Lyrics.* Boston: Small, Maynard & Co., 1912.

———. *A Century of Texas Cattle Brands.* Forth Worth, 1936.

Carrington, Frances C. *My Army Life and the Fort Phil Kearney Massacre.* Philadelphia 1910.

Carrington, Henry B. *Ab-Sa-Ra-Ka.* 3d edition of Mrs. Margaret Irvin Carrington's narrative. Philadelphia, 1878.

Carter, Robert G. *On the Border with Mackenzie.* Washington, D.C., 1935.

Case, Victoria. *We Called It Culture.* Garden City, N.Y.: Doubleday, 1948.

Casey, Robert J. *Pioneer Railroad.* New York: Whittlesey House, 1948.

Chapman, Arthur. *Out Where the West Begins.* Boston: Houghton, 1917.

Chittenden, Hiram M. *The American Fur Trade of the Far West.* New York: F. P. Harper, 1902.

Clancy, Foghorn. *My Fifty Years in Rodeo.* San Antonio: Naylor Co., 1952.

Clark, Charles Badger. *Sun and Saddle Leather.* Boston: Badger, 1922.

Clark, O. S. *Clay Allison of the Washita.* Attica, Ind.: G. M. Williams, 1922.

Clarke, Robert D. *The Works of Sitting Bull.* Chicago: Knight and Leonard, 1878.

Clay, John. *My Life on the Range.* Chicago: privately printed, 1924.

Clemen, Rudolph A. *The American Livestock and Meat Industry.* New York: Ronald Press, 1923.

Clemens, Samuel L. *Roughing It.* Hartford, Conn., 1891.

Clum, Woodworth. *Apache Agent.* Boston, 1936.

Coburn, Wallace David. *Rhymes from a Round-up Camp.* New York: Putnam, 1903.

Cody, William F. *Buffalo Bill's Own Story of His Life and Deeds.* Chicago: Homewood Press, 1917.

Colbert, Walter. *The Cattle Industry: What It Is Now and What It Was 65 to 70 Years Ago.* Ardmore, Okla., 1941.

Collings, Ellsworth. *The 101 Ranch.* Norman: University of Oklahoma Press, 1937.

Collins, Hubert E. *Warpath and Cattle Trail.* New York: Morrow, 1928.

Colorado Brand Book. Denver, 1887.

Conard, Howard Louis. *Uncle Dick Wootton.* Chicago: Dibble, 1890.

Conn, William. *Cowboys and Colonels.* London: Griffith, Farran, Okedon and Welsh, n.d.

Connelly, William E. *Wild Bill and His Era.* New York: Press of the Pioneers, 1933.

Cook, James H. *Fifty Years on the Old Frontier.* New Haven: Yale University Press, 1923.

———. *Longhorn Cowboy.* New York: Putnam, 1942.

Cook, John R. *The Border and the Buffalo.* Topeka, Kansas: Crane & Co., 1907.

Cooke, Jay, & Co. *The Northern Pacific Railroad.* Philadelphia, 1871.

Coolidge, Dane. *Texas Cowboys.* New York: Dutton, 1937.

———. *Arizona Cowboys.* New York: Dutton, 1938.

———. *Old California Cowboys.* New York: Dutton, 1939.

Coutant, C. G. *History of Wyoming.* Laramie, Wyo.: Chaplin, Spafford and Mathison, 1899.

Cox, James. *Historical and Biographical Record of the Cattle Industry and the Cattlemen of Texas and Adjacent Territory.* St. Louis: Woodward & Tiernan, 1895.

Craig, John R. *Ranching with Lords and Commons, or Twenty Years on the Range.* Toronto: privately printed, 1903.

Crawford, Captain Jack. *Lariattes.* Sigourney, Iowa: William A. Bell, 1904.

———. *The Poet Scout, a Book of Song and Story.* New York: Funk and Wagnalls, 1886.

Crawford, Lewis F. *Badlands and Broncho Trails.* Bismarck, N. Dak., 1922.

———. *Rekindling Camp Fires.* Bismarck, N. Dak., 1926.

Crawford, Medorem. Letters, 1846–1860. Manuscript, University of Oregon Library.

Crawford, Samuel Johnson. *Kansas in the Sixties.* Chicago: McClurg, 1911.

Crissey, F. *Alexander Legge.* Chicago: privately printed, 1936.

Crofutt, George. *Crofutt's New Overland Tourist and Pacific Coast Guide.* Chicago, 1878.

Croke, James. Letters, 1854. Manuscript, University of Oregon Library.

Crook, George. *Resume of Operations against Apache Indians, 1882 to 1886.* Omaha, 1886.

———. *General George Crook.* Norman: University of Oklahoma Press, 1946.

Cross, F. J. *The Free Lands of Dakota.* Yankton: South Dakota, 1876.

Cross, Joe. *Cattle Clatter: History of Cattle from the Creation to the Texas Centennial in 1936.* Kansas City, Mo.: Walker Publishing Co., 1938.

Cruse, Thomas. *Apache Days and After.* Caldwell, Idaho, 1941.

Culley, John H. *Cattle, Horses and Men of the Western Range.* Los Angeles: Ward Ritchie, 1940.

Cummins, Henry. Letters, 1859–1862. Manuscript, University of Oregon Library.

Cunningham, Eugene. *Triggernometry: A Gallery of Gunfighters.* New York: Press of the Pioneers, 1934.

Custer, Geroge A. *Wild Life on the Plains and Horrors of Indian Warfare.* St. Louis, 1891.

Dale, Edward Everett. *The Range Cattle Industry.* Norman: University of Oklahoma Press, 1930.

————. *Cow Country.* Norman: University of Oklahoma Press, 1942.

David, Robert B. *Finn Burnett.* Glendale, Arizona: Arthur H. Clark, 1937.

Davidson, Jay Brownlee. *Farm Machinery and Farm Motors.* Orange Judd Co., N.Y., 1908.

Davis, Britton. *The Truth about Geronimo.* New Haven, 1929.

Davis, John Patterson. *The Union Pacific Railway.* Chicago: S. C. Griggs and Co., 1894.

Dayton, Edson C. *Dakota Days, May 1886–August 1898.* Hartford, Conn., 1937.

De Lacy Lacy, Charles. *The History of the Spur.* n.p.: n.d.

Delano, Alonzo. *Pen-knife Sketches.* San Francisco: Grabhorn Press, 1934.

Denhardt, Robert M. *The Horse of the Americas.* Norman: University of Oklahoma Press, 1948.

De Voto, Bernard. *Mark Twain's America.* Boston: Little, Brown, 1932.

Dick, Everett N. *The Sod-house Frontier.* New York: D. Appleton-Century, 1937.

Diggs, Annie L. *The Story of Jerry Simpson.* Wichita, Kansas, 1908.

Dimsdale, Thomas J. *The Vigilantes of Montana.* Norman: University of Oklahoma Press, 1953.

Dobie, J. Frank. *A Vaquero of the Brush Country.* Dallas: Southwest Press, 1929.

————. *On the Open Range.* Dallas: Southwest Press, 1931.

————. *Tales of the Mustang.* Dallas: Book Club of Texas, 1936.

————. *Mustangs and Cowhorses.* Austin: Texas Folklore Society, 1940.

————. *The Longhorns.* Boston: Little, Brown, 1941.

————. *Guide to Life and Literature of the Southwest.* Dallas: Southern Methodist University Press, 1952.

Dodd, E. P. Scrapbook history. Manuscript, University of Oregon Library.

Dodge, Richard Irving. *The Hunting Grounds of the Great West.* London: Chatto & Windus, 1877.

Donoho, M. H. *Circle Dot.* Topeka, Kansas: Crane & Co., 1907.

Dorson, Richard M. *Davy Crockett, American Comic Legend.* New York: Rockland Editions, 1939.

Doubleday, Russell. *Cattle-ranch to College.* New York: Doubleday and McClure, 1899.

Douglas, C. L. *Cattle Kings of Texas.* Dallas: Regional Press, 1938.

Driggs, Benjamin W. *History of Teton Valley.* Caldwell, Idaho: Caxton Printers, 1926.

Dunn, Jacob P. *Massacres of the Mountains, a History of the Indian Wars of the Far West.* New York, 1886.

Dustin, Fred. *The Custer Tragedy.* Ann Arbor, Mich., 1939.

Duval, John C. *Adventures of Big-Foot Wallace.* Macon, Ga.: J. W. Burke and Co., 1885.

———. *Early Times in Texas.* Austin, Texas: H.P.N. Gammel and Co., 1892.

Dyer, Mrs. D. B. *Fort Reno.* New York: G. W. Dillingham, 1896.

Edwards J. B. *Early Days in Abilene.* Abilene, Texas, 1938.

Ellard, Harry. *Ranch Tales of the Rockies.* Canyon City, Colo., 1899.

Elliot, William J. *The Spurs.* Spur, Texas: The Texas Spur, 1939.

Ellis, Edward S. *The Great Cattle Trail.* Philadelphia: Coates, 1894.

———. *Cowmen and Rustlers: A Story of the Wyoming Cattle Ranges in 1892.* Philadelphia: Coates, 1898.

Ellis, William T. *Memories.* Eugene, Oregon: J. H. Nash, 1939.

Farley, Frank Webster. *Raising Beef Cattle on Farm and Range.* Kansas City, Mo.: Walker Publications, Inc., 1931.

Fee, Chester A. *Chief Joseph, the Biography of a Great Indian.* New York, 1936.

Finerty, John F. *War-path and Bivouac.* Chicago, 1890.

Fitzpatrick, Lilian. *Nebraska Place Names.* Lincoln: University of Nebraska, 1925.

Foy, Eddie, and Alvin F. Harlow. *Clowning through Life.* New York: Dutton, 1928.

French, William. *Some Reflections of a Western Ranchman: New Mexico 1883–1889.* New York: Stokes, 1928.

Frewen, Moreton. *Melton Mowbray and Other Memories.* London: Jenkins, 1924.

Furlong, Charles W. *Let 'er Buck, a Story of the Passing of the Old West.* New York: G. P. Putnam's Sons, 1923.

Gann, Walter. *Tread of the Longhorns.* San Antonio: Naylor, 1949.

Gard, Wayne. *Frontier Justice.* Norman: University of Oklahoma Press, 1949.

Gardner, Charles M. *The Grange—Friend of the Farmer.* Washington, D.C.: National Grange, 1949.

Garland, Hamlin. *A Son of the Middle Border.* New York: Macmillan, 1925.

Garrett, Pat F. *The Authentic Life of Billy, the Kid . . .* Santa Fe: New Mexican Printing and Publishing Co., 1882.

Gibson, J. Watt. *Recollections of a Pioneer.* St. Joseph, Mo.: privately printed, 1912.

Gillett, J. B. *Six Years with the Texas Rangers, 1876–1881.* Austin, Texas: Van Broeckman-Jones Co., 1921.

Goodnight, Charles, and others. *Pioneer Days in the Southwest, 1850–1879.* Guthrie, Okla., 1909.

Graham, William A. *The Story of the Little Big Horn*. Harrisburg, Pa., 1941.

Grand, W. Joseph. *Illustrated History of the Union Stockyards*. Chicago, 1896.

Greeley, Horace. *An Overland Journey from New York to San Francisco in 1859*. New York: Saxton, Barker & Co., 1860.

Greenburg, Dan W. *Sixty Years: A Brief Review of the Cattle Industry in Wyoming*. Cheyenne, Wyo.: Stock Growers' Association, 1932.

Grinnell, George B. *The Fighting Cheyennes*. New York, 1915.

———. *Two Great Scouts and Their Pawnee Battalion*. Cleveland, 1928.

Grinnell, J. B. *The Cattle Industries of the United States*. New York: Jos. H. Reall, 1882.

Guernsey, Charles A. *Wyoming Cowboy Days*. New York: Putnam, 1936.

Hafen, Le Roy R., and Ann W. Hafen. *Colorado*. Denver: Old West Publishing Co., 1945.

Hagedorn, Herman. *Roosevelt in the Bad Lands*. Boston: Houghton, 1921.

Hale, Will. *24 Years a Cowboy and Ranchman in Southern Texas and Old Mexico*. O. T. Hedrick and W. H. Stone, n.p.: 1905.

Haley, J. Evetts. *The XIT Ranch*. Chicago: Lakeside Press, 1929.

———. *Charles Goodnight, Cowman and Plainsman*. Boston: Houghton, 1936.

———. *George W. Littlefield, Texan*. Norman: University of Oklahoma Press, 1943.

———. *Jeff Milton: A Good Man with a Gun*. Norman: University of Oklahoma Press, 1948.

———. *The Heraldry of the Range*. Canyon, Texas: Panhandle-Plains Historical Society, 1949.

Hall, Caroline Arabella. *Songs for the Grange, Set to Music and Dedicated to the Order of Patrons of Husbandry in the United States*. Philadelphia: J. A. Wagenseller, 1873.

Halsell, H. H. *Cowboys and Cattleland*. Nashville: Parthenon Press, 1937.

Hamner, Laura Vernon. *The No-gun Man of Texas, 1835–1929*. Amarillo, Texas, 1935.

———. *Short Grass and Longhorns*. Norman: University of Oklahoma Press, 1943.

Hardin, John Wesley. *Life of . . . Written by Himself*. Seguin, Texas: Smith & Moore, 1896.

Harlow, Alvin F. *Old Waybills*. New York: : D. Appleton-Century, 1934.

Harper, Minnie Timms, and George Dewey Harper. *Old Ranches*. Dallas: Dealey and Lowe, 1936.

Harris, Frank. *My Reminiscences as a Cowboy*. New York: Boni, 1930.

Hastings, Frank S. *A Ranchman's Recollections*. Chicago: Breeders' Gazette, 1921.

Hebard, Grace R. *Washakie.* Cleveland, 1930.

Hebard, Grace R., and Earl A. Brininstool. *The Bozeman Trail.* Cleveland, 1922.

Hendricks, George David. *The Bad Men of the West.* San Antonio: Naylor, 1941.

Henry, Stuart. *Conquering Our Great American Plains.* New York: Dutton, 1930.

Hibben, Paxton. *The Peerless Leader, William Jennings Bryan.* New York: Farrar and Rinehart, 1929.

Hicks, John D. *The Populist Revolt.* Minneapolis: University of Minnesota Press, 1931.

Hill, J. L. *The End of the Cattle Trail.* Long Beach, Calif.: G. W. Moyle, 1923.

Hill, Luther B. *History of the State of Oklahoma.* Chicago: Lewis Publishing Co., 1908.

Hinkle, J. F. *Early Days of a Cowboy on the Pecos.* Roswell, N. Mex., 1937.

Historical Records Survey. *Checklist of Kansas Imprints, 1854–1876.* Topeka, Kansas, 1939.

Hodge, Frederick W. *Handbook of American Indians North of Mexico.* Washington, D.C., 1907–10.

Holbrook, Stewart. *Holy Old Mackinaw.* New York: Macmillan, 1938.

Holden, William Curry. *Alkali Trails.* Dallas: Southwest Press, 1930.

———. *The Spur Ranch.* Boston: Christopher, 1934.

Hough, Emerson. *The Story of the Outlaw.* New York: Outing Publishing Company, 1907.

———. *Story of the Cowboy.* New York: Appleton, 1924.

———. *North of 36.* New York: Appleton, 1929.

Howard, Helen A. *War Chief Joseph.* Caldwell, Idaho, 1941.

Howard, Joseph Kinsey. *Montana: High Wide and Handsome.* New Haven: Yale University Press, 1944.

Howard, Oliver O. *My Life and Experiences among Our Hostile Indians.* Hartford, Conn., 1907.

———. *Famous Indian Chiefs I Have Known.* New York, 1908.

Howe, Edgar. *Plain People.* New York: Dodd, Mead, 1929.

Howe, George F. *Chester A. Arthur.* New York: Dodd, Mead, 1934.

Huidekoper, Wallis. *The Land of the Dakotas.* Helena, Mont., n.d.

Humphrey, Seth K. *Following the Prairie Frontier.* Minneapolis: University of Minnesota Press, 1931.

Hunt, Frazier, and Robert Hunt. *Horses and Heroes.* New York: Charles Scribner's Sons, 1949.

Hunter, J. Marvin, and Noah H. Rose. *The Album of Gunfighters.* Bandera, Texas, 1951.

Hunter, J. Marvin, ed. *The Trail Drivers of Texas.* 2d ed., revised. Nashville: Cokesbury Press, 1925.

Hyde, George E. *Red Cloud's Folk.* Norman, Okla. 1937.

Inman, Henry. *The Old Santa Fe Trail.* Topeka, Kansas: Crane & Company, 1899.

Interstate Agricultural Convention, 1880. *Proceedings.* Springfield, Ill., 1881.

Jackson, A. P., and E. C. Cole. *Oklahoma.* Kansas City, Mo.: Millett & Hudson, 1885.

Jackson, Joseph Henry. *Anybody's Gold.* New York: Appleton-Century, 1941.

Jackson, W. H., and S. A. Long. *The Texas Stock Directory, or Book of Marks and Brands.* San Antonio: Herald Office, 1865.

James, W. S. *Cowboy Life in Texas, or 27 Years a Maverick.* Chicago: Donahue, 1898.

James, Will. *Cowboys North and South.* New York: Scribners, 1924.

———. *Smoky, the Cowhorse.* New York: Scribners, 1926.

———. *Sand.* New York: A. L. Burt, 1929.

———. *Lone Cowboy.* New York: Scribners, 1930.

———. *Cow Country.* New York: Scribners, 1931.

Jaques, Mary J. *Texan Ranch Life.* London: Horace Cox, 1894.

Jennewein, J. Leonard. *Calamity Jane of the Western Trails.* Huron, S. Dak.: Dakota Books, 1953.

Jocelyn, Stephen P. *Mostly Alkali.* Caldwell, Idaho: Caxton Printers, 1953.

Johannsen, Albert. *The House of Beadle and Adams and Its Dime and Nickel Novels; the Story of a Vanished Literature.* Norman: University of Oklahoma Press, 1950.

Johnson, Francis W. *A History of Texas and Texans.* Chicago: American Historical Society, 1918.

Johnson, Phil. *Life on the Plains.* Chicago, 1888.

Kansas and Pacific Railway Company. *Guide map of the best and shortest cattle trail to the Kansas Pacific Railway.* Kansas City, Mo.: Ramsey, Millett and Hudson, 1874.

Kansas City Stockyards Company. *Seventy-five Years of Kansas City Livestock Market History, 1871–1946.* Kansas City, Mo., 1946.

Keithley, Ralph. *Buckey O'Neill.* Caldwell, Idaho: Caxton Printers, 1949.

King, Edward. *The Southern States of North America.* London: Blackie & Son, 1875.

King, Frank M. *Pioneer Western Empire Builders.* Pasadena, Calif.: Trail's End Publishing Co., 1946.

Kipling, Rudyard. *American Notes.* New York: G. Munro's Sons, 1896.

Knibbs, Henry Herbert. *Songs of the Trail.* Boston: Houghton, 1920.

LaFrentz, F. W. *Cowboy Stuff.* New York: Putnam, 1927.

Lake, Stuart. *Wyatt Earp, Frontier Marshal.* Boston: Houghton, 1931.

Lampman, C. P. *Great Western Trail.* New York: Putnam, 1939.

Lang, Lincoln A. *Ranching with Roosevelt.* Philadelphia: Lippincott, 1926.

Larkin, Margaret. *Singing Cowboy.* New York: Knopf, 1931.

Larson, Agnes M. *History of the White Pine Industry in Minnesota.* Minneapolis: University of Minnesota Press, 1949.

Latham, Henry. *Trans-Missouri Stock Raising: The Pasture Lands of North America.* Omaha: Daily Herald Steam Printing House, 1871.

Lavender, David S. *One Man's West.* New York: Doubleday, 1943.

Leech, Harper, and John C. Carroll. *Armour and His Times.* New York: Appleton-Century, 1938.

Leigh, William R. *The Western Pony.* New York: Huntington Press, 1933.

Lewis, Alfred Henry. *Wolfville.* New York: Stokes, 1897.

Lewis, Lloyd, and Stanley Pargellis. *Granger Country, a Pictorial Social History of the Burlington Railroad.* Boston: Little, Brown, 1949.

Lockwood, Frank C. *Arizona Characters.* Los Angeles: Times-Mirror Press, 1928.

———. *The Apache Indians.* New York, 1938.

Lomax, John A. *Songs of the Cattle Trail and Cow Camps.* New York: Macmillan, 1919.

Long, J. C. *Bryan the Great Commoner.* New York: Appleton, 1928.

Long, Richard M. *Wichita, 1866–1883.* Wichita, Kansas: McCormick-Armstrong Company, 1945.

Luce, Edward S. *Keogh, Comanche and Custer.* St. Louis, 1939.

Mackay, Malcolm S. *Cow Range and Hunting Trail.* New York: Putnam, 1925.

Major, Mabel. *Southwest Heritage.* Albuquerque: University of New Mexico Press, 1938.

Majors, Alexander. *Seventy Years on the Frontier.* Chicago: Rand McNally, 1893.

Malin, James C. *Dust Storms, 1850–1900.* Reprint from *Kansas Historical Quarterly.* 1946.

Marshall, James. *Santa Fe: The Railroad that Built an Empire.* New York: Random House, 1945.

McArthur, Lewis A. *Oregon Geographic Names.* Portland, Ore.: Binfords and Mort, 1944.

McCarty, John L. *Maverick Town, the Story of Old Tascosa.* Norman: University of Oklahoma Press, 1946.

McCauley, James Emmitt. *Stove-up Cowboy's Story.* Austin, Texas: Folklore Society, 1943.

McComas, Evans. Diary, 1864–1866. Manuscript, University of Oregon Library.

McCoy, Joseph G. *Historic Sketches of the Cattle Trade of the West and Southwest.* Kansas City, Mo.: Ramsey, Millett & Hudson, 1874.

———. *Historic Sketches of the Cattle Trade.* Edited by Ralph P. Bieber. Glendale, Calif.: A. H. Clark, 1940.

McDonald, James. *Food from the Far West.* London: Nimmo, 1878.

McMurry, Donald L. *Coxey's Army.* Boston: Little, Brown, 1929.

McMurtrie, Douglas C. *Oregon Imprints, 1847–1870.* Eugene: University of Oregon Press, 1950.

McNeal, T. A. *When Kansas was Young.* New York: Macmillan, 1922.

Meeker, Ezra. *Ventures and Adventures of Ezra Meeker.* Seattle: Rainier Publishing Co., 1908.

Mercer, Asa Shinn. *The Banditti of the Plains, or the Cattlemen's Invasion of Wyoming.* San Francisco: Grabhorn Press, 1935.

Miles, Nelson A. *Personal Recollections and Observations.* Chicago: Werner, 1896.

———. *Serving the Republic.* New York: Harper, 1911.

Miller, Benjamin S. *Ranching in the Southwest.* New York: privately printed, 1896.

Mills, Anson. *My Story.* Washington, D.C., 1918.

Missouri, Kansas and Texas Railroad. *Reports and Statements.* St. Louis, 1879.

Monaghan, Jay. *Last of the Bad Men, Tom Horn.* Indianapolis: Bobbs-Merrill, 1946.

———. *The Great Rascal, the Life and Adventures of Ned Buntline.* Boston: Little, Brown, 1952.

Montana Stock Grower's Association. *Brand Book.* Helena, 1885.

Mooney, James. *The Ghost-Dance Religion.* Washington, D.C., 1896.

Mora, Joseph J. *Trail Dust and Saddle Leather.* New York: Scribners, 1946.

———. *Californios, the Saga of the Hard-riding Vaqueros, America's First Cowboys.* Garden City, N.Y.: Doubleday, 1949.

Mott, Frank L. *American Journalism.* New York: Macmillan, 1950.

Mowry, Sylvester. Letters, 1855–1856. Manuscript, University of Oregon Library.

Myers, John M. *The Last Chance: Tombstone's Early Years.* New York: Dutton, 1950.

Myrick, Herbert. *Cache la Poudre: The Romance of a Tenderfoot in the Days of Custer.* New York: Orange Judd, 1905.

Nickerson, Azor H. "Major General George Crook and the Indians." Manuscript, Army War College Library, Washington, D.C., n.d.

Nimmo, Joseph. *The Range and Ranch Cattle Business of the United States.* Washington, D.C.: Government Printing Office, 1885. (Also published as *House Exec. Doc. 7,* Part III, 48th Congress, 2d session.)

Nordyke, Lewis R. *Cattle Empire: The Fabulous Story of the 3,000,000 Acre XIT.* New York: Morrow, 1949.

North, Escott. *Saga of the Cowboy.* London: Jerrolds, 1942.

Noyes, Alva J. *In the Land of Chinook.* Helena, Mont.: State Publishing Co., 1917.

Nye, Edgar Wilson. *Nye and Riley's Railway Guide.* Chicago: Dearborn Pub. Co., 1888.

O'Beirne, Harry F. *The Indian Territory: Its Chief Legislators and Leading Men.* St. Louis: Woodward, 1892.

Ogle, Ralph H. *Federal Control of the Western Apaches, 1848–1886.* Albuquerque, 1940.

O'Keefe, Rufus. *Cowboy Life.* San Antonio: Naylor, 1936.

Olmstead, Frederick Law. *A Journey through Texas.* New York: Mason Brothers, 1859.

Orchard, Hugh. *Old Orchard Farm.* Ames: Iowa State College Press, 1952.

O'Reilly, Harrington. *Fifty Years on the Trail.* New York: F. Warne, 1889.

Osgood, Ernest S. *The Day of the Cattleman.* Minneapolis: University of Minnesota Press, 1929.

Otero, Miguel A. *My Life on the Frontier.* New York: Press of the Pioneers, 1935–39.

———. *The Real Billy the Kid.* New York: R. R. Wilson, 1936.

Owen, John. *The Journals and Letters of Major John Owen, Pioneer of the Northwest, 1850–1871.* Edited by Paul C. Philips. New York: Eberstadt 1927.

Paine, Albert Bigelow. *Captain Bill MacDonald, Texas Ranger.* New York: Little & Ives, 1909.

Paine, Bayard H. *Pioneers, Indians and Buffaloes.* Curtis, Nebr.: Curtis Enterprise, 1935.

Palmer, Joel. *Journal of Travels over the Rocky Mountains.* Cleveland: A. H. Clark Co., 1906.

Parrish, Randall. *The Great Plains.* Chicago: McClurg, 1907.

Paxson, Frederick Logan. *History of the American Frontier.* New York: Houghton, 1924.

Payne, Doris Palmer. *Captain Jack, Modoc Renegade.* Portland, Oreg., 1938.

Peake, Ora Brooks. *The Colorado Range Cattle Industry.* Glendale, Calif.: A. H. Clark, 1937.

Pearson, Edmund. *Dime Novels; or, Following an Old Trail in Popular Literature.* Boston: Little, Brown, 1929.

Pelzer, Louis. *The Cattlemen's Frontier.* Glendale, Calif.: A. H. Clark, 1936.

Poe, John W. *The Death of Billy the Kid.* Boston: Houghton, 1933.

Pollock, J. M. *The Unvarnished West: Ranching as I Found It.* London: Simpkin, Marshall, 1911.

Ponting, Tom Candy. *Life of Tom Candy Ponting.* Decatur, Ill., 1904.

Porter, Robert P. *The West: From the Census of 1880.* Chicago: Rand McNally, 1882.

Post, C. C. *Ten Years a Cowboy.* Chicago: McClurg, 1886.

Potter, Jack M. *Cattle Trails of the Old West.* Clayton, N. Mex.: Laura H. Krehbiel, 1939.

———. *Lead Steer and Other Tales.* Clayton, N. Mex., n.d.

Powell, Cuthbert. *Twenty Years of Kansas City's Live Stock Trade and Traders.* Kansas City, Mo.: Pearl Printing Company, 1893.

Powell, John W. *Report on the Lands of the Arid Regions of the United States.* Washington, D.C.: U.S. Interior Department, 1879.

Price, Con. *Trails I Rode.* Pasadena, Calif.: Trail's End Publishing Co., 1947.

Prose and Poetry of the Live Stock Industry of the United States, with Outlines of the Origin and Ancient History of Our Live Stock Animals. Volume 1 (no others published). Denver and Kansas City: National Live Stock Historical Association, 1905.

Raine, William MacLeod. *Famous Sheriffs and Western Outlaws.* New York: Doubleday, 1929.

———. *Guns of the Frontier.* Boston: Houghton, 1940.

Raine, William MacLeod, and Will C. Barnes. *Cattle.* New York: Doubleday, 1930.

Rainey, Mrs. George. *Cherokee Strip Brands.* Enid, Okla., 1949.

Rak, Mary Kidder. *A Cowman's Wife.* Boston: Houghton, 1934.

———. *Mountain Cattle.* Boston: Houghton, 1936.

Rankin, M. Wilson. *Reminiscences of Frontier Days.* Denver, 1935.

Raymond, Elvira. Letters, 1842–1843. Manuscript, University of Oregon Library.

Reid, Elizabeth. *Mayne Reid, a Memoir of His Life.* London: Ward and Downey, 1890.

Remington, Frederic. *Pony Tracks.* New York: Harper, 1895.

———. *Drawings.* New York: Russell, 1897.

———. *Crooked Trails.* New York: Harper, 1898.

———. *Done in the Open.* New York: Russell, 1902.

Reminiscences of Oregon Pioneers. Pendleton, Oreg., 1937.

"Report of a Board of Officers Convened by the Commanding General, Department of the Platte to Examine into and Report the Facts Attending the Arrest, Confinement, Disarmament, Escape and Recapture of a Number of Cheyenne Indians Recently at and in the Vicinity of Fort Robinson, Nebraska, February 7, 1879." Manuscript, Army War College Library, Washington, D.C.

Rhodes, Eugene Manlove. *Good Men and True*. New York: Holt, 1910.

Richardson, Rupert N. *The Comanche Barrier to South Plains Settlement*. Glendale, Calif., 1933.

Richter, Francis C. *Richter's History and Records of Baseball*. Philadelphia: F. C. Richter, 1914.

Richthofen, Walter von. *Cattle Raising on the Plains of North America*. New York: Appleton, 1885.

Ricketts, William P. *Fifty Years in the Saddle*. Sheridan, Wyo.: Star Publishing Co., 1942.

Riddle, Jeff C. D. *The Indian History of the Modoc War and the Causes that Led to It*. San Francisco, 1914.

Ridings, Sam P. *The Chisholm Trail, a History of the World's Greatest Cattle Trail*. Guthrie, Okla.: Cooperative Publishing Co., 1936.

Riegel, Robert Edgar. *Story of the Western Railroads*. New York: Macmillan, 1926.

Rister, Carl C. *The Southwestern Frontier*. Cleveland: A. H. Clark, 1928.

———. *Border Command: General Phil Sheridan in the West*. Norman, Okla., 1944.

———. *No Man's Land*. Norman: University of Oklahoma Press, 1948.

———. *Oil! Titan of the Southwest*. Norman: University of Oklahoma Press, 1949.

Robinson, Doane. *A History of the Dakota or Sioux Indians*. Aberdeen, S. Dak., 1904.

Rollins, Philip Ashton. *The Cowboy, His Characteristics, His Equipment*. New York: Scribners, 1922.

Rollinson, John K. *Hoofprints of a Cowboy and a U.S Ranger*. Caldwell, Idaho: Caxton, 1941.

———. *Wyoming Cattle Trails*. Caldwell, Idaho: Caxton, 1948.

Rolt-Wheeler, Francis W. *A Book of Cowboys*. Boston: Lothrop, 1921.

Roosevelt, Theodore. *Hunting Trips of a Ranchman*. New York: Putnam, 1885.

———. *Ranch Life and the Hunting Trail*. New York: Century, 1888.

———. *The Rough Riders*. New York: P. F. Collier & Son, 1899.

Root, Frank A. *The Overland Stage to California*. Topeka, Kansas, 1901.

Rourke, Constance. *Troupers of the Gold Coast*. New York: Harcourt, Brace, 1928.

Ruede, John. *Sod-house Days, Letters from a Kansas Homesteader, 1877–78*. Edited by John Ise. New York: Columbia University Press, 1937.

Rush, Oscar. *The Open Range*. Caldwell, Idaho: Caxton, 1936.

Rusling, James Fowler. *The Railroads! The Stockyards! The Eveners! An Expose of the Railroad Ring*. Washington, D.C.: R. O. Polkinhorn, 1878.

Russell, Charles M. *Studies of Western Life*. New York: Albertype Company, 1890.

———. *Rawhide Rawlins Stories.* Great Falls: Montana Newspaper Association, 1921.

———. *More Rawhides.* Great Falls: Montana Newspaper Association, 1925.

———. *Trails Plowed Under.* Garden City, N.Y.: Doubleday, 1928.

———. *Good Medicine.* Garden City, N.Y.: Garden City Publishing Co., 1936.

Rye, Edgar. *The Quirt and the Spur, Vanishing Shadows of the Texas Frontier.* Chicago: W. B. Conkey, 1909.

Sabin, Edwin L. *Kit Carson Days.* Chicago: A. C. McClurg, 1914.

Sage, Lee. *The Last Rustler.* Boston: Little, Brown, 1930.

Sanders, Alvin H. *Shorthorn Cattle.* Chicago: Sanders, 1901.

———. *Story of the Herefords.* Chicago: Breeders' Gazette, 1914.

———. *Cattle of the World.* Washington, D.C.: National Geographic Society, 1926.

Sandoz, Mari. *Crazy Horse.* New York, 1942.

Santee, Ross. *Men and Horses.* New York: Century, 1926.

———. *Cowboy.* New York: Grossett and Dunlap, 1928.

Sass, Herbert R. *Hear Me, My Chiefs.* New York, 1940.

Schatz, August H. *Opening of a Cow Country.* Ann Arbor, Mich.: Edwards Brothers, 1939.

Seely, Howard. *A Lone Star Bo-peep, and Other Tales of Texan Ranch Life.* New York: W. L. Mershon, 1885.

Sheldon, Addison E. *Land Systems and Land Policies in Nebraska.* Lincoln, Nebr., 1936.

Sheldon, Henry D. Papers, 1903. Manuscript, University of Oregon Library.

Shepherd, Major W. *Prairie Experiences in Handling Cattle and Sheep.* New York: Orange Judd, 1885.

Siringo, Charlie. *A Texas Cow Boy; or, Fifteen Years on the Hurricane Deck of a Spanish Pony.* Chicago: M. Umbdenstock & Co., 1885.

———. *Riata and Spurs.* Boston: Houghton, 1927.

Smalley, Eugene Virgil. *History of the Northern Pacific Railroad.* New York: Putnam, 1883.

Smith, Henry Nash. *Virgin Land, the American West as Symbol and Myth.* Cambridge: Harvard University Press, 1950.

Smythe, William E. *Conquest of Arid America.* New York: Macmillan, 1905.

Sonnichsen, C. L. *Roy Bean, Law West of the Pecos.* New York: Macmillan, 1944.

Sowell, Andrew Jackson. *Rangers and Pioneers of Texas.* San Antonio: Shepard Brothers, 1884.

Spring, Anges Wright. *Seventy Years, a Panoramic History of the Wyoming Stock Growers' Association.* Cheyenne, Wyo., 1943.

———. *The Cheyenne and Black Hills Stage and Express Route.* Glendale, Calif.: A. H. Clark Co., 1949.

Stanley, Clark. *True Life in the Far West, by the American Cowboy.* Worcester, Mass.: Musinger Printing Co., n.d.

Stansbery, Lon R. *The Passing of 3-D Ranch.* Tulsa, Okla.: G. W. Henry, 1930.

Stanton, G. Smith. *When the Wildwood was in Flower . . . Fifteen Years Experiences of a Stockman.* New York: J. S. Ogilvie, 1909.

Steedman, Charles J. *Bucking the Sage Brush.* New York: Putnam, 1904.

Steinel, A. T., and D. W. Working. *History of Agriculture in Colorado.* Fort Collins: State Agriculture College, 1926.

Stoddard, Henry Luther. *Horace Greeley.* New York: G. P. Putnam's Sons, 1946.

Stone, Arthur. *Following Old Trails.* Missoula, Mont.: M. J. Elrod, 1913.

Stout, Tom. *Montana, Its Story and Biography.* Chicago: American Historical Society, 1921.

Strahorn, Robert E. *The Handbook of Wyoming and Guide to the Black Hills and Big Horn Regions for Citizen, Emigrant and Tourist.* Cheyenne, Wyo.: Knight & Leonard, 1877.

———. *The Resources of Montana Territory.* Helena, Mont., 1879.

Strand, J. *Memories of Old Western Trails in Texas Longhorn Days.* Willeston, N. Dak.: Interstate Press, 1931.

Streeter, Floyd B. *Prairie Trails and Cow Towns.* Boston: Chapman and Grimes, 1936.

Stuart, Granville. *Montana as It Is.* New York: Westcott, 1865.

———. *Forty Years on the Frontier.* Edited by Paul C. Philips. Cleveland: A. H. Clark, 1925.

Sturmberg, Robert. *History of San Antonio and the Early Days in Texas.* San Antonio: Standard Printing Company, 1920.

Sullivan, John H. *Life and Adventures of the Original and Genuine Cowboys, by Broncho John.* Valparaiso, Ind., 1905.

———. *Life and Adventures of Broncho John; His Second Trip Up the Trail.* Valparaiso, Ind., 1908.

Sullivan, W. John L. *Twelve Years in the Saddle for Law and Order.* Austin, Texas: Von Boeckmann-Jones Co., 1909.

Sutley, Zack T. *The Last Frontier.* New York: Macmillan, 1930.

Sutton, Fred E., and A. B MacDonald. *Hands Up! Stories of the Six-Gun Fighters of the Old Wild West.* Indianapolis: Bobbs-Merrill, 1927.

Sweet, Alexander E., and J. Armoy Knox. *On a Mexican Mustang through Texas.* Hartford, Conn.: S. S. Scranton, 1883.

Swenson Brothers. *The Story of the S M S Ranch.* Stamford, Texas, 1919.

Swift, Louis F. *The Yankee of the Yards; the Biography of Gustavus Franklin Swift.* Chicago: A. W. Shaw, 1937.

Swisher, James. *How I Know; or Sixteen Years on the Western Frontier.* Cincinnati: printed by the author, 1881.

Taft, Robert. *Photography and the American Scene.* New York: Macmillan, 1938.

———. *Artists and Illustrators of the Old West, 1850–1900.* New York: Charles Scribner's Sons, 1953.

Tait, Samuel W., Jr. *The Wildcatters, an Informal History of Oil-Hunting in America.* Princeton: Princeton University Press, 1946.

Talbot, Ethelbert. *My People of the Plains.* New York: Harper & Brothers, 1906.

Taylor, Frank J., and Earl M. Welty. *Black Bonanza.* New York: Whittlesey House, 1950.

Taylor, Thomas U. *Chisholm Trail and Other Routes.* San Antonio: Naylor, 1936.

Thayer, William M. *Marvels of the New West.* Norwich, Conn.: Henry Bill Publishing Company, 1887.

Thoburn, Joseph B. *Standard History of Oklahoma.* Chicago: American Historical Society, 1916.

Thompson, Albert W. *They Were Open Range Days.* Denver: World Press, 1946.

Thompson, George G. *Bat Masterson; the Dodge City Years.* Fort Hays, Kansas State College (Language and Literature Series, No. 1), 1943.

Thorp, N. Howard (Jack). *Songs of the Cowboys.* Boston: Houghton, 1921.

Thorp, N. Howard (Jack), and N. M. Clark. *Pardner of the Wind.* Caldwell, Idaho: Caxton, 1945.

Thrall, Homer S. *A Pictorial History of Texas.* St. Louis: Thompson, 1879.

Tilghman, Zoe A. *Outlaw Days.* Oklahoma City: Harlow Pub. Co., 1926.

———. *Quanah, the Eagle of the Comanches.* Oklahoma City, 1938.

Tompkins, Colonel Frank. *Chasing Villa, the Story Behind the Story of Pershing's Expedition into Mexico.* Harrisburg, Pa.: Military Service Pub. Co., 1934.

Topping. E. S. *Chronicles of the Yellowstone.* St. Paul: Pioneer Press Co., 1883.

Townshend, Richard B. *A Tenderfoot in New Mexico.* New York: Dodd Mead, 1924.

Treadwell, Edward F. *The Cattle King.* New York: Macmillan, 1931.

Trenholm, Virginia Cole. *Footprints on the Frontier.* Douglas, Wyo.: Douglas Enterprise Co., 1945.

Triggs, J. H. *History of Cheyenne and Northern Wyoming.* Omaha: Herald Publishing Company, 1876.

Trottman, Nelson. *History of the Union Pacific.* New York: Ronald Press, 1923.

Turnbull, George S. *History of Oregon Newspapers.* Portland, Oreg.: Binfords & Mort, 1939.

Turner, Frederick Jackson. *The Frontier in American History.* New York: Holt, 1920.

Twitchell, Ralph Emerson. *Leading Facts of New Mexican History.* Cedar Rapids, Iowa: Torch Press, 1911–17.

Union Pacific Railway, Passenger Department. *The Oregon Short Line Country.* Omaha, 1885.

Van de Water, Frederic F. *Glory-Hunter, a Life of General Custer.* Indianapolis, 1934.

Van Zant, Henry Clay. Letters, 1838. Manuscript, author's private collection.

Vestal, Stanley. *Sitting Bull.* Boston, 1932.

———. *Warpath.* Boston, 1934.

Vincent, Henry. *Story of the Commonweal.* Chicago: W. B. Conkey Co., 1894.

Wallace, Charles. *Mrs. Nat Collins, the Cattle Queen of Montana.* St. James, Minn.: C. W. Foote, 1894.

Walsh, C. C. *Early Days on the Western Range.* Boston: Sherman, French and Co., 1917.

Walsh, Richard J. *The Making of Buffalo Bill.* Indianapolis: Bobbs-Merrill, 1928.

Walters, Lorenzo D. *Tombstone's Yesterdays.* Tucson, 1928.

Webb, Walter Prescott. *The Great Plains.* Boston: Ginn, 1931.

———. *The Texas Rangers.* Boston: Houghton, 1935.

Wellman, Paul I. *The Trampling Herd.* New York: Carrick & Evans, 1939.

Wells, Evelyn, and Harry C. Peterson. *The '49ers.* Garden City, N.Y.: Doubleday, 1949.

Wendt, Lloyd, and Herman Kogan. *Bet a Million! The Story of John W. Gates.* Indianapolis: Bobbs-Merrill, 1948.

Westermeier, Clifford P. *Man, Beast, Dust; the Story of Rodeo.* Denver: World Press, 1947.

Wharton, Clarence. *Satanta: The Great Chief of the Kiowas and His People.* Dallas, 1935.

Wheeler, Homer W. *The Frontier Trail.* Los Angeles: Times-Mirror Press, 1923.

———. *Buffalo Days; Forty Years in the Old West; the Personal Narrative of a Cattleman.* Indianapolis: Bobbs-Merrill, 1925.

White, Owen, P. *Them Was the Days.* New York: Minton, Balch, 1925.

———. *Trigger Fingers.* New York: Putnam, 1926.

———. *Lead and Likker.* New York: Minton, Balch, 1932.

White, William Allen. *Autobiography.* New York: Macmillan, 1946.

Wiest, Edward. *Agricultural Organization in the United States.* Lexington: University of Kentucky, 1923.

Wik, Reynold M. *Steam Power on the American Farm.* Philadelphia: University of Pennsylvania Press, 1953.

Williams, J. E. *Fifty-eight Years in the Panhandle of Texas.* Austin, Texas: privately printed, 1944.

Williams, Moses A. Diaries, 1850–1896. Manuscript, University of Oregon Library.

Wilson, Bushrod. Letters, 1850–1854. Manuscript, University of Oregon Library.

Wilson, Mrs. Augustus. *Memorial Sketch and Official Report of the First National Convention of Cattlemen, November 17–22, 1884.* St. Louis: McCoy, 1884.

Wilson Parson's Memorial and Historical Library Magazine, containing scenes and incidents, etc. of the First National Cattlegrower's Convention. St. Louis, 1885.

Wilstach, Frank J. *Wild Bill Hickok, the Prince of Pistoleers.* Garden City, N.Y.: Doubleday, Page, 1926.

Winch, Frank. *Thrilling Lives of Buffalo Bill and Pawnee Bill.* New York: S. L. Parsons, 1911.

Winslow, Edith Black. *In Those Days.* San Antonio: Naylor, 1950.

Wister, Owen. *The Virginian.* New York: Macmillan, 1925.

Wright, Robert M. *Dodge City, the Cowboy Capital.* Wichita, Kansas: Wichita Eagle Press, 1913.

Writers Program, Colorado. *Colorado.* New York: Hastings House, 1943.

Writers Program, Wyoming. *Wyoming.* New York: Oxford University Press, 1941.

2. Articles and Other Short Pieces

Aeschbacher, W. D. "Development of Cattle Raising in the Sand Hills." *Nebraska History* 28 (1947): 41–64.

Arnold, Frazer. "Ghost Dance and Wounded Knee." *Cavalry Journal* 43 (May/June 1934): 19–20.

Barnes, Will C. "Col. James Harvey McClintock, Pioneer, Historian, Soldier and Citizen." *Arizona Historical Review* 6, no. 1 (January 1935): 67–74.

Blake, Henry N. "The First Newspaper of Montana." Historical Society of Montana, *Contributions* 5 (1904): 253–73.

Boatright, Mody C., and Donald Day. *Backwoods to Border* (Texas Folklore Society, Publication No. 18). Austin, 1943.

Botkin, Theodosius. "Among the Sovereign Squats." Kansas State Historical Society, *Transactions* 7 (1902): 418–41.

Brandon, C. Watt. "Building a Town on Wyoming's Last Frontier." *Annals of Wyoming* 22 (1950): 27–46.

Brecht, Frederick G. "Reminiscences." *Arizona Historical Review* 6, no. 1 (January 1935): 85–86.

Britt, Albert. "Ride 'Im, Cowboy!" *Outlook* 135 (1923): 136–39.

Brownsville (Nebraska) *Advertiser,* June 6 and October 18, 1856, as quoted in *Nebraska History* 26 (1945): 240, 242.

Bryan, O. S. "An Early Dakota Camp Meeting." *South Dakota Historical Collections* 20 (1940): 281–298.

Buchanan, John R. "The Great Railroad Migration into Northern Nebraska." Nebraska State Historical Society, *Proceedings* 15 (1907): 25–34.

Burdick, Usher L. "Recollections and Reminiscenses of Graham's Island." *North Dakota History* 16 (1949): 5–29, 165–91.

Buxbaum, Katherine. "A Rural Literary Society." *Palimpsest* 21 (1940): 23–30.

"Camel breeding in Texas." *National Live-Stock Journal* 9 (1878): 299.

Chatterton, Fenimore. "A Unique Campaign." *Annals of Wyoming* 19 (1947): 32–38.

Clancy, Foghorn. "Rodeo Progress." *Hoofs and Horns* 23, no. 2 (August 1953): 17.

Coffin, William H. "Settlement of the Friends in Kansas." Kansas State Historical Society, *Transactions* 7 (1902): 322–61.

Coletta, Paolo E. "The Youth of William Jennings Bryan—Beginnings of a Christian Statesman." *Nebraska History* 31 (1950): 1–24.

Cox, W. W. "Reminiscences of Early Days in Nebraska." Nebraska Historical Society, *Transactions* 5 (1893): 63–81.

Coyle, James. "Letter to Arizona Pioneers Historical Society." *Arizona Historical Review* 6, no. 5 (July 1935): 87.

Crawford, Nelson Antrim. "The Making of a Hero." *Kansas Magazine* (1949): 1–5.

Creigh, Thomas Alfred. "From Nebraska City to Montana, 1866"; diary edited by James C. Olson. *Nebraska History* 29 (1948): 208–37.

Dale, Edward E. "The Social Homesteader." *Nebraska History* 25 (1944): 155–71.

———. "Wood and Water: Twin Problems of the Prairie Plains." *Nebraska History* 29 (1948): 87–104.

Dickinson County Chronicle (Abilene, Kansas). June 28, 1878, as quoted in *Kansas Historical Quarterly* 12 (1943): 325.

———, June 7, 1878, as quoted in *Kansas Historical Quarterly* 14 (1946): 233.

Diggs, Annie L. "Women in the Alliance Movement." *Arena* 6 (1892): 160–79.

Dolbee, Cora. "The Fourth of July in Early Kansas." *Kansas Historical Quarterly* 11 (1942): 130–72.

Doran, Thomas F. "Kansas Sixty Years Ago." Kansas State Historical Society, *Collections* 15 (1923): 482–501.

Dunn, Nora G. "Reminiscences of Fourscore Years and Eight." *Annals of Wyoming* 19 (1947): 125–135.

Dykes, J. C. "Dime-novel Texas; or, the subliterature of the Lone Star State." *Southwestern Historical Quarterly* 49 (1946): 327–40.

Ellis, A. N. "Recollections of an Interview with Cochise, Chief of the Apaches." *Kansas State Historical Society Collections* 13 (Topeka, Kansas, 1915): 387–92.

Eureka (Kansas) *Herald,* May 10, 1877, as quoted in *Kansas Historical Quarterly* 11 (1942): 96.

"Expeditions of Capt. Jas. L. Fisk to the Gold Mines of Idaho and Montana, 1864–1866." *North Dakota State Historical Collections* 2 (1906): 421–61.

Fox, John J. "The Far West in the 80's." Edited by T. A. Larson. *Annals of Wyoming* 21 (1949): 3–87.

Frantz, Joe B. "Moses Lapham: His Life and Selected Correspondence." *Southwestern Historical Quarterly* 54 (1950–51) 324–32, 462–75.

Gallego, Hilario. "Reminiscences of an Arizona Pioneer." *Arizona Historical Review* 6, no. 1 (January 1935): 75–81.

Gard, Wayne. "The Fence-Cutters." *Southwestern Historical Quarterly* 51 (1947): 1–15.

Giles, Barney M. "Early Military Aviation in Texas." *Southwestern Historical Quarterly* 54 (1950): 143–58.

Goldberg, Isaac. "Reminiscences." *Arizona Historical Review* 6, no. 2 (April 1935): 74–82.

Hadley, James A. "A Royal Buffalo Hunt." Kansas State Historical Society, *Transactions* 10 (1908): 564–80.

Hansen, George W. "A Tragedy of the Oregon Trail." Nebraska State Historical Society, *Transactions* 17 (1913): 110–26.

Harrington, W. P. "The Populist Party in Kansas." Kansas State Historical Society, *Collections* 16 (1923–25): 403–50.

Hickman, Ervin. "Fredricksburg, Texas: 100 Years of Progress." *Cattleman* 33 (January 1947): 29–30, 110–12.

Hill City (Kansas) *New Era,* June 18, 1908, as quoted in *Kansas Historical Quarterly* 19 (1951): 216–17.

Hoeltje, Hubert H. "The Apostle of the Sunflower in the State of the Tall Corn." *Palimpsest* 18 (1937): 186–211.

Horton, James C. "Peter D. Ridenour and George W. Baker." Kansas State Historical Society, *Transactions* 10 (1908): 589–621.

Hough, Emerson. "Texas Transformed." *Putnam's Magazine* 7 (November 1909): 200–207.

House, Boyce. "Spindletop." *Southwestern Historical Quarterly* 50 (1946): 36–43.

Irwin, Clark. "Early Settlers en Route." Nebraska State Historical Society, *Transactions* 3 (1892): 191–200.

Jack, Frances E. "P. E.O. Beginnings." *Palimpsest* 23 (1942): 85–98.

Jeffries, Charlie. "Reminiscences of Sour Lake." *Southwestern Historical Quarterly* 50 (1946): 25–35.

Johnson, Walter. "Politics in the Midwest." *Nebraska History* 32 (1951): 1–17.

Johnson, Willard D. "The High Plains and Their Utilization." U. S. Geological Survey, *Twenty-first Annual Report,* pt. 4 (1899–1900): 609–741.

Jones, Alf D. "Omaha's Early Days." Nebraska State Historical Society, *Transactions* 4 (1892): 152–54.

Junction City (Kansas) *Union,* July 8, 1871, as quoted in *Kansas Historical Quarterly* 10 (1941): 329–30.

———, July 27, 1867, as quoted in *Kansas Historical Quarterly* 16 (1948): 411.

Kansas Chief (White Cloud), January 5, 1860, as quoted in *Kansas Historical Quarterly* 14 (1946): 447.

———, August 6, 1857, as quoted in *Kansas Historical Quarterly* 20 (1952): 298.

Kansas Daily Commonwealth (Topeka), June 16, 1872, as quoted in *Kansas Historical Quarterly* 11 (1942): 402.

Kautz, August V. "From Missouri to Oregon in 1860." *Pacific Northwest Quarterly* 37 (1946): 193–230.

Kendall, Jane R. "History of Fort Francis E. Warren." *Annals of Wyoming* 18 (1946): 3–66.

Kinsley (Kansas) *Graphic,* January 17, 1880, as quoted in *Kansas Historical Quarterly* 18 (1950): 429.

Kiowa (Kansas) *Herald,* January 8, 1885, as quoted in Kansas Historical Quarterly 17 (1949): 302.

Koller, Joe. "Indian Rodeos in the Dakotas." *Hoofs and Horns* 22 (June 1953): 14.

Lakin (Kansas) *Eagle,* August 27, 1879, as quoted in *Kansas Historical Quarterly* 6 (1937): 104–105.

Lamb, Ted. "Trick Riding." *Hoofs and Horns* 22 (March 1953): 15.

"Laramie City, a Review for 1868–1869," reprinted from Laramie Weekly *Sentinel,* May 5, 1883, in *Annals of Wyoming* 15 (1943): 391–402.

Levinson, Harry. "Mary Elizabeth Lease: Prairie Radical." *Kansas Magazine* (1948): 18–24.

Lomax, Susan F. "A Trip to Texas." Edited by John A. Lomax. *"Southwestern Historical Quarterly* 48 (1944): 254–61.

Lutrell, Estelle. "Arizona's Frontier Press." *Arizona Historical Review* 6 (1935): 14–26.

Mahnken, Norbert R. "William Jennings Bryan in Oklahoma." *Nebraska History* 31 (1950): 247–74.

Martin, George W. "A Chapter from the Archives." Kansas State Historical Society, *Collections* 12 (1912): 259–375.

McCampbell, C. W. "W. E. Campbell, Pioneer Kansas Livestockman." *Kansas Historical Quarterly* 16 (1948): 245–73.

McCann, Leo P. "Ride 'Im, Cowboy!" *Sunset Magazine* 59 (September 1927): 18–20, 62.

McNeal, Thomas A. "Southwestern Kansas." Kansas State Historical Society, *Transactions* 7 (1902): 90–95.

Munro, J. A. "Grasshopper Outbreaks in North Dakota, 1808–1948." *North Dakota History* 16 (1949): 143–64.

Munson, Lyman E. "Pioneer Life in Montana." Historical Society of Montana, *Contributions* 5 (1904): 200–34.

Owen, Mary A. "Social Customs and Usages in Missouri during the Last Century." *Missouri Historical Review* 15 (1920): 176–90.

Palmer, Alma B. "Fire! Fire! Fire!" *Nebraska History* 33 (1952): 180–85.

Peterson, Harold F. "Some Colonization Projects of the Northern Pacific Railroad." *Minnesota History* 10 (1929): 127–44.

"Pioneering in Waubausee County." Kansas State Historical Society, *Transactions* 11 (1910): 594–613.

"The Pioneers." *Palimpsest* 8 (1927): 1–56.

Platt, M. F. "Reminiscences of Early Days in Nebraska." Nebraska Historical Society, *Transactions* 4 (1892): 87–95.

Porter, Willard H. "Rope, Trip and Tie." *Cattleman* 34 (January 1948): 31–32, 96–100.

Pound, Louise, "Old Nebraska Folk Customs." *Nebraska History* 28 (1947): 3–31.

Prentis, Noble L. "Pike of Pike's Peak." Kansas State Historical Society, *Transactions* 6 (1900): 325–36.

Regur, Dorothy. "In the Bicycle Era." *Palimpsest* 14 (1933): 349–62.

Richardson, Warren. "History of the First Frontier Days Celebrations." *Annals of Wyoming* 19 (1947): 39–44.

Rise, Cyrus. "Experiences of a Pioneer Missionary." Kansas State Historical Society, *Collections* 13 (1915): 298–318.

Roberts, T. F. "Pioneer Life in Western Dakota." *North Dakota History* 15 (1948): 154–68.

Schmitt, Martin. "Frontier Mule Power." *Cattleman* 81 (October 1946): 36ff.

Scott, Willard. "Associational Sermon." Nebraska State Historical Society, *Transactions* 3 (1892): 230–42.

Sharp, Mildred J. "Early Cabins in Iowa." *Palimpsest* 2 (1921): 16–29.

Shipman, Mrs. O. L. "Letter to Texas State Historical Association." *Southwestern Historical Quarterly* 52 (1948): 237.

Smith, Ralph. "The Farmers' Alliance in Texas, 1875–1900." *Southwestern Historical Quarterly* 43 (1945): 346–69.

"A Steam Wagon Invented by an Early Resident of South Dakota." *South Dakota Historical Collections* 10 (1920): 362–87.

Studer, Carl L. "The First Rodeo in Texas." *Southwestern Historical Quarterly* 48 (1945): 370–72.

Swisher, J. A. "Billy Sunday." *Palimpsest* 11 (1930): 343–54.

Taft, Robert. "The Pictorial Record of the Old West, Pt. V." *Kansas Historical Quarterly* 16 (1948): 113–35.

Thompson, Roy. "The First Dunker Colony of North Dakota." *North Dakota Historical Collections* 4 (1913): 81–100.

"Town Boomers and Their Advertising." *Kansas Historical Quarterly* 9 (1940): 97–99.

Tuttle, Daniel S. "Early History of the Episcopal Church in Montana." Historical Society of Montana, *Contributions* 5 (1904): 289–324.

Walker, Arthur L. "Recollections of Early Day Mining in Arizona." *Arizona Historical Review* 6 (April 1935): 14–43.

Warner, C. A. "Texas and the Oil Industry." *Southwestern Historical Quarterly* 50 (1946): 1–24.

Wells, Philip F. "Ninety-six Years among the Indians of the Northwest—Adventures and Reminiscences of an Indian Scout and Interpreter in the Dakotas, as Told to Thomas E. Odell." *North Dakota History* 15, (1948): 265–312.

Westermeier, Clifford P. "Cowboy Capers." *Annals of Wyoming* 22 (July 1950): 13–25.

White, William Allen. "Steam Power on the American Farm, 1830–1880." *Agricultural History* 25 (1951): 181–86.

Willson, C. E. "From Variety Theater to Coffee Shoppe." *Arizona Historical Review* 6 (1935): 2–13.

Winslow, Charles Frederick. "Nantucket to the Golden Gate in 1849, from Letters in the Winslow Collection." Transcribed by Helen Irving Oehler. California Historical Society, *Quarterly* 29 (1950): 1–18, 167–72, 255–60.

Wright, Carl C. "Reading Interests in Texas from the 1830's to the Civil War." *Southwestern Historical Quarterly* 54 (1951): 301–15.

Wyman, Walker D. "California Emigrant Letters." California Historical Society, *Quarterly* 24 (1945): 17–46, 117–38, 235–60, 343–64.

Young, Hiram H. "A Hoosier in Kansas, Diary, 1886–1895." Edited by Powell Moore. *Kansas Historical Quarterly* 14 (1946): 166–212, 297–352, 414–46.

3. Periodicals, Reports, and Other Serials

Agricultural History
American Agriculturist
American Cattle Producer
Annals of Iowa
Annals of Wyoming
Breeders' Gazette
Cattleman
Chicago Board of Trade, Annual Reports
Chronicles of Oklahoma
Colorado Farmer and Livestock Journal
Denver Board of Trade, Annual Reports
Frontier Times
Illinois State Historical Society, Journal of the
Illinois State Historical Society, Publications
Iowa Journal of History and Politics
Kansas City Stockyards, Receipts and Shipments of Livestock
Kansas Farmer
Kansas Historical Quarterly
Kansas State Board of Agriculture, Reports
Kansas State Historical Society, Biennial Reports
Matador Land and Cattle Company, Annual Reports
Mississippi Valley Historical Review
Montana Board of Live Stock Commissioners, Annual Reports
Montana Historical Society, *Contributions*
National Cattle Growers' Association of America, *Proceedings*
National Livestock Journal
Nebraska History
Nebraska State Board of Agriculture, Annual Reports
Nebraska State Historical Society, Publications
New Mexico Historical Review
North Dakota Historical Quarterly
North Dakota State Historical Society, *Collections*
Northwestern Live Stock Journal
Omaha Board of Trade, Annual Reports
Outing Magazine
Panhandle-Plains Historical Review

Prairie Farmer
Rocky Mountain Husbandman
South Dakota Historical Collections
Southwestern Historical Quarterly
Swan Land and Cattle Company, Annual Reports
Union Stockyard and Transit Company, Annual Reports
Union Stockyard and Transit Company, Receipts and Shipments of Livestock
U.S. Bureau of American Ethnology, *Seventeenth Annual Report, Part I,* Washington, D.C., 1898
U.S. Bureau of Animal Industry, Annual Reports
U.S. Commissioner of Patents, Annual Reports
U.S. Congress, Senate, 21st Congress, 2d Session, *Executive document 38*
U.S. Congress, 43d, 1st Session, *House Document 122* (Copies of the Correspondence and Papers Relative to the War with the Modoc Indians in Southern Oregon and Northern California, during the Years 1872 and 1873), Washington, D.C., 1874
U.S. Congress, 44th, 2d Session, *Senate Ex. Document 9* (Message from the President of the United States Communicating the Report and Journal of the Proceedings of the Commission Appointed to Obtain Certain Concessions from the Sioux Indians), Washington, D.C., 1877
U.S. Congress, 46th, 2d Session, *Senate Report 708* (Report of the Select Committee to Examine into the Circumstances Connected With the Removal of the Northern Cheyennes from the Sioux Reservations to the Indian Territory), Washington, D.C., 1880
U.S. Congress, 50th, 1st Session, *Senate Ex. Document 33* (Indian Operations on the Plains), Washington, D. C., 1887
U.S. Department of Agriculture, Annual Reports
U.S. War Dept., *Report of the Secretary of War, 1880, Part I,* Washington, D.C., 1880

INDEX

▲▲▲▲▲▲▲▲▲▲▲▲▲▲▲▲▲